Essential Clinical Guide to Understanding and Treating Autism

Essential Clinical Guide to Understanding and Treating Autism

Fred R. Volkmar

Lisa A. Wiesner

WILEY

Published by John Wiley & Sons, Inc., Hoboken, New Jersey.
Published simultaneously in Canada.

This publication is designed to provide accurate and authoritative information in regard to the subject matter covered. It is sold with the understanding that the publisher is not engaged in rendering professional services. If legal, accounting, medical, psychological or any other expert assistance is required, the services of a competent professional should be sought.

For general information on our other products and services, please contact our Customer Care Department within the U.S. at 800-956-7739, outside the U.S. at 317-572-3986, or fax 317-572-4002.

Wiley publishes in a variety of print and electronic formats and by print-on-demand. Some material included with standard print versions of this book may not be included in e-books or in print-on-demand. If this book refers to media such as a CD or DVD that is not included in the version you purchased, you may download this material at http://booksupport.wiley.com. For more information about Wiley products, visit www.wiley.com.

Library of Congress Cataloging-in-Publication Data:
Names: Volkmar, Fred R., author. | Wiesner, Lisa A., author.
Title: Essential clinical guide to understanding and treating autism / by
    Fred R. Volkmar, Lisa A. Wiesner.
Description: First edition. | Hoboken, New Jersey : Wiley, [2018] | Includes
    bibliographical references and index. |
Identifiers: LCCN 2017015023 (print) | LCCN 2017015963 (ebook) | ISBN
    9781119427049 (pdf) | ISBN 9781119427124 (epub) | ISBN 9781118586624 (pbk.)
Subjects: | MESH: Autistic Disorder—therapy | Autistic Disorder—psychology
    | Autism Spectrum Disorder—therapy | Autism Spectrum Disorder—psychology
    | Infant | Child | Adolescent | Adult
Classification: LCC RC553.A88 (ebook) | LCC RC553.A88 (print) | NLM WS
    350.8.P4 | DDC 616.85/882—dc23
LC record available at https://lccn.loc.gov/2017015023

Cover image: © Ilya Terentyev/iStockphoto; © OkinawaPottery/Getty Images
Cover design: Wiley

Printed in the United States of America

First Edition

PB Printing 10 9 8 7 6 5 4 3 2 1

Contents

Preface

The last several years have seen major changes in the health care delivery system. Increasingly, primary care providers are being asked to assume a greater role in the management of medical care for individuals with developmental and behavioral problems. These responsibilities can range from early screening and case management to the care of adults with continuing difficulties. To further complicate things, the system for mental health coverage varies quite widely (and wildly) with many specialist providers taking no insurance. Somewhat paradoxically, at least in the United States (and to some extent in other countries), there is a three-tiered approach with basic care covered under insurance programs such as Medicaid for individuals who quality for it, privately reimbursed coverage for those who can afford it (often, but not always, the highest level of service), and, for much of the middle class, insurance coverage that is remarkably spotty—with some providers who often are under tremendous pressure and scrutiny. Yet another set of issues arises for individuals who receive services from various providers and agencies, for example, child psychiatrists, social workers, educators, psychologists, speech pathologists, behavior specialists, and so on. The primary care provider has an increasingly important role in care coordination and provision of a "medical home" (Hyman & Johnson, 2012; Knapp et al., 2013). This book is written to address the needs of primary care providers for what we hope is an accessible and straightforward guide to medical care for individuals with autism, Asperger's, and the broader autism spectrum group of conditions.

We are, respectively, an academic child psychiatrist (clinician researcher) and a pediatric primary care provider. We hope that our different backgrounds have helped us focus on what is most important for primary care providers to know about autism and related conditions. We have tried to be concise but reasonably comprehensive. You will see that chapters have references and often lists of additional reading resources. One of the challenges in doing a book of this kind is the tremendous growth in the scientific and lay literature on the topic. There are now nearly 30,000 scientific papers on the topic, not to mention the many books and chapters; a quick Google search will yield an initial set of over 25,000 hits. Accordingly, we have tried to identify the most relevant and accessible resources for those who desire additional information or to read primary sources.

There are many excellent resources not included here, although we've tried to give a reasonable sample of the best ones available. We have tried to combine a life-span approach with a focus, in some chapters, on specific age groups. As we note somewhat sadly, the literature is most limited when it comes to adults with autism spectrum disorder (ASD) (a growing and important population and a population not always well served by the health care system). You will see that we also have included a chapter on alternative treatments—obviously here we're not recommending treatments but are giving primary care providers relevant information. In our experience a majority of parents of children with autism will engage in at least one such treatment, and it is important that they be able to have a discussion with their child's primary care providers about these treatments. We also include a chapter on behavior management issues as well as another on medications—we emphasize that primary care physicians (PCPs) who are less familiar with these medications should use local resources and consultations and always be aware that research is ongoing and there may be changes in indications, doses, and so forth.

Increasingly with earlier diagnosis and intervention more children with autism and related conditions are becoming self-sufficient adults—often with some continued vulnerability—but they are able to live independently and have productive and fulfilling lives. For others, unfortunately, longer-term involvement of parents and family is needed, and these individuals also need PCPs who are knowledgeable about autism.

As you will see from this book many professionals are involved throughout the individual's life. PCPs have an important role in helping these specialists talk with each other, the individual, and his or her family. As one of our teacher's often said, "if you meet one person with autism you've met one person with autism." As you work more with this group of patients you'll likely agree with this point of view.

We are grateful to a number of our colleagues who have reviewed parts of this book in our efforts to make it helpful to primary care providers who deal with individuals with autism and their families. We have profited from their wisdom and comments. They include Karen Bailey, MSW; Leah Booth, CC-SPL; Kasia Chawarska, PhD; Michelle Goyette-Ewing, PhD; Roger Jou, MD, PhD; Kathy Koening, MSN, APRN; James McPartland, PhD; and Nancy Moss, PhD. We also particularly thank Ellen Keene, JD, for her extremely helpful review of the chapter on legal issues. We also are grateful to our editor, Patricia Rossi, and the staff at Wiley for their unflagging support and help in making this book as readable as possible. We also thank Lori Klein and Evelyn Pomichetr for their secretarial assistance and Logan Hart for helping us identify resources. Finally, we thank our own children, who have taught us much about child development, and, of course, our patients and their families, who have taught us much about autism.

◾ REFERENCES

Hyman, S. L., & Johnson, J. K. (2012). Autism and pediatric practice: Toward a medical home. *Journal of Autism and Developmental Disorders, 42*(6), 1156–1164.

Knapp, C., Woodworth, L., Fernandez-Baca, D., Baron-Lee, J., Thompson, L., & Hinojosa, M. (2013). Factors associated with a patient-centered medical home among children with behavioral health conditions. *Maternal and Child Health Journal, 17*(9), 1658–1664.

Essential Clinical Guide to Understanding and Treating Autism

CHAPTER 1

What Is Autism?

Diagnostic Concepts, Causes, and Current Research

Autism and related conditions (now widely known as ***autism spectrum disorders,*** or ***ASDs***) are disorders that share significant social disability as a major defining feature. This social disability is quite severe, and its severity and early onset lead to more general and pervasive problems in learning and adaptation. Over the years there have been a number of changes in classification, and for purposes of completeness we'll give a brief summary of these conditions here. Then we'll go on to briefly review what we know about causes and review some of the current research on the condition. For primary care providers it is helpful to understand how our understanding of autism has changed over time and how it is manifested clinically. Subsequent chapters will review aspects of autism and related conditions in more depth. This chapter gives an overview of diagnostic concepts, causes of the condition, and current research.

THE DISCOVERY OF AUTISM

The condition known as ***autistic disorder, childhood autism,*** or ***infantile autism*** (all three names mean the same thing) was first described by Dr. Leo Kanner in 1943 (although cases had likely been noted earlier). Kanner reported on 11 children with what he termed "an inborn disturbance of affective contact," that is, these children came into the world without the usual interest in other people and in dealing with the social world. (For an interesting, and somewhat divergent, set of views on the development of autism as a concept see the books by Donvan and Zuker [2016] and Silberman [2015] in the reading list at the end of this chapter.) Dr. Kanner gave a careful and detailed description of the unusual behaviors these cases exhibited. Kanner mentioned that these children exhibited "resistance to change." He also identified them as having an "insistence on sameness." For example, these children might require that their parents take the same route to school or church and become very upset if there was any deviation from this routine. They might panic if anything in their living room was out of place. They might be very rigid about what kinds of clothes they would wear or foods they would eat. The term *resistance to change* also was used to refer to some of the unusual behaviors frequently seen in children with autism, for example, the apparently purposeless motor behaviors (**stereotypies**) such as body rocking, toe walking, and hand flapping; Kanner felt that these behaviors might be helping the child "maintain sameness."

Kanner mentioned that when language developed at all it was unusual. For example, the child with autism might fail to give the proper tone to his or her speech (that is, might speak like a robot) or might echo language (echolalia) or confuse personal pronouns (pronoun reversal). Or, when asked if he or she wanted a cookie, the child might respond "Wanna cookie, wanna cookie, wanna cookie." Sometimes the language that was echoed was from the distant past (delayed echolalia). Sometimes it happened immediately (immediate echolalia). Sometimes part of it was echoed but part had been changed (mitigated echolalia).

In his original report Kanner thought there were two things essential for a diagnosis of autism—first the autism that is social isolation and second the unusual behaviors and insistence on sameness. (See Box 1.1.)

BOX 1.1 KANNER'S DESCRIPTION OF AUTISM

The outstanding, "pathognomonic," fundamental disorder is in the children's *inability to relate themselves* in the ordinary way to people and situations for the beginning of life. Their parents referred to them as having always been "self-sufficient"; "like in a shell"; "happiest when left alone"; "acting as if people weren't there"; "perfectly oblivious to everything about him"; "giving the impression of silent wisdom"; "failing to develop the usual amount of social awareness"; "acting almost as if hypnotized." This is not, as in schizophrenic children or adults, a departure from an initially present relationship; it is not a "withdrawal" from formerly existing participation. There is from the start an *extreme autistic aloneness* that, whenever possible, disregards, ignores, shuts out anything that comes into the child from outside. Direct physical contact or such motion or noise as threatens to disrupt the aloneness is either treated "as if it weren't there" or, if this is no longer sufficient, resented painfully as a distressing interference.

... This insistence on sameness led several children to become greatly disturbed upon the sight of anything broken or incomplete. A great part of the day was spent in demanding not only the sameness of the wording of a request but also the sameness of the sequence of events.

... The dread of change and incompleteness seems to be a major factor in the explanation of the monotonous repetitiousness and the resulting *limitation in the variety of spontaneous activity*. A situation, a performance, a sentence is not regarded as complete if it is not made up of exactly the same elements that were present at the time the child was first confronted with it. If the slightest ingredient is altered or removed the total situation is no longer the same and this is not accepted as such, or it is resented with impatience "or even with a reaction of profound frustration."

Source: Kanner (1943, pp. 242, 245, 246).

By the late 1970s there was a consensus that autism was characterized by (1) impaired social development of a type quite different from that in normal children, (2) impaired language and communication skills—again of a distinctive type, (3) resistance to change or insistence on sameness as reflected in inflexible adherence to routines, motor mannerisms, and stereotypies, and other behavioral oddities; and (4) an onset in the first years of life. There have been some changes in how autism is diagnosed since that time and we'll discuss them shortly, but we should also note some important (and persistent) mistakes about autism.

SOME EARLY MISTAKES ABOUT AUTISM

Although Kanner's description remains a "classic," it was not, of course, the last word on the subject. Some aspects of his original report misled early clinicians and investigators.

Autism and Intelligence

Kanner originally thought that children with autism probably had normal intelligence. He thought this because they did rather well on some parts of intelligence (IQ) tests. On other parts of these tests, however, they did quite poorly or refused to cooperate at all. Kanner assumed that, if they did as well on all parts of the IQ test as they did on the one or two parts that they seemed to do well on, the child would not be retarded. Unfortunately, it turns out that often cognitive or intellectual skills are difficult to assess, in large part because these are frequently very scattered. Put in another way, children with autism often do some things well such as solving puzzles but they may have tremendous difficulty with more language-related tasks. The degree of discrepancy among different skill areas is very unusual in the typically developing population but very frequent in children with autism.

As time went on it became clear that overall many children with autism have an **intellectual disability** (IQ below 70). In the past this was true for the majority of cases, but fortunately with earlier diagnosis and more effective interventions, this number has gone down so that probably only a minority of cases now do so. However, the pattern of performance in autism is usually rather different from that seen in mental retardation without autism, often with highly discrepant scores in various parts of the

IQ test, for example, strengths in nonverbal abilities but great weakness in verbal or more socially related tasks. Occasionally (maybe 10% of the time) children with autism have some unusual ability, such as drawing, playing music, memorizing things, or sometimes calculating days of the week for events in the past or future (calendar calculation). These abilities are usually isolated (the otherwise very wonderful version of autism in *Rain Man* is misleading in this respect). These individuals are usually referred to as **autistic savants.** Savant skills typically fall into a specific set of categories: calendar calculation, artistic ability, mathematical-calculating skills, music, and visual-spatial skills. Stephen Wiltshire, for example, is an extraordinarily productive artist who captures amazing architectural detail of a city after a single viewing (go to www.stephenwiltshire.co.uk). Sometimes savant skills diminish with age; for example, Nadia (Selfe, 1979) had truly amazing drawing abilities as a young child but lost these as she became older. However, one young man we know has had long-standing abilities to do calendar calculations extending at least 10,000 years before and after the current date and has not lost these abilities as he aged (Thioux, Stark, Klaiman, & Schultz, 2006). Box 1.2 provides an example of a child with unusual drawing ability. Keep in mind that even when these abilities are present (at most in 10% of cases) they are often isolated areas of strength and should not lead teachers, parents, and care providers to overestimate other levels of ability!

These isolated abilities are often noted in the presence of overall intellectual disability. During the 1970s and 1980s most children with autism exhibited intellectual disability; as we discuss in other chapters of this book, this is now much less true.

Autism and Parenting

Kanner's (1943) report also mentioned that cases often came from families in which a parent was remarkably successful; in the first 11 cases he described a parent was either in *Who's Who of America* or *American Men and Women of Science*. This led to the idea, in the 1950s that perhaps the parent's success had led them to somehow neglect the child so concepts such as "refrigerator mother" were invoked to account for autism. As you'll

BOX 1.2 AN EXAMPLE OF UNUSUAL DRAWING ABILITY IN A BOY WITH AUTISM.

"Bim Gets Breakfast in the Love Kitchen" Drawn by a child with autism; Bim is the child's made-up cartoon character.
Source: Reprinted with permission from Volkmar and Pauls (2003, p. 1134).

see in the rest of this chapter there is no evidence to support this and considerable evidence that shows that autism is a strongly genetically and brain-based disorder. But this myth of poor parenting traumatized an entire generation of parents and led to inappropriate and ineffective treatments for the child. Fortunately as it became clear during the 1970s that autism was strongly genetic and brain-based, and it also became clear that structured educational and behavioral interventions could help the child with autism to learn (National Research Council, 2001; Reichow, Doehring, Cicchetti, & Volkmar, 2011).

OTHER CONDITIONS ON THE AUTISM SPECTRUM AND CHANGES WITH *DSM-5*

By the late 1970s a consensus on the **validity** of autism as a concept had emerged, and by 1980 it was included in the landmark third edition of the American Psychiatric Association's official diagnostic guidelines (a book called *Diagnostic and Statistical Manual of Mental Disorders; DSM-III* (APA,1980). *DSM-III* had to have a class of disorder to which autism belonged and the term *pervasive developmental disorder (PDD)* was chosen. In retrospect a term such as *autism and related conditions* or *autism spectrum disorders* might have been better. Over the next decade some revisions were made as research became available, and in 1994 the fourth edition of the book (DSM-IV, APA, 1994) recognized a number of conditions in addition to autism within the broader PDD class. These concepts have their own history and an attempt was made to expand the range of conditions in *DSM-IV* (and its companion international volume *ICD-10* [WHO, 1993]). For autism and related conditions the American *DSM* and international *ICD-10* were essentially the same as DSM-IV, and even in the new DSM-5 individuals with "well-established" diagnoses under DSM-IV are "grandfathered" in (APA, 2013), so DSM-IV effectively remains in effect. The "new" conditions identified in the fourth edition of the *DSM* and in *ICD-10* are described in the next sections.

Asperger's Disorder

Hans Asperger, a medical student working at the University of Vienna during the Second World War, wrote a paper (1944) on boys who had marked social problems but good language (in some ways) (see Box 1.3). They also had all-encompassing special interests (he described them as "little professors") and he made the important point that the child's special interests actually interfered with other aspects of their learning (and often dominated family life). These boys also tended to have significant motor problems, and in several cases it appeared that other family members, particularly fathers, had similar kinds of problems. The special interests can focus on any of a host of topics—we've seen children with interests as diverse as dinosaurs and snakes, the stock market, spelling, the operas of Wagner, and time—to give just a few examples. Box 1.4 provides an example of such interests.

BOX 1.3 ASPERGER'S DISORDER (AS)

Hans Asperger, a medical student at the University of Vienna, wrote his medical school thesis on boys who couldn't form groups—he used the term *autistic personality disorder* in describing these boys.

Problem Areas

- Marked social and motor problems
- Unusual circumscribed interests (that interfered with learning)

Areas of Strength

- Good language vocabulary and speech but issues with social language
- Apparently good cognitive skills

The family history was often positive for similar problems in fathers. Over time several modifications were made as new cases were identified, for example, in girls, in lower IQ individuals, and in some individuals with language problems.

BOX 1.4 CIRCUMSCRIBED INTERESTS IN ASPERGER'S DISORDER

In contrast to unusual abilities, circumscribed interests are more typical of individuals with Asperger's syndrome. In his initial description of the condition Asperger (1944) mentioned several such interests (e.g., train schedules, dinosaurs, American gangsters) and noted that because of their intensity these interfered with other areas of learning for the child and had a negative impact on family life. Among the more cognitively able individuals on the autism spectrum such interests are common. Rather than being more mechanical than savant abilities these interests have to do with acquisition of knowledge and the intense fixation on a topic. The figure shows an example of one such interest, and although drawing is involved in the child's presentation of his interest, it is not itself extraordinary in contrast to his long-standing and highly intense interest in time (Volkmar, Klin, Schultz, Rubin, & Bronen, 2000).

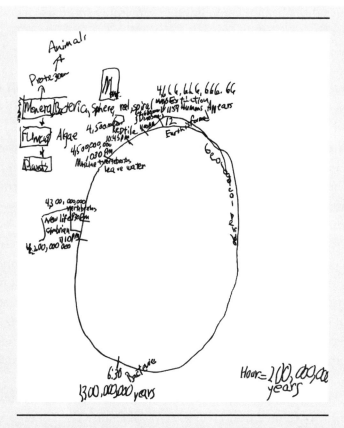

Drawing made by a boy with Asperger's disorder, illustrating his interest in time. His autobiographical statement made at the same time indicated what his drawing referred to:

> My name is … I am an intelligent unsociable, but adaptable person would like to dispel any untrue rumors about me. I cannot fly. I cannot use telekinesis. My brain is not large enough to destroy the entire world when unfolded. I did not teach my long-haired guinea pig, Chronos, to eat everything in sight. That is the nature of the long-haired guinea pig.

Source: Reprinted with permission from Volkmar et al. (2000, p. 263).

The drawing illustrates the history of the universe from the moment of its creation (12:00 midnight) through geologic time, for example, the appearance of bacteria (6:30 a.m.). It illustrates the patient's profound interest (and knowledge) regarding this topic, which tended to be all-encompassing, as well as his less-developed fine motor abilities.

Asperger thought of the condition as something more like a personality trait rather than a developmental disorder. He speculated that the condition was not usually recognized until after about age 3. His original German term for the condition was *autistic psychopathy* (probably better translated as *autistic personality disorder*); thus he used the word *autism* (as had Kanner) but was not aware of Kanner's report in the United States the year before. Asperger, who lived for many years after describing this condition, saw many cases in his lifetime. Even at the end of his life, he felt that the condition was different from infantile autism. The condition began to receive attention with the publication of a large case series in 1980, although, over time, the concept of Asperger's came to be used in several different ways. This inconsistency has been a complication in the way the term is used. The category of Asperger's disorder was officially recognized in *DSM-IV* but by *DSM-5* a decision was made to drop it. In the meantime, of course, the concept is frequently to refer to individuals who have what seem to be good verbal skills but who also have a serious social disability. It is interesting that before DSM-IV appeared a series of terms had been proposed (from a range of disciplines) to account for similar patterns of social disability. These terms came from different disciplines, for example, from pediatric neurology, right hemisphere learning disability syndrome; from speech pathology, semantic-pragmatic processing disorder; from psychiatry, schizoid personality disorder; and from psychology, a profile of termed nonverbal learning disability. The last term refers to a profile on psychological testing in which strengths early in life are in the verbal domain and weaknesses in the nonverbal one. This profile is associated with a range of conditions but does seem more commonly associated with Asperger's than autism. It has specific implications for treatment (e.g., emphasizing verbal approaches).

As a practical matter, children with AS have better verbal skills and we can sometimes use language-based treatments, such as very structured and problem-oriented psychotherapy and counseling. These therapies might not work with many typical autistic children. Poor motor skills in AS may also have important implications for vocational training. A comprehensive review of work on Asperger's is available (McPartland, Klin, & Volkmar, 2014).

Childhood Disintegrative Disorder (CDD)

Although it is fortunately rather rare, **childhood disintegrative disorder,** or **CDD,** is of interest for several reasons. It first was described almost 100 years ago by a specialist in special education, who noted the onset of what we would now describe as autism but only after a period of several years of normal development. The term *disintegrative psychosis* was used to refer to the condition but more recently the term *CDD* has been used. This condition clearly is quite rare, although it's also the case that many times children with the condition probably have not been adequately diagnosed or studied. Children with CDD develop normally for several years of life. Typically they talk on time, walk on time, acquire the capacity to speak in sentences, are normally socially related, and are toilet trained but, usually between the ages of 3 and 4 years the child experiences a marked and enduring **regression** in skills. Many behaviors that resemble those in autism develop, such as the motor mannerisms (stereotypies) and the profound lack of interest in other people typical of autism. One of the interesting questions for present research is whether children with autism who have a major regression in their development are exhibiting something like this condition (Volkmar, Koenig, & State, 2005).

Rett's Disorder

In 1966, Andreas Rett described a group of girls with an unusual history and clinical features. They were apparently normal at birth and developed normally for the first months of life. However, usually within the first year or so of life their head growth rate began to decrease. In addition, they started to lose the developmental skills they had acquired. As time went on they lost purposeful hand movements and various unusual symptoms began to develop. They seemed to lose interest in other people in the preschool years—which is why there was the potential to misdiagnose the girls as having autism. As they became somewhat older the developmental losses became more progressive and quite different from those in autism. Unusual hand-washing or hand-wringing stereotypies developed (see Figure 1.1).

The girls developed other unusual respiratory symptoms, such as breath holding spells or air swallowing (aerophagia). Seizure disorders sometimes developed as well. Problems in walking and in posture were seen and, over time, scoliosis often developed. By adulthood the girls had become severely retarded young women. However, their course was different from that seen in autism. The degree of problems in breathing, in loss of hand movements and other motor difficulties, scoliosis, and so on suggested that this was a

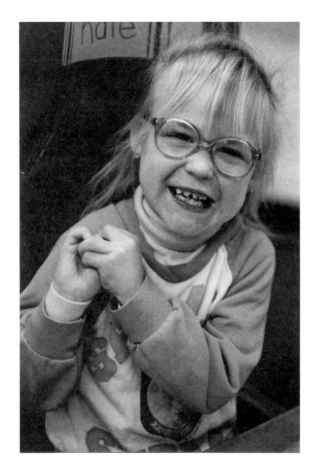

FIGURE 1.1   **Handwashing: Stereotyped Hand Movements in Rett's Disorder.**

Source: Reprinted from Van Acker, Loncola, and Van Acker (2005, p. 127).

very distinct condition. And indeed the condition has now been related to a defect in a single gene (Rutter and Thapar, 2014).

Pervasive Developmental Disorder Not Otherwise Specified (Atypical Autism, the "Broader" Autism Phenotype)

Beginning with DSM-III (1980) a group of individuals who had some features of autism but not the full condition was recognized. This turns out to be a relatively large group of individuals. Various terms have been used in describing these cases: *atypical autism, pervasive developmental disorder not otherwise specified, the broader autism spectrum,* and so forth. Given its very nature of being not quite autism but resembling the concept it is a bit complicated to think about. Over time, however, as we've become aware of the complex genetics of autism and the clinical manifestation of this group it is clear that such cases are relatively frequent and of considerable clinical and research interest (Ingersoll and Wainer, 2014; Rutter & Thapar, 2014). Indeed these cases outnumber the more "classically" autistic ones and likely account for much of the apparent increase in rates of autism and related conditions (Presmanes Hill, Zuckerman, & Fombonne, 2014). Practitioners should be aware that terms are often used rather loosely, and someone may tell you about a child with some oddities and eccentricities and equate this with autism.

CHANGES WITH *DSM-5*

The most recent version, ***DSM-5*** (APA, 2013), has introduced a number of changes based on a review of the two decades of work that followed *DSM-IV*. The rather awkward term pervasive developmental disorder that had been used for many years was dropped as the overall label for the category and replaced with autism spectrum disorder. This was a welcome change.

The new definition of autism spectrum disorder is simpler than that used in *DSM-IV* with fewer criteria for the diagnosis but probably overfocuses on more "classic" autism, because a number of studies have now shown that several groups, including the more cognitively able adolescents and adults as well as infants, would "lose" their diagnosis in *DSM-5* (Smith, Reichow, & Volkmar, 2015). As a result of these concerns the *DSM-5* definition does allow cases with "well-established" diagnoses under *DSM-IV* to keep the diagnosis. *DSM-5* also includes a new category—**social communication disorder**—for individuals with problems primarily in the area of pragmatic language. The rationale for this new category was poorly made and it is clearly the case that this new term does not simply replace the older PDD–NOS term.

EPIDEMIOLOGY OF AUTISM AND RELATED CONDITIONS

Numerous epidemiological studies of autism have been conducted. Their interpretation is complicated given differences in case findings, diagnostic criteria used, and other factors. There has been much interest in whether autism is increasing, with public service messages in the media suggesting that autism is very common. However, much of these claims are based on school records or school-assigned diagnosis for educational purposes, and it is well known that often a diagnosis of autism is desired in terms of getting more services (a problem referred to as *diagnostic substitution*). Furthermore children diagnosed by schools or inexperienced clinicians are more likely to outgrow and "lose" their diagnosis as time goes on (Blumberg, Zablotsky, Avila, Colpe, Pringle, & Kogan, 2016). A recent comprehensive review (Presmanes Hill, Zuckerman, & Fombonne, 2014) noted that the prevalence of autism (looking at the most recent studies) is about 1 in 152 children. The authors of this review did not find evidence supporting a major increase in the condition. Clearly the more stringent the criteria used the lower the rates noted, particularly if the data are based on direct examination rather than school report.

ASDs are clearly more common in males by three- to fivefold. In lower-IQ groups this is much less pronounced but in the more intellectually able the male predominance increases. There is some suggestion that higher rates of disability (overall) in females may reflect an even stronger genetic risk (see Rutter & Thapar, 2014). Studies of social class and autism in the United States typically note lower prevalence rates in Black and Hispanic children, a difference not so consistently observed in other countries with more uniform approaches to screening and medical care.

What Causes Autism?

There was much confusion in the first decade or two after autism was first described relative to its causes. Speculation began in the 1950s to center on psychosocial factors. However, during the 1960s and 1970s evidence began to strongly accumulate to show that autism was a brain-based and strongly genetic condition.

Neurobiological Aspects of Autism

It took several decades for it to become clear that autism was a strongly brain-based disorder. In his original report Kanner (1943) emphasized that autism was congenital (i.e., present from birth if not before), but he also observed that the children in his sample were attractive (i.e., not dysmorphic) and that parents were remarkably successful. These observations, combined with considerable diagnostic confusion about childhood psychosis and a strong psychosocial approach generally used in understanding mental illness, led early workers to suggest psychotherapy to "remedy" the difficulties in parenting that presumably caused autism. As time went on, however, it became clear that there was strong evidence that autism was brain-based given the frequent development of seizure disorder during childhood, a topic we discuss in more detail in subsequent chapters. Researchers began in earnest to look at the brain basis of the disorder.

A host of theories speculate about what brain region or regions may be involved, although over time models have become more sophisticated as we understand more about the complexity of the "social brain" (Pelphrey, Shultz, Hudac, & Vander Wyk, 2011; Volkmar, 2011). The significance and severity of the difficulties in processing social and other information across various areas of development are now taken to suggest that a rather diverse and widely distributed set of neural systems are implicated. At the same time it is clear that some aspects of neurocognitive functioning are spared and may even, in some cases, be highly superior, for example with savant skills sometimes present.

Scientists have conducted neuroimaging studies of the brain's structure and function. It appears that there are differences in the amygdala as well as in overall brain size. The latter appears to increase during toddlerhood (ages 2 to 4 years) with growth decelerating after that time so that by the end of adolescence brain size is only slightly larger. The nature of this difference remains the focus of research and speculation and theories have centered on abnormal connectivity in individuals with autism with more connections "locally" and fewer "long-range" connections. One of the best-replicated fMRI findings came from our group (Schultz et al., 2000) when we observed that a part of the ventral surface of the temporal lobe (the fusiform gyrus) was underactive during a face perception task. This area in typically developing individuals seems to have a high specificity for processing faces.

Overall the literature on neuroimaging suggests volume differences in specific brain regions with brain overgrowth the most replicated finding in one subgroup of cases and atypical structural and functional connectivity with some changes observed with age (Anagnostou & Taylor, 2011). These studies have been complemented by other approaches. For example, autopsy studies are relatively uncommon, but the available work has suggested differences in cortical structure particularly in those brain regions involved in social-affective processing, specifically, the amygdala, hippocampus, septum, anterior cingulate, and mammillary bodies; these strongly interconnected regions comprise the limbic system. Newer work has used stem cell technology to replicate early brain development.

New methods have also been used to understand social information processing. For example, methods using eye tracking (infrared cameras are able to follow the exact point of regard as an individual watches social situation) note major differences in the way social scenes are viewed. The following figure shows the focus of interest for a person with autism and a typically developing adult viewing a short film clip from the movie classic *Who's Afraid of Virginia Wolf?* The person with autism who is cognitively high functioning tracks the mouth during the playing of this clip while the typically developing adult focuses on the eye region—(see Figure 1.2) the latter giving much more social affective information than the former.

As might be expected, attempts have been made to produce animal models of autism. Early work focused on lesion studies or exposure to various teratogens in utero. Interpretation of behavioral change was challenging. Furthermore developmental aspects of autism did not seem to be simply observed. However, with the discovery of single-gene disorders such as Fragile X syndrome and Rett's syndrome, it is now possible to produce genetically modified animal models, and exciting work on basic genetic mechanisms is proceeding and may even lead to treatments.

Genetic Factors

A strong role of genetic factors was suggested in the first twin study of autism (Folstein & Rutter, 1977). Subsequent twin studies have confirmed these findings with estimates of heritability in the 60% to 90% range. This line of research has also suggested vulnerability in family members for a broader range of neuropsychiatric disorders including ADHD, anxiety, and learning and language problems. Subsequent work in the area has exploded in the past decade, particularly over the last few years as genetic methods and techniques have become much more sophisticated (and relatively cheaper!). We've moved from the 1980s, when we were looking at karyotypes, to now having the potential for genomic sequencing. Several critical findings have emerged over the last decade or so (Rutter & Thapar, 2014).

It is clear that genetic influences are very important in autism and that in a small group of cases (clearly less than 10%) associations with conditions such as Fragile X and tuberous sclerosis are identified. These associations are, however, important in terms of initial work; for example, screening for these conditions and their presence has important implications for genetic counseling of parents and family members. It has become apparent that there is a wide range of variability in the phenotypes of autism and that a number of genes and mechanisms create considerable genetic heterogeneity. More commonly it appears that the genes involved in autism are multiple and are involved as well in the potential expression of a broader range of conditions (the "broader phenotype"). Many of the genes identified have made sense in that they often seem to be involved in aspects of brain development or neural connectivity.

FIGURE 1.2 **Visual focus of a typically developing adult (top line) and a high-functioning man with autism (bottom line) while viewing a short movie clip from the classic film *Who's Afraid of Virginia Woolf?* The typically developing individual focuses on the top portion of the face while observing the interaction; the individual with autism focuses on the mouth region (losing much of the social-emotional information).**

Source: Reprinted, with permission from Klin, Jones, Schultz, Volkmar, and Cohen (2002, p. 899).

Obstetrical Risk and Environmental Factors in ASD

Given that the concordance rate in identical twins is less than 100% some potential importance might be attached to issues of obstetrical risk or environmental factors—perhaps interacting with genetic vulnerability (Lyall, Schmidt, & Hertz-Picciotto, 2014). Research has addressed the relevance of possible environmental factors or specific toxins, but findings have not been conclusive in terms of proving strong environmental connections. Similarly a recent meta-analysis of more than 40 studies looking at prenatal factors in autism evaluated 50 potential risk factors. Those factors observed included advanced parental age, medication use by the mother, early- or later-born children, and gestational diabetes among others, although, of course, one of the difficulties here is that problems in the fetus might themselves increase obstetric risk. The study concluded that there was not sufficient evidence to implicate any one single prenatal factor in the pathogenesis of autism (Gardener, Spiegelman, & Buka, 2009). In a large study from Finland (including a broad diagnostic approach encompassing cases with **subthreshold** autism) low Apgars at birth were noted to be a risk (Polo-Kantola, Lampi, Salomaki, Gissler, et al., 2014).

SERVICES FOR CHILDREN WITH AUTISM

Initial treatment approaches in the 1950s and 1960s often focused on correcting a putative problem related to emotional deprivation. In the 1960s this began to change as research suggested a strong brain basis for the disorder (Rimland, 1964). During the 1970s other work appeared that showed that structured interventions with strong behavioral and special education components were more effective than unstructured psychotherapy (Bartak & Rutter, 1973). Most important, increased legislative interest in children with disabilities of all kinds resulted in the passage of the Education for All Handicapped Children Act in 1975. Before then parents often were told by schools that there was no way their child could be educated. Often parents were advised to place their child in a residential or large state institution where the child got little in the way of intervention.

Now schools in the United States are mandated to provide a **free and appropriate public education (FAPE)** for all individuals with disabilities. This is a radically different approach. As programs have become increasingly sophisticated schools have done an increasingly better job of providing education for children with autism (NRC, 2001). This means that schools now provide the major focus of intervention for this population. As a result it appears that more children are being identified in schools and receiving services and, importantly, it also seems that, as a group, children with autism are doing better as services are provided. A considerable, and expanding, body of work on evidence-based treatments in autism is now available (Reichow, Doehring, Cicchetti & Volkmar, 2011).

Diagnostic and intervention practice are rather similar in the United States and most English-speaking countries as well as in Northern Europe and Japan. In other parts of the world interest is increasing. Although autism is seen in all cultures there are only a few studies of cultural issues in autism (Freeth, Milne, Sheppard, & Ramachandran, 2014). Within the United States high socioeconomic status (SES) and high-income families are more likely to seek a diagnosis and access services; conversely, families in poverty may be less aware of the condition and less likely to receive a diagnosis or access services (Palmer, Walker, Mandell, Bayles, & Miller, 2010). Sadly it is the case that few attempts have been made to examine differences in practice across states in the United States (Doehring, 2014).

CURRENT RESEARCH

Research in autism has expanded tremendously over the last several decades as a result of increased federal and private support and the potential for investigators to understand more about what makes us uniquely human—the social brain. Work has proceeded using a variety of techniques that look at actual brain processes in a host of ways; for example, fMRI, EEG, and new methods such as eye tracking have been used to clarify some of the basic ways in which social engagement differs in individuals with ASD. Work on genetic mechanisms is now beginning to link to other areas, including work on brain development and connectivity.

Work has also proceeded on evaluating treatments with a view toward establishing treatments as being evidence based—something we will discuss in Chapter 12 when we talk about alternative treatments (see Box 1.5). Treatment studies are among the most difficulty to obtain federal funding for, unfortunately, for both psychosocial and pharmacological research.

Furthermore the knowledge base among the various disciplines involved in the care of individuals with autism varies tremendously. And, unfortunately and notably, work on and with older adults is quite limited indeed. This relates, in part, to the enthusiasm over the potential for early diagnosis and treatment and the hope for better outcomes. But it does reflect the unfortunate tendency to overlook the very significant needs of adolescents and adults. A number of practice guidelines and books on evidence-based treatments in autism are now available (McClure, 2014; Volkmar et al., 2014).

BOX 1.5 EVIDENCE-BASED MEDICINE AND EVIDENCE-BASED PRACTICE

Evidence-based medicine approaches clinical decision making based on well-conducted research. In development of recommendations such as practice guidelines, several levels of support are typically identified (procedures vary somewhat), typically giving the most credence to the strongest types of support (meta-analyses of multiple studies, systematic reviews, and well-conducted randomized controlled trials). Intermediate levels of support typically derive from case-controlled studies, particularly if these are well conducted and free of potential confounds and bias. The weakest levels of evidence are case reports or, ultimately, clinical opinion. It is important to note that some procedures are in common use but have never, ever been subject to a randomized trial (e.g., jumping out of airplanes with and without parachutes!). For psychological research, issues may arise relative to the kinds of studies that can be designed and conducted, for example, in the move of a treatment program from specialized treatment (academic) centers to more real-world settings. Official practice guidelines typically will attempt to summarize the strength of available evidence in making recommendations about potential treatments.

Evidence-based practice has its origins in evidence-based medicine but has expanded to a range of other fields, including psychology, speech-communication, education, and others. It strives to use the best available research evidence on the selection of treatment in the context of the individual needs and treatment preferences.

Summary

This chapter has provided some background information on autism-related concepts that now fall within the broad term of *autism spectrum disorder*. All these share, as a basic and essential feature, major problems in social interaction. These social learning disorders have important ramifications for the ways children learn from the social and nonsocial world. Autism and related conditions are strongly genetic and brain-based. They can be associated with eventual intellectual deficiency but, and fortunately increasingly often, with earlier diagnosis and intervention, outcomes may well be substantially improved. Various medical conditions are associated with autism including, more frequently, seizure disorders (epilepsy) and, less commonly, specific genetic conditions, notably Fragile X and tuberous sclerosis.

REFERENCES

American Psychiatric Association. (1980). *Diagnostic and statistical manual of mental disorders (DSM-III;* 3rd. ed.). Arlington, VA: American Psychiatric Press.

American Psychiatric Association. (1994). *Diagnostic and statistical manual of mental disorders (DSM-IV;* 4th ed.). Arlington, VA: American Psychiatric Press.

American Psychiatric Association. (2013). *Diagnostic and statistical manual (DSM-5;* 5th ed.). Arlington, VA: American Psychiatric Association.

Anagnostou, E., & Taylor, M. D. (2011). Review of neuroimaging in autism spectrum disorders: What we have learned and where we go from here. *Molecular Autism, 2*(4), 1–9.

Asperger, H. (1944). Die "autistichen psychopathen" im kindersalter. *Archive fur Psychiatrie und Nervenkrankheiten, 117,* 76–136. Reprinted [in part] in Frith, U. (Ed.). (1991). *Autism and Asperger syndrome.* Cambridge, UK: Cambridge University Press.

Bartak, L., & Rutter, M. (1973). Special educational treatment of autistic children: A comparative study. 1. Design of study and characteristics of units. *Journal of Child Psychology and Psychiatry and Allied Disciplines, 14*(3), 161–179.

Blumberg, S., Zablotsky, B., Avila, R., Colpe, L., Pringle, B. A., & Kogan, M. (2016). Diagnosis lost: Differences between children who had and who currently have an autism spectrum disorder diagnosis. *Autism, 20*(7), 783–795. doi:10.1177/1362361315607724

Doehring, P. (2014). Translating research into effective social policy. In F. R. Volkmar, S. J. Rogers, R. Paul, & K. A. Pelphrey (Eds.), *Handbook of autism and pervasive developmental disorders* (4th ed., Vol. 2, pp. 1107–1126). Hoboken, NJ: Wiley.

Folstein, S., & Rutter, M. (1977). Genetic influences and infantile autism. *Nature, 265*(5596), 726–728.

Freeth, M., Milne, E., Sheppard, E., & Ramachandran, R. (2014). Autism across cultures: Perspectives from non-western cultures and implications for research. In F. R. Volkmar, S. J. Rogers, R. Paul, & K. A. Pelphrey (Eds.), *Handbook of autism and pervasive developmental disorders* (4th ed., Vol. 2, pp. 997–1013). Hoboken, NJ: Wiley.

Gardener, H., Spiegelman, D., & Buka, S. L. (2009). Prenatal risk factors for autism: Comprehensive meta-analysis. *British Journal of Psychiatry, 195*(1), 7–14.

Ingersoll, B., & Wainer, A. (2014). The broader autism phenotype. In F. R. Volkmar, S. J. Rogers, R. Paul, & K. A. Pelphrey (Eds.), *Handbook of autism and pervasive developmental disorders* (4th ed., Vol. 1, pp. 28–56). Hoboken, NJ: Wiley.

Klin, A., Jones, W., Schultz, R., Volkmar, F. R., & Cohen, D. J. (2002). Defining and qualifying the social phenotype in autism. *American Journal of Psychiatry, 159,* 895–908.

Lyall, K., Schmidt, R. J., & Hertz-Picciotto, I. (2014). Environmental factors in the preconception and prenatal periods in relation to risk for ASD. In F. R. Volkmar, S. J. Rogers, R. Paul, & K. A. Pelphrey (Eds.), *Handbook of autism and pervasive developmental disorders* (4th ed., Vol. 1, pp. 424–456). Hoboken, NJ: Wiley.

McClure, I. (2014). Developing and implementing practice guidelines. In F. R. Volkmar, S. J. Rogers, R. Paul, & K. A. Pelphrey (Eds.), *Handbook of autism and pervasive developmental disorders* (4th ed., Vol. 2, pp. 1014–1035). Hoboken, NJ: Wiley.

McPartland, J. C., Klin, A., & Volkmar, F. R. (2014). Asperger syndrome: Assessing and treating high-functioning autism spectrum disorders. *Asperger syndrome: Assessing and treating high-functioning autism spectrum disorders* (2nd ed.) New York, NY: Guilford Press.

National Research Council. (2001). *Educating young children with autism.* Washington, DC: National Academy Press.

Palmer, R. F., Walker, T., Mandell, D., Bayles, B., & Miller, C. S. (2010). Explaining low rates of autism among Hispanic schoolchildren in Texas. *American Journal of Public Health, 100*(2), 270–272.

Pelphrey, K. A., Shultz, S., Hudac, C. M., & Vander Wyk, B. C. (2011). Research review: Constraining heterogeneity; The social brain and its development in autism spectrum disorder. *Journal of Child Psychology and Psychiatry and Allied Disciplines, 52*(6), 631–644.

Polo-Kantola, P., Lampi, K. M., Salomaki, S. Gissler, M., et al. (2014). Obstetric risk factors and autism spectrum disorders in Finland. *Journal of Pediatrics, 164*(2), 358–365.

Presmanes Hill, A., Zuckerman, K., & Fombonne, E. (2014). Epidemiology of autism spectrum disorders. In F. R. Volkmar, S. J. Rogers, R. Paul, & K. A. Pelphrey (Eds.), *Handbook of autism and pervasive developmental disorders* (4th ed., Vol. 1, pp. 57–96). Hoboken, NJ: Wiley.

Reichow, B., Doehring, P., Cicchetti, D. V., & Volkmar, F. (2011). *Evidence-based practices and treatments for children with autism.* New York, NY: Springer.

Rimland, B. (1964). *Infantile autism: The syndrome and its implications for a neural theory of behavior.* New York, NY: Appleton-Century-Crofts.

Rutter, M., & Thapar, A. (2014). Genetics of autism spectrum disorders. In F. R. Volkmar, S. J. Rogers, R. Paul, & K. A. Pelphrey (Eds.), *Handbook of autism and pervasive developmental disorders* (4th ed., Vol. *1*, pp. 411–423). Hoboken, NJ: Wiley.

Schultz, R. T., Gauthier, I., Klin, A., Fulbright, R. K., Anderson, A. W., Volkmar, F., Skudlarski, P., Lacadie, C., Cohen, D. J., & Gore, J. C. (2000). Abnormal ventral temporal cortical activity during face discrimination among individuals with autism and Asperger syndrome. *Archives of General Psychiatry, 57*(4), 331–340.

Selfe, L. (1979). *Nadia: A case of extraordinary drawing ability in an autistic child.* New York, NY: Harcourt.

Smith, I. C., Reichow, B., & Volkmar, F. R. (2015). The effects of *DSM-5* criteria on number of individuals diagnosed with autism spectrum disorder: A systematic review. *Journal of Autism and Developmental Disorders, 45*(8), 2541–2552.

Thioux, M., Stark, D. E., Klaiman, C., & Schultz, R. T. (2006). The day of the week when you were born in 700 ms: Calendar computation in an autistic savant. *Journal of Experimental Psychology: Human Perception & Performance, 32*(5), 1155–1168.

Van Acker, R., Loncola, J. A., & Van Acker, E. Y. (2005). Rett syndrome: A pervasive developmental disorder. In F. Volkmar, A. Klin, R. Paul, & D. J. Cohen (Eds.), *Handbook of autism and pervasive developmental disorders* (3rd ed., Vol. *1*, pp. 126–164). New York: Wiley.

Volkmar, F. R. (2011). Understanding the social brain in autism. *Developmental Psychobiology, 53*(5), 428–434.

Volkmar, F. R., Klin, A., Schultz, R. T., Rubin, E., & Bronen, R. (2000). Asperger's disorder. *American Journal of Psychiatry, 157*(2), 262–267.

Volkmar, F. R., Koenig, K., & State, M. (2005). Childhood disintegrative disorder. In F. Volkmar, A. Klin, R. Paul, & D. J. Cohen (Eds.), *Handbook of autism and pervasive developmental disorders* (3rd ed., Vol. *1*, pp. 70–86). New York: Wiley.

Volkmar, F., & Pauls, D. (2003). Autism. *The Lancet, 2362,* 1134.

Volkmar, F., Siegel, M., Woodbury-Smith, M., King, B., McCracken, J., State, M., & the American Academy of and Child and Adolescent Psychiatry (AACAP) Committee on Quality Issues (CQI). (2014). Practice parameter for the assessment and treatment of children and adolescents with autism spectrum disorder. *Journal of the American Academy of Child and Adolescent Psychiatry, 53*(2), 237–257.

World Health Organization (WHO). (1993). *International classification of diseases (ICD-10;* 10th ed.). Geneva, Switzerland: Author.

SUGGESTED READING

Attwood, T. (2006). *The complete guide to Asperger's syndrome.* Philadelphia, PA: Jessica Kingsley.

Baron-Cohen, S. (2004). *The essential difference: Male and female brains and the truth about autism.* New York, NY: Basic Books.

Donvan, J., & Zuker, C. (2016). *In a different key: The story of autism.* New York, NY: Penguin Random House.

Hermelin, B. (2001). Bright splinters of the mind: A personal story of research with autistic savants. London, UK: Jessica Kingsley.

Frith, U., & Hill, E. (Eds.). (2004). *Autism: Mind and brain.* New York, NY: Oxford University Press.

Grinker, R. R. (2007). *Unstrange minds: Remapping the world of autism.* New York, NY: Basic Books.

Romanowski-Bashe, P., Kirby, B. L., Baron-Cohen, S., & Attwood, T. (2005). *The OASIS guide to Asperger syndrome: Completely revised and updated; Advice, support, insight, and inspiration.* New York, NY: Crown.

Silberman, S. (2015). *Neurotribes: The legacy of autism and the future of neurodiversity.* New York, NY: Penguin Books.

CHAPTER 2

Screening and Diagnostic Assessment

A wareness by primary care providers is essential in providing the earliest opportunities for screening and diagnosis of ASD. Earlier diagnosis and provision of effective treatments helps us optimize, to the extent possible, the child's ultimate outcome.

THE ROLE OF DIAGNOSIS

The diagnosis of autism is important in helping the child and family secure needed services. There are good data to suggest that with earlier diagnosis and intervention children with autism (as a group) are doing better and better. Issues of screening are often most relevant to primary health care providers with definitive diagnosis often established by specialists. It is important to be aware of, at least in the United States, that eligibility for services can be granted for young children (those under 3) even before a diagnosis is definitively established and also that for children over 3 schools are mandated service providers. As we discussed in Chapter 1, autism is a strongly genetic disorder associated with a handful of (generally also) strongly genetic conditions. Although our awareness of possible genetic mechanisms has increased dramatically, even with our understanding of some of the specific genetic risk factors, the diagnostic assessment remains a clinical diagnosis best made by experienced clinicians rather than a genetic test or single assessment instrument. Other conditions can either coexist with autism or be confused with autism and are reviewed subsequently in this chapter; we touch on this again when we discuss treatments.

Primary care providers have an important role in screening for autism because they see children many times during their first years of life. As we'll discuss in this chapter a number of warning signs are frequent, and some **screening tests** have been developed that make use of these. Although delays in detection are less frequent than in the past they still sometimes happen. Early provision of service seems to be very important in determining ultimate outcome, and for some children the difference is between a child who grows up to be independent and self-sufficient or one who is in **residential services.**

Similar to all diagnoses, an autism diagnosis has potential limitations. It gives us a general sense of the child's needs but does not tell us a lot about the specifics. As mentioned, particularly in the United States the autism label may have important implications for service eligibility. Clinicians rely on observation and history to make the diagnosis. Various guidelines, rating scales, and checklists have been developed and may help in the process, but they augment and don't replace thoughtful clinical thinking.

As we discussed in Chapter 1, guidelines to the categorical diagnosis of autism have evolved over time; this has reflected changes in our understanding of autism. The move to autism spectrum disorder in the *DSM-5* (APA, 2013) is, in many ways, a good one although aspects of the *DSM-5* system are problematic since the actual definition is rather narrow and many individuals with previous diagnoses would now potentially lose their official diagnosis and thus, at least in the United States, potentially their eligibility for educational services (Smith, Reichow, & Volkmar, 2015). It appeared that the higher-cognitive-functioning cases (with what *DSM-IV* would have termed *Asperger's disorder* or *PDD-NOS* as well those with higher-cognitive functioning) were at risk of losing their diagnosis (and thus access to services) as were very young children. As a result of these concerns a decision was made for the final version of *DSM-5* to grandfather in well-established previous diagnoses, that is, effectively creating a new system and, at least for those already diagnosed, keeping the older one. Given all this, issues of diagnosis are less clear than in the past. That said, and as we'll discuss subsequently, a number of well-designed screening and diagnostic instruments continue to be used and can facilitate the diagnostic process regardless of which specific categorical approach one desires to use. It is important to realize that these instruments often rely on dimensional assessments rather than simple categorical ones; for example, multiple items may be evaluated based on a current exam or past history and rated based on severity with a total score suggesting the likelihood or severity of autism. Often these assessments require training, sometimes extensive, in their administration and interpretation. Similarly, as we will discuss shortly, the use of dimensional instruments such as tests of intelligence, language, communication, and **adaptive behavior (functioning)** remain important parts of the evaluative process (see Appendix 2, "Understanding School and Specialist Assessment," for a review of such instruments). As a practical matter in the real world our approach to the actual patient tends to be ideographic, that is, we want to see the entire person with his or her whole pattern of strengths and weaknesses.

WARNING SIGNS IN YOUNG CHILDREN

Although parents are mostly concerned in the first year of life some become more concerned as language fails to develop after the first birthday; 90% of parents are concerned by age 2. In the other 10% of cases the child is either somewhat more cognitively able (this may delay diagnostic concern) or, occasionally, a child develops normally and then has a regression of development (see Chapter 7). Concerns are more likely to develop earlier if parents are well educated and may be delayed in families of lower socioeconomic status. Sometimes, particularly for higher cognitively functioning individuals, concerns may not be raised until much later. Concern may also increase for children with siblings who are known to have autism or it may come, particularly for first-time parents, when grandparents or aunts and uncles (or the primary care provider) raise concern. We are increasingly aware that the earlier estimates of recurrent risk in siblings (2% or so) are significantly less than what we now observe (10%–20%) (Schaefer, Mendelsohn, & Professional and Clinical Guidelines Committee, 2013).

Early concern may come as parents note developmental differences. For example, in retrospect the mother may report that the baby was hard to hold, seemed distant or less interested in others. Sometimes the child may not respond to human voice but be overly sensitive to the sound of the vacuum cleaner, and parents may be worried about a possible hearing problem. The infant may not participate in the social games or routines of infancy and be happy to be left alone. Even before language develops, potential problems in communication may be observed with limited response to language (including his or her own name). Unusual interests (in moving things such as fans) and attachments (to hard rather than soft objects) may develop. We talk more about these warning signs in detail in Chapter 7, which focuses on infants and young children. Occasionally a child seems to develop normally and stops (usually this is reported after the first birthday), although it can be hard to disentangle, at times, an actual regression from a failure to progress (essentially developmental stagnation).

Parents may report that, as infants get a bit older, the child responds idiosyncratically to some sounds or may communicate her or his wants in odd ways, such as taking a parent's hand to a desired object without making eye contact (i.e., using the hand as a tool as if there is not a person connected to it) or failures in **joint attention** (e.g., rarely pointing to show things to parents).

It is important to take parent concern seriously. In the past it was frequent to reassure parents that the child was "'just language delayed." But children who have only language delay are usually socially related and don't have the unusual behaviors we see in autism. A history or observation of regression—particularly if this is marked (e.g., a child who had phrase speech and then stops speaking) should also prompt significant clinical concern. We'll discuss issues that arise relative to regression further on in this chapter and discuss early warning signs in greater detail in Chapter 7.

Once concern arises, what can be done? Fortunately a number of tools are available to primary care providers. These include general developmental screeners (Level 1 screeners) that can be used to assess overall development and determine whether more specific evaluation is needed. Typically primary care providers will have had some experience with one or more of these during their training. In addition other instruments (Level 2 screeners) have been developed that are specific to autism (see Box 2.1). Features of some of these screeners are provided in Table 2.1.

BOX 2.1 SCREENING FOR AUTISM AND INITIAL ASSESSMENT
LEVEL 1 AND LEVEL 2 SCREENERS

Level 1: Routine Developmental Surveillance
- Performed on all children at all well-child visits
- Identifies children at risk for atypical development
- Red flags indicating additional screening

Level 2: Diagnosis and Evaluation of Autism
- In-depth evaluation of children identified as at-risk
- Differentiates autism from other developmental disorders
- Can help with diagnosis (but should *not* be the *sole* determination of diagnosis)

The American Academy of Pediatrics has recommended screening at 18 and 24 months of age. Concerns can and do arise even before 18 months, and warning signs or suggestive features on reports or from examinations can also lead to referral for early intervention services. Many of the screeners currently available are designed as Level 1 screens—that is, to be used for general screening for autism by primary care providers—and other screeners (Level 2 screeners) are more focused on a diagnosis of autism, for example, in at-risk populations. Level 1 screeners typically require relatively little training. A few screeners have aspects of more general (Level 1) and autism-specific (Level 2) items. As a general rule Level 1 screeners are a bit more concerned with sensitivity, that is, correctly picking up a high proportion of children at risk for possible autism (or in the case of the general screeners children at any developmental risk). However, the Level 2 screeners focus on autism and generally try to be efficient and pick up only those children with autism (that is minimizing false positives for the diagnosis). As with all screeners there is a trade-off between these two tensions. These instruments often tend to pick up children at risk for autism *and* for other developmental problems. Of the various screeners summarized in Table 2.1 the M-CHAT is the most commonly used. The "Suggested Reading" list at the end of the chapter provides information on other screeners that will

TABLE 2.1 SELECTED SCREENING INSTRUMENTS FOR AUTISM

Scale Name (Abbreviation)	Age Range; Type of Screener	Administration	Comment
Modified Checklist for Autism in Toddlers (M-CHAT)	16–30 months Level 1	First-stage 23-item yes-no (parent) with follow-up for screen positives	Readily and frequently used Tends to over-identify
Early Screening of Autistic Traits Questionnaire (ESAT)	14 months Level 1	14 yes-no items, parent report	Good Se* but lower Sp**
Social Communication Questionnaire (SCQ)	4 years+ Level 2	40-item scale	Looks at current and lifetime behaviors
Gilliam Autism Rating Scale, 2nd ed. (GARS-2)	3–22 years Level 2	42 items	May underdiagnose
Childhood Autism Rating Scale, 2nd ed. (CARS-2)	2 years to adult Level 2	15 items 4-point scale (0 = normal to 4 = very autistic)	Can be used for diagnosis; requires some (minimal) training
Screening Tool for Autism in Two-Year-Olds (STAT)	24–35 months Level 2	12-item scale administered to child	Good balance of Se* and Sp**
Social Responsiveness Scale, 2nd ed. (SRS-2)	>2.5 years Level 2	Easily done, different forms for different ages	Caregiver (or self-) report with an overall total score to reflect severity and five subscale scores; different forms for different age groups (adults can self-report); readily administered and scored; aids clinical diagnosis
Autism Behavior Checklist (ABC)	5–22 years Level 2	47 yes-no items, teacher or parent	Readily used in school settings

*Sensitivity
**specificity

be discussed in less detail (see Ibanez, Stone, & Coonrod, 2014, for a very detailed review).

The M-CHAT helps in identifying children at risk—thus many children who score positive do not, in the end, receive an autism diagnosis. It can be used for toddlers between 16 and 30 months of age. Parents are asked to answer a series of yes–no questions about their child's development and behavior. The screen is positive if any three features of autism are said by parents to be present or if the child fails two of the six items identified by the authors as more central to autism. These critical items focus on interest in other children, responding to name, pointing (following a parent or child pointing to show), and **imitation.** A follow-up interview (M-CHAT FUI) has been developed and seeks additional information about the specific behaviors. The M-CHAT was developed as an extension of an older British instrument but was modified to be based on parent report. The M-CHAT has been widely translated and is readily available. The instrument has been shown to have a reasonable balance of sensitivity and specificity; but as would be expected false positive screens are fairly common.

Given some of the concerns about the M-CHAT a revised version (Robins, Casagrande, Barton, Chen, Dumont-Mathieu, & Fein, 2014) has been developed. The M-CHAT-R requires little or no training for health care professionals and is readily available (www.mchatscreen .com). In the first stage parents respond to 20 yes–no questions (this takes only a few minutes). If children screen positively for autism risk then parents are asked a more structured series of follow-up questions to obtain additional information (5–10 minutes estimated time). The new version was modified in several ways including dropping several items that did not seem to work well in the initial version, language was simplified for parents, and examples given to clarify items. Children with a total score of >3 on the initial screen and >2 at the follow-up interview were at about a 48% risk of being diagnosed with ASD and a 95% risk of some developmental concerns.

With various screeners now available, it is clear that given the importance of early diagnosis and the major role primary care providers have in monitoring early development some screening should be undertaken.

Sometimes issues of screening arise for older children (as late as school-age). This can happen in a range of situations, for example, a child is 4 but in a non-English-speaking household, or a child is of school-age but is more cognitively able and social vulnerabilities are less apparent until he or she is exposed to groups of peers, or sometimes diagnosis is delayed if the family is economically disadvantaged and don't have access to regular health care or get health care in settings like walk in clinics or even the emergency room where little attention may be paid to developmental issues. Care providers should remain alert to the issue of a possible missed or delayed autism spectrum diagnosis in individuals of all ages.

Screening in Older Children, Adolescents, and Adults

Although it is typical for autism or ASD to be recognized in young children the diagnosis is sometimes missed. This can occur for different reasons. Probably most commonly the child is more cognitively able and somewhat less severely socially impaired (or at least appears to be). Asperger suggested this back in 1944 because concern arose for the boys he described as they entered preschool, when unusual social overtures and a lack of social sensitivity led to initial worry on the part of teachers. Indeed, many such children, particularly if somewhat less impaired, may manage to get by and, in their own way and often in some specialized area, be relatively successful. For example, in one recent study of a large sample of college students (White, Ollendick, & Bray, 2011) between 1% and 2% screened positive for symptoms of autism, none of whom had been previously diagnosed. Occasionally one of us has seen individuals well into adulthood who wondered (or whose spouses wondered) if they had autism, Asperger's, or ASD!

As we noted, poverty and lack of parental education, particularly in strained educational systems, may also lead to serious underdiagnosis of autism and misdiagnoses of other problems such as intellectual deficiency or emotional or behavioral problems and may overshadow autism detection and service provision in school systems. This can be a major problem and challenge for primary care providers who may need to educate educators about autism! For adults, particularly, issues of comorbidity (having more than one disorder) can complicate diagnosis and screening. For example, an adult might also have depression or anxiety problems as the initial presenting complaint. Some of the screeners mentioned previously will work with school-age and adolescent children. For adults many of the diagnostic instruments we'll review further on in this chapter can be used.

WHAT TO DO IF A SCREEN IS POSITIVE

If a screen is positive, or if parental concern (for whatever reason) is raised (e.g., because of a relative), or if you are concerned based on your observation of the child or parent's report, it is imperative to obtain a careful history and examination. This should include a history of the pregnancy, birth, and delivery, as well as family history (particularly for a history of autism or recurrent developmental problems). If the child is not previously known to you, review with the parents what the child's early development was like—were milestones on time or delayed? Was the baby overly difficult or "too easy"? Did he or she respond appropriately to parents (and to you)? For less sophisticated parents and for parents with multiple children, remembering specific dates may be easier if you ask the parent to remember a specific time (first birthday or Christmas) and describe the child's behavior. Are there any symptoms suggestive of seizures? Of hearing loss? Has the child had frequent ear infections? Be alert for factors that might account for language delay (e.g., a child who is hearing two languages spoken at home)—but even in these cases look for warning signs of possible autism (in the past year one of us has seen two children in which over a year went by between parental concern and diagnosis because of bilingualism in the home). Has the child had any other evaluations already? Are the parents familiar with what services might be available from Birth to Three or Child Find or similar agencies, that is, evaluation only, evaluation and treatment services, or help in securing treatment? It is helpful if primary care providers can put parents in touch with relevant state agencies (such as Birth to Three, Child Find, or other agencies) and then follow up with the parents to be sure an evaluation was done. The follow-up is critical for several reasons. Sometimes parents want to minimize troubles or have obstacles (because of poverty, language barriers, and so forth) in accessing service or following through with interventions, and unfortunately many children who screen positive don't get a further evaluation. At least one study suggests that even when screening is done, there are many obstacles to getting the child assessed and then into an appropriate intervention program. In 2010 King and colleagues examined factors that contributed to success and failure in screening. In this project 17 different practices attempted to implement the American Academy of Pediatrics recommendations on screening. Quantitative data (based on chart reviews) and qualitative data from phone interviews were used. Nearly all the practices implemented parent-completed screening instruments and a large number of cases (85%) were screened, although doing so could have been a challenge. Only about 60% of children who failed (i.e., were positive on) the screen actually were referred and families often failed to follow up on referrals. This underscores the need for practices to have a sound system in place that ensures screening, referral, and systematic follow-up (King et al., 2010).

Comprehensive Diagnostic Assessments

Often the state-designated early child intervention providers will conduct an initial, although often somewhat limited, assessment. Practices vary from state to state and often within a state. These early assessments often serve to define eligibility for service and to direct aspects of early intervention. Definitive diagnosis often is done as the child reaches between ages 3 and 5. This reflects the fact that assessment instruments become more elaborate (often moving from screening or parent report to more traditional tests of development, intelligence, or communication—see Appendix 2). Also it is at about 3 years of age that we can become most certain of a diagnosis of autism (Lord, 1995). Because children become eligible for school-based programs at age 3 schools may conduct more comprehensive assessments or refer parents to specialists or centers where people are knowledgeable in the area. Sometimes, of course, parents wish to obtain more detailed assessments or a second opinion and additional services.

Various specialists and organizations around the country provide comprehensive diagnostic assessments for children at risk of having autism. Sometimes these more detailed assessments are provided by specialists working as individuals (who may or may not collaborate with professionals from other disciplines) and sometimes groups of providers may work as a team (Volkmar, Booth, McPartland, & Wiesner, 2014). States vary tremendously in terms of what is available: In some states there are diagnostic centers that service this need as part of a more comprehensive package of autism-related interventions. Some of the excellent centers (and there are others, too) are provided in the resource list for this chapter. Often university-based medical schools, clinics, or children's hospitals will have such programs, and some parent organizations such as Autism Speaks (www.autismspeaks.org) and the Center for Disease Control (https://www.cdc.

gov/ncbddd/autism/index.html), the American Academy of Pediatrics (https://www.aap.org/en-us/about-the-aap/Committees-Councils-Sections/Council-on-Children-with-Disabilities/Pages/Autism.aspx), the American Academy of Child and Adolescent Psychiatry (https://www.aacap.org/AACAP/Families_and_Youth/Facts_for_Families/FFF-Guide/The-Child-With-Autism-011.aspx), and university websites such as the one at Yale (www.autism.fm) provide links to helpful information and resources.

A comprehensive assessment will usually include a number of elements, varying a bit depending on the child's age and current levels of functioning. Typically this will include a careful history (important for establishing a diagnosis and also clarifying what additional studies might be needed) and psychological testing, including tests of development or intelligence as well as adaptive (real-world) functioning. The results of the psychological assessment typically serve as a baseline (against which subsequent progress can be assessed) and as an aid in treatment planning. Typically observation and results of tests can help clarify areas of strength and weakness important for programming and also help with a differential diagnosis. Often a speech-language pathologist will do an assessment of language and communication skills; this is frequently an area that is deferred to the school. If the school person is experienced, it may be fine, but it is important that an experienced individual does this. Testing is not just limited to vocabulary. Some children with autism may have a large vocabulary, sometimes as a result of extensive teaching, but they don't always use their vocabulary to communicate. The speech pathologist will assess language levels and help develop a plan for intervention with a broad focus on fostering communication skills. Occupational and physical therapy assessments focus on sensory issues as well as gross and fine motor skills. Depending on the history and examination, other professionals can also be involved, for example, an audiologist, ophthalmologist, neurologist, or geneticist. Appendix 2 provides a summary of some aspects of assessments and how to understand reports from specialists and schools.

As was true for screening instruments, a number of measures have been developed for diagnosis—some of these rely on parent report, others on observations; some require very extensive training and others relatively little. These instruments are designed to help (but to not replace) good clinical work (see Lord, Corsello, & Grzadzinski, 2014, for a comprehensive summary of diagnostic instruments). Be wary if an experienced clinician or team makes a definitive diagnosis based solely on a single instrument.

Many different issues are involved in the use of these instruments (again, a little knowledge can be a dangerous thing), and sometimes people will use them in ways that were not intended. For example, we encountered a well-meaning school administrator who got access to a rating scale, and, with no training in how to use it and very little experience with autism, decided a child "couldn't have autism based on her [incorrect] completion of the rating scale" (to make matters worse, her score, which was done with no training at all, came out half a point below the usual cutoff for autism). Some of the scales require very specific, and sometimes extensive, training to complete. None of these scales are a substitute for a careful, thoughtful assessment by an experienced clinician. Many (but not all) of these instruments are listed in Table 2.2.

The two instruments that are probably most commonly used at present are the **Autism Diagnostic Interview–Revised (ADI-R)** and the **Autism Diagnostic Observation Schedule (ADOS).** The ADI-R is an interview done with parents that focuses on the child's social and communication skills, as well as other behaviors. This test, which can take a while to complete, was originally designed for research (to be sure that researchers in different parts of the world were diagnosing autism in the same way). It has the considerable advantage of being explicitly keyed, or linked, to the diagnostic criteria for autism in *DSM-IV* and the new *DSM-5*. The ADOS is a companion instrument to the ADI-R; it focuses on assessment of the child using various activities. Other instruments commonly used at present include the **Childhood Autism Rating Scale, 2nd ed. (CARS-2),** along with several others. These scales measure severity of autism either on the basis of parent or teacher report or observation of the child. Instruments for assessment of possible Asperger's disorder have been developed as well (see Volkmar & Wiesner, 2009, p. 71, for a brief summary of these; also see Lord et al., 2014, for a detailed discussion of diagnostic instruments).

Several other instruments are available for assessment of individuals with Asperger's disorder. Given that, at least as an official diagnosis, Asperger's has been around for comparatively much less time than autism, it is probably not surprising that there is less agreement about which of these scales is best to use.

TABLE 2.2 **SELECTED DIAGNOSTIC ASSESSMENT INSTRUMENTS FOR AUTISM**

Name	Format and Comments
Autism Diagnostic Interview–Revised (ADI-R) (Lord, Rutter, & Le Courteur 1994)	Interview with parents to verify diagnosis of autism based on history of child (requires substantial training). Very well done test used for research as well. Items keyed to categorical (*DSM/ICD*) criteria. Typically takes 90 minutes or more. Used for children with chronological and mental ages above 2 years. Issues with borderline cases.
Autism Diagnostic Observation Schedule (ADOS) (Lord et al., 2000)	Assessment of the child, covering a wide span in ability levels; assesses behaviors and features relevant to diagnosis of autism. Companion instrument to ADI-R, also very well done. Requires significant training. Items designed to elicit behaviors of type seen in autism. Four modules based on levels of individual's language. Less useful for nonverbal adults or adolescents. Versions for different levels of language ability.
Childhood Autism Rating Scale, 2nd ed. (CARS-2) (Schopler & Van Bourgondian, 2010)	A revision of an older instrument often used in schools. Can be learned very readily. Fifteen items rated on 4-point score (normal to very autistic). Scores >30 suggest autism. Looks at severity of autism.
Gilliam Autism Rating Scales, 3rd ed. (GARS-3) (Gilliam, 2014)	**Norm-referenced test:** focus is on ages 3–22. Takes 5–10 minutes. Forty-two items grouped in three categories. Fifty-six items grouped in 6 subscales. Rapidly administered.
Social Responsiveness Scale, 2nd ed. (SRS-2) (Constantino & Gruber, 2012)	Caregiver (or self-) report with an overall total score to reflect severity and five subscale scores. Different forms for different age groups (adults can self-report). Readily administered and scored.

MEDICAL EVALUATIONS AND ASSESSMENT

The assessment should include a review of the pregnancy, labor and delivery, review of the early development, and developmental milestones as well as nature of first concerns. Depending on the age of the child, parents may be aided by use of baby books, videos, and so on (this becomes more important as children age because **telescoping effects** on recall are sometimes observed). The exposure of the mother to any unusual environmental factors (viral illness, known toxins including alcohol and cigarettes) should be noted as well as results of an earlier screening of other developmental assessments. As we mentioned sometimes these instruments will pick up developmental problems other than autism, so the primary care provider also needs to be able to follow up with appropriate testing and referral. Again various guidelines and practice parameters are available (McClure, 2014; Volkmar, Siegel, et al., 2014; Wilson, Robert, Gillian, Ohlsen, Robertson, & Zinkstok, 2014).

The differential diagnosis of autism includes other developmental disorders (language disorder, intellectual disability, and mental retardation); sensory impairments; along with a number of potentially associated medical conditions (seizure disorders, Fragile X syndrome, and tuberous sclerosis). For older, more cognitively able children (who may come to diagnosis somewhat later) other issues can include anxiety disorders. Some children who have been reared in situations of profound deprivation may exhibit some autistic-like symptoms, but these usually remit with provision of adequate care (this can be an issue for children adopted from orphanages in other countries). To complicate matters further, some of these conditions (notably intellectual disability) can coexist with autism, and as children become older many also do exhibit anxiety problems in addition to their autism. Occasionally developmental language disorders may seem to suggest possible autism, but children with language problems typically (unlike children with autism) will make normal use of conventional gestures and also usually point to things of interest (to show parents). Differentiation from intellectual disability without autism can be difficult particularly because many children with intellectual disability also have associated social delays and exhibit repetitive, stereotyped movements (the latter are the single least reliable sign of autism for just this reason). Social problems in autism typically are much more severe than would be expected given the child's overall developmental level, but differentiation can be difficult in the youngest and most cognitively impaired children. For children with more classical autism, there is reasonably good agreement and diagnosis stability after age 3 years. Provision of intervention should not be delayed because issues of diagnosis are unclear.

For children with autism attentional problems are frequent—an additional diagnosis of ADHD is not usually made unless these difficulties are more substantial than expected given the child's developmental level. The issue of associated problems in autism is a complex one for several reasons. Typically children will have major problems in communication (or may initially be mute), have cognitive impairments, but they can be difficult to assess. Furthermore, there are differences in approaches to comorbidity in the US (*DSM*) and international (*ICD*) systems with the former generally more tolerant of multiple diagnosis and the latter discouraging them. Given the multiple areas that autism affects, many behavior problems can be seen ranging from hyperactivity, aggression, and self-injury to seemingly obsessive compulsive symptoms and mood-anxiety problems.

Medical evaluations can be conducted even when referral for early intervention or more comprehensive diagnostic assessments are in process. Typically this includes the following: physical examination, a hearing screen (at a minimum), and full audiological evaluation if language is delayed, as well as screening for Fragile X and assessment for tuberous sclerosis. There have been significant changes in our understanding of the genetic basis of autism over the past several decades and in recommendations for genetic testing.

Genetic testing in autism is in a state of flux. We have moved from simple karyotype analysis to much more sophisticated assessments that look for variations in chromosomal structure, duplications and deletions, and other manifestations (not always associated with known problems). Indeed, this is an area where knowledge has increased dramatically and cost has diminished markedly. The American College of Human Genetics has updated their recommendations (Schaefer et al., 2013) and as those recommendations note it is important for clinicians to be aware of the current guidelines as well as new research and to carefully document clinical reasoning in terms of pursuing (or not pursuing) more advanced testing, for example, specific dysmorphic features might suggest additional testing. These new guidelines suggest two tiers of assessment. The first tier is expected to have the highest yield and recommends chromosomal microarray (CMA) and Fragile X testing (expected yield is about 10% to 15% of cases). The second tier of tests (with lower diagnostic yield) is suggested if the first-tier tests are negative; this would include testing for the MPEC-2 gene associated with Rett's (it can be considered in both females and males—especially if the latter have some clinical features suggestive of Rett's).

Abnormal or questionable result often suggests need for further genetic evaluation and counseling; this is particularly true for younger parents who may be considering having additional children. Over the last several years the positive yield of genetic testing (if clinical suspicions are present) has increased. In a recent study CMA and whole-exome sequencing (WES) were compared in a large sample of children with ASDs who were grouped based on the severity of associated physical dysmorphology. The two methods yielded somewhat different results based on morphological group. In the children who had both forms of testing, the identifiable genetic etiology rate was nearly 16% (Tammimies et al., 2015).

In the absence of significant findings on examination or history (such as seizures) structural MRI is not usually indicated. It may be justified in the presence of seizures, regression, microcephaly, or other relevant findings on history or examination (routine use is not typically indicated).

One might reasonably ask what the actual yield is of more complex and sophisticated medical assessments. In one study done some years ago (Majnemer & Shevell, 1995) a series of young children with suspected developmental delay were identified and 50 children with an autistic spectrum disorder were assessed. History or physical exam was suggestive of associated conditions in a minority of cases; not all cases had every test but only a single child with a possible Landau-Kleffner variant (on a sleep EEG) was identified.

A history of loss of skills particularly should prompt a thorough medical assessment. In a large sample of children with autism, parents report some aspect of regression in about 20% of cases—although often it turns out that some degree of delay was already present. This is a complication for interpreting much of the work done on the topic (when sometimes a parent report is equated with true regression). When you think about it, of course, it is understandable that sometimes parents become worried only as skills fail to develop.

PROVISION OF SERVICES

Having had a positive screen or, if significant concerns are present regardless of the screening, the obvious question is what to do next. We discuss these issues in detail in Chapters 5 and 6. For younger children early intervention and Birth to Three services can be used, and after age 3 years (in the United States) schools assume responsibility. As we have noted there is potential for children to fall through the cracks, so it is important to be sure that follow-through has occurred and the child and family are connected to services.

Summary

In this chapter we reviewed issues of screening and early diagnosis:

- Screening should be conducted for all young children. This should include review of possible red flags for an autism diagnosis (difficulties in social relatedness, language development, and unusual behavior). Screening instruments have been developed based on clinical observation and parent report. Some children, particularly more cognitively able ones, may come to diagnosis somewhat later than the preschool years.

- A screen positive or presence of warning signs of autism should prompt a thorough diagnostic evaluation and, as appropriate, referral for evaluation of eligibility of early intervention services. Areas relevant to a differential diagnosis (positive family history, possible hearing or visual impairment, unusual movements, or possible seizures) should inform the evaluation. Observation of the child should focus on problems in social interaction and communication as well as unusual responses to the environment.

- Screening procedures should take into account the child's age and development level.

- Clinical sensitivity to any important ethnic, cultural, or socioeconomic factors is indicated.

- For children who screen positive, more comprehensive diagnostic assessment may need to be conducted over and above any additional assessments from early intervention services.

The primary care provider has an important role in screening, in coordination of assessment results and care coordination, and, over time, in helping the family obtain appropriate, evidence-based services. The primary care providers should also be aware of the local and regional resources available to parents and be able to refer them to parent support groups and advocacy programs. Box 2.2 from the CDC website provides a helpful summary of screening flow (see the figure) and emphasizes the importance of following up at all stages of the process. An awareness of state and federal mandates for services and the importance of school-based interventions (after age 3 years) are also essential.

BOX 2.2 EVALUATION PROCEDURES: AUTISM AND PERVASIVE DEVELOPMENTAL DISORDERS

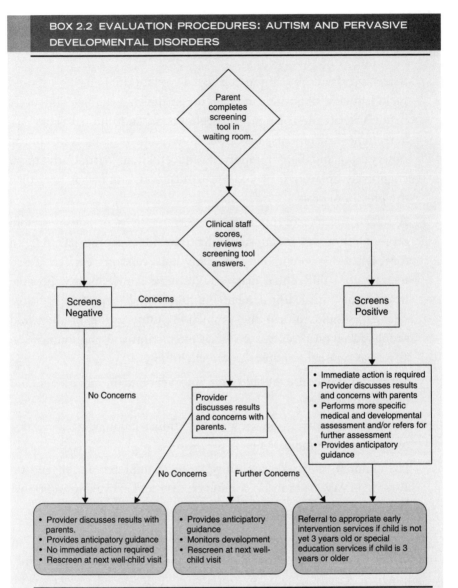

Pediatric Developmental Screening Flowchart *Source:* Centers for Disease Control (2017).

1. Historical Information
    a. Early development and features of development
    b. Age and nature of onset (e.g., gradual or dramatic)

   c. Medical and family history (especially for autism but other conditions as well)

2. Psychological and Communicative Examination
   a. Estimate(s) of intellectual level (particularly nonverbal IQ) depending on age and level of functioning either developmental testing or IQ test
   b. Communicative assessment (receptive and expressive language, use of nonverbal communication, pragmatic use of language)
   c. Adaptive behavior (how does the child cope with the real world and generalize skills?)
   d. Social and communicative skills evaluation relative to nonverbal intellectual abilities (is there a marked discrepancy?)

3. Psychiatric Examination
   a. Nature of social relatedness (eye contact, joint attention, imitation, attachment behaviors)
   b. Behavioral features (stereotypy or self-stimulation, resistance to change, unusual sensitivities to the environment, self-injurious behaviors, etc.)
   c. Play skills (nonfunctional use of play materials, developmental level of play activities) and communication, ability to play with peers
   d. Can use various rating scales, checklists, and instruments specific to autism

4. Medical Evaluation
   a. Search for any associated medical conditions (genetic, infectious, pre- and perinatal risk factors, etc.)
   b. Genetic testing (first tier including chromosomal microarray and Fragile X testing) with more specialized testing if these are negative (see American College of Human Genetics [Schaefer et al., 2013] for current recommendations)
   c. Hearing test (always indicated and not limited to simple three-tone screening)
   d. Vision screening
   e. Other tests and consultations as indicated by history and current examination (e.g., EEG, CT, MRI scan) if unusual features are present (seizures, physical anomalies, microcephaly, regression)

5. Additional Consultations
   a. Occupational or physical therapy as needed
   b. Respiratory therapy or orthopedic specialists
      (Rett's syndrome)

Source: Adapted from Volkmar, Cook, and Lord (2002).

REFERENCES

American Psychiatric Association. (2013). *Diagnostic and statistical manual of mental disorders* (5th ed.). Washington, DC: Author.

Centers for Disease Control. (2017). Pediatric developmental screening flowchart. Child Development. Retrieved from www.cdc.gov/ncbddd/childdevelopment/documents/screening-chart.pdf

Constantino, J. N., & Gruber, C. P. (2012). *Social responsiveness scale* (2nd ed.). Los Angeles, CA: Western Psychological Services.

Gilliam, J. E. (2014). *Gilliam Autism Rating Scale* (3rd ed.). Austin, TX: PRO-ED.

Huerta, M., Bishop, S. L., Duncan, A., Hus, V., & Lord, C. (2012). Application of DSM-5 criteria for autism spectrum disorder to three samples of children with DSM-IV diagnoses of pervasive developmental disorders. *American Journal of Psychiatry, 169*(10), 1056–1064. doi:10.1176/appi.ajp.2012.12020276

Ibanez, L. V., Stone, W. L., & Coonrod, E. E. (2014). Screening for autism in young children. In F. R. Volkmar, S. J. Rogers, R. Paul, & K. A. Pelphrey (Eds.), *Handbook of autism and pervasive developmental disorders* (4th ed., Vol. 2, pp. 585–604). Hoboken, NJ: Wiley.

Kanner, L. (1943). Autistic disturbances of affective contact. *Nervous Child (2)*, 217–250.

King, T. M., Tandon, S. D., Macias, M. M., Healy, J. A., Duncan, P. M., Swigonski, N. L., Skipper, S. M., & Lipkin, P. H. (2010). Implementing developmental screening and referrals: Lessons learned from a national project. *Pediatrics, 125*(2), 350–360.

Krug, D. A., Arick, J. R., & Almond, P. J. (1980). *Autism screening instrument for educational planning.* Portland, OR: ASIEP Educational.

Lord, C. (1995). Follow-up of two-year-olds referred for possible autism. *Journal of Child Psychology & Psychiatry & Allied Disciplines, 36*(8), 1365–1382

Lord, C., Corsello, C., & Grzadzinski, R. (2014). Diagnostic instruments in autistic spectrum disorders. In F. R. Volkmar, S. J. Rogers, R. Paul, & K. A. Pelphrey (Eds.), *Handbook of autism and pervasive developmental disorders* (4th ed., Vol. 2, pp. 610–650). Hoboken, NJ: Wiley.

Lord, C., Risi, S., Lambrecht, L., Cook, E. H., Leventhal, B. L., DiLavore, P. C., … Rutter, M. (2000). The Autism Diagnostic Observation Schedule—Generic:

A standard measure of social and communication deficits associated with the spectrum of autism. *Journal of Autism & Developmental Disorders, 30*(3), 205–223.

Lord, C., Rutter, M., & Le Couteur, A. (1994). Autism Diagnostic Interview—Revised: A revised version of a diagnostic interview for caregivers of individuals with possible pervasive developmental disorders. *Journal of Autism & Developmental Disorders, 24*(5), 659–685.

Lord, C., Wagner, A., Rogers, S., Szatmari, P., Aman, M., Charman, T., & Yoder, P. (2005). Challenges in evaluating psychosocial interventions for autistic spectrum disorders. *Journal of Autism & Developmental Disorders, 35*(6), 695–708; discussion 709–611.

Majnemer, A., & Shevell, M. I. (1995). Diagnostic yield of the neurologic assessment of the developmentally delayed child. *Journal of Pediatrics, 127*(2), 193–199. [See comments.]

McClure, I. (2014). Developing and implementing practice guidelines. In F. R. Volkmar, S. J. Rogers, R. Paul, & K. A. Pelphrey (Eds.), *Handbook of autism and pervasive developmental disorders* (4th ed., Vol. 2, pp. 1014–1035). Hoboken, NJ: Wiley.

Robins, D. L., Casagrande, K., Barton, M., Chen, C.-M. A., Dumont-Mathieu, T., & Fein, D. (2014). Validation of the Modified Checklist for Autism in Toddlers, Revised with Follow-up (M-CHAT-R/F). *Pediatrics, 133*(1), 37–45. doi:https://dx.doi.org/10.1542/peds.2013–1813

Schaefer, G. B., Mendelsohn, N. J., & Professional and Clinical Guidelines Committee. (2013). Clinical genetics evaluation in identifying the etiology of autism spectrum disorders: 2013 guideline revisions. *Genetics in Medicine, 15*(5), 399–407. [Erratum appears in (2013). *Genetics in Medicine, 15*(8), 669.]

Schopler, E., & Van Bourgondian, M. (2010). *Childhood Autism Rating Scale* (2nd. ed., CARS-2). Los Angeles, CA: Western Psychological.

Smith, I. C., Reichow, B., & Volkmar, F. R. (2015). The effects of *DSM-5* criteria on number of individuals diagnosed with autism spectrum disorder: A systematic review. *Journal of Autism and Developmental Disorders, 45*(8), 2541–2552.

Tammimies, K., Marshall, C. R., Walker, S., Kaur, G., Thiruvahindrapuram, B., Lionel, A. C., Yuen, R. K., Uddin, M., Roberts, W., Weksberg, R., Woodbury-Smith, M., Zwaigenbaum, L., Anagnostou, E., Wang, Z., Wei, J., Howe, J. L., Gazzellone, M. J., Lau, L., Sung, W. W., Whitten, K., Vardy, C., Crosbie, V., Tsang, B., D'Abate, L., Tong, W. W., Luscombe, S., Doyle, T., Carter, M. T., Szatmari, P., Stuckless, S., Merico, D., Stavropoulos, D. J., Scherer, S. W., & Fernandez, B. A. (2015). Molecular diagnostic yield of chromosomal microarray analysis and whole-exome sequencing in children with autism spectrum disorder. *JAMA, 314*(9), 895–903.

Volkmar, F. R., Booth, L. L., McPartland, J. C., & Wiesner, L. A. (2014). Clinical evaluation in multidisciplinary settings. In F. R. Volkmar, S. J. Rogers, R. Paul, & K. A. Pelphrey (Eds.), *Handbook of autism and pervasive developmental disorders* (4th ed., Vol. 2, pp. 661–672). Hoboken, NJ: Wiley.

Volkmar, F., Cook, E., & Lord, C. (2002). Autism and pervasive developmental disorders. In M. Lewis (Ed.), *Child and adolescent psychiatry: A comprehensive textbook.* Baltimore, MD: Williams & Wilkins.

Volkmar, F. R., Klin, A., Siegel, B., Szatmari, P., et al. (1994). Field trial for autistic disorder in *DSM-IV. The American Journal of Psychiatry, 151*(9), 1361–1367.

Volkmar, F., Siegel, M., Woodbury-Smith, M., King, B., McCracken, J., State, M., & the American Academy of and Child and Adolescent Psychiatry (AACAP) Committee on Quality Issues (CQI). (2014). Practice parameter for the assessment and treatment of children and adolescents with autism spectrum disorder. *Journal of the American Academy of Child & Adolescent Psychiatry, 53*(2), 237–257.

Volkmar, F., & Wiesner, L. (2009). *A practical guide to autism.* Hoboken, NJ: Wiley.

White, S. W., Ollendick, T. H., & Bray, B. C. (2011). College students on the autism spectrum: Prevalence and associated problems. *Autism, 15*(6), 683–701. doi:https://dx.doi.org/10.1177/1362361310393363

World Health Organization (WHO). (1993). *International classification of diseases (ICD-10;* 10th ed.). Geneva, Switzerland: Author.

Wilson, C., Roberts, G., Gillan, N., Ohlsen, C., Robertson, D., & Zinkstok, J. (2014). The NICE guideline on recognition, referral, diagnosis and management of adults on the autism spectrum. *Advances in Mental Health and Intellectual Disabilities, 8*(1), 3–14.

▨ SUGGESTED READING

Autism Genome Project Consortium, Szatmari, P., Paterson, A. D., Zwaigenbaum, L., Roberts, W., Brian, J., & Shih, A. (2007). Mapping autism risk loci using genetic linkage and chromosomal rearrangements. *Nature Genetics, 39*(3), 319–328.

Bolton, P. F., Carcani-Rathwell, I., Hutton, J., Goode, S., Howlin, P., & Rutter, M. (2011). Epilepsy in autism: Features and correlates. *British Journal of Psychiatry, 198,* 289–294.

Coonrod, E. E., & Stone, W. L. (2005). Screening for autism in young children. In F. Volkmar, A. Klin, R. Paul, & D. J. Cohen (Eds.), *Handbook of autism and pervasive developmental disorders* (3rd ed., Vol. 2, pp. 707–729). New York: Wiley.

Gardener, H., Spiegelman, D., & Buka, S. L. (2009). Prenatal risk factors for autism: Comprehensive meta-analysis. *British Journal of Psychiatry, 195*(1), 7–14.

Geschwind, D. H. (2009). Advances in autism. *Annual Review of Medicine, 60,* 367–380.

Mandell, D. S., Ittenbach, R. F., Levy, S. E., & Pinto-Martin, J. A. (2007). Disparities in diagnoses received prior to a diagnosis of autism spectrum disorder. *Journal of Autism & Developmental Disorders, 37*(9), 1795–1802.

McClure, I., & Melville, C. A. (2007). Early identification key in autism spectrum disorders. *Practitioner, 251*(1697), 31.

Palmer, R. F., Blanchard, S., Jean, C. R., & Mandell, D. S. (2005). School district resources and identification of children with autistic disorder. *American Journal of Public Health, 95*(1), 125–130.

Rutter, M. (2006). Autism: Its recognition, early diagnosis, and service implications. *Journal of Developmental & Behavioral Pediatrics, 27*(2 Suppl), S54–S58.

State, M. W. (2010). Another piece of the autism puzzle. *Nature Genetics, 42*(6), 478–479.

Volkmar, F. R., & McPartland, J. C. (2014). From Kanner to *DSM-5*: Autism as an evolving diagnostic concept. *Annual Review of Clinical Psychology, 10*, 193–212. doi:https://dx.doi.org/10.1146/annurev-clinpsy-032813–153710

Zwaigenbaum, L. (2010). Advances in the early detection of autism. *Current Opinion in Neurology, 23*(2), 97–102.

CHAPTER 3

Approaches to Providing Medical Care

Not surprisingly, two of the major challenges in autism—difficulties with communication and social interaction—pose significant challenges for provision of health care. Acute disease can present in various ways in a person with limited verbal ability, for example, irritability, decreased appetite or refusal to eat, acute weight loss, or in behavioral changes such as head banging or **self-injury.** Difficulties with social interaction and sensitivity to change may mean a child does not like to be touched or won't cooperate when being examined, and even the most minor procedures can pose challenges. The rapid pace of medical care can further exacerbate these difficulties as does the volume of patients needing care. This is very challenging when the care provider is unfamiliar with the individual or where the environment is unfamiliar and overstimulating (e.g., the emergency room). For persons with autism the long-term goal is to help them participate as much as possible in the process of getting good health care and leading a healthy lifestyle (Volkmar & Wiesner, 2009).

Preventive care is particularly important. Routine screening by physical exam and laboratory testing can detect problems early—when treatments can prevent more severe or permanent conditions. It cannot be emphasized enough that regular well-child visits are critically important. Participation in these visits helps the provider and patient get to know each other. This facilitates care provision when the individual is ill. Regular screening for common health problems and immunizations is also part of this process.

As we discuss further on in the chapter the adoption of a medical home model for care facilitates coordination of care and helps make optimal use of resources.

Other challenges arise given our complex health care system. These issues can come about through difficulties concerning insurance, for example: finding providers who accept certain insurance plans or, for adults, finding an insurance provider. Often health care is delivered by different providers, for example, specialists such as psychiatrists, neurologists, psychologists, or speech pathologists can all be involved. One important way to prevent this problem, as we discuss subsequently, is having a medical home with a provider or provider group who takes a leadership role in integrating care and services. A number of more general and more specific resources are available (e.g., Durand, 2014).

In this chapter, we discuss some of the issues involved in providing quality health care to individuals on the autism spectrum. We review some practical approaches to making visits more successful, coping with the emergency department and hospitalization, coordination of care issues, and the medical home for individuals with ASDs. Some excellent resources are available for families, and we include them in either the References or the "Suggested Reading" list at the end of this chapter. Unfortunately it is also important to note that there is very little scholarly work, much less research studies, relevant to health care for adults with ASDs (Piven, Rabins, & Autism-in-Older Adults Working Group, 2011; also see Howlin, 2014). We conclude the chapter with a discussion of practice guidelines and evidence-based treatments.

Helping Medical Visits Be Successful

Parents and the doctor and his or her staff can take steps to make visits to the office successful (see Box 3.1). This starts with making regular visits go well. Routine visits are important for many reasons. Having the child become familiar with the doctor's office and procedures when he or she is well also makes cooperation during an illness much more likely. Routine visits also offer the chance for preventative care. Several steps can be taken to facilitate successful medical visits: (1) preparation of the child for the visit, (2) being sensible about visit schedules and waiting time, (3) planning activities to help keep the child occupied, and (4) giving extra time for examination to enable the child to be more familiar with procedures and the examiner (Volkmar et al., 2014; Volkmar & Wiesner, 2009).

BOX 3.1 MAKING MEDICAL VISITS SUCCESSFUL

Prepare the Child for the Visit
- Picture books, visual schedules, or even the various computer applications available for autism (e.g., showing a schedule, the physical office, pictures of the staff and doctor) may be helpful.
- For children who are interested provide play medical equipment.
- For parents there are various books (including board books for the child) to minimize the newness of procedures.

Schedule
- Schedule appointments early in morning or afternoon—minimize waiting time.
- If possible have a quiet (separate) waiting area.
- If possible have staff members who know (or come to know) the child well.

Activities
- Have favorite activities available for the child if possible.
- Use the phone or iPad to keep the child occupied—potentially showing information to help the child familiarize him- or herself with what will happen.

In Conducting the Physical Exam
- Be deliberate, predictable, consistent, and thoughtful—do more intrusive things at the end of the exam.
- Give the child extra time for processing.
- Keep language simple.
- Encourage (reinforce) cooperation and compliance.
- Try to end on a positive note (for parents and child).

DENTAL CARE

Prevention is a critically important aspect of dental care and one that is often overlooked or avoided given the multiple difficulties of a child with ASD (Lai, Milano, Roberts, & Hooper, 2012). Children who have inadequate prevention are at risk for major problems as they age, for example, dental pain may cause self-injurious behavior and untreated dental problems can lead to other medical problems—sometimes severe ones. A growing body of work on dental care for children with autism is available (see the "Suggested Reading" list at the end of the chapter). One large survey (Kopycka-Kedzierawski, Auinger, Kopycka-Kedzierawski, & Auinger, 2008) assessed dental status and needs of a large nationally representative sample of children and adolescents with and without autism. About half of the children and adolescents with autism were reported to have excellent or good dental status (as compared to nearly 70% of typically developing children). Given the increased rates of accident and injury it is not surprising that traumatic dental injuries may be even more likely in children with ASDs (Altun, Guven, Yorbik, & Acikel, 2010).

Guidelines on caring for individuals with autism for professionals are available (e.g., Green & Flanagan, 2008) as are guidelines and suggestions for parents to encourage successful dental visits (Marshall, Sheller, Williams, Mancl, & Cowan, 2007; Volkmar & Wiesner, 2009). As with visits to the family doctor or pediatrician, a variety of procedures may be used to prepare the child. Engaging in some toothbrushing and dental care will facilitate cooperation with the dentist (other predictors of successful dental visits include overall cognitive and communicative ability and the ability to sit for a haircut). Box 3.2 provides some suggestions for ensuring good dental hygiene.

BOX 3.2 STEPS FOR PARENTS IN ENSURING GOOD DENTAL CARE

- Start early. Toothbrushing should be started as soon as the teeth begin to come in. Parents should try to make this an enjoyable game or have a special (favorite) activity after.
- Try different toothpastes. Different flavors are available. Brushing without toothpaste is better than not brushing at all!
- Talk to the dentist (also maybe to the pharmacist) about ways to give the toothbrush a taste that is interesting.

- For children who don't tolerate the toothbrush, work on a plan to help introduce it.
- Try brushing teeth in front of a mirror. Sometimes children are interested in watching themselves. You can also try toothbrushing as a family activity (occasionally children with autism will get into the swing of this).
- If the child won't brush her teeth, encourage water drinking immediately after meals (to try to clean out as much food as possible from the teeth and give the bacteria that cause cavities less food to grow on). You can do this with a bottle for very young children or through a straw or squeeze bottle for older children.
- Think about other approaches. Some children like mechanical things and might be willing to try an electric toothbrush or one of the water irrigators.
- Avoid foods that are known to cause cavities. This means limiting sweets, particularly sticky sweets. Some foods are particularly likely to stick to children's teeth, such as fruit roll-ups and dried fruits such as raisins. Keep in mind that many drinks have large amounts of sugar as well. Try to encourage use of other (nonsweet) foods as snacks. For children who receive foods as reinforcers, try to encourage a range of foods.
- If the child has motor difficulties talk with the occupational therapist or physical therapist about adapted toothbrushes that may give the child more stability and control.
- For more-cognitively able children (those who can follow verbal direction), disclosing tablets (which show areas where more brushing is needed) might be helpful and instructive providing visual feedback to child and caregiver.

SPECIAL HEALTH CARE SITUATIONS: EMERGENCY DEPARTMENT AND HOSPITAL STAYS

The fast pace of medical care, particularly in emergency department (ED) settings, can present challenges for the child with ASD. A lack of familiarity with ASD on the part of ED staff members may also complicate the situation, sometimes further worsening the child's anxiety or behavior.

Parents can be effective advocates and a comforting presence. The primary care provider should be contacted if at all possible and certainly should be included in any follow-up.

Although some literature exists for ED staff on children with disabilities in general (e.g., Grossman, Richards, Anglin, & Hutson, 2000), specific information on autism for these professionals has been minimal. This lack of information (and training) can also be a problem for emergency responders. Schools should have basic information needed for emergency situations, and use of a Medic-Alert bracelet can be helpful in indicating allergies, medications, conditions, and so on. On the ED side, it is important to avoid overstimulation of the individual, to keep the pace of interaction somewhat slower than usual, and to listen to reports of parents or school staff members who will know the child best. Obviously in some truly urgent situations this is not possible and the bare minimum of facts may be all that can be conveyed. Guidelines for parents are available (e.g., Volkmar & Wiesner, 2009). The more cognitively able individual may present special sources of confusion for ED staff members who should be helped to understand the nature of the social disability present (Raja & Azzoni, 2001). Education of staff members is also helpful (Nadler, 2014).

Unlike visits to the ED, hospitalizations are often planned in advance. This gives an opportunity for preparation with a tour and engagement between the patient and nursing or pediatric staff members (if they are available). In some cases procedures can be done so that the child is discharged on the same day. The individual's health care provider can facilitate the process of hospitalization. Various steps can be taken to minimize the individual's anxiety and make the hospital stay as pleasant (and short) as possible. Familiar activities, videos, materials, and so forth may help lessen the child's anxiety as will the presence of familiar family members. As much as possible the person's routines should be followed—including schoolwork if possible and relevant. Hospital staff members should be aware of the child's difficulties and take extra precautions about safety issues.

For surgical and other procedures careful explanation should be provided if possible. For elective surgery there is often an opportunity for the patient and parents to meet the staff members, see the recovery room, and so on (Volkmar & Wiesner, 2009). If necessary, medications can be used to reduce pain and anxiety.

Issues of care coordination for individuals with autism are complex. This complexity reflects several factors:

- Autism itself is associated with a wide range of clinical expressions and risk for other medical problems.
- Many services are provided in school settings.
- A very large number of disciplines are potentially involved in the care of the individuals.
- Patterns of treatment and entitlements to available services vary considerably with age and developmental level of the person (Lokhand-wala, Khanna, & West-Strum, 2012).

Unfortunately parents of children with ASDs report themselves three times more likely than parents of other children with special needs to have difficulties in obtaining needed services (Montes, Halterman, & Magyar, 2009). Sadly, these unmet needs result in lower quality of health care and a more adverse impact on the family (Zuckerman, Lindly, Bethell, & Kuhlthau, 2014). Even if considering only potential medical specialists, a large number might be involved, for example, a neurologist, geneticist, mental health consultant, dentist, GI specialist, and sleep specialist. Within the schools the school psychologist, social worker, speech pathologist, occupational therapist, physical therapist, and educators and special educators are all frequently involved. Behavioral interventions may be provided in school or at home and also need to be well coordinated. An important function of the primary care provider, particularly in the context of providing a medical home for the individual, is to work to ensure that all the various specialists involved are aware of each other's work and, as much as possible, coordinated relative to the overall care plan.

One important potential ally in this effort is the school nurse or, in some cases, the school-based health clinic (Bellando & Lopez, 2009; Minchella & Preti, 2011). Although sometimes needing additional information and resources (Staines, 2010), the school nurse is in an unusual position of bridging the gap between school staff members and medical professionals and has a critically important function in coordinating communication and discussion among all the professionals involved in the care for individuals with ASDs who have concurrent medical problems.

Primary care providers can take several steps to improve coordination of care. First they can ensure that all the various professionals involved, particularly those prescribing medications or conducting treatments, are aware of each other and each other's work. The primary care provider is in an important position for providing overall monitoring and ensuring that members of the treatment team are neither working at cross-purposes nor ignorant of each other's efforts. At times, particularly when working with members of multiple disciplines, this can be a challenge, but it is an important one that needs to be addressed. The social worker or school psychologist can be an important ally in this regard, particularly when it comes to finding ancillary services.

DRUG INTERACTIONS AND SIDE EFFECTS

It is not uncommon for the child, adolescent, or adult with ASD to be receiving multiple medications. Sometimes medications are added for new or emergent problems. At other times a second medication may be given to control for side effects of another one. It is important for the primary care provider to be kept in the loop regarding addition of medications to the treatment program. These new medications may be prescribed because of neurological issues (seizures) or behavioral issues (agitation, anxiety, irritability, mood, or sleep problems). They may be prescribed by neurologists or psychiatrists who may not always be aware of other relevant medical problems or concurrent medication interactions. These issues tend to arise as children become adolescents and adults, but there are other potential issues that can come up, and it is critical that the primary care provider is always involved and informed regarding changes in treatment programs.

IMMUNIZATIONS AND AUTISM

The prevention of communicable diseases through immunization has been a major accomplishment in medicine during the last century. Unfortunately a single paper published some years ago in the *Lancet* (Wakefield et al., 1998) led to major concern that immunization with MMR might increase autism risk. Other concerns were expressed about the use of thimerosal (a mercury-containing preservative) in some vaccines. Both concerns led to panic among parents and decreasing vaccinations rates.

A body of strong research now has failed to show any connection between autism and immunization. These concerns were increased by extensive media coverage, but these issues have been extensively examined and the link between immunization and autism has been discounted (Offit, 2008). Primary care providers should continue to encourage parents to engage in sensible immunization programs. Clearly, if more children remain unimmunized there will be a growing threat of the return of illnesses such as measles, mumps, and rubella.

RISKS ASSOCIATED WITH MEDICATION USE

With increasing age, behavior-modifying medication use becomes more common. We discuss these agents in greater detail in following chapters in this book but emphasize that the primary care provider should always be careful to review current medications, including psychotropic medications and any alternative-complementary treatments. There are a number of likely reasons for medication use to increase with age. Behavior-modifying medications are frequently started, at least as trials, in childhood and increase with age. For the school-age child a stimulant may be used for attention issues, and some of the atypical neuroleptics may be used for irritability and agitation. In adolescence, particularly for more-cognitively able and more verbal individuals, problems with anxiety or depression may lead to trials of SSRIs. In adulthood increased behavioral difficulties, particularly in the absence of good programs, and the pressure for speedy treatment effects often lead to multiple agents being used (in our experience the greatest number of medications we've seen used—all for behavioral or psychiatric issues—is 10!). In their sample of nearly 500 adolescents and adults with ASD the average number of agents used was 1.6 with more than 60% of the sample taking at least one medication (Stoddart et al., 2013). Poor insurance coverage, involvement of multiple providers, and poor monitoring contribute to overuse of medication and the potential for side effects and drug interactions. Long-term monitoring is important because for some agents such as the neuroleptics, routine use—over time—may be associated with adverse effects. For some individuals it is the case that such use can be justified but should be carefully monitored and, as appropriate, the individual and parents or guardians should be involved in decision making.

In any initial contact it is important for the primary care provider to review current and past medication use and be alert for a history of significant side effects, allergies, and adverse reactions. Be alert to the common confusion of allergies and side effects. Issues of interactions and side effects can also arise with alternative and complementary treatments, for example, with high doses of vitamins or use of treatments that potentially have serious metabolic side effects.

NEW MODELS OF CARE: THE MEDICAL HOME

As noted there is a growing role for the primary care provider to coordinate the many providers of health care and to serve, at times, as a liaison to schools and other services providers. This has led to the development of new conceptualizations of the role of the primary care provider so that the emerging best practice model for pediatric primary care is the medical home. The American Academy of Pediatrics (AAP) originally developed the medical home model to address the needs of children and youth with special health care needs (American Academy of Pediatrics, 2002). A **medical home** is a primary care practice that provides health care that is comprehensive including preventive, acute, and chronic care; coordinated across primary and specialty care; accessible; continuous from birth through the transition to adulthood; family-centered; compassionate; and culturally sensitive. It should emphasize a partnership with families. The primary health care professionals should assume a major role in coordinating care with the team of other care providers.

The medical home model is now seen as the standard of care for all children but is an approach that is especially effective for those with special needs. A review of 33 studies supports the fact that when children with special health care needs receive their primary health care through a medical home, their health status, timeliness of care, family-centeredness, and family functioning are improved (Homer et al., 2008).

Because of the particular complexity of conditions experienced by children with ASDs, the medical home model of health care delivery is especially tailored to meet their needs. These children are reported to have less comprehensive and coordinated care and greater unmet needs, when compared to the broader cohort of children and youth with special health care needs. Several studies based on national survey data found that parents of children with autism were less likely to report care consistent with that in a medical home such as family-centered, comprehensive, or coordinated, and less satisfaction with their children's primary care than were parents of children with other special health care needs regardless of severity of condition, personal characteristics, or insurance status (Brachlow, Ness, McPheeters, & Gurney, 2007; Carbone et al., 2010; Carbone, 2013). They were more likely to report difficulty in accessing subspecialty care and less likely to be offered help with education, therapy, or support groups.

When receiving care through a medical home, however, families report improved health and decreased financial burdens (Golnik, Scal, Wey, & Gaillard, 2012). The functions of a medical home that are central to health care for children with ASDs include developmental screening to identify signs and symptoms at the earliest point in time, referral for more comprehensive evaluation and intervention, coordination of care with specialists and all other agencies and professionals involved, ongoing monitoring and management of ASD and coexisting medical problems, medication management and support, education for families in seeking interventions including complementary and alternative medicine, and **transition** to adult services.

Screening for ASD should be incorporated into well-child visits at 18 and 24 months of age. The challenges to universal screening for ASD include concerns about the accuracy of existing validated instruments, the time and costs involved, comfort in managing children with ASDs before other services and supports are in place, and limited resources in the community once the diagnosis is made (Hyman & Johnson, 2012). However, child health providers report several barriers to serving children with ASDs that include lack of necessary skills such as recognizing signs and symptoms and addressing the medical and behavioral comorbid conditions, lack of time and resources to provide extensive care coordination, and lack of familiarity with local resources unique to children with ASDs (Williams, Tomchek, Grau, Bundy, Davis, & Kleinert, 2012).

Because of the special challenges in treating children with autism, specific efforts may be needed to ensure optimal care is provided in a medical home model. Golnik et al. (2012) evaluated a primary care medical home designed specifically to address the needs of children with ASDs at the Fairview Children's Clinic in Minneapolis. Elements of this medical home included individualized care plans, care coordination with ASD-specific resources including dentists, tools to improve patient visits including ASD-specific toys, longer visits, and pictures and stories written in tailored formats. They found that designing a medical home specifically to address the unique needs of children with ASDs results in an increased likelihood of children receiving care that meets medical home criteria as well as increased satisfaction among parents of children with ASDs. In a qualitative study that included focus groups with pediatricians, the following resources were cited as helpful to them in providing a medical home for children with ASDs: a website of community resources, evidence-based guidelines for younger children with ASDs, and insurance-reimbursed care coordinators.

PRACTICE GUIDELINES AND EVIDENCE-BASED PRACTICE

As we discuss in other chapters, a number of evidence-based treatments and programs are now available, and the literature on medical problems associated with autism has grown significantly. Several practice guidelines are now available, and although these take somewhat different approaches, it is interesting to see that they converge in many ways (Isaksen, Bryn, Diseth, Heiberg, Schjolberg, & Skjeldal, 2013; McClure 2014; Volkmar et al., 2014). Similarly a number of excellent scholarly reviews and research papers have now appeared on medical conditions and problems associated with autism (Coury, 2010; Levy et al., 2010). Fortunately there is a tiny but growing literature on medical conditions in adults with autism (Burke & Stoddart 2014). We will revisit the issue of evidence-based interventions and programs in Chapter 5 relative to educational interventions.

SUMMARY

As in the rest of medicine an ounce of prevention is worth a pound of cure! Familiarity with typical patterns of vulnerability and strength can lead to informed medical practice that engages individuals and their families more fully in the health care process and anticipates and prevents some major long-term health problems. From early in life a series of steps can be taken with parents to make well-child and sick visits more successful. Anticipating the child's needs by having a familiar routine, use of visuals (books, schedule, apps), avoiding excessive waits, having familiar materials or activities to help with waiting, thinking about the need for a more consistent and informed approach, and giving extra time will help. If well-child visits go better, then sick visits will also go more smoothly. For older children, adolescents, and adults an awareness of the typical age-related issues and concerns as well as those more specific to ASD is helpful.

Preventive dental care is also important. Unmet dental care needs can lead to major difficulties later in life—even later in childhood. The use of an experienced pediatric dentist can be very helpful but even a dentist in general practice can take steps to engage the child in tolerating dental visits and encouraging good dental hygiene.

Children with autism are at increased risk for accidental injury, and some data show increased ED visits; often these can be minimized if there is a strong working relationship with the primary care provider. Steps to facilitate the ED visits as well as hospitalizations (particularly if anticipated) can make life less stressful for the individual with ASD and his or her caregivers (and the hospital staff members).

Given the number of potential medical and mental health problems, particularly as individuals age, it is especially important that the primary care provider be familiar with all medications being taken as well as any engagement in any relevant complementary and alternative treatments (diets, vitamins, and so forth). The use of the medical home approach is strongly associated with higher levels of health care and more efficient health care delivery. As the evidence base for treatments and intervention procedures has grown, a number of practice guidelines and resources for clinicians are now available and provide a good initial reference for the primary care provider confronted with a sometimes dizzying array of treatments.

▨ REFERENCES

Altun, C., Guven, G., Yorbik, O., & Acikel, C. (2010). Dental injuries in autistic patients. *Pediatric Dentistry, 32*(4), 343–346.

American Academy of Pediatrics, Medical Home Initiatives for Children with Special Needs Project Advisory Committee. (2002). Policy statement: The medical home. *Pediatrics, 110,* 184–186.

Bellando, J., & Lopez, M. (2009). The school nurse's role in treatment of the student with autism spectrum disorders. *Journal for Specialists in Pediatric Nursing, 14*(3), 173–182.

Brachlow, A. E., Ness, K. K., McPheeters, M. L., & Gurney, J. G. (2007). Comparison of indicators for a primary care medical home between children with autism or asthma and other special health care needs: National Survey of Children's Health. *Archives of Pediatrics & Adolescent Medicine, 161*(4), 399–405.

Burke, L., & Stoddart, K. P. (2014). Medical and health problems in adults with high-functioning autism and Asperger syndrome. *Adolescents and adults with autism spectrum disorders* (pp. 239–267). New York, NY: Springer Science + Business Media.

Carbone, P. S. (2013). Moving from research to practice in the primary care of children with autism spectrum disorders. *Academic Pediatrics, 13*(5), 390–399. doi:https://dx.doi.org/10.1016/j.acap.2013.04.003

Carbone, P. S., Bhel, D. D., Azor, V., & Murphy, N. A. (2010). The medical home for children with autism spectrum disorders: Parent and pediatrician perspectives. *Journal of Autism & Developmental Disorders, 40*(3), 317–324.

Carbone, P. S., Farley, M., & Davis, T. (2010). Primary care for children with autism. *American Family Physician, 81*(4), 453–460.

Coury, D. (2010). Medical treatment of autism spectrum disorders. *Current Opinion in Neurology, 23*(2), 131–136. doi:https://dx.doi.org/10.1097/WCO.0b013e3283 3722fa

Durand, V. M. (2014). *Autism spectrum disorder: A clinical guide for general practitioners.* Washington, DC: American Psychological Association.

Golnik, A., Scal, P., Wey, A., & Gaillard, P. (2012). Autism specific primary care medical home intervention. *Journal of Autism and Developmental Disorders, 42*(6), 1087–1093.

Green, D., & Flanagan, D. (2008). Understanding the autistic dental patient. *General Dentistry, 56*(2), 167–171.

Grossman, S. A., Richards, C. F., Anglin, D., & Hutson, H. R. (2000). Caring for the patient with mental retardation in the emergency department. *Annals of Emergency Medicine, 35*(1), 69–76.

Homer, C. J., Klatka, K., Tomm, D., et al. (2008). A review of the evidence for the medical home for children with special health care needs. *Pediatrics, 122*(4), e922–e937.

Howlin, P. (2014). Outcomes in adults with autism spectrum disorders. In F. R. Volkmar, S. J. Rogers, R. Paul, & K. A. Pelphrey (Eds.), *Handbook of autism and pervasive developmental disorders* (4th ed., Vol.1, pp. 97–116). Hoboken, NJ: Wiley

Hyman, S. L., & Johnson, J. K. (2012). Autism and pediatric practice: Toward a medical home. *Journal of Autism and Developmental Disorders, 42*(6), 1156–1164.

Isaksen, J., Bryn, V., Diseth, T. H., Heiberg, A., Schjolberg, S., & Skjeldal, O. H. (2013). Children with autism spectrum disorders: The importance of medical investigations. *European Journal of Paediatric Neurology, 17*(1), 68–76. doi:https://dx.doi.org/10.1016/j.ejpn.2012.08.004

Kopycka-Kedzierawski, D. T., Auinger, P., Kopycka-Kedzierawski, D. T., & Auinger, P. (2008). Dental needs and status of autistic children: Results from the National Survey of Children's Health. *Pediatric Dentistry, 30*(1), 54–58.

Lai, B., Milano, M., Roberts, M. W., & Hooper, S. R. (2012). Unmet dental needs and barriers to dental care among children with autism spectrum disorders. *Journal of Autism and Developmental Disorders, 42*(7), 1294–1303. doi:https://dx.doi.org/10.1007/s10803–011–1362–2

Levy, S. E., Giarelli, E., Lee, L. C., Schieve, L. A., Kirby, R. S., Cunniff, C., et al. (2010). Autism spectrum disorder and co-occurring developmental, psychiatric, and medical conditions among children in multiple populations of the United States. *Journal of Developmental & Behavioral Pediatrics, 31*(4), 267–275. doi:https://dx.doi.org/10.1097/DBP.0b013e3181d5d03b

Lokhandwala, T., Khanna, R., & West-Strum, D. (2012). Hospitalization burden among individuals with autism. *Journal of Autism and Developmental Disorders, 42*(1), 95–104.

Marshall, J., Sheller, B., Williams, B. J., Mancl, L., & Cowan, C. (2007). Cooperation predictors for dental patients with autism. *Pediatric Dentistry, 29*(5), 369–376.

McClure, I. (2014). Developing and implementing practice guidelines. In F. R. Volkmar, S. J. Rogers, R. Paul, & K. A. Pelphrey (Eds.), *Handbook of autism and pervasive developmental disorders* (4th ed., Vol. 2, pp. 1014–1035). Hoboken, NJ: Wiley.

Minchella, L., & Preti, L. (2011). Autism spectrum disorder: Clinical considerations for the school nurse. *NASN School Nurse, 26*(3), 143–145.

Montes, G., Halterman, J. S., & Magyar, C. I. (2009). Access to and satisfaction with school and community health services for US children with ASD. *Pediatrics, 124*(Suppl 4), S407–S413.

Nadler, C. B. (2014). Development and evaluation of educational materials for pre-hospital and emergency department personnel on the care of patients with autism spectrum disorder. *Journal of Developmental and Behavioral Pediatrics, 35*(7), 473.

Offit, P. (2008). *Autism's false prophets.* New York, NY: Columbia University Press.

Piven, J., Rabins, P., & Autism-in-Older Adults Working Group. (2011). Autism spectrum disorders in older adults: Toward defining a research agenda. *Journal of the American Geriatrics Society, 59*(11), 2151–2155.

Raja, M., & Azzoni, A. (2001). Asperger's disorder in the emergency psychiatric setting. *General Hospital Psychiatry, 23*(5), 285–293.

Staines, R. (2010). School nurses can help identify children with undiagnosed autism. *Paediatric Nursing, 22*(2), 7.

Stoddart, K. P., Burke, L., Muskat, J., Duhaime, S., Accardi, C., Burnh Riosa, P., et al. (2013). *Diversity in Ontario's youth and adults with autism spectrum disorders: Complex needs in unprepared systems* (p. 52). Toronto, ON, Canada: The Hanen Centre.

Volkmar, F., Siegel, M., Woodbury-Smith, M., King, B., McCracken, J., State, M., & the American Academy of and Child and Adolescent Psychiatry (AACAP) Committee on Quality Issues (CQI). (2014). Practice parameter for the assessment and treatment of children and adolescents with autism spectrum disorder. *Journal of the American Academy of Child and Adolescent Psychiatry, 53*(2), 237–257.

Volkmar, F. R., & Wiesner, E. A. (2009). *A practical guide to autism: What every parent, family member, and teacher needs to know.* Hoboken, NJ: Wiley.

Wakefield, A. J., Murch, S. H., Anthony, A., Linnell, J., Casson, D. M., Malik, M., et al. (1998). Ileal-lymphoid-nodular hyperplasia, non-specific colitis, and pervasive developmental disorder in children. *Lancet, 351*(9103), 637–641.

Williams, P. G., Tomchek, S., Grau, R., Bundy, M. B., Davis, D. W., & Kleinert, H. (2012). Parent and physician perceptions of medical home care for children with autism spectrum disorders in the state of Kentucky. *Clinical Pediatrics (Phila), 51*(11), 1071–1078. doi:10.1177/0009922812460333

Zuckerman, K. E., Lindly, O. J., Bethell, C. D., & Kuhlthau, D. (2014). Family impacts among children with autism spectrum disorder: The role of health care quality. *Academic Pediatrics, 14*(4), 398–407.

▓ SUGGESTED READING

Acs, G., & Ng, M. W. (2009). Dental care for your child with special needs. In M. L. Batshaw (Ed.), *When your child has a disability: The complete sourcebook for daily and medical care.* Baltimore, MD: Brookes.

Batshaw, M. (2002). *Children with disabilities* (5th ed.). Baltimore, MD: Brookes.

Batshaw, M. (2012). *Children with disabilities* (12th ed.). Baltimore, MD: Brookes.

Civardi, A., & Bates, M. (Eds.). (2009a). *Going to the dentist (first experiences).* Tulsa, OK: EDC.

Civardi, A., & Bates, M. (Eds.). (2009b). *Going to the hospital.* Tulsa, OK: EDC.

Dias, G. G., Prado, E.F.G. B., Vadasz, E., & Siqueira, J.T.T. (2010). Evaluation of the efficacy of a dental plaque control program in autistic patients. *Journal of Autism & Developmental Disorders, 40*(6), 704–708.

Fombonne, E., & Cook, J.E.H. (2003). MMR and autistic enterocolitis: Consistent epidemiological failure to find an association. *Molecular Psychiatry, 8,* 933–934.

Hollins, S., Avis, A., & Cheverton, S. (1998). *Going into hospital.* London, UK: Gaskell and St. George's Hospital Medical School.

Hollins, S., Bernal, J., & Gregory, M. (1996). *Going to the doctor.* London, UK: St. George's Mental Health Library.

Mayer, M. (1990). *Just going to the dentist.* New York, NY: Golden Books.

Ming, S. X., & Pletcher, B. A. (Eds.). (2014). *Navigating the medical maze with a child with autism spectrum disorder: A practical guide for parents.* Philadelphia, PA: Jessica Kingsley.

Murkoff, H. (2002). *What to expect when you go to the dentist.* New York, NY: Harper Festival.

Pace, B. (2002). *Chris gets ear tubes.* Washington, DC: Gallaudet University Press.

Rogers, F. (2002). *Going to the hospital.* Tulsa, OK: EDC.

Stratton, K., Gable, A., & McCormick, M. (Eds.). (2001). *Immunization safety review: Thimerosal containing vaccines and neurodevelopmental disorders.* Immunization Safety Review Committee–Institute of Medicine. Washington, DC: National Academies Press. (Can be ordered online at www.nap.edu.)

Stratton, K., Gable, A., Shetty, P., & McCormick, M. (Eds.). (2009). *Immunization safety review: Measles-mumps-rubella vaccine and autism.* Immunization Safety Review Committee–Institute of Medicine. Washington, DC: National Academies Press. (Can be ordered online at www.nap.edu.)

Taylor, B., Miller, E., Farrington, C. P., Petropoulos, M. C., Favot-Mayaud, I., Li, J., et al. (1999). Autism and measles, mumps, and rubella vaccine: No epidemiological evidence for a causal association. *Lancet, 353*(9169), 2026–2029. [See comments.]

Taylor, B., Miller, E., Lingam, R., Andrews, N., Simmons, A., & Stowe, J. (2002). Measles, mumps, and rubella vaccination and bowel problems or developmental regression in children with autism: Population study. *British Medical Journal, 324*(7334), 393–396.

Volkmar, F. R., Rowberry, J., de Vinck-Baroody, O., Gupta, A. R., Leung, J., Meyers, J., et al. (2014). Medical care in autism and related conditions In F. Volkmar, A. Klin, R. Paul, & D. J. Cohen (Eds.), *Handbook of autism and pervasive developmental disorders* (4th ed., Vol. 1, pp. 532–555). New York: Wiley.

Weber, J. D. (2000). *Children with Fragile X syndrome: A parents' guide.* Bethesda, MD: Woodbine House.

CHAPTER 4

Frequent Medical Conditions and Problems

S ince 1943 when Kanner first described autism, there have been many suggestions as to its cause and associations with different medical conditions. During the 1970s and 1980s a series of case reports began to accumulate suggesting associations of autism with a host of conditions (Gillberg & Coleman, 2000). Several factors complicated the interpretation of this literature. Most important, only "positive" case reports were published (i.e., you don't hear about cases *not* associated with autism); the real issue was whether the frequency of the associations in reports was greater than by chance. As the literature was reinterpreted (Rutter, Baily, Bolton, & Le Couteur, 1994) the major associations clearly related to seizures and two genetic disorders. Seizure disorders were very clearly increased in autism. The rates of autism associated with Fragile X and tuberous sclerosis, although not high in autism, were higher than by chance alone. As individuals with autism were followed over time it became clear that a number of other medical conditions and vulnerabilities were also of concern.

Autism is currently understood to be brain-based. Differences have been shown by fMRI in the brains of people with autism. It is clear that there is a strong genetic component, although most likely not a single gene.

SEIZURE DISORDERS

Seizure disorders are the most frequently encountered medical complications associated with ASD. Perhaps as many as 15% of children will have a seizure disorder, and this does not include febrile seizures. In the general population, about 5% of all children experience a seizure by the time they are 15 years old; more than half of these will be seizures associated with a high fever. Of course febrile seizures do not, of themselves, constitute epilepsy.

The literature on the association between autism and epilepsy is complex, with many case reports and few large-scale studies (Bolton, Carcani-Rathwell, Hutton, Goode, Howlin, & Rutter, 2011). One meta-review (Amiet, Gourfinkel-An, Consoli, Perisse, & Cohen, 2010) noted strong associations of seizures with lower cognitive function and with girls (themselves often with greater intellectual disability). Complications in comparing studies relate to changes in diagnostic practice (broad versus narrow views of the diagnosis) and the need to take a developmental perspective; for example, adolescents with autism develop seizures more frequently than those without autism. Sadly, there are few studies of adults.

The data in the following figure present rates of seizure in two different samples of children with autism and a normative sample of British children. The risk for developing epilepsy is increased in autism relative to the normal population throughout childhood with an increased risk early in life and again starting in early adolescence. All various seizure types are observed. Generalized seizures account for about 40% of seizure disorders in the general population and about 80% or more of those seen in autism. Absence seizures account for roughly 10% to 15% of all seizures in autism. Atonic seizures are also sometimes seen. Partial seizures, either simple or complex, account for perhaps 10% of seizures in autism (see Figure 4.1).

Referral should be made for an EEG and neurological consultation if seizures are suspected. EEGs (including 24-hour EEGs) are now easier to do, but sometimes either behavioral or even pharmacological help may be needed to augment cooperation (the latter, of course, has the potential for affecting the EEG and so is not ideal). Odd behaviors can sometimes be mistaken for seizures so it can be helpful to have good reporting of the episode and even a video of the event for clinical correlation. Parents and teachers should be taught basic first aid relative to seizures and if medications

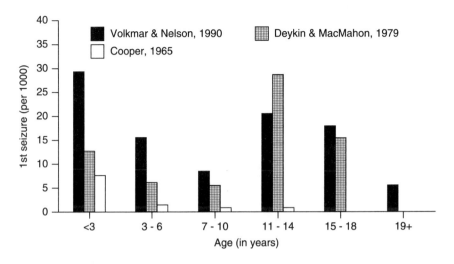

FIGURE 4.1   **Rates of first seizure, excluding febrile seizures, in two samples of individuals with autism (Deykin & MacMahon, 1979; Volkmar & Nelson, 1990) and a normal British sample (Cooper, 1975).**

Source: Reprinted with permission from Volkmar and Wiesner (2009, p. 389).

become an issue then risks and side effects need to be balanced. For children with ASDs it is important to minimize, to the extent possible, potential sedation and interference with school participation.

GENETIC CONDITIONS RELATED (OR POTENTIALLY RELATED) TO AUTISM

As research on autism began to increase in the late 1970s and 1980s a host of case reports noted associations of autism with a range of conditions. The problem with case reports is that, by their very nature, they are newsworthy but lack framing information relative to rates of conditions in the general population. The issue is not whether syndrome *x* (of any type) is *ever* associated with autism; rather, the issue is whether it is observed at a rate greater than that observed in the population (Rutter et al., 1994). If this standard is applied, a much reduced number of conditions become of interest. Several of these have strong genetic components.

Fragile X Syndrome

This X-linked disorder is now one of the most frequently identified causes of intellectual deficiency. It is found in 1% to 2% of cases of autism (in individuals with Fragile X the rate of associated autism varies by gender with about 25% of boys and 5% of girls affected) (Abrahams & Geschwind, 2008). The condition arises as a result of an absent or decreased expression of the Fragile X mental retardation protein (FMRP) resulting from a mutation in the FMR1 gene on chromosome X. Usually there is a loss of functioning because of an unstable expansion of a trinucleotide repeat. If there are more than 200 repeats of this trinucleotide the FMRI gene is silenced and a full mutation results; in individuals with 50 and 200 repeats a range of findings may be observed. Because the condition is X-linked, males are more likely severely affected, with females exhibiting a greater range of impairment.

Physical features of the condition may not be immediately apparent at birth, and it is not uncommon for a family to have a second child before the disorder is diagnosed in the first child; this is unfortunate because genetic counseling and prenatal testing are available. Physical features include relative macrocephaly, long face, and large ears. Frequently hypotonia is observed, as is an arched palate. Testicular enlargement is noted particularly in adolescence. Various associated medical problems include seizures, mitral valve prolapse, and recurrent ear and sinus infections. Intellectual difficulty and learning problems are frequent.

The degree of intellectual impairment correlates with the FMRP produced by the individual (Visootsak, Warren, Anido, & Graham, 2005). On psychological testing weaknesses in mathematics, visuospatial abilities, attention, and **executive functioning** as well as **visual–motor** coordination issues, are noted (Van Esch, 2012). A small number of cases are totally nonverbal; most will have some language and speech problems. Social anxiety is fairly common and suggests ASD (even when full criteria are not met); other symptoms suggestive of autism can include difficulties with gaze and sensory issues. Given that this is a single-gene disorder there is some potential for targeted gene therapy; this is an active area of current work (Roach, 2014).

Tuberous Sclerosis (TS)

This condition is found in perhaps 1% of children with autism, although as many as 20% of children with tuberous sclerosis are noted to have autism

(Abrahams & Geschwind, 2008) and others exhibit some features of autism. It appears that the risk for autism is increased with the presence of temporal lobe tubers, greater intellectual disability, and seizure disorder. Unlike the usual patterns in autism, the male-to-female ratio is about equal.

This neurocutaneous disorder can potentially affect many organ systems; these commonly include brain, skin, eyes, heart, and kidney. There is a broad range of syndrome expression and the diagnosis is made based on the presence of at least two major features and two minor ones (Roach & Sparagana, 2004). Major features include facial angiofibromas, renal angiomyolipoma, cortical tubers, cardiac rhabdomyoma, and more than three hypomelanotic macules; minor features include multiple renal cysts, bone cysts, and gingival fibromas, among others.

The condition occurs because of an abnormality in the TSC-1 or TSC-2 gene, usually because of a de novo mutation, and is an autosomal-dominant condition. Genetic testing is not required for the diagnosis of the condition, but usually patients who meet the criteria will exhibit a mutation on testing. The range of expression can vary significantly within the same family. A high index of suspicion should arise based on the presence of major or minor features. For young children the presence of seizures along with delayed development and hypomelanotic skin patches is suggestive. These are best seen with a Wood's lamp examination and a careful physical. MRI or CT cranial imaging may be used along with a kidney ultrasound and an echocardiogram. Abnormalities may be seen on retinal examination as well.

In young children seizures and cardiac rhabdomyosarcoma may alert the clinician to the diagnosis. With age, the skin features and learning and cognitive problems become more apparent. Epilepsy is common (up to 90% of cases) as is intellectual disability (40% to 60% of cases).

There have been several hypotheses about the relationship between autism and TS. It is possible that this linkage is direct because of some aspects of gene expression or the effects of the tuber location. As can be imagined the help of a clinician experienced in the management of TS is invaluable. Treatment of seizure disorders is particularly important, and a regression in skills should prompt consideration of new-onset seizure disorder.

Dup15q Syndrome

This duplication syndrome (Chromosome 15q11.2–13.1) occurs in several forms. If the duplication is inherited from the father, development may be normal, but when inherited from the mother, developmental difficulties often result. Most frequently, however, the duplication occurs in the fetus at conception. The condition is associated with a wide range of severity. There are a number of potential physical findings including hypotonia, which can result in feeding difficulties and motor delays. There may be some similar facial features with a flat nasal bridge, epicanthal folds, and high palate. In a minority of cases there may be small stature. Variable degrees of cognitive delay are reported as is a higher than expected frequency of autism (still the condition accounts for perhaps 1% to 2% of all cases of autism) (Abrahams & Geschwind, 2008), and diagnostic complications arise with severe motor or cognitive delay. About half of all cases will have one or more seizures.

OTHER GENETIC CONDITIONS

Additional genetic conditions that have been found to have an increased rate of autism include Angelman syndrome, Down syndrome, phenylke-tonuria, Smith-Lemli-Opitz syndrome, Joubert syndrome, and 22q deletion syndrome, among others. The significance of such associations remains unclear because associations are based largely on case reports, although for many of these conditions genes associated with the condition are now known. As we discussed in Chapter 3, consideration of genetic conditions and evaluation should be part of an initial comprehensive medical assessment.

Regression

When he first described autism, Leo Kanner mentioned that he thought autism was congenital. Subsequently, it has become clear that approximately 20% of children eventually diagnosed with autism seem to be relatively normal at birth and in the early months—or sometimes even for the first year or two of life—but then are reported by their parents to lose skills and develop autism. This number is probably an overestimate of the number who actually show dramatic regression. See Table 4.1 for the different type of regression.

It is important to take a careful history, because the issues surrounding the characterization of the regression are often complicated. Sometimes with a careful developmental history it appears that there were some red flags even

TABLE 4.1   TYPES OF REGRESSION IN AUTISM

Condition Name or Observance	Description
Dramatic skill loss with development of autism (Child Disintegrative Disorder [CDD])	Quick development of autistic-like behaviors in a previously normal child; a special category in *ICD-10* (and in *DSM-IV* as well) for this called *childhood disintegrative disorder*; rare; dramatic loss of skills and unequivocal onset usually between 3 and 4 years
Developmental stagnation	Often reported in younger children (1–2 years) as less skill loss but failure to progress
Rett's disorder	Onset in first years of life with loss of skill development, loss of purposeful hand movements; associated with marked regression and a host of neurological signs and symptoms; associated with a specific gene
Landau-Kleffner syndrome (acquired aphasia with epilepsy)	Loss mostly in expressive language; can be confused with autism; characteristic EEG pattern
Skill loss in relation to other medical and neurological disease	Central nervous system (CNS) infections, mitochondrial disease, inherited disorders, other specific medical conditions
Skill loss in adolescence	Sometimes observed in individuals with autism; loss of skills not marked but adolescent fails to make major gains

before the parents noted trouble (i.e., it may be less a case of regression than failure to appreciate a gradual onset of development). Sometimes a child will have a couple of words or possible words and then not develop more words or do so only very slowly. It is sometimes not clear whether the child really had a good grasp of the words or was simply playing with making sounds as many babies do.

Difficulties in defining regression complicate the interpretation of available research. Treatments for children with autism who have had a regression are no different than for other children with autism—unless a medical condition is found to explain the deterioration. Careful physical examination and selected laboratory studies suggested by the exam or history may be needed. With the exception of unrecognized seizure activity, the chances of finding an underlying condition are rather low.

A diverse group of conditions can be associated with developmental regression. These include seizures, CNS infection, mitochondrial deficits (e.g., Leigh disease), hypothyroidism, subacute sclerosing panencephalitis, neurolipidosis, metachromatic leukodystrophy, Addison–Schilder disease, Angelman syndrome, gangliosidosis, lipofuscinosis, and the aminoacidopathies (e.g., phenylketonuria [PKU]), among others (Dyken & Krawiecki, 1983).

DSM-IV and *ICD-10* recognized a rare condition, childhood disintegrative disorder, in which autism develops in a rather distinctive way after a fairly long period (usually 3 to 4 years) of normal development. The onset of this condition can be relatively sudden (days to weeks) or more prolonged (weeks to months). Often the child becomes more anxious or agitated and is aware of losing abilities. As he or she becomes less interested in the environment a more classic autism clinical picture develops—often with language loss. Language loss can be total or the child may have a few single words (having previously had fluent and complex speech). Despite extensive medical evaluations no specific medical cause is otherwise found, and although the child's progress is usually limited there is no further deterioration (as in a childhood onset dementia) (Westphal & LeMaistre, 2014). In girls (and very rarely in boys) Rett's disorder may be associated with a loss of skills. A genetic test for this single-gene disorder is now available.

Similarly **Landau–Kleffner syndrome** (also known as *acquired epileptic aphasia*) presents with onset of aphasia and is associated with a specific EEG abnormality. Onset is usually in the preschool to early school years with perhaps a slight male predominance. Sometimes (but not always) clinical seizures are observed. The potential for confusion with autism is probably greatest in the youngest cases, because of later onset use of visual and other aides usually make it clear that a strong desire to communicate is present and the child is socially related.

Any clear history of regression should lead to a thorough history, review of systems, and physical examination. Typically a series of studies including EEG and others looking for signs of associated medical conditions (as previously listed) will be conducted. It is important to note that sometimes seizure disorders are difficult to recognize but are expressed in disrupted or delayed development.

HEARING AND VISION PROBLEMS

The most common sensory sensitivities reported among children with ASDs are probably those that involve sensitivity (over or under) to sounds and noises. As infants become a bit older parents often will notice a lack of attention to the human voice (sometimes in striking contrast to the child's response to other sounds). Concerns about deafness are fairly frequent. Fortunately in the United States the vast majority of infants are screened at birth and congenital hearing loss is now diagnosed at a much younger age than in the past. There is potential for confusion of autism and hearing loss, and brain stem auditory-evoked response is helpful. It is the case that autism and deafness can coexist in a small number of cases. Typically hearing loss is diagnosed first these days and only when the child fails to respond to treatment is autism suspected; by that time other symptoms suggestive of autism may develop. If both diagnoses are present, it is important to know because thoughtful coordination of treatments is needed. The primary care provider also should be alert to fluctuating hearing loss, for example, with recurrent otitis media. Some children with deafness who might initially appear to exhibit symptoms of autism will no longer do so if intervention is provided through hearing aids, implants, implementation of visual sign, and so forth. Occasionally children will exhibit a mixed hearing loss involving conductive and sensorineural hearing.

The school and family can respond to children with sound sensitivities and provide minimally distracting environments; some school buildings and classrooms seem almost perversely designed to complicate life for the child with an ASD, because concrete block construction and linoleum floors contribute to an echo chamber effect. For some children using earphones to attenuate extraneous noises may help.

For many children with autism, some aspects of visual skills represent an area of strength (e.g., skills of the type used in putting together puzzles). However, unusual visual preferences may also be seen. Some children will spend long periods of time engaged in visual mannerisms (such as flicking a string back and forth in front of their eyes) or may be interested in unusual visual aspects of materials (focusing on minor details of a toy).

Children with visual difficulties sometimes exhibit unusual body movements that may be mistaken for those seen in autism. Concerns about vision should be promptly addressed with specialist help (presuming that the child is minimally cooperative). Issues of diagnosis can be most complicated in children who are blind and deaf; fortunately, such cases are rare.

EATING AND FEEDING PROBLEMS

Children with autism and related disorders can have a number of problems with eating and food. These include unusual food preferences and sensitivities as well as eating of nonnutritive substances (pica), discussed subsequently. Although sometimes described as hard to feed, it is interesting that food problems or issues tend to become more pronounced as the child gets a bit older. Some children will have profound sensitivities to food textures or tastes or smells, for example, foods of a certain consistency or color. Other children are resistant to new foods, eating only a limited diet. Attempts to introduce new foods can be fraught with difficulty. Often parents report issues with food sensitivities starting more or less from the moment that solid foods are introduced. It is interesting, however, that we've seen only a handful of children with autism who exhibit failure to thrive.

To some extent the unusual food preferences of some children with ASDs may be understood as having some resemblance to problems seen in typically developing toddlers who struggle with food. The things that help the typically developing child cope—for example, being motivated to imitate the models provided by family members eating a range of foods or enjoying praise from parents for trying new foods—don't work nearly as well in children with ASDs. This gets even more complicated when parents are also pursuing complementary and alternative dietary interventions.

Unfortunately, dealing with unusual food preferences is not easy. Occupational therapists and speech therapists may be helpful. Strategies can include practices such as *gradual* change. Depending on the child's preferences, it may be possible to add to foods he or she does like. For example, if she will drink smoothies or milkshakes, you can try adding different kinds of foods to the shake. Sometimes varying the way foods are presented makes them more tolerable, for example, freezing pureed vegetables into popsicles may make them more interesting. For some children it helps if they are involved in food preparation—visual approaches can be used to make a simple cookbook on index cards, and sometimes the child is more motivated if he or she has been involved in the cooking. Similarly, getting the child involved in grocery shopping might help.

Behavior approaches can be used and might include praise, time-limited meals, ignoring food refusals, and more frequent mini-meals (with limited snacks in between).

Pica

Eating nonfood substances (**pica**) is noted in individuals with intellectual disability as well as with autism. Items eaten can include dirt, paint chips, string, or even clothing. The materials may be chewed and retained in the mouth and may or may be not swallowed. Obviously, substances that are poisonous are of concern as, indeed, is the potential for bowel obstruction. Parents should be aware of any existing sources of lead or toxins.

A number of strategies are available to deal with this problem, including behavioral interventions (Piazza et al., 1998) as well as pharmacological ones (Lerner, 2008). The choice of intervention strategy depends on several factors, including age and cognitive level of the child and on the specific behavior(s) that are at issue. Support from the speech pathologist and occupational therapist at school may be helpful. For some children it is the experience of moving their mouth and chewing that is critically important. In such instances use of crunchy foods or foods with interesting textures, gum, and so on can be helpful. Obviously parents should be aware of the potential for adding sugar to the child's diet. Occasionally pica is associated with the child's being overstimulated, and in such cases reducing the level of environmental stimulation may help. A good behavior analyst may also be very helpful, for example, in noting the contexts or situations in which the behavior occurs as well as its antecedents and consequences. For some children use of an electric toothbrush (sometimes several times a day) can provide oral simulation. For other children one sometimes can find a substitute or alternative behavior such as eating ice chips (with or without flavor). Sometimes reactions to the behavior may be an important part of what keeps it going. Depending on the context any of a number of medical or laboratory studies may be indicated (abdominal x-ray, hemoglobin lead level, etc.).

Gastrointestinal Problems

In recent years there has been considerable interest in gastrointestinal problems in children with ASDs. A number of factors including lack of exercise, sedentary lifestyle, and poor or rather limited diet all may contribute. A review by the British Medical Research Council suggested that there were no epidemiological data documenting the incidence and prevalence of gastrointestinal disturbances in children with ASDs. Kuddo and Nelson (2003) similarly failed to find evidence of increased GI problems.

Constipation and diarrhea appear to be the most frequently reported gastrointestinal symptoms (Chaidez, Hansen, & Hertz-Picciotto, 2014; Wang, Tancredi, & Thomas, 2011). It is not clear that there are strong associations either with severity of autism or level of intellectual disability (Chandler et al., 2013). Differences in gut permeability are also not observed (Dalton et al., 2014) and well-controlled studies do not show a relationship of gluten- or casein-free diets to behavior change in autism (Hyman et al., 2016; Millward, Ferriter, Calver, & Connell-Jones, 2008). Clearly GI problems may predispose to other difficulties, for example, sleep problems or irritability. We hope future research will include better controlled and rigorous studies to further evaluate GI problems in autism. Evidence-based guidelines are currently not available for gastrointestinal disease in children with ASDs, and so standard practice should prevail.

Obesity

About a third of children in the United States are now overweight—a major increase over the last several decades. Obesity is significantly related to a range of medical problems, including type 2 diabetes, hypertension, orthopedic problems, and hyperlipidemia, among others. If these problems continue they place the adult at increased risk for health problems. Unfortunately relatively little is known about the prevalence of obesity in individuals with ASDs. There are good a priori reasons to suspect that rates would be increased (see Box 4.1).

BOX 4.1 RISK FACTORS FOR OVERWEIGHT AND OBESITY IN ASD

- Limited **social skills** ➔ isolation from peer activities including play and sports activities
- Executive function difficulties ➔ difficulties with team sports

- Social isolation ➜ engagement in solitary and sedentary activities, for example, video games
- Food can be a major source of pleasure
- Medications ➜ decrease activity levels; may directly stimulate appetite (e.g., Risperidone)

The limited literature on this topic has produced variable results with increased prevalence of overweight ranging from about 10% to over 30% of children with autism. Zuckerman, Hill, Guion, Voltolina, and Fombonne (2014) evaluated obesity in a large sample of children with ASDs in Oregon and found that overall 18% met criteria for overweight and an additional 17% for obesity. Obesity was also associated with sleep and behavior problems. Risk factors have included severity of autism and associated medication administration. One study has noted nutritional deficiencies even in the presence of overweight, presumably reflecting idiosyncratic eating patterns (Shmaya, Eilat-Adar, Leitner, Reif, & Gabis, 2015).

As with typically developing youth (and adults) intervention is important, although options, unfortunately, can be rather limited. Effective intervention programs must recognize the needs of the individual and his or her situation. When possible the person should be involved and engaged. Setting realistic weight targets is important (Grondhuis & Aman, 2014). A few programs designed specifically to benefit children with ASDs have been developed (Gillette et al., 2014; Sharp, Burrell, & Jaquess, 2014). Appropriate exercise programs (Srinivasan, Pescatello, & Bhat, 2014) may help. In a few locations around the United States special recreational programs for children with ASD have been developed either through free-standing facilities or in conjunction with schools.

SLEEP AND SLEEP PROBLEMS

Needs for sleep vary considerably over children's development. Problems in sleep are among some of the most difficult to cope with. Parents, often already stressed, can become chronically tired and frustrated by their child's late bedtimes and by the frequent awakenings during the night. More than half of children with autism will, at some point, have problems with sleep that last more than a month; these are distressing to them or their parents and are associated with behavior problems (Park et al., 2012). The nature of the problem changes somewhat over time (Goldman, Richdale, Clemons, & Malow, 2012), but problems can persist well into adolescence.

Sometimes parents will tell us that sleep has never been a problem. Other times parents will tell us that their child slept pretty well as an infant, but then sleep seemed to get more disorganized. For example, as a toddler, she might have started to wake during the night and climbed into her parents' bed or demand attention. Also, it seems that many children with autism may not sleep through the night on a regular basis until much later in life. They may stay up late and sometimes cause trouble for themselves and their parents as they wander about the house at night. Sometimes the problem is that they wake up early. Or they may be highly dependent on quite specific and precise bedtime routines, which sometimes get more and more complicated over time, with any violation of the routine leading to a rough night.

Many parents are up for a good part of the night waiting until the child finally goes to sleep so that they can go to bed. As parents become more tired and stressed, they may have more difficulty coping with their child (and other parts of their lives) in the daytime, which may further contribute to the child's troubles.

There is a small but growing body of research in this area but few longitudinal studies have been conducted. Some research suggests that it is younger children with autism who are most likely to have sleep problems. Others suggest that the issue has less to do with age and more with the child's overall level of development. Still others suggest that differences are not strongly related to either the child's age or developmental level (Goldman et al., 2012). Recent data suggest that, if anything, sleep problems are much more common in children with ASDs than other children with disabilities.

At least 50% of children will have problems by school-age. If anything, parents probably underreport sleep problems, most likely because they have become used to them! Limited physical exercise may contribute. Some investigators have suggested that perhaps problems with brain chemistry that affect the neurotransmitters or hormone levels of the child may be responsible for sleep disturbances. Basic problems in the day-night cycle may also be involved. Although children with ASDs are more likely than typically developing children to have sleep problems, the types of sleep problems they have are the same. Box 4.2 suggests some ways to solve sleep problems.

BOX 4.2 SUGGESTIONS FOR HOW TO SOLVE SLEEP DISORDERS

- Keep a sleep diary for 1 to 2 weeks to help understand the problem.
- Make sure the child is tired by increasing exercise, decreasing daytime sleeping, or changing type, dose, or timing of medications.
- Avoid foods, drinks, or activities that overstimulate the child at bedtime.
- Work toward having the child fall asleep on his or her own at the beginning of the night.

There are a number of steps you can take to help parents. Keeping a sleep diary for at least a week to give detailed accounting of the times, routines, and problems can be very helpful. One of the simple things to try first, as with other behavior problems in autism, is to attempt to capitalize on the child's desire for structure and consistency. That is, try to use the child's desire for routine and predictability to help establish a reasonable sleep pattern. This means having a consistent bedtime routine. Approximately 15 to 30 minutes for the entire routine seems to work well. Parents should also be consistent in the choice of the predetermined bedtime routine. They can make a bedtime book or a story board with pictures that outline the bedtime routine and then turn over a picture as each bedtime activity is completed. Parents should avoid any activities or foods that the child would find very stimulating. Too much exercise just before bedtime may make it harder for the child to fall asleep. Also, they should avoid all drinks or food with caffeine for at least 6 hours before bedtime. Care providers should also be alert to any medications that might disrupt sleep.

For parents it is important to keep in mind that although the goal is to help the child get to sleep at a reasonable hour, what you can actually control is only that the child is in bed on time. If the child stays up for a while but is quiet in her bedroom that may be perfectly fine. The child should not be dependent on the parents for falling and staying asleep. For many parents, the most burdensome part of sleeping difficulties is coping with the child's need for the parent(s) every night as part of his bedtime routine. When children have this need parents can quickly find themselves sleep deprived. Sometimes a parent will end up sleeping with his or her child, although then the child's tendency to wake up frequently may make it difficult for the parent to get a good night's sleep (not to mention complicating relationships with the spouse).

Parents should pay attention to the environment in the bedroom. Is it one that will help the child get to sleep (and stay asleep) or is it one that will jazz him up and make getting to sleep even more difficult? Occasionally, parents tell us that working to quiet the various noises in the house (dishwasher, laundry, etc.) helps. Other parents buy a white noise machine or similar device to hide or mask other noises that bother their child; there are many variations available, some with a choice of sounds such as rain, waves at the beach, and so on.

Whatever, parents should not make the mistake of encouraging problematic sleep patterns, for example, by letting the child miss school because she had a bad night. This is a surefire ticket to disaster because it can reinforce the behavior that is causing trouble in the first place!

Excessive sleep (naps) during the day can cause trouble with nighttime sleep. Some excellent resources for parents are available (e.g., Durand, 2013). There is an entire chapter devoted to sleep in the book that we (Volkmar & Wiesner, 2009) authored explicitly for parents.

Parents frequently seek pharmacological interventions. If the problem is of new onset it is important to take a comprehensive history and examination searching for factors that may contribute to new onset of sleep issues, for example, medical problems such as ear infections or urinary tract (bladder) infections or recent changes that might affect sleep. As with other children, breathing issues related to enlarged tonsils and adenoids or severe obesity can also contribute. Medications may also affect the sleep cycle.

Diphenhydramine (Benadryl™) may sometimes be sufficient. Otherwise a range of prescription medicines can be used as with other individuals, keeping in mind that occasionally, the individual with ASD becomes paradoxically more agitated rather than relaxed.

There has been great interest in Melatonin as a sleep aid. In one recent study a 14-week intervention with supplemental melatonin improved sleep latency in most children at the 1 mg or 3 mg dosages. The treatment was safe and well tolerated and improved behavior and decreased parenting stress (Malow et al., 2012). If sleep problems are severe and intractable, engagement with a specialist may be helpful.

SAFETY

Accidents are the leading cause of death in individuals with autism (Shavelle & Strauss, 1998). It remains somewhat unclear the extent to which associated medical problems such as seizures contribute to risk (Bilder et al., 2013; Gillberg, Billstedt, Sundh, & Gillberg, 2010). Increased risk in autism reflects several factors: lack of appreciation of danger, impulsivity, limited social and communication skills, unusual sensory interests, and so forth. Further increasing risk, motor skills are often relatively preserved. The child who is otherwise fearful of new things or situations may seem driven to explore a new construction site, or the child who is otherwise afraid of the water may be preoccupied with a neighbor's swimming pool. In addition to the usual counseling of parents on issues of safety, health care providers have an important additional role in this regard for children with autism (see Box 4.3).

BOX 4.3 ACCIDENTS AND INJURIES

- Injuries are the leading cause of death in children and adolescents in the United States.
- Fatal injuries are just the tip of the iceberg: For every fatal injury, another 18 children end up in the hospital and more than 200 are treated in the ED.
- Less cognitively able children are at great risk as are those with seizure disorders (children have drowned in bathtubs with only a little water).
- The good (but sad) news is that most of these injuries are preventable.
- In autism, the available data suggest that children with autism are at increased risk for serious injury and even death because of accidents such as drowning and suffocation.

What might not interest other children might be of great interest to children with autism. Parents should safety proof the house, paying special attention to the usual danger areas (kitchen and bathroom) as well as to the child's bedroom. Windows that can be opened, neighboring pools, and other attractive hazards should all be considered. For younger children, audio or visual monitoring can be helpful—particularly in children with sleeping problems. Poisonings can occur at any age, and it is important for health care providers to educate parents about common household poisons—cleaners, medications, and so forth. Parents should have ready access to the local Poison Control Center number and should also understand the warning signs that the child may have gotten into something (stains on clothing or mouth, sudden onset of vomiting, etc.).

Some children on the autism spectrum have trouble with running away or bolting from caregivers, which is a major safety issue (Solomon & Lawlor, 2013). Anderson et al. (2012) noted that almost 50% of children had run away after age 4 years and that in half of these cases (i.e., 25% of children with autism) the length of the time they were missing was a source of concern. Traffic injury and drowning are areas of risk, and severity of autism is associated with running-away risk. At home, parents can use special locks that are harder to open, or for younger children put a hook-and-eye-type lock well out of the child's reach. Another choice is to put alarms on the windows or doors that go off when they are opened, alerting parents to a child's trying to leave the house. If the child has a tendency to wander, it might be helpful to have him wear a MedicAlert bracelet. The bracelet can have the child's name, parents' names, and cell phone number and can even state that the child has autism or ASD. We have seen one instance in which the child's tendency to bolt or wander was so severe that her parents obtained a very large helper dog that went with the child everywhere. The child and dog were basically tied together and the dog was trained that when the child started to bolt the dog would just sit! Other options are increasingly available—for example, GPS systems that provide a tracker of the child.

Outside the home, the yard and, particularly, swimming pools or bodies of water present an obvious hazard and need to be surrounded by secure gates and fences as well as alarms that go off if a child goes through them or gets into the water. Even without a pool a yard can be the source of many dangers. Parents should be encouraged to walk around their yard to look for safety hazards and should very much be encouraged to help the child learn to swim (and observe water safety). Crossing the street, being careful walking, responding to strangers, and so forth can all be taught, and there are now even a few computer programs specifically designed for children with ASDs (Steinborn & Knapp, 1982).

Safety issues can also arise at school. These issues can be more complex to deal with, and having a school nurse who is involved and proactive can be extremely helpful. Accidents and incidents often are associated with transition times and, seemingly paradoxical, less-structured activities (recess, gym, cafeteria)—this is understandable in that children with autism often do better with schedules and structure. Teachers should all be trained in basic safety issues and simple first aid. Explicit teaching about safety can occur. As at home, parents and teachers should be mindful of potential dangers, for example, in play equipment or physical space, or for factors in the child that may present risk, for example, children who are fearless climbers. Teachers should not assume that having a fence around a playground makes up for adequate supervision.

BULLYING

Being bullied can be a major problem for individuals with ASDs. It can begin in the elementary school years and tends to increase in frequency as children become older—particularly for more cognitively able students. This is unfortunate for many reasons, including the fact that it is just this group who are most likely to be mainstreamed. Factors predisposing to bullying include problems in reading social cues and in dealing with the fast pace of social interaction. Unusual interests may also make the student with ASD stand out from peers—at a point in development when standing out is generally not a good thing. Language issues—particularly social language issues—may be a problem because challenges in dealing with more sophisticated language and figures of speech may lead to confusion. It is typical for the teenager with ASD to say something that is perceived as funny by peers (even if this was not intended and conversely, the attempt to actually make a joke may go over like a lead balloon). As a result the more-able individuals with ASDs may frequently have the experience of seeming to be laughed at (for reasons not apparent to him or her). The need to cooperate with others presents challenges for team sports. Even small groups can also present a challenge, and, at times, deciding what is or isn't bullying (e.g., the teacher who uses sarcasm or ridicule) can be difficult.

This can also be an issue when the more cognitively able child, for example, with Asperger's, doesn't understand classroom etiquette, such as constantly disrupting the class by asking questions. Occasionally teachers will join typical peers in mocking the student!

Bullying can be an isolated instance but can also be ongoing and frequent. Types of bullying vary with developmental level. Heinrichs (2003) notes that younger children are more likely to exhibit physical or verbal aggression toward same-sex peers, and in early adolescence social bullying become more common. In later adolescence, sexual aspects of bullying may be more prominent as is cyber bullying. Severity of social difficulties, social isolation, and difficulties with social language use apparently increase risk. Individuals who have idiosyncratic styles of relating and communication are also at increased risk (Maiano, Normand, Salvas, Moullec, & Aime, 2015). The presence of additional problems in the child with ASD, for example, anxiety or mood issues, further increases risk.

Bullying can lead to stress-related problems as well as contribute to or worsen anxiety and depression. It may also precipitate aggression or present with physical symptoms. Bullying is probably most common in situations without adequate adult monitoring (unfortunately just the situations in which the individuals with an ASD will have more trouble). It can also be seen in nonschool settings.

Some of the same problems that contribute to bullying in the first place also make it less likely that the more-able child with an ASD will report it. Awareness on the part of parents and teachers may come only after some specific incident. Primary care providers should be alert to the potential for bullying in children of all ages but particularly those with disabilities.

A range of bullying-prevention programs have been developed, and bullying rates vary dramatically from country to country. Some countries, such as Norway, have well-established policies that have lowered the rates of bullying. Although a policy of zero tolerance of bullying might, at first blush, seem to be a simple solution, it presents its own issues. Effective programs need to be broad based and start early and include sensible strategies for helping children who are bullied, are bullies, or both.

Summary

The early impression that autism was not associated with other medical conditions proved incorrect. As children were followed over time it became clear that there was a significant risk for seizure disorder. Genetic studies made it clear that autism was strongly heritable. However, early claims for vast numbers of medical conditions associated with autism proved incorrect. Autism is strongly associated with a risk for seizure disorder (particularly with onset in early childhood and adolescent). It is also increased in association with some genetic conditions such as Fragile X and tuberous sclerosis. Connections to other genetic conditions also have been noted (although their evidence is somewhat less strong).

Regression in development is reported in perhaps 25% of children with autism, but clear-cut regression is relatively uncommon. Various types and patterns of regression are observed. Occasionally associated medical problems are noted, although this is usually not the case.

Hearing and visual problems are sometimes observed, and primary care providers should be alert to them. Eating and feeding issues are fairly frequent, although data in favor of the gut connection with autism are rather limited. It appears that obesity and GI problems such as constipation may result from limited activity levels, poor diet, and so on. That said, problems with poor eating and nutrition are important and should be addressed. Obesity is a frequent long-term health problem.

Sleep problems in autism are common, and parents probably underreport them. Various steps can be taken to address these issues and can contribute to lessened parental stress and improved child behavior.

Safety concerns are a major issue in autism with an increased (doubled) risk for accidental death. Parents and teachers should be familiar with common issues, for example, bolting, and be prepared to address them. Similarly, bullying, particularly for the higher cognitive functioning student, can be a major problem and may present to primary care providers with behavioral issues such as school avoidance or nonspecific physical complaints including headaches, stomachaches, and so forth.

Although concern about associations of autism with immunizations was fanned by the media, there is no evidence supporting such claims. There is clearly increased risk for children in developing communicable diseases if population rates of vaccination decrease. Parents should be encouraged, as should other parents, to engage in appropriate immunizations.

▓ REFERENCES

Abrahams, B. S., & Geschwind, D. H. (2008). Advances in autism genetics: On the threshold of a new neurobiology. *Nature Reviews Genetics, 9*(5), 341–355. [Erratum appears in *Nature Reviews Genetics, 9*(5), 493.]

Amiet, C., Gourfinkel-An, I., Consoli, A., Perisse, D., & Cohen, D. (2010). Epilepsy and autism: A complex issue. *Archives de Pediatrie, 17*(6), 650–651.

Anderson, C., Law, J., Daniels, A., Rice, C., Mandell, D. S., Hagopian, L., & Law, P. A. (2012). Occurrence and family impact of elopement in children with autism spectrum disorders. *Pediatrics, 130*(5), 870–877.

Bilder, D., Botts, E. L., Smith, K. R., Pimentel, R., Farley, M., Viskochil, J., McMahon, W. M., Block, H., Ritvo, E., Ritvo, R. S., & Coon, H. (2013). Excess mortality and causes of death in autism spectrum disorders: A follow-up of the 1980s Utah/UCLA autism epidemiologic study. *Journal of Autism & Developmental Disorders, 43*(5), 1196–1204.

Bolton, P. F., Carcani-Rathwell, I., Hutton, J., Goode, S., Howlin, P., & Rutter, M. (2011). Epilepsy in autism: Features and correlates. *British Journal of Psychiatry, 198,* 289–294.

Chaidez, V., Hansen, R. L., & Hertz-Picciotto, I. (2014). Gastrointestinal problems in children with autism, developmental delays or typical development. *Journal of Autism & Developmental Disorders, 44*(5), 1117–1127.

Chandler, S., Carcani-Rathwell, I., Charman, T., Pickles, A., Loucas, T., Meldrum, D., Simonoff, E., Sullivan, P., & Baird, G. (2013). Parent-reported gastro-intestinal symptoms in children with autism spectrum disorders. *Journal of Autism & Developmental Disorders, 43*(12), 2737–2747.

Cooper, J. E. (1975). Epilepsy in a longitudinal survey of 5000 children. *British Medical Journal, 1,* 1020–1022.

Dalton, N., Chandler, S., Turner, C., Charman, T., Pickles, A., Loucas, T., Simonoff, E., Sullivan, P., & Baird, G. (2014). Gut permeability in autism spectrum disorders. *Autism Research: Official Journal of the International Society for Autism Research, 7*(3), 305–313.

Deykin, E. Y., & MacMahon, B. (1979). The incidence of seizures among children with autistic symptoms. *American Journal of Psychiatry, 136*(10), 1310–1312.

Durand, M. V. (2013). *Sleep better.* Baltimore, MD: Brookes.

Dyken, P., & Krawiecki, N. (1983). Neurodegenerative diseases of infancy and childhood. *Annals of Neurology, 13,* 351–364.

Gillberg, C., Billstedt, E., Sundh, V., & Gillberg, I. C. (2010). Mortality in autism: A prospective longitudinal community-based study. *Journal of Autism & Developmental Disorders, 40*(3), 352–357.

Gillberg, C., & Coleman, M. (2000). *The biology of the autistic syndromes* (3rd ed.). London, UK: Mac Keith Press.

Gillette, M. L., Stough, C. O., Beck, A. R., Maliszewski, G., Best, C. M., Gerling, J. K., & Summar, S. (2014). Outcomes of a weight management clinic for children with special needs. *Journal of Developmental & Behavioral Pediatrics, 35*(4), 266–273.

Goldman, S. E., Richdale, A. L., Clemons, T., & Malow, B. A. (2012). Parental sleep concerns in autism spectrum disorders: Variations from childhood to adolescence. *Journal of Autism and Developmental Disorders, 42*(4), 531–538.

Grondhuis, S. N., & Aman, M. G. (2014). Overweight and obesity in youth with developmental disabilities: A call to action. *Journal of Intellectual Disability Research, 58*(9), 787–799.

Heinrichs, R. (2003). *Perfect targets: Asperger syndrome and bullying—Practical solutions for surviving the social world.* Lenexa, KS: Autism Asperger.

Hyman, S. L., Stewart, P. A., Foley, J., Cain, U., Peck, R., Morris, D. D., Wang, H., & Smith, T. (2016). The gluten-free/casein-free diet: A double-blind challenge trial in children with autism. *Journal of Autism and Developmental Disorders, 46,* 205–220.

Kuddo, T., & Nelson, C. B. (2003). How common are gastrointestinal disorders in children with autism? *Current Opinion in Pediatrics, 15,* 339–343.

Lerner, A. J. (2008). Treatment of pica behavior with olanzapine. *CNS Spectrums, 13*(1), 19.

Maiano, C., Normand, C. L., Salvas, M. C., Moullec, G., & Aime, A. (2015). Prevalence of school bullying among youth with autism spectrum disorders: A systematic review and meta-analysis. *Autism Research, International Society for Autism Research (INSAR), 9*(6), 601–615.

Malow, B., Adkins, K. W., McGrew, S. G., Wang, L., Goldman, S. E., Fawkes, D., & Burnette, C. (2012). Melatonin for sleep in children with autism: A controlled trial examining dose, tolerability, and outcomes. *Journal of Autism and Developmental Disorders, 42*(8), 1729–1737.

Millward, C., Ferriter, M., Calver, S., & Connell-Jones, G. (2008). Gluten- and casein-free diets for autistic spectrum disorder. *Cochrane Database of Systematic Reviews* (2). [Update of (2004). *Cochrane Database of Systematic Reviews* (2).

Park, S., Cho, S. C., Cho, I. H., Kim, B. N., Kim, J. W., Shin, M. S., Chung, U. S., Park, T. W., Son, J. W., & Yoo, H. J. (2012). Sleep problems and their correlates and comorbid psychopathology of children with autism spectrum disorders. *Research in Autism Spectrum Disorders, 6*(3), 1068–1072.

Piazza, C. C., Fisher, W. W., Hanley, G. P., LeBlanc, L. A., Worsdell, A. S., Lindauer, S. E., & Keeney, K. M. (1998). Treatment of pica through multiple analyses of its reinforcing functions. *Journal of Applied Behavior Analysis, 31*(2), 165–189.

Roach, E. S. (2014). Mechanism-based therapy of genetic neurological disease. *Pediatric Neurology, 50*(4), 285–286.

Roach, E. S., & Sparagana, S. P. (2004). Diagnosis of tuberous sclerosis complex. *Journal of Child Neurology, 19*(9), 643–649.

Rutter, M., Bailey, A., Bolton, P., & Le Couteur, A. (1994). Autism and known medical conditions: Myth and substance. *Journal of Child Psychology & Psychiatry & Allied Disciplines, 35*(2), 311–322.

Sharp, W. G., Burrell, T. L., & Jaquess, D. L. (2014). The autism MEAL plan: A parent-training curriculum to manage eating aversions and low intake among children with autism. *Autism, 18*(6), 712–722.

Shavelle, R. M., & Strauss, D. (1998). Comparative mortality of persons with autism in California, 1980–1996. *Journal of Insurance Medicine (Seattle), 30*(4), 220–225.

Shmaya, Y., Eilat-Adar, S., Leitner, Y., Reif, S., & Gabis, L. (2015). Nutritional deficiencies and overweight prevalence among children with autism spectrum disorder. *Research in Developmental Disabilities, 38,* 1–6.

Solomon, O., & Lawlor, M. C. (2013). And I look down and he is gone: Narrating autism, elopement and wandering in Los Angeles. *Social Science & Medicine, 94,* 106–114.

Srinivasan, S. M., Pescatello, L. S., & Bhat, A. N. (2014). Current perspectives on physical activity and exercise recommendations for children and adolescents with autism spectrum disorders. *Physical Therapy, 94*(6), 875–889.

Steinborn, M., & Knapp, T. J. (1982). Teaching an autistic child pedestrian skills. *Journal of Behavior Therapy and Experimental Psychiatry, 13*(4), 347–351.

Van Esch, H. (2012). Clinical features and diagnosis of Fragile X syndrome in children and adolescents. *UpToDate,* pp. 1–16.

Visootsak, J., Warren, S. T., Anido, A., Graham, J. M., Jr. (2005). *Clinical Pediatrics (Phila.), 44*(5), 371–381.

Volkmar, F., & Nelson., D. (1990). Seizures disorders in autism. *Journal of the American Academy of Child and Adolescent Psychiatry, 29*(1), 127–129.

Volkmar, F., & Wiesner, L. (2009). *A practical guide to autism.* Hoboken, NJ: Wiley.

Wang, L. W., Tancredi, D. J., & Thomas, D. W. (2011). The prevalence of gastrointestinal problems in children across the United States with autism spectrum disorders from families with multiple affected members. *Journal of Developmental & Behavioral Pediatrics, 32*(5), 351–360.

Westphal, A., & LeMaistre, E. (2014). Childhood disintegrative disorder. In H. Friedman (Ed.), *Encyclopedia of mental health* (2nd ed.). Waltham, MA: Academic Press/Elsevier.

Zuckerman, K. E., Hill, A. P., Guion, K., Voltolina, L., & Fombonne, E. (2014). Overweight and obesity: Prevalence and correlates in a large clinical sample of children with autism spectrum disorder. *Journal of Autism & Developmental Disorders, 44*(7), 1708–1719.

▪ SUGGESTED READING

Amir, R. E., Van den Veyver, I. B., Wan, M., Tran, C. Q., Francke, U., & Zoghbi, H. Y. (1990). Rett syndrome is caused by mutations in X-linked MeCP2, encoding methyl-CpG-binding protein 2. *Nature Genetics, 23,* 985–988.

Andersen, I. M., Kaczmarska, J., McGrew, S. G., & Malow, B. A. (2008). Melatonin for insomnia in children with autism spectrum disorders. *Journal of Child Neurology, 23*(5), 482–485.

Buie, T., Campbell, D. B., Fuchs, G. J., Furuta, G. T., Levy, J., Vandewater, J., Whitaker, A. H., Atkins, D., Bauman, M. L., Beaudet, A. L., et al. (2010). Evaluation, diagnosis, and treatment of gastrointestinal disorders in individuals with ASDs: A consensus report. *Pediatrics, 125*(Suppl 1), S1–S18.

Burke, L., & Stoddart, K. P. (2014). Medical and health problems in adults with high-functioning autism and Asperger syndrome. *Adolescents and adults with autism spectrum disorders* (pp. 239–267). New York, NY: Springer Science + Business Media.

Catalano, R. A. (1998). *When autism strikes: Families cope with childhood disintegrative disorder*. New York, NY: Perseus.

Coury, D. (2010). Medical treatment of autism spectrum disorders. *Current Opinion in Neurology, 23*(2), 131–136.

DeMyer, M. K., Barton, S., DeMyer, W. E., Norton, J. E., Allen, J., & Steele, R. (1973). Prognosis in autism. *Journal of Autism and Childhood Schizophrenia, 4,* 42–60.

Durand, V. M. (1998). *Sleep better! A guide to improving sleep for children with special needs*. Baltimore, MD: Brookes.

Durand, V. M. (2008). *When children don't sleep well: Interventions for pediatric sleep disorders; Parent workbook*. New York, NY: Oxford University Press.

Ferber, R. (1985). *Solve your child's sleep problems*. New York, NY: Simon & Schuster.

Ferber, R. (2006). *Solve your child's sleep problems: New, revised, and expanded edition (rev. ed.)*. New York, NY: Simon & Schuster.

Giarelli, E., & Fisher, K. M. (2016). *Integrated health care for people with autism spectrum disorder*. Springfield, IL: Charles Thomas Publishing.

Isaksen, J., Bryn, V., Diseth, T. H., Heiberg, A., Schjolberg, S., & Skjeldal, O. H. (2013). Children with autism spectrum disorders: The importance of medical investigations. *European Journal of Paediatric Neurology, 17*(1), 68–76.

Johnson, K. P., & Malow, B. A. (2008). Assessment and pharmacological treatment of sleep disturbance in autism. *Child and Adolescent Psychiatric Clinics of North America, 17,* 773–785.

Johnson, K. P., & Malow, B. A. (2008). Sleep in children with autism spectrum disorders. *Current Neurology and Neuroscience Reports, 8*(2), 155–161.

Levy, S. E., Giarelli, E., Lee, L. C., Schieve, L. A., Kirby, R. S., Cunniff, C., Nicholas, L., Reaven, J., & Rice, C. E. (2010). Autism spectrum disorder and co-occurring developmental, psychiatric, and medical conditions among children in multiple populations of the United States. *Journal of Developmental & Behavioral Pediatrics, 31*(4), 267–275.

Maglione, M. A., Das, L., Raaen, L., Smith, A., Chari, R., Newberry, S., Shanman, R., Perry, T., Goetz, M. B., & Gidengil, C. (2014). Safety of vaccines used for routine immunization of U.S. children: A systematic review. *Pediatrics, 134*(2), 325–337.

McClure, I. (2014). Developing and implementing practice guidelines. In F. R. Volkmar, S. J. Rogers, R. Paul, & K. A. Pelphrey (Eds.), *Handbook of autism and pervasive developmental disorders* (4th ed., Vol. 2, pp. 1014–1035). Hoboken, NJ: Wiley.

Offit, P. (2008). *Autism's false prophets*. New York, NY: Columbia University Press.

Pantley, E., & Sears, W. (2002). *The no-cry sleep solution: Gentle ways to help your baby sleep through the night*. Columbus, OH: McGraw-Hill.

Polimeni, M. A., Richdale, A. L., & Francis, A. J. (2005). A survey of sleep problems in autism, Asperger's disorder and typically developing children. *Journal of Intellectual Disability Research, 49*(Pt. 4), 260–268.

Stoddart, K. P., Burke, L., Muskat, J., Duhaime, S., Accardi, C., Burnh Riosa, P., et al. (2013). *Diversity in Ontario's youth and adults with autism spectrum disorders: Complex needs in unprepared systems* (p. 52). Toronto, ON, Canada: The Hanen Centre.

Volkmar, F., Siegel, M., Woodbury-Smith, M., King, B., McCracken, J., State, M., & the American Academy of Child and Adolescent Psychiatry (AACAP) Committee on Quality Issues (CQI). (2014). Practice parameter for the assessment and treatment of children and adolescents with autism spectrum disorder. *Journal of the American Academy of Child and Adolescent Psychiatry, 53*(2), 237–257.

Wakefield, A. J. (1999). MMR vaccination and autism. *Lancet, 354*(9182), 949–950.

Weiskop, S., Richdale, A., & Matthews, J. (2005). Behavioural treatment to reduce sleep problems in children with autism or Fragile X syndrome. *Developmental Medicine and Child Neurology, 47*(2), 94–104.

Weissbluth, M. (2005). *Healthy sleep habits, happy child.* New York, NY: Ballantine Books.

CHAPTER 5

Overview of Educational Programs and Interventions

The social, communication, and behavioral problems in individuals with autism present major challenges for learning from very early on in life. In the first years after autism was identified by Kanner there was little consensus on what to do apart from psychotherapy (which had little benefit) (Reichow & Volkmar, 2011). As time went on, however, it became more apparent that structured teaching could be effective and that some of the basic principles of learning derived from behavioral work in psychology could be used effectively (Rutter & Bartak, 1973). Until Public Law 94–142 (which we'll talk more about in Chapter 6), many schools simply refused to provide programs for children they believed were "uneducable," and as a result many parents were left with little choice but to put the child into a state residential or institutional program where often children aged into adulthood and old age. However, with the mandate for schools to provide education for all, schools began to, and now do, assume a central, if not *the* central, role in intervention. As we will talk about in Chapter 6, a variety of issues arise, but for more disabled children an individualized program must be developed tailored to fit each child's current needs and abilities consistent with the long-term plan or vision for the child. Areas of intervention typically address the core diagnostic features of autism—deficits with social interaction and communication—but also must focus on other issues, including problems in learning. Schools must help students compensate for challenges in forward planning and organizational skills (what are often called *executive function issues*), and there is a major need for learning to generalize things over settings (adaptive skills). And of course schools also have to provide an education.

In the first decades after autism was described, specific intervention programs began, often started by parents desperate to avoid institutional placement. Some of the programs still exist today. Over time researchers also became interested in best approaches to treatment, and a number of model programs developed around the country (National Research Council, 2001). Many of these programs continue to exist although often these programs have evolved in terms of their approach to delivering services. For example, often early programs were center-based, that is, parents took the child to the center for service. Over time more home-based programs were developed (particularly for younger children), and finally programs began to move into public school settings. It is not uncommon to see that many of the older and more established programs have evolved over time.

In this chapter we provide a quick review of selected model programs, all of which are, to some degree, evidence-based; this will illustrate the range of effective approaches employed. We then go on to discuss specific aspects of evidence-based interventions relevant to all schools—often these were pioneered in the programs we've described. As a primary care provider, you do not need to be aware of all the fine points of intervention—rather you should know about some of the effective models so that you can help parents ask good questions about programs and services. Keep in mind that intervention research is some of the most difficult to do and get funded; there is a stronger database focused on specific interventions as compared to evidence-based program assessments (Reichow, Barton, Volkmar, Paul, Rogers, & Pelphrey, 2014).

MODEL PROGRAMS: AN OVERVIEW

Several different kinds of programs have developed over time and share many similarities as well as some important differences (see Box 5.1). These programs have variable degrees of evidence showing that the program is effective (this is a complicated issue for many [Paul & Fahim, 2016; Reichow et al., 2014]). Keep in mind that in discussing any of these approaches, in reality the issue relates to what a specific child needs! Primary care providers can be effective sources of information and support, especially if they really get to know the schools in the area they serve.

- *Center-based programs* provide services in a special setting. This might be in a special school or clinic (possibly affiliated with a college or university program in some way). These programs may be *segregated* (only children with ASDs or special needs) or *inclusive* (include some typically developing children).
- *Home-based programs* provide services mostly within the home (although sometimes there is additional time in outside programs such as actual classrooms and other intervention time outside the home). These are often used for young children.
- *School-based programs* provide services within the schools. This might be in an integrated, inclusive classroom (a mix of typically developing children and some children with ASDs or other problems) or a specialized (segregated) autism or special ed classroom (and many variations in between).

Model programs for intervention can be grouped into several general groups. This grouping reflects differences in approach or theoretical orientation.

- Behaviorally based and focused programs or **applied behavior analysis (ABA)** programs employ principles of behavioral psychology in fostering learning—particularly learning-to-learn skills (such as sitting and paying attention). Rewards are used to shape behavior. **Discrete trial teaching** is one of the more frequently used ABA techniques. In discrete trial teaching there is an antecedent, a behavior, and a consequence. For example, if you are trying to have the child say the word *orange* you might hold out an orange and ask "what is this?" There would then be a behavior from the child (e.g., saying the word for orange or just reaching for it or maybe just making a sound) and then a consequence (giving the child the orange if he says the word or some approximation or even some sound—depending on the child—but withholding it if he does not).

Typically, the desired behavior is broken down into smaller steps, each of which is then taught (often many times) using prompts and rewards, which are then gradually faded over time. There is a very large and impressive literature on the effectiveness of these interventions, although it should be noted that it is almost entirely based on single-case reports and case studies (Odom, Boyd, Hall, & Hume, 2014). A number of such programs have been developed around the country (e.g., the Douglas Developmental Disabilities Center program [Harris & Handleman, 2000]; the Lovaas approach [Lovaas & Smith, 1988]; Princeton Child Development Institute [McClannahan & Krantz, 2004]; these all have moderate to strong evidence supporting their efficacy).

- Developmentally oriented programs such as the one developed by Sally Rogers (Rogers, Dawson, & Vismara, 2012; Rogers & Vismara, 2014) build on the child's interest using developmentally guided approaches to intervention. The Rogers model (originally referred to as the **Denver model** where it was first developed and more recently as the early start developmental model) has mild to moderately strong support at the present time (see Dawson et al., 2010; Rogers & Vismara, 2014). The Greenspan floortime model is also developmentally oriented and has an elaborate theoretical basis (Greenspan & Wieder, 2009), although the evidence base for this approach is relatively limited (Reichow et al., 2014). The SCERTS model (Prizant, Wetherby, Rubin, Laurent, & Rydell, 2004) focuses on social interaction, communication, and emotional regulation.

- **Pivotal response training (PRT)** is a bit of a hybrid in that interventions are also based on ABA procedures, but it has a developmental orientation in that it focuses on behaviors seen as being key to learning and other skills (Koegel & Koegel, 2006). An important goal of this intervention is **generalization** of skills (use of same skills across settings with different people or materials). PRT procedures have been used to facilitate language, play, and social skills. There is moderately strong evidence in support of this method (Koegel & Koegel, 2006; Koegel, Koegel, Vernon, & Brookman-Frazee, 2010).

- Eclectic approaches such as **TEACCH** (Schopler, 1997) draw from various techniques and methods. Aspects of this program, the first statewide autism program in the United States, are unique and some have strong empirical support. At the same time this kind of approach is, perhaps, one of the most challenging to validate in the era of evidence-based treatments because it is indeed eclectic (Mesibov & Shea, 2010). With that being said there are important and unique aspects of these programs and some portions of them can be considered to be evidence-based.

Other treatment models are available as well (see Reichow et al., 2014, for a review of programs and evidence and Volkmar & Wiesner, 2009, for information specifically for parents on these programs). Some of these programs depend heavily on developing social relationships, for example, Relationship Development Intervention developed by Gutstein and Sheely (2002) and to some extent the Greenspan model, although only some evidence is available for each and they should be regarded as emerging rather than well-established evidence-based treatments (Paul & Fahim, 2016).

The original report from the National Research Council (NRC) (2001) and a subsequent review by the AAP Council on Children with Disabilities (Myers, Johnson, & The American Academy of Pediatrics Council on Children with Disabilities, 2007) summarize important aspects of intervention programs (note that, although the focus on these reviews is often on young children, the priorities—with some adaption—are relevant at all ages). The consensus from the NRC report was that there were a number of commonalities among the programs for younger children that could point to at least one (or sometimes more) evaluation or outcome studies (see Box 5.2).

BOX 5.2 COMMON FEATURES OF EFFECTIVE PROGRAMS

- Provision of a relatively intensive program (in terms of hours and levels of teacher support) as early as possible
- Development of functional, spontaneous communication
- Social instruction in various settings
- For younger children enhancing play skills and peer play abilities (for older individuals this can be expanded to include the range of leisure-time activities)

- Enhanced academic and cognitive growth including a range of abilities and problem-solving skills and multitasking
- Positive behavioral interventions for problem behaviors and reduction of behaviors that interfere with learning
- Use of aids such as visual supports, augmentative communication, and so forth
- Functional academic skills as appropriate
- Inclusion of a family component (this is particularly helpful for fostering generalization)
- Opportunities for interaction with typically developing peers relative to specific goals
- Provision of an appropriate and supportive physical environment for learning (e.g., relative to minimizing distractions)

The overarching goal is to help individuals acquire as many skills as possible to enable them to be as productive and self-sufficient as possible as an adult. And we, and others, have repeatedly emphasized family involvement is essential to this effort. To the extent possible the individual also needs to be a part of the planning process, particularly as he or she matures. By law this should clearly be in place by high school.

Autism-Focused Curricula

An effective curriculum will be individualized and include observable goals and objectives within the context of a longer-term vision for the student (Hume & Odom, 2007; Olley, 2005). It cannot be overemphasized that the curriculum should fit the child and not vice versa. The curriculum for students who are fully included requires special planning. This typically entails a well-done individualized education plan (IEP) with critical support from teachers and aides. Interestingly, sometimes the commitment to full inclusion (Hume & Odom, 2007) can present significant obstacles for the child with autism or ASD; for example, it may require the child to learn some activities in the community, but this will remove the child from the traditional classroom settings.

Sometimes children with ASD exhibit one or more isolated academic areas of real strength. They often seem to have an interest in iconic (visual) images. This may start with things such as signs or hood ornaments on cars but often this interest extends into letters and numbers; it is not uncommon for very young children with autism to be more fascinated by the letters or numbers on building blocks and ignore their use as building materials. Some children become early readers. *Hyperlexia* is the isolated ability to read single words with greater proficiency than you would otherwise expect given the child's age or other areas of difficulties. Some children with autism or other ASDs (e.g., those with Asperger's) can become effective early readers. Sometimes, however, reading to decode (to say the word out loud) may greatly exceed the child's ability to understand. Good tests of reading ability are available, and it is important to make sure that good reading includes understanding as well as decoding before making this a major part of the child's program.

Careful attention has to be paid to the learning environment and other factors that affect the child's ability to learn within his or her program. For example, the use of simple organization aides—such as visual schedules or use of functional routines and activity schedules—can enhance learning by helping with transitions, providing a structure for learning, and decreasing problem behaviors.

Evidence-Based Intervention Methods

Approaches to establishing the evidence basis of interventions stem from medicine and psychology as well as other disciplines. These approaches share some similarities and some differences, based partly on the specific discipline as well as the topic being addressed. In the next sections we review some of the approaches used. Keep in mind that, in the real world, these are often used side by side; this can complicate evaluation of their effectiveness!

Behavioral Techniques   The early observation that structured teaching was more helpful to children with autism inspired a large body of behaviorally based interventions using the principles of learning theory. The various ABA approaches to intervention use these techniques very effectively—particularly when the clinician is experienced and has a good sense of the individual's needs and challenges. We talk about specific methods in greater detail in the chapter on behavioral intervention

(Chapter 10). Keep in mind that these interventions typically have a very strong research base—although most in the form of single cases studies, that is, the same children before, during, and after intervention. Some of the strongest model programs in the country use these methods.

Social Skills Social skills are an obvious area for support given the centrality of social difficulties in the expression of children with autism. Having better social (and social-communicative) skills helps students to achieve higher levels of peer acceptance and integration into the community. There are essentially three approaches to teaching social skills: adult-led approaches (teacher or clinician instruction and therapy), peer-based approaches, and combination approaches (e.g., social skills groups with peers with an adult or adults present). The peer-based approaches have, by far, the strongest base in the research literature and tend to integrate preschoolers and young school-age children into mainstream education (Kohler, Strain, & Goldstein, 2005). Peers can be highly effective teachers but need to be given (simple) instructions on how to interact, for example, the "stay, play, and talk with your buddy approach" (Goldstein, Kaczmarek, Pennington, & Shafer, 1992).

Social skills become increasingly sophisticated and complex during the school years because there is a shift from play to games with rules (including sports). For typically developing children the first more intense friendships also typically develop at this time, and the child with ASD may become aware of feeling isolated. Social skills interventions in the school-age group tend to more frequently involve adults (that is, with one-on-one instruction) or hybrid methods (social skills group in which an adult and other children are present). Adult-based approaches range from more-focused, ABA activities for more cognitively or socially impaired students to more naturalistic ones (Reichow, Steiner, & Volkmar, 2013). Teaching social skills may go on in individual sessions with the speech pathologist with additional work then done with teacher and parents to help generalize skills. Behavioral techniques and visual supports can be used as well (Myles, 2013). Several good models have been developed including **Social Stories,** which teaches new strategies for solving problems and producing more socially acceptable solutions (Gray, 1998).

For the typically developing adolescent a very high level of social awareness is usual (even when done in a decidedly casual way, adolescents are extremely social creatures). For the adolescent or young adult with ASD this can be a source of great discomfort because the tendency to be overly literal and rule oriented comes just at the time when the typical adolescent is highly aware of the uses of ironic and figurative language. The UCLA Peers Program (Laugeson, Frankel, Gantman, Dillon, & Mogil, 2012; Laugeson, Gantman, Kapp, Orenski, & Ellingsen, 2015) has been well supported in controlled trials and can be effective when used with teenagers and young adults.

Social skills groups are one of the most frequently used methods for teaching social skills, particularly in the elementary and middle school years. These groups can be limited to children with difficulties or can include typical peers—the latter becoming valuable role models. The adult(s) monitor the ongoing group activity, intervening as appropriate but with the goal, as much as possible, of having group members provide helpful feedback. A number of excellent resources for social skills groups and social skills training are provided in the "Suggested Reading" list at the end of this chapter. Parents looking for social skills groups outside the school setting should talk with other parents about their experiences and obtain the names of experienced group leaders. It is important to realize that social skills groups are conducted by individuals with a range of training (there is no formal certification program). Groups are overseen frequently by psychologists, social workers, speech pathologists, and others. Teachers also can be encouraged to think about teaching social skills directly in the classroom.

Unfortunately, there is relatively little research on adolescent and adult social skills interventions, although more resources are appearing (Walton & Ingersoll, 2013). Many of the methods previously described can be used, particularly for individuals who are less verbal. Sadly, by this age typical peers have dramatically moved ahead in their social experience, and peer-based methods are not promising. However, adult-based approaches can be quite effective, particularly for helping the individual learn specific skills and tasks. Some valuable guides to teaching common social problem-solving have been developed; for example, *The Hidden Curriculum* (Myles, Trautman, & Schelvan, 2004) provides an overview and discussion of some of the more common social situations and ways that more-able individuals on the autism spectrum can be helped to deal with them. One meta-analysis found that overall social skills intervention had a moderate effect on individuals with autism (Reichow et al., 2013).

Communication and Language   The development of communication skills broadly defined (i.e., not just speech) is a critical component of intervention programs. Some excellent resources for parents are available (Paul & Fahim, 2016). For the typically developing child the onset of language proceeds seamlessly during the first months of life. At birth typically developing babies will orient to the faces and sounds of their parents. By 6 months they vocalize with good intonation (the musical aspect of speech), are beginning to respond to voices even without a visual cue, are starting to detect feelings conveyed by the voice, and are beginning to respond to their own name. By 1 year, a truly tremendous amount of development has occurred even before the child says his or her first word. Between the first and second year of life a tremendous explosion of language ability typically occurs, with infants able to begin to think more symbolically, and by the second birthday the child will often have several hundred words.

The situation in autism and related disorders is a very different one, and communication problems are a core challenge and important target area for early intervention given their importance for long-term outcome. The infant with autism may not babble or will produce the entire range of sounds rather than developing those unique to the language he or she is immersed in. As Kanner first noted, when language does develop unusual features are present. For children with no spoken language there are problems in establishing intentionality, joint attention, limited reciprocity, and nonverbal abilities. As language begins to emerge in children with ASD it often is limited and tends to be inflexible. As a function of the **gestalt processing** (learning in chunks) style, echoed language is common. **Echolalia** (repeating things over and over) was noted by Kanner but over time the child may start to break the language chunk apart and change it (mitigated echolalia). Problems with the musical aspects of language (**prosody**) take the form of **monotonic,** or robot-like, speech. Problems with pronouns and the social use of language (pragmatic problems) are found. Some children use **idiosyncratic language**—meanings that are unique to them. Some children learn to say many words, but their language understanding lags behind what they can say (the reverse of what happens in normal development). Interestingly some areas of language development are not typically impaired, for example, articulation or the ways words are said. Social language skills typically are very important targets for intervention at whatever level of language the child has. As children start to develop some language and use it to express their experience, social interchange becomes more important. Prior to that the meaning or intention must be inferred through behavior or sometimes through use of nonverbal visual aids or supports (picture exchange or object exchange).

A host of procedures and approaches have been used to teach communication and language skills; the recent book by Paul and Fahim (2016) has an excellent review of approaches and the evidence supporting these. The approaches will be selected in consultation with the treatment team at school and may be delivered or supervised by the speech pathologist (or sometimes by others, such as the school psychologist) and will vary depending on the child's age, cognitive ability, and level of communicative ability. Methods are available for parents at home to stimulate language, and use of peers and small groups can be an excellent opportunity for stimulating language learning.

Several different approaches are used in fostering communication abilities (Tager-Flusberg, Paul, & Lord, 2014). Some are more didactic, teacher-directed methods that are based in learning theory. Other approaches are more naturalistic, using similar principles but in more natural settings, often trying to incorporate the child's natural motivations. Another set of approaches is sometimes called *developmental* or *pragmatic*; here, the emphasis is on using a range of materials and methods on a trial-and-error basis to see what works. Some methods are more heavily teacher directed; others try to maximize naturalistic methods.

It is important to realize that the ability to communicate is very closely related to behavior. When children on the autism spectrum have either limited or very unusual (and sometimes very idiosyncratic) ways of communicating, behavior problems may result. Communication issues also can arise, somewhat paradoxically, in older and more-able children and adults. The person with Asperger's may talk on and on but have real trouble having a genuine conversation with a back-and-forth information exchange. Accordingly, a focus on communication should always be a major part of the program for any individual with an autism spectrum diagnosis.

Some children with autism never learn to talk (fortunately, this is less so than in the past). Special methods can be used to foster communication (more broadly defined). Parents sometimes worry that if these augmentative communication approaches are used in a young child that it means the school is giving up on the child talking; in fact, anything that helps the child be more communicative will help and may foster speech (Mirenda, 2014). These approaches vary in a number of ways and are adapted to the child's level and patterns of difficulties and can be used in combination with other approaches. A somewhat different approach is embodied in the use of computers or applications that help the child to communicate and organize. Yet another approach uses devices that essentially talk for the child. For example, the child may push a button and the machine says "hello" or "cookie." These devices are very sophisticated but, unfortunately, their ability to produce a broad range of language initiations or responses is rather limited. For some children all these approaches are still too advanced. In these cases, use of actual objects may be helpful.

Another line of intervention for early language development in children with autism has focused on more naturalistic and developmental approaches. One approach of this type was developed at the Hanen Centre to help parents stimulate language development in children with various disabilities; the book *More Than Words* by Sussman (1999) uses this approach to outline a series of developmentally based interventions, including imitating the child's sounds and words, modeling and engaging in games, using visual support and music, and following any leads produced by the child. In this model any behavior is treated as a form of communication.

The Denver model developed by Sally Rogers similarly has emphasized developmental methods and approaches in fostering language development. Another popular program, the social communication emotional regulation transactional support (SCERTS) model (Prizant et al., 2004), uses a multidisciplinary approach focused on communication and social-emotional development of young children with autism and related disorders. Areas of emphasis include social communication, helping children regulate their emotions, and supporting transactions with others. Families are actively involved in this process. More information on the SCERTS approach is provided by Prizant and Wetherby (2005) and at the SCERTS website (www.scerts.com).

Quill (2000) similarly has developed a curriculum focused on enhancing social and communication skills. Her approach draws on a range of methods including highly structured and more natural settings. Typical peers are given coaching and then are used to help the child with ASD learn to be more effective as a communicator and play partner.

The more naturalistic and developmentally based methods are very popular with schools and parents. However, rigorous research comparing all the various approaches is pretty limited. In contrast to the much more structured, behaviorally oriented approaches, naturalistic ones require considerable training of all concerned and, to some extent, can be much more dependent on the presence of a sensitive member of the treatment team who gets the importance of the particular approach. It is important to realize that use of one of these more naturalistic teaching methods still requires considerable planning and work if it is to be implemented successfully.

Expanding Language Abilities and Unusual Language Features   Once children start using some words, and maybe start putting words together, a wide range of methods can be employed to enhance communication skills. These can include ABA-based discrete trial or pivotal response approaches as well as more naturalistic approaches, for instance, setting up situations in which children will be tempted to use their language. The *Teach Me Language* book (Freeman & Dake, 1997) has a well-developed approach to help children move from single words to more sophisticated language.

For the more cognitively able and older individuals, for example, with Asperger's and higher-functioning autism, similar and somewhat different issues arise. For these students, communication issues often have less to do with saying words and vocabulary building and much more to do with social language use. Problems can arise in several ways. For some children prosody and talking in a very loud voice can be a major problem. Work on correcting prosody can include the use of audio or videotape recorders or other devices (for practice and feedback). Some computer programs have been developed for prosody problems in other conditions and may be useful in autism. For children who speak in a very loud voice (what speech pathologists call **register**) it probably doesn't make much sense to try to develop the many different levels of voice that most of us have. Rather it may make more sense to focus on three voice loudness levels—soft, medium, and loud—and then teach which one goes where: loud voice at recess, medium voice in class, soft voice at place of worship. Work on conversational and social skills can dovetail nicely with social skills groups or social skills teaching programs. This can include work on listening and turn taking, inviting feedback, use of language to express feelings, and for self-regulation. Explicit teaching of social conventions can be helpful. The tendency for individuals on the autism spectrum to be highly literal can lead to all kinds of miscommunications. Accordingly, teaching aspects of figurative language, idioms, and slang can be explicitly taught (see Myles et al., 2004, for some helpful examples). A number of good resources are available.

The evidence supporting these various language and communication interventions is rather variable, with some methods having reasonably extensive bodies of research and others very little. The Paul and Fahim (2016) book provides helpful information, and many parents (and teachers) can use it to research specific methods.

Organizational Issues and Supportive Technology

Children, adolescents, and adults with ASDs face many challenges for learning because of their problems with multitasking (executive functioning). It is likely that some of these are the direct result of the social disability itself, and others come about basically as a fallout of the social problems. Often there may be early problems in acquiring learning-to-learn skills, such as sharing a focus of attention, staying seated, focusing on the teachers, and so on. These issues are important throughout life for all of us but can have serious consequences for learning (see Table 5.1).

TABLE 5.1 **EXECUTIVE FUNCTIONING DEFICITS AND DIFFICULTIES IN CHILDREN WITH AUTISM AND ASPERGER'S**

Problem Area	Resulting Difficulty
Planning and ongoing evaluation	Difficulties in forward planning and monitoring lead to focus on short-term goals and failure to see big picture.
Flexibility	Given the often rigid thinking pattern, the child sees only one solution to a problem, getting stuck on one step or stage of a project. The child can't do work-arounds; novelty can create behavioral issues.
Inhibition	The child has a tendency to perseverate, stick with previous responses and strategies, and can't shift to change problems.

Various strategies can be used very effectively to deal with problems of organization and executive functioning deficits. These can take many forms. One of the simplest to use in the classroom (and at home) is visual supports. Say, for example, that a 4-year-old child with autism has significant difficulties with transitions. One approach would be to put up a visual schedule with pictures of the daily activities. Depending on the child's language and cognitive levels, variations on this theme can be adopted; for instance, at school there can be a written label *circle time* if that is appropriate. Similarly, at home, the child's day can be put up on the fridge with magnets, with each photograph turned over when an activity is done. At the end of the day, parents can review what the child did. An entire literature on visual supports now exists and has proven very helpful to teachers and parents alike. A series of excellent books by Linda Hodgdon (2003, 2011) on the use of visual strategies is very practical and gives helpful guidance to teachers and parents on how to use these approaches in the classroom.

A range of more sophisticated apps and other computer-based supports and learning programs are available as well. Some focus more on organization (with visual lists, timers, reminders, and so forth). Others are more focused on projects, for example, writing papers or taking notes. The reading list includes a number of relevant resources.

For students who need visual reminders, a timer that gives students a clear visual sense of what time is left for a task can be helpful. Particularly when students have trouble and get stuck (this often happens in activities such as spelling), using a timer to indicate when studying is done helps. Other aids can include electronic organizers, tape recorders, and computers. Even within the high-tech end, some approaches are fairly simple to implement. For example, a fourth-grade boy who was very high functioning (but quite disorganized) had the task of writing a two- to three-page paper on the history of Egypt. The boy was excited to be able to use the computer and quickly amassed literally hundreds of facts and pictures from the Internet and other sources. His problem was in how to translate this into a paper. We suggested that the father get out his computer and boot up his slide-maker program and set up a series of several slides, each with a title only. The first slide was "Egypt: A History" and had the child's name, the next slide was "Egypt at the Time of the Pharaohs," the next "Egypt at the Time of Jesus," the next "Egypt at the Time of Mohammed," and finally "Egypt Today." The boy then went back and filled in the bottom half of the slide with five or six relevant points and facts. The father and boy then turned this visual presentation into an outline and each of the slides became a paragraph of the paper, with each of the five or six bullet points becoming a sentence. Keep in mind that in our increasingly computer- and Internet-focused society, knowing how to use the computer can be a very handy skill as children get older and think about job choices.

For children with Asperger's in particular, the use of a laptop computer from very early on in school has considerable advantages. Often, cursive writing is a real struggle for children with Asperger's, and the laptop offers a highly functional work-around.

Laptop and keyboard skills also can provide access to other important technologies, for example, spell-checking (if the parents and teachers wish it to). It is important for parents and teachers to understand that this can indeed be a reasonable accommodation. Depending on the circumstance, computers can be equipped with all kinds of supports in addition to spell-check, including text-to-speech **voice synthesizers**. Organizational software such as Inspiration and Kidspiration (www.inspiration.com) can be a benefit. For more-able students, it is very much worth having parents and teachers visit websites focused on the needs of children with other problems such as learning disabilities (www.ldpride.net) or **attention deficit disorder (ADD)** (e.g., www.addwarehouse.com) to look for new materials, software, and so forth.

Keep in mind that, depending on the context, some of the lower-tech approaches can be very helpful, such as the book *Smart but Scattered* (Dawson & Guare, 2009). There are other excellent books that discuss executive function and organizational issues and are included in the "Suggested Reading" list at the end of the chapter.

ADAPTIVE SKILLS AND GENERALIZATION TO REAL-WORLD SETTINGS

The term *adaptive skills* applies to the application of concepts learned in school to real-world settings outside the classroom—for example, math facts help you solve math problems and also teach how to pay for items at a grocery store. Generalization of skills across settings is often a very major challenge for students with ASD of all ages and levels of functioning. These abilities are one of the major factors that determine ultimate independence and self-sufficiency.

The goal for students with ASD is to make the student as independent as possible. Unfortunately, the real world is unpredictable—a problem if you have a preference for sameness. Second, the real world is highly social—a problem if you have social vulnerabilities. Third, the real world is fast-paced, with many demands and bits of information coming at you at a time. And, finally, if you tend to learn things in a very narrow kind of way, you will have significant problems generalizing skills. If, for example, you can use the toilet at home but not at school, that is a problem. Similarly, if you can solve complex math equations in your head but not order a cheeseburger in a fast-food restaurant, you're in trouble.

It is almost always the case that individuals with ASDs exhibit lower—and often very much lower—levels of ability in real-world contexts than they exhibit in familiar and highly structured settings. Accordingly, it is critical that schools and parents specifically consider the issues of generalization and adaptive skills as part of the child's program (see Box 5.3).

BOX 5.3 TEACHING ADAPTIVE SKILLS

As with other skills, an explicit and focused approach is helpful.

- Try to use the child's natural motivations as much as possible.
- Be explicit in teaching.
- Use routines and scripts, which can then be faded.
- Teach generalization (different materials, situations, and contexts for the same behavior).
- Use the same methods used in schools:
  - Visual schedules
  - Written materials
  - Photographs
- Be consistent (gradually introduce variations).
- Use natural environments (rewards and consequences) as much as possible.

Appendix 2 discusses some of the ways adaptive skills can be assessed. Particularly as students become older an explicit focus on such skills should be an important part of the educational program. Of course, much of the work on social skills and communication we've already discussed is concerned with translating abilities learned in the classroom into real-world settings. There are a number of approaches to teaching daily living, coping, and **self-help skills** as well. The "Suggested Reading" section provides some helpful resources for parents and teachers.

WORKING WITH SCHOOLS

For the primary care provider there are important opportunities to interface with school personnel. In addition to the regular and special classroom teachers (who often know the child very well) there will typically be a school psychologist as well as a speech-language therapist who can be invaluable in helping parents obtain quality services. Particularly for those individuals of school-age, a school nurse may be a very important point of contact for primary care providers. The school nurse has an important role in care coordination, and when children have other medical problems or are receiving medications for behavioral or psychiatric difficulties, the school nurse may play a central role in the interface of the educational and medical systems (Bellando & Lopez, 2009; Minchella & Preti, 2011).

SUMMARY

In this chapter, we surveyed some of the various approaches to teaching particular skills and have discussed several interventions in different areas: curriculum issues, social skills, communication skills, daily life (adaptive) skills, and organizational issues. It is important for parents and educators to work together in developing IEPs that address the strengths and weaknesses of the particular child. Parents and families have a particularly important role in helping generalize skills across settings, that is, in helping the child learn to use what he or she learns in school in other contexts.

Although we wish there was more research on these various intervention methods, there is at least some, and fortunately there are more and more tools for parents and teachers to work with. It is particularly important to include a focus on real-world skills and generalization given the learning style of individuals with autism and related disorders. Parents (and teachers) should not be misled by isolated areas of strength—when these are present, they can be important considerations in program development, but keep in mind that other areas will need intensive work.

Many different approaches to teaching have been developed with a number of model programs that now are evidence based. Keep in mind that schools can employ any one of these various models and any of the various evidence-based intervention methods. For purposes of monitoring the individual child the IEP should be a helpful guide with a clear statement of targets for intervention, objectives, and ways to monitor progress. As we note, a number of school personnel can be useful allies for the primary care provider in advocating for the individual student.

▓ REFERENCES

Bellando, J., & Lopez, M. (2009). The school nurse's role in treatment of the student with autism spectrum disorders. *Journal for Specialists in Pediatric Nursing, 14*(3), 173–182.

Dawson, P., & Guare, R. (2009). *Smart but scattered: The revolutionary "executive skills" approach to helping kids reach their potential.* New York, NY: Guilford Press.

Dawson, G., Rogers, S., Munson, J., Smith, M., Winter, J., Greenson, J., et al. (2010). Randomized, controlled trial of an intervention for toddlers with autism: The early start Denver model. *Pediatrics, 125*(1), e17–e23.

Freeman, S., & Dake, L. (1997). *Teach me language: A language manual for children with autism, Asperger's syndrome, and related developmental disorders.* Langley, BC, Canada: SKF Books.

Goldstein, H., Kaczmarek, L., Pennington, R., & Shafer, K. (1992). Peer-mediated intervention: Attending to, commenting on, and acknowledging the behavior of preschoolers with autism. *Journal of Applied Behavior Analysis, 25*(2), 289–305.

Gray, C. A. (1998). Social stories and comic strip conversations with students with Asperger syndrome and high-functioning autism. In E. Schopler & G. B. Mesibov (Eds.), *Asperger syndrome or high-functioning autism? Current issues in autism* (pp. 167–198). New York, NY: Plenum Press.

Greenspan, S. I., & Wieder, S. (2009). *Engaging autism: Using the floortime approach to help children relate, communicate, and think.* Cambridge, MA: Da Capo Lifelong Books.

Gutstein, S. E., & Sheely, R. K. (2002). *Relationship development intervention with young children: Social and emotional development activities for Asperger syndrome, autism, PPD and NLD.* Philadelphia, PA: Jessica Kingsley.

Harris, S., & Handleman, J. S. (2000). *Preschool education programs for children with autism.* Austin, TX: PRO-ED.

Hodgdon, L. (2003). *Solving behavior problems in autism: Improving communication with visual strategies.* Troy, MI: QuirkRoberts Publishing.

Hodgdon, L. (2011). *Visual strategies for improving communication.* Troy, MI: QuirkRoberts Publishing.

Hume, K., & Odom, S. (2007). Effects of an individual work system on the independent functioning of students with autism. *Journal of Autism and Developmental Disorders, 37*(6), 1166–1180.

Koegel, R. L., & Koegel, L. K. (Eds.). (2006). *Pivotal response treatments for autism: Communication, social, & academic development.* Baltimore, MD: Brookes.

Koegel, R. L., Koegel, L. K., Vernon, T. W., & Brookman-Frazee, L. I. (2010). *Empirically supported pivotal response treatment for children with autism spectrum disorders: Evidence-based psychotherapies for children and adolescents* (pp. 327–344). New York, NY: Guilford Press.

Kohler, F. W., Strain, P. S., & Goldstein, H. (2005). Learning experiences, an alternative program for preschoolers and parents: Peer-mediated interventions for young children with autism. In E. D. Hibbs & P. S. Jensen (Eds.), *Psychosocial treatments for child and adolescent disorders: Empirically based strategies for clinical practice* (2nd ed., pp. 659–687). Washington, DC: American Psychological Association.

Laugeson, E. A., Frankel, F., Gantman, A., Dillon, A. R., & Mogil, C. (2012). Evidence- based social skills training for adolescents with autism spectrum disorders: The UCLA PEERS program. *Journal of Autism and Developmental Disorders, 42*(6), 1025–1036.

Laugeson, E. A., Gantman, A., Kapp, S. K., Orenski, K., & Ellingsen, R. (2015). A randomized controlled trial to improve social skills in young adults with autism spectrum disorder: The UCLA PEERS program. *Journal of Autism and Developmental Disorders, 45*(12), 3978–3989.

Lovaas, O. I., & Smith, T. (1988). Intensive behavioral treatment for young autistic children. In B. B. Lahey & A. E. Kazdin (Eds.), *Advances in clinical child psychology* (pp. 285–324). New York, NY: Plenum Press.

McClannahan, L. E., & Krantz, P. J. (2004). Some guidelines for selecting behavioral intervention programs for children with autism. In H. E. Briggs & T. L. Rzepnicki (Eds.), *Using evidence in social work practice: Behavioral perspectives* (pp. 92–103). Chicago, IL: Lyceum Books.

Mesibov, G. B., & Shea, V. (2010). The TEACCH program in the era of evidence-based practice. *Journal of Autism and Developmental Disorders, 40*(5), 570–579.

Minchella, L., & Preti, L. (2011). Autism spectrum disorder: Clinical considerations for the school nurse. *NASN School Nurse, 26*(3), 143–145.

Mirenda, P. (2014). Augmentative and alternative communication. In F. R. Volkmar, S. J. Rogers, R. Paul, & K. A. Pelphrey (Eds.), *Handbook of autism and pervasive developmental disorders* (4th ed., Vol. 2, pp. 813–825). Hoboken, NJ: Wiley.

Myers, S. M., Johnson, C. P., & The American Academy of Pediatrics Council on Children with Disabilities. (2007). Management of children with autism spectrum disorders. *Pediatrics, 120*(5), 1162–1182.

Myles, B. S. (2013). Building social skills instruction for children with Asperger syndrome. *Asperger syndrome: A guide for professionals and families* (pp. 91–111). New York, NY: Springer Science + Business Media.

Myles, B. S., Trautman, M. L., & Schelvan, R. L. (2004). *The hidden curriculum: Practical solutions for understanding unstated rules in social situations.* Shawnee Mission, KS: Autism Asperger.

National Research Council. (2001). *Educating young children with autism.* Washington, DC: National Academies Press.

Odom, S. L., Boyd, B. A., Hall, L. J., & Hume, K. A. (2014). Comprehensive treatment models for children and youth with autism spectrum disorders. In F. R. Volkmar, S. J. Rogers, R. Paul, & K. A. Pelphrey (Eds.), *Handbook of autism and pervasive developmental disorders* (4th ed., Vol. 2, pp. 770–787). Hoboken, NJ: Wiley.

Olley, J. G. (2005). Curriculum and classroom structure. In F. Volkmar, A. Klin, R. Paul, & D. J. Cohen (Eds.), *Handbook of autism and pervasive developmental disorders* (3rd ed., Vol. 2, pp. 863–881). New York: Wiley.

Paul, R. & Fahim, D. (2016). *Let's talk.* Baltimore, MD: Brookes.

Prizant, B., Wetherby, A. M., Rubin, E., Laurent, A. C., & Rydell, P. J. (2004). *The SCERTS model: Enhancing communication and socioemotional abilities of children with autism spectrum disorder.* Baltimore, MD: Brookes.

Reichow, B., & Barton, E. E., Volkmar, F. R., Paul, R., Rogers, S. J., & Pelphrey, K. A. (2014). Evidence-based psychosocial interventions for individuals with autism spectrum disorders. In F. R. Volkmar, S. J. Rogers, R. Paul, & K. A. Pelphrey (Eds.), *Handbook of autism and pervasive developmental disorders* (4th ed., Vol. 2, pp. 969–992). Hoboken, NJ: Wiley.

Reichow, B., Steiner, A. M., & Volkmar, F. (2013). Social skills groups for people aged 6 to 21 with autism spectrum disorders (ASD). *Evidence-Based Child Health: A Cochrane Review Journal, 8*(2), 266–315.

Reichow, B., & Volkmar, F. R. (2011). Evidence-based practices in autism: Where we started. *Evidence-based practices and treatments for children with autism* (pp. 3–24). New York, NY: Springer Science + Business Media.

Rogers, S. J., Dawson, G., & Vismara, L. A. (2012). *An early start for your child with autism: Using everyday activities to help kids connect, communicate, and learn.* New York, NY: Guilford Press.

Rogers, S. J., &Vismara, L. (2014). Interventions for infants and toddlers at risk for autism spectrum disorder. In F. R. Volkmar, S. J. Rogers, R. Paul, & K. A. Pelphrey (Eds.), *Handbook of autism and pervasive developmental disorders* (4th ed., Vol. 2, pp. 739–769). Hoboken, NJ: Wiley.

Rutter, M., & Bartak, L. (1973). Special educational treatment of autistic children: A comparative study. II. Follow-up findings and implications for services. *Journal of Child Psychology & Psychiatry & Allied Disciplines, 14*(4), 241–270.

Schopler, E. (1997). Implementation of TEACCH philosophy. In D. J. Cohen & F. R. Volkmar (Eds.), *Handbook of autism and pervasive developmental disorders* (pp. 767–795). Hoboken, NJ: Wiley.

Sussman, F. (1999). *More than words; Helping parents promote communication and social skills in children with autism spectrum disorder.* Toronto, ON, Canada: The Hanen Centre.

Tager-Flusberg, H., Paul, R., & Lord, C. (2014). Language and communication in autism. In F. R. Volkmar, S. J. Rogers, R. Paul, & K. A. Pelphrey (Eds.), *Handbook of autism and pervasive developmental disorders* (4th ed., Vol. 1, pp. 335–364). Hoboken, NJ: Wiley.

Volkmar, F. R., & Wiesner, L. A. (2009). *A practical guide to autism: What every parent, family member, and teacher needs to know.* Hoboken, NJ: Wiley.

Walton, K. M., & Ingersoll, B. R. (2013). Improving social skills in adolescents and adults with autism and severe to profound intellectual disability: A review of the literature. *Journal of Autism and Developmental Disorders, 43*(3), 594–615.

▨ SUGGESTED READING

Adreon, D., & Myles, B. S. (2001). *Asperger syndrome and adolescence: Practical solutions for school success.* Shawnee Mission, KS: Autism Asperger.

Al-Ghani, K. I. (2009). *The red beast: Controlling anger in children with Asperger's syndrome.* Philadelphia, PA: Jessica Kingsley.

Anderson, S. R., Jablonski, A. L., Thomeer, M. L., & Knapp, V. M. (2007). *Self-help skills for people with autism: A systematic teaching Approach.* Bethesda, MD: Woodbine House.

Ando, H. (1977). Training autistic children to urinate in the toilet through operant conditioning techniques. *Journal of Autism and Childhood Schizophrenia, 7*(2), 151.

Arick, J. R., Krug, D. A., Loos, L., & Falco, R. (2005). School-based programs. In F. Volkmar, A. Klin, R. Paul, & D. J. Cohen (Eds.), *Handbook of autism and pervasive developmental disorders* (3rd ed., Vol. 2, pp. 1003–1028). New York: Wiley.

Baker, J. (2001). *Social skills picture book: Teaching play, emotion, and communication to children with autism.* Arlington, TX: Future Horizons.

Barbera, M. L., & Rasmussen, T. (2007). *The verbal behavior approach: How to teach children with autism and related disorders.* Philadelphia, PA: Jessica Kingsley.

Beukelman, D. R., & Mirenda, P. (2005). *Augmentative and alternative communication: Supporting children and adults with complex communication needs* (3rd ed.). Baltimore, MD: Brookes.

Bondy, A., & Frost, L. (1998). The picture exchange communication system. *Seminars in Speech and Language, 19,* 373–389.

Buron, K. D., & Myles, B. S. (2004). *When my autism gets too big! A relaxation book for children with autism spectrum disorders.* Shawnee Mission, KS: Autism Asperger.

Carter, M. A., & Santomauro, J. (2007). *Pirates: An early-years group program for developing social understanding and social competence for children with autism spectrum disorders and related challenges.* Shawnee Mission, KS: Autism Asperger.

Charlop, M., & Trasowech, J. (1991). Increasing children's daily spontaneous speech. *Journal of Applied Behavior Analysis, 24,* 747–761.

Cohen, M. J., & Sloan, D. L. (2007). *Visual supports for people with autism: A guide for parents and professionals.* Bethesda, MD: Woodbine House.

Coulter, D. (Producer/Director). (2005). *Manners for the real world: Basic social skills* [DVD]. Winston Salem, NC: Coulter Video

Dunlap, G., & Fox, L. (1996). Early intervention and serious problem behaviors: A comprehensive approach. In L. K. Koegel, R. L. Koegel, & G. Dunlap (Eds.), *Positive behavioral support: Including people with difficult behavior in the community* (pp. 31–50). Baltimore, MD: Brookes.

Dunlap, G., & Fox, L. (1999a). A demonstration of behavioral support for young children with autism. *Journal of Positive Behavioral Interventions, 2,* 77–87.

Dunlap, G., & Fox, L. (1999b). Supporting families of young children with autism. *Infants and Young Children, 12,* 48–54.

Dawson, P., & Guare, R. (2003). *Executive skills in children and adolescents: A practical guide to assessment and intervention.* New York, NY: Guilford Press.

Delmolino, L., & Harris, S. L. (2004). *Incentives for change: Motivating people with autism spectrum disorders to learn and gain independence.* Bethesda, MD: Woodbine House.

Dunn, M. A. (2005). *SOS. Social skills in our schools: A social skills program for children with pervasive developmental disorders, including high-functioning autism and Asperger syndrome, and their typical peers.* Shawnee Mission, KS: Autism Asperger.

Durand, V. M., & Carr, E. G. (1987). Social influences on "self-stimulatory" behavior: Analysis and treatment application. *Journal of Applied Behavioral Analyses, 20*(2), 119–132.

Fein, D., & Dunn, M. (2007). *Autism in your classroom.* Bethesda, MD: Woodbine House.

Fovel, J. T. (2002). *The ABA program companion: Organizing quality programs for children with autism and PDD.* New York, NY: DRL Books.

Gagnon, E. (2001). *Power cards: Using special interests to motivate children and youth with Asperger syndrome and autism.* Shawnee Mission, KS: Autism Asperger.

Goldstein, A. P., Sprafkin, R. P., Gershaw, N. J., & Klein, P. (1980). *Skill-streaming the adolescent: A structured learning approach to teaching prosocial skills.* Champaign, IL: Research Press.

Goldstein, H. (2002). *Promoting social communication: Children with developmental disabilities from birth to adolescence.* Baltimore, MD: Brookes.

Goldstein, H., English, K., & Shafer, K. (1997). Interaction among preschoolers with and without disabilities: Effects of across-the-day peer intervention. *Journal of Speech, Language, and Hearing Research, 40,* 33–48.

Gray, C. (1994). *Comic strip conversations.* Arlington, TX: Future Horizons.

Gray, C. (2000). *The new social story book: Illustrated edition* (2nd ed.). Arlington, TX: Future Horizons.

Greenspan, S. I. (2006). *Engaging autism: Helping children relate, communicate and think with the DIR floortime approach.* New York, NY: Da Capo Lifelong Books.

Greenspan, S. I., & Wieder, S. (2009). *Engaging autism: Using the floortime approach to help children relate, communicate, and think.* Cambridge, MA: Da Capo Lifelong Books.

Grigorenko, E. L., Klin, A., & Volkmar, F. (2003). Annotation: Hyperlexia; Sisability or superability? *Journal of Child Psychology and Psychiatry, 44*(8), 1079–1091.

Gutstein, S. E., & Sheely, R. K. (2002). *Relationship development intervention with children, adolescents and adults.* Philadelphia, PA: Jessica Kingsley.

Handleman, J. S., Harris, S. L., & Martins, M. P. (2005). Helping children with autism enter the mainstream. In F. Volkmar, A. Klin, R. Paul, & D. J. Cohen (Eds.), *Handbook of autism and pervasive developmental disorders* (3rd ed., Vol. 2, pp. 1029–1042). New York: Wiley.

Harris, S. L., & Handleman, J. S. (1994). *Preschool education programs for children with autism.* Austin, TX: PRO-ED.

Harris, S. L., Handleman, J. S., & Jennett, H. (2005). Models of educational intervention for students with autism: Home, center and school-based programming. In F. Volkmar, A. Klin, R. Paul, & D. J. Cohen (Eds.), *Handbook of autism and pervasive developmental disorders* (3rd ed., Vol. 2, pp. 1043–1054). New York: Wiley.

Heflin, L. J., & Alaimo, D. F. (2007). *Students with autism spectrum disorders: Effective instructional practices.* Upper Saddle River, NJ: Prentice Hall.

Ivannone, R., Dunlap, G., Huber, H., & Kincaid, D. (2003). Effective educational practices for students with autism spectrum disorders. *Focus on Autism and Other Developmental Disabilities, 18,* 150–165.

Kanner, L. (1943). Autistic disturbances of affective contact. *Nervous Child, 2,* 217–250.

Keating-Velasco, J. L. (2007). *A is for autism, F is for friend: A kid's book for making friends with a child who has autism.* Shawnee Mission, KS: Autism Asperger.

Koegel, L., Carter, C., & Koegel, R. (2003). Teaching children with autism self-initiations as a pivotal response. *Topics in Language Disorders, 23,* 134–145.

Koegel, L. K., & LaZebnik, C. (2004). *Overcoming autism.* New York, NY: Penguin Books.

Koegel, R. L., & Koegel, L. K. (1995). *Strategies for initiating positive interactions and improving learning opportunities.* Baltimore, MD: Brookes.

Koegel, R. L., & Koegel, L. K. (Eds.). (2006). *Pivotal response treatments for autism: Communication, social, & academic development.* Baltimore, MD: Brookes.

Koegel, L. K., Koegel, R. L., & Carter, C. A. (1998). Pivotal responses and the natural language teaching paradigm. *Seminars in Speech and Language, 19,* 355–371.

Koegel, R., O'Dell, M., & Koegel, L. (1987). A natural language teaching paradigm for non–verbal autistic children. *Journal of Autism and Developmental Disorders, 17,* 187–200.

Kranowitz, C. S. (1995). *101 activities for kids in tight spaces.* New York, NY: St. Martin's Press.

Laski, K., Charlop, M., & Schreibman, L. (1988). Training parents to use the natural language paradigm to increase their autistic children's speech. *Journal of Applied Behavior Analysis, 21,* 391–400.

Lovaas, O. I. (1981). *Teaching developmentally disabled children: The me book.* Austin, TX: PRO-ED.

Lovaas, O. I. (1987). Behavioral treatment and normal educational and intellectual functioning in young autistic children. *Journal of Consulting and Clinical Psychology, 55,* 3–9.

Lovaas, O. I. (2003). *Teaching individuals with developmental delays: Basic intervention techniques.* Austin, TX: PRO-ED.

Marans, W. D., Rubin, E., & Laurent, A. (2005). Addressing social communication skills in individuals with high-functioning autism and Asperger syndrome: Critical priorities in educational programming. In F. Volkmar, A. Klin, R. Paul, & D. J. Cohen (Eds.), *Handbook of autism and pervasive developmental disorders* (3rd ed., Vol. 2, pp. 977–1002). New York: Wiley.

Matson, J. L., Benavidez, D. A., Compton, L. S., Paclawskyj, T., & Baglio, C. (1996). Behavioral treatment of autistic persons: A review of research from 1980 to the present. *Research in Developmental Disabilities, 17,* 433–465.

Maurice, C. R., Foxx, R. M., & Greene, G. (2001). *Making a difference: Behavioral intervention for children with autism.* Austin, TX: PRO-ED.

Maurice, C., Green, G., & Luce, S. C. (1996). *Behavioral intervention for young children with autism: A manual for parents and professionals.* Austin, TX: PRO-ED.

McAfee, J. (2002). *Navigating the social world.* Arlington, TX: Future Horizons.

McClannahan, L. E., & Krantz, P. J. (1999). *Activity schedules for children with autism: Teaching independent behavior.* Bethesda, MD: Woodbine House.

McClannahan, L. E., & Krantz, P. J. (2001). Behavior analysis and intervention for preschoolers at the Princeton Child Development Institute. In J. S. Handleman & S. L. Harris (Eds.), *Preschool education programs for children with autism* (Rev. ed., pp. 191–213). Austin, TX: PRO-ED.

McClannahan, L. E., & Krantz, P. J. (2005). *Teaching conversation to children with autism: Scripts and script fading.* Bethesda, MD: Woodbine House.

McGee, G., Krantz, P., Mason, D., & McClannahan, L. (1983). A modified incidental teaching procedure for autistic youth: Acquisition and generalization of receptive object labels. *Journal of Applied Behavior Analysis, 16,* 329–338.

McGee, G. G., & Morrier, M. J. (2005). Preparation of autism specialists. In F. Volkmar, A. Klin, R. Paul, & D. J. Cohen (Eds.), *Handbook of autism and pervasive developmental disorders* (3rd ed., Vol. 2, pp. 1123–1160). New York: Wiley.

McGee, G. G., Morrier, M. J., & Daly, T. (2001). The Walden early childhood programs. In J. S. Handleman & S. L. Harris (Eds.), *Preschool education programs for children with autism* (2nd ed., pp. 157–190). Austin, TX: PRO-ED.

Meltzer, L. (Ed.). (2007). *Executive function in education: From theory to practice.* New York, NY: Guilford Press.

Mesibov, G. B., Shea, V., & Schopler, E. (2004). *The TEACCH approach to autism spectrum disorders.* New York, NY: Springer.

Mirenda, P., & Iacono, T. (2009). *Autism spectrum disorders and AAC.* Baltimore, MD: Brookes.

Myles, B., & Southwick, J. (2005). *Asperger syndrome and difficult moments: Practical solutions for tantrums, rage and meltdowns.* Shawnee Mission, KS: Autism Asperger.

Patrick, N. J. (2008). *Social skills for teenagers and adults with Asperger syndrome: A practical guide to day-to-day life.* London, UK: Jessica Kingsley.

Paul, R., & Sutherland, D. (2005). Enhancing early language in children with autism spectrum disorders. In F. Volkmar, A. Klin, R. Paul, & D. J. Cohen (Eds.),

Handbook of autism and pervasive developmental disorders (3rd ed., Vol. 2, pp. 946–976). New York: Wiley.

Pepper, J., & Weitzman, E. (2004). *It takes two to talk: A practical guide for parents of children with language delay.* Toronto, ON, Canada: The Hanen Centre.

Perske, R. (1988). *Circles of friends: People with disabilities and their friends enrich the lives of one another.* Nashville, TN: Abingdon Press.

Plass, B. (2008a). *Functional routines for adolescents & adults—community.* East Moline, IL: LinguiSystems.

Plass, B. (2008b). *Functional routines for adolescents & adults—home.* East Moline, IL: LinguiSystems.

Plass, B. (2008c). *Functional routines for adolescents & adults—leisure & recreation.* East Moline, IL: LinguiSystems.

Plass, B. (2008d). *Functional routines for adolescents & adults—work.* East Moline, IL: LinguiSystems.

Potter, C., & Whittaker, C. (2001). *Enabling communication in children with autism.* London, UK: Jessica Kingsley.

Prizant, B. M., & Duchan, J. F. (1981). The functions of immediate echolalia in autistic children. *Journal of Speech and Hearing Disorders, 46*(3), 241–249.

Prizant, B. M., &Wetherby, A. M. (2005). Critical issues in enhancing communication abilities for persons with autism spectrum disorders. In F. Volkmar, A. Klin, R. Paul, & D. J. Cohen (Eds.), *Handbook of autism and pervasive developmental disorders* (3rd ed., Vol. 2, pp. 925–945). New York: Wiley.

Prizant, B. M., Wetherby, A. M., Rubin, E. M., Laurent, A. C., & Rydell, P. J. (2005). *The SCERTS model: A comprehensive educational approach for children with autism spectrum disorders* (2 vol.). Baltimore, MD: Brookes.

Quill, K. (1995). *Teaching children with autism: Strategies to enhance communication and socialization.* New York, NY: Delmar.

Quill, K. (2000). *Do watch listen say: Social and communication intervention for children with autism.* Baltimore, MD: Brookes.

Rogers, S. J. (1998). Empirically supported comprehensive treatments for young children with autism. *Journal of Clinical Child Psychology, 27,* 168–179.

Rogers, S. J., Hall, T., Osaki, D., Reaven, J., & Herbison, J. (2000). The Denver model: A comprehensive, integrated educational approach to young children with autism and their families. In J. S. Handleman & S. L. Harris (Eds.), *Preschool education programs for children with autism* (2nd ed., pp. 95–133.) Austin, TX: PRO-ED.

Rogers, S. J., Herbison, J. M., Lewis, H. C., Pantone, J., & Reis, K. (1986). An approach for enhancing the symbolic, communicative, and interpersonal functioning of young children with autism or severe emotional handicaps. *Journal of the Division for Early Childhood, 10,* 135–148.

Rogers, S. J., & Lewis, H. (1988). An effective day treatment model for young children with pervasive developmental disorders. *Journal of the American Academy of Child and Adolescent Psychiatry, 28,* 207–214.

Rosaler, M. (2004). *Asperger syndrome.* New York, NY: Rosen.

Sabin, E. (2006). *The autism acceptance book: Being a friend to someone with autism.* New York, NY: Watering Can Press.

Sanders, R. S. (2002). *Overcoming Asperger's: Personal experience & insight.* Murfreesboro, TN: Armstrong Valley.

Savner, J. L., & Myles, B. S. (2000). *Making visual supports: Work in the home and community; Strategies for individuals with autism and Asperger syndrome.* Shawnee Mission, KS: Autism Asperger.

Schetter, P., & Lighthall, K. (2009). *Homeschooling the child with autism.* San Francisco, CA: Jossey-Bass.

Schlieder, M. (2007). *With open arms: Creating school communities of support for kids with social challenges using Circle of Friends, extracurricular activities, and learning teams.* Shawnee Mission, KS: Autism Asperger.

Schreibman, L. (2005). *The science and fiction of autism.* Cambridge, MA: Harvard University Press.

Smith, T. (1996). Are other treatments effective? In C. Maurice, G. Green, & S. Luce (Eds.), *Behavioral intervention for young children with autism: A manual for parents and professionals* (pp. 45–59). Austin, TX: PRO-ED.

Smith, T., & Buch, G. A., et al. (2000). Parent-directed, intensive early intervention for children with pervasive developmental disorder. *Research in Developmental Disabilities, 21*(4), 297–309.

Strain, P. S., & Cordisco, L. (1994). LEAP preschool. In J. S. Handleman & S. L. Harris (Eds.), *Preschool education programs for children with autism* (2nd ed., pp 225–244). Austin, TX: PRO-ED.

Stewart, K. (2002). *Helping a child with nonverbal learning disorder or Asperger's syndrome: A parent's guide.* Oakland, CA: New Harbinger.

Sundberg, M., Michael, J., Partington, J., & Sundberg, C. (1995). The role of automatic reinforcement in early language acquisition. *Analysis of Verbal Behavior, 13,* 21–37.

Wheeler, M. (2007). *Toilet training for individuals with autism or other developmental issues* (2nd ed.). Arlington, TX: Future Horizons.

White, S. W., Koenig, K., & Scahill, L. (2006). Social skills development in children with autism spectrum disorders: A review of the intervention research. *Journal of Autism and Developmental Disorders, 37,* 1858–1868.

Wrobel, M. (2003). *Taking care of myself: A hygiene, puberty and personal curriculum for young people with autism.* Arlington, TX: Future Horizons.

Zeedyk, M. S. (2008). *Promoting social interaction for individuals with communication impairments: Making contact.* London, UK: Jessica Kingsley.

CHAPTER 6

Securing Services

Having helped parents get a diagnosis, how do you help them get services? In this chapter we discuss legal rights and key concepts relative to the rights to educational services. It is important that parents and teachers have some basic understanding of these concepts and rights and know that primary care providers can be major sources of information and help. Keep in mind that, as in other areas, parents and parent support groups may be good sources of information. Also keep in mind that things can evolve—either through changes in the laws (by Congress) or new judicial decisions (by the courts)—so it is important that everyone involved be aware of current requirements. We also will touch on the complex issues of services for adults with ASD.

This chapter is primarily concerned with the United States. Laws in other countries will differ. Before 1975 only a small number, maybe about 20%, of children with disabilities received an education within public schools. The diagnosis of autism at that time focused on classic Kanner's autism and not the broader spectrum. In many schools, parents would be turned away and told to put their children in institutional settings where there was little proactive programming. Such placements helped them learn to live in (i.e., remain in) institutions, and outcome was often poor. There were, of course, exceptions, but these usually were situations in which parents wouldn't accept a lack of services and advocated for, or sometimes started, their own private schools or programs. Many of the earliest schools for children with autism in the United States were started this way, and some remain active to the present. This changed dramatically in 1975 when Congress passed the Education for All Handicapped Children Act (**Public Law 94–142**), which mandated school services for *all* children. This law has been revised and amended many times. The current version is called the **Individuals with Disabilities Education Act (IDEA).** (The IDEA is an alphabet soup of abbreviations that we will introduce to you in this chapter; see Table 6.1.) This law applies to several areas, including early education as well as school-based and transition services and mandates meeting the educational needs of children with disabilities from the time they are born until they reach 21 years of age. Although the IDEA is thought of as a civil rights law, it technically does not require states to participate; rather, it gives them incentives to do so by funding programs when states meet certain requirements. All the states participate. The IDEA was most recently amended in 2004.

TABLE 6.1   KEY TERMS AND CONCEPTS

Term	Concept
IDEA	The Individuals with Disabilities Education Act is an act of Congress giving specific rights to children with disabilities for educational services.
PL 94–142	Public Law 94–142 is the original (1975) law passed by Congress mandating school services to children with disabilities.
FAPE	Free and appropriate public education
IEP	Individualized education plan
LRE	Least restrictive environment
ADA	Americans with Disabilities Act
504 plan	A plan developed to accommodate the special needs of a child with a handicap; it is less commonly used in autism than the IEP.
IFSP	Individualized family service plan is a plan similar to the IEP but for younger children (under age 3).
Inclusion	Having children with ASDs in classes or other settings where there are typically developing peers (also referred to as *mainstreaming*); this can be full or part time and with or without the support of an aid or teacher
Extended school year (ESY)	Special education services beyond the usual school year; specified in the Individuals with Disabilities Education Act; eligibility is determined by a child's IEP—often on the basis of potential for loss of skills over the summer

It is important to understand what the law does and doesn't require. There are some key concepts that we'll review shortly. Also, it is important to realize that the age of the child has some relevance here. For example, after age 21 the IDEA does not apply, but other laws, such as the Americans with Disabilities Act (ADA), may apply, such as in college or vocational school. The requirements for early intervention (before age 3) programs are different from those of public schools, and some of the terms and concepts will vary depending on the age of the child and a bit from state to state. Also keep in mind that a vast number of children, over 6 million in 2006, were educated under the provisions of this law. This number includes children with a range of disabilities, not just autism. Autism is, however, mentioned specifically in the IDEA law as one of the conditions that meet the requirement for disability. This is an area in which diagnostic labels are very important. The intent of the law is to identify children whose disabilities interfere with their learning. Thus, even if a child with autism has normal cognitive ability, he or she can still qualify for services. The "Suggested Reading" list at the end of this chapter provides information on a number of resources that can be helpful in understanding this law and how it works. Be aware, however, that in the legal arena, changes can happen at any time. These changes can come from changes in the statute (the underlying law), from court decisions (which interpret the law), from regulations enacted by the state and federal education agencies to implement the law.

Changes can also occur because of local issues that affect school services and programs. For example, a gifted director of special educational services in a district can retire or be replaced, and sometimes, literally overnight, there can be a dramatic shift in the quality and nature of programs. We provide a brief overview here. If parents have trouble securing services a parent advocate or lawyer may be needed. This chapter is as accurate as we could make it at the time of publication; however, it is not a substitute for the advice of a lawyer. Parents should consult with an attorney (or other advocate) who has experience in the area (Mayerson, 2014).

Some states may have additional provisions about the regulation of special education services. In general, federal statutes usually supersede state laws and regulations (called *preemption*). However, a state or **local education agency (LEA)** may choose to provide even more services or more protections than are guaranteed by the federal statute. Box 6.1 provides a history of IDEA.

BOX 6.1 THE HISTORY AND EVOLUTION OF THE IDEA

Legislative History

1975: The Education for All Handicapped Children Act (PL 94–142) mandates the right to education for all children with disabilities.

1990: The law is renamed the Individuals with Disabilities Education Act (IDEA).

1997: IDEA was amended in several ways including provision of coverage to delayed children between ages 3 and 9 years, and the use of mediation to resolve disputes was encouraged.

2004: The Individuals with Disabilities Education Improvement Act of 2004 (IDEIA) modified the law to conform with No Child Left Behind and also dealt with disciplinary issues for students in special education.

Supreme Court Decisions

A series of decisions by the Supreme Court have relevance:

Board of Education of the Hendrick Hudson Central School District v. Rowley (1982) clarified that the standard was of an adequate, not optimal, special education program.

Schaffer v. Weast (2005) held that the "moving" party (usually the parent) in a placement challenge had the burden of persuasion.

Winkelman v. Parma City School District (2007) found that, under IDEA, parents have independent enforceable rights that include the entitlement to a free appropriate public education for their child and can bring action (with or without a lawyer or representing themselves) to enforce their own rights, which are the same as their child's rights.

Arlington Central School District v. Murphy (2006) found that parents who prevail in legal action can be awarded "reasonable attorney fees" by the court but cannot recover fees for expert witnesses.

THE MANDATE FOR IDENTIFICATION

The states are required to locate and evaluate children with disabilities who may need special services. This is known as the "Child Find" obligation. Children can be identified and referred for evaluation by parents or by health care providers (usual for autism), as well as by school personnel. Given the key importance of health care providers, it is especially important that they be aware of these rights, be familiar with programs and services, and be available to advise parents. The Child Find requirement—to identify and evaluate—applies to all children, including children attending private schools and children who are homeless or migrant. Special provisions are made for children under age 3. Once a child has been identified, the local school district (the local education authority or EA in legal speak) must determine whether the child is eligible for services under IDEA. Parents of children under the age of 18 are asked to give their consent for an evaluation. The evaluation should be sufficiently detailed so it can provide a determination of whether the child does or does not meet the eligibility requirement of having a disability such that the child requires special education and **related services** in order to benefit from his or her education. Given the many different manifestations of autism and related conditions, multiple disciplines and evaluations are frequently required to be able to provide a comprehensive assessment. For example, many children on the autism spectrum require speech and language evaluations as well as psychoeducational evaluations and occupational therapy assessments. The purpose of the assessment is to establish whether or not the child is entitled to services and to assist the team in planning the individual educational plan (IEP) that will provide and direct the services.

Parents can, of course, submit their own evaluations. The school district must take the evaluation into consideration, but it is not required to accept such evaluations or to follow their recommendations. If the parents disagree with the evaluation provided by the school, they can also request an independent evaluation. If parents are careful to document that they disagree with the school's assessment, the school either has to pay for the independent evaluation or request a hearing (often called *due process*) to defend their evaluation and to show that an independent evaluation is not needed. Why would a parent want to ask for an independent evaluation? There are several situations when this would make sense. If a school district does not identify a child as having a disability and the parent disagrees, an independent evaluation can be helpful. In other cases, sometimes the district identifies the child as disabled but does not offer services because their evaluation does not show that the disability interferes with the child's ability to benefit from education. A review (usually repeat testing) at least every 3 years (triennial review) is required, with additional testing as needed to show continued need for services.

FREE AND APPROPRIATE PUBLIC EDUCATION

One of the core key concepts of the IDEA is that students must be provided with a free and appropriate public education (FAPE). Note the words *free* and *appropriate*. The meaning of *free* is clear: that parents do not have to pay. However, the question of what is *appropriate* for a particular child is often one that turns into a sticking point. Parents, understandably, want the best for their child. The law, however, uses the word *appropriate,* not *best*. Put another way, as set out by the US Supreme Court in the case of *Board of Education of the Hendrick Hudson Central School District v. Rowley,* a school district satisfies its duty by providing an "adequate" education. In that case, Amy Rowley, a hearing-impaired child, was able to advance from grade to grade without the benefit of the requested sign language interpreter. The Supreme Court stated that law required "personalized instruction and related services calculated ... to meet [a child's] educational need." The Court added that, because in this case they were presented with a handicapped child who was receiving substantial specialized instruction and related services and who was performing above average in the regular classrooms of a public school system, they confined their analysis to that situation. Unfortunately, later court decisions and hearings of other decisions have frequently ignored the Court's limitation of Rowley (because that was a situation in which the child was performing above average). The Rowley case has limited the services required by the IDEA to minimally adequate in order to pass a child from grade to grade. This issue remains an important one and a source of frequent dispute between parents and schools.

As a practical matter, there also are considerable regional variations in how services are provided and what services are available. This can be very dramatic across states and sometimes even within states. In our particular state of Connecticut, for example, variations from town to town can be quite noticeable, and sometimes moving across the street can result in a major change for the better (or worse) in terms of the quality of a program (Doehring & Becker-Conttrill, 2013).

Eligibility for Services

The IDEA includes a very specific list of covered disabilities, including autism as well as mental retardation, speech-language impairment, visual impairment, and hearing impairment. In addition, the law requires that the child must, as a result of this condition, require special education services. In other words, simply having a disability or a diagnosis alone does not make a child eligible for special education and related services. So if a hearing-impaired child, for example, could be helped with a hearing aid so that his disability was not interfering with his ability to learn, he would not necessarily qualify for services under the IDEA unless there was some other condition that interfered with educational progress.

We want to stress two additional points: It is very important to keep in mind that educational progress is not limited to academic progress. The term *special education* is much broader than book learning. It is, under the law, "specially designed instruction, at no cost to parents, to meet the unique needs of a child with a disability." This definition includes these services:

- Instruction in the classroom and also in other settings
- Instruction in physical education
- Transition services designed to help the child move from school to employment, vocational school, or other setting
- Services based on the individual child's needs that take the child's strengths, preferences, and interests into account
- Instruction, related services, community experiences, the development of employment and other post-school adult living objectives, and, when appropriate, acquisition of **daily living skills** and functional vocational evaluation

This is a broad definition of education, well beyond academic subjects, and covers areas of critical importance for children with ASDs. Transition services must be available, and usually are delivered, after a child has completed and graduated from high school.

The second point is that even if a student doesn't technically qualify under the IDEA, there are other federal laws, notably the ADA and section 504 of the **Rehabilitation Act of 1973,** which may apply, and the child may qualify for some **accommodations** or services under these laws. Both of these laws prohibit discrimination based on a person's disability and require equal access to services. The ADA applies to public accommodations and governmental services, and the Rehabilitation Act applies to recipients of federal funds. Thus, it is likely that almost every public school system would fall under both acts. Both laws require that entities make reasonable accommodations, which are modifications to their policies and procedures that are required to permit a person with a disability to access the services or benefits provided. This applies in schools and means that even if it is determined that a child with a disability does not need special education in order to make progress in school, if she needs another modification to receive equal access it must be provided. Such modifications can be modified curriculum or transportation, preferential seating, or even being permitted to enter and leave classes early to avoid the difficulties of the crowds and disorder of the halls between classes. One important difference about accommodations under these acts from special education mandated under IDEA is that reasonable accommodations must be requested by the student or her parents—there is no requirement to seek out eligible students and offer such accommodations.

For young children, the possibility of a "developmental delay" category is given for children between 3 and 9 years of age so that children with developmental delays do not have to have a specific disability label. As a result of the emphasis on autism, there is often pressure to have children on the autism spectrum (more broadly defined) included within the autism category. Practices vary considerably from state to state and sometimes within states. It is also possible for children with ASDs to qualify under different categories, for example, speech and language impairment, intellectual delay, even "other health impaired." In theory the emphasis should be on the child's needs and not the child's label; in reality the label is important.

INDIVIDUALIZED EDUCATION PLAN (IEP)

The IDEA requires schools to create an **individualized education plan (IEP)** for any child who is eligible for special education. This is the most important element of the student's intervention program. This document is developed by parents and teachers and others (an "interdisciplinary team") using the information gathered by all of them and presented in the evaluation. The document will be the guide for the school program and should set out exactly what kinds of services are to be provided, including the number of hours of each service, how much of that service will be provided in a setting with nonhandicapped peers, and what special arrangements or accommodations are made for the student. It should also include measurable goals and objectives.

The IEP is an individualized plan—a blueprint. The child should not be pigeonholed into whatever autism classroom the school or district has. Rather, the IEP should reflect the unique needs of the child. In theory, the IEP will include long-term goals. Short-term objectives should be developed without regard to what is available in the district's existing programs. Making goals measurable is truly important.

Parents should understand that the IEP is developed by an interdisciplinary team (called by different names in different states, that is, planning and placement team [PPT], committee on special education [CSE or CSPE], or in many states simply IEP team), which includes mainstream and special education teachers, specialists (i.e., school psychologist, social worker, speech-language pathologist), and parents in a process that aims to achieve a consensus. The IEP is not something you vote on such as a committee meeting. The law requires that parents (and teenagers) be invited to all formal meetings and be able to participate in a meaningful way. It is also important to realize that the IEP can include provisions for extending the school day or school year if that is necessary to the child's education. This is available particularly (but not only) if there is risk of regression for the child. The IEP also can include transition services even beyond high school graduation until the age of 21 (in many states, until the end of the school year in which a child turns 21). The primary care provider can also be invited to attend—this may be particularly important in terms of children with chronic medical conditions.

Parents are also free to bring advocates to the meeting. This could be a friend, another parent, an attorney, or professionals (e.g., physicians and psychologists). The IEP is not limited to speech-language services, occupational therapy, physical therapy, psychological services, counseling, and assistive technology. School health services as well as social work services in school are also covered, as are transportation services. Any accommodations or modifications the child needs to benefit from the program should be spelled out; this includes any accommodations for standardized district or state tests. The IEP is a written document, and parents should always have a copy.

Academic goals should be reasonable relative to levels of cognitive ability. It is important that parents and teachers not be misled by the sometimes isolated special abilities seen in children with the autism spectrum disorders: some children may be able to read to decode, but their understanding of what they read may be quite poor. Social skills should be explicitly targeted. This can be done in a variety of ways through individualized small groups and classrooms. If properly supported, opportunities for mainstreaming are very helpful. A common mistake is to mainstream older school-aged children into settings where they are most vulnerable, such as cafeteria, recess, or gym; these can be some of the worst settings for children on the spectrum because of the lower level of structure and lack of adult support and monitoring.

Communication needs to be encouraged, starting at whatever level the child is functioning at. Some individuals with Asperger's syndrome and higher functioning autism have better vocabulary abilities that may mislead school staff members into thinking the child does not need to work with the speech pathologist. In fact, it is communication and not just vocabulary work that these children need. Daily living skills become increasingly important determinants of self-sufficiency and independence as the child gets older. Sometimes an extended-day program is necessary to generalize daily living skills in the home.

Motor and sensory issues can be addressed with the help of occupational and physical therapists. Consideration can be given to providing additional supports, for example, assistive technology such as computers for children with motor coordination issues. Behavior issues and challenges need to be viewed in the context of the overall goals of the program and the safety of the child and classmates. This is an area in which the efforts of behavioral psychologists can be extremely helpful and where objective data can really be useful in informing the intervention plan.

If there are major issues or problems, it is important that the school know about them. For example, if the child has seizures, is allergic to a food, or is receiving medications that affect behavior, it is important that school staff members be adequately informed. Appropriate accommodations can be made for medical problems. Vocational planning should start as children move through high school. We'll discuss this further in the chapter on adolescents and adults (Chapter 9).

Given that often many different people and specialties are involved in the child's life at school, it is good to specifically address issues of coordination of services and communication among service providers. How (and how often) will the team pass information back and forth to each other? How will they communicate with parents? Who will be the point person in talking with the parents? Who should parents primarily communicate with? When parents are appropriately involved and knowledgeable, the system can work well to help the child learn to generalize his or her knowledge from school to home and other settings.

The IEP should be a plan for action with a reasonable presentation of the child's various abilities. Based on these strengths and needs, there should be an explicit statement of goals for the child's educational program—along with short-term goals and benchmarks for reaching those goals. The IEP should be explicit about what services will be provided, including how frequent these are and their form and duration (e.g., 30 minutes of individual speech-language work with the school speech pathologist twice a week and one 30-minute group of three to four students and the speech pathologist each week for social skills training). The goals should be operationalized in some way, so you will know when the goals have been met. The law requires measurable goals, and therefore the IEP should set out how progress will be measured. This can be done in a number of different ways, but it is important that the IEP be explicit about how this is to be done. The degree to which mainstream activities are planned should also be made clear and what plans are in place (if needed) to help the student to be successful in mainstream settings. The IEP usually states the amount of time spent with typically developing peers. Several excellent books and resources are available to guide parents; some are listed in the "Suggested Reading" list at the end of this chapter.

Regardless of whether the evaluations are done as part of the IEP process (i.e., by the school) or parents have independent evaluations, it is important that the evaluator understand the question(s) being asked. For example, is this an assessment primarily focused on diagnosis and eligibility, or is the main goal to establish patterns of strength and weakness and to make program recommendations or primarily to monitor progress? Independent evaluations are most often needed in situations in which parents and schools see a child and her needs so differently that they cannot agree on an appropriate program. The evaluation should translate into goals that will move the child along the developmental line toward as independent an adulthood as possible and objectives that can be measured in order to monitor the child's progress toward those goals. Goals should cover academic and nonacademic areas.

There are some things parents can do to be effective participants in the IEP process. First, they can bring (or, even better, supply ahead of time) any reports or documents relevant to the meeting, for example, reports from a private speech pathologist or documentation that the child has a need for occupational or physical therapy. Sometimes a pre-IEP meeting is helpful to review results of assessments or discuss preliminary plans. This can give parents an opportunity to digest the reports and discuss them with each other and any outside professionals before the planning meeting takes place. Parents can always bring someone to the meeting; this can be the other parent, an advocate, a professional, or an attorney. If appropriate, the child can also be part of the meeting. Parents can keep their own notes of the meeting and should remember to always have everything put down on paper—a verbal promise without written documentation won't work as well as a written promise. After the IEP meeting, the parents should receive a copy of the IEP and any documentation from the meeting. When it arrives, parents should read it carefully and submit additions or corrections, if there are any, in writing. Parents should try to participate actively in the meeting—they are the people who know the child best and who are in the best position to speak for him or her.

The legal standard is *appropriate* education, not the *best*. The school is not required to provide the specific method of instruction that parents chose; for example, they do not have to provide only applied behavior analysis (ABA)-based instruction. It is the school's responsibility to be sure that parents understand the range of programs and services potentially available. This may include private schools or even residential programs. The fact, by itself, that the school has, for example, an autism classroom does not mean that this will always be the right placement for a child with autism. Consistent with the law, the goal should be the least restrictive placement possible. Therefore, private schools and, particularly, residential programs are often tried only after other placements have not worked out. The child can have a wonderful IEP, but if the school doesn't follow it, it won't be much help. On rare occasions, we've been surprised that the IEP was pretty poorly done but the school program was very good. We've also seen occasions when, in the attempt to capture every possible issue, the IEP was more than 100 single-spaced pages long; in this case, the attempt to get everything right resulted in a document that was too complicated to be useful.

SPECIAL EDUCATION AND RELATED SERVICES

IDEA encompasses special education and "related services." The latter includes the range of other interventions designed to meet the child's needs and enable him or her to participate in and benefit from special education, for example, speech and language therapy, occupational and physical therapy, or the services of a psychologist or an aide or paraprofessional. Assistive technology is also included. Transportation also falls into this category, for example, a special bus to and from school. Most medical services are specifically excluded. We'll talk briefly about insurance coverage of medical issues at the end of this chapter.

Least Restrictive Environment (LRE)

Keep in mind that PL 94–142 was passed at a time when there was great interest in civil rights for minority groups, including individuals with special needs. Some of the terms (*integrated* or *segregated*) carry some of the broader context of the time the law was passed.

The law mandates that children be educated in the **least restrictive environment (LRE)** appropriate to the child's learning. The intent of the law is for children to be educated in settings that are normative, that is, where they are with typically developing, nondisabled peers. There is a body of work on how to do this in autism and particularly in young children with autism (Kohler & Strain, 1999; Martins, Harris, & Handleman, 2014). As children become older this can be a more complicated problem. Some schools will insist that they appropriately include everyone throughout high school; this can sometimes result in unfortunate situations. For example, we've seen a 16-year-old nonverbal and cognitively impaired child with autism included in mainstream high school classes even at a time when he was not able to shower independently much less understand the material presented; he should have been helped with relevant self-care and other issues and in classes looking at his potential for adult activities.

As you might expect the issue of inclusion and special schools (i.e., "segregated") settings has been the focus of much litigation, and in many states the standard is now twofold: (1) can the child be adequately educated in the general classroom setting if additional services are provided, and (2) if the child is in a more restricted setting, how can he be integrated into mainstream settings to the maximum extent appropriate? This right not to be segregated is considered a civil rights issue, although some parents believe that their children will receive better or more appropriate services in separate specialized settings, given that these may have more experienced teachers and specialized resources.

In helping parents think about choices, several considerations can apply here. These include the benefits to the student of being in a regular classroom with support versus a self-contained special education classroom or other more segregated classroom, the benefits to the students and peers who don't have disabilities of being in an integrated classroom, and the disruption to the education of other students, if any, caused by the student's behavior. A child cannot be placed in an inappropriate setting because it is less costly.

Participation in Decision Making and Legal Protections

Families are specifically included in the decision-making process under IDEA. Parents and, to the extent possible, students should participate in meaningful ways in decision making. Parents have an important role in the entire process, and a series of safeguards are in place to protect their rights and those of the child. Primary care providers can also participate and should especially in complex situations. In reality, of course, many different things can affect parents' abilities to be strong advocates, for example, their levels of sophistication, language barriers, and other competing concerns. Protections written into the law include the rights of parents to review and receive copies of records, to attend IEP meetings, to participate in decision making, and to consent (or not) to the proposed program (IEP). There are specific requirements about notification of meetings, rights to request independent evaluations, and the provision to parents of notices and explanations of their rights. There is also a procedure to resolve disputes between parents and schools that is designed to promote agreement among the parties and to protect the rights of the student. These dispute resolution mechanisms are mediation or what are called ***due process hearings.*** Due process is what the US Constitution requires before depriving anyone of life, liberty, or property. By calling the special education appeal hearing *due process,* Congress was emphasizing the importance of the right to an education and of the process used to develop the plan. The courts consider adherence to these rights to due process as important as the content of the IEP and the nature of the educational program. In fact, ironically, the courts and hearing officers are more likely to reverse a decision of a school district because of a failure to provide due process safeguards than because of an educational decision. The hope and expectation is that a fair and open process should produce an appropriate educational program. Box 6.2 describes the common terms associated with the rights and safeguards under IDEA.

BOX 6.2 RIGHTS AND SAFEGUARDS UNDER IDEA

Notice requirements. The school must give written notice to parents of proposed changes (e.g., in placement or program) and of the parents' rights (e.g., to voice complaints or contest a planned change).

Consent of parents. Parents must give consent for an evaluation to be done, or if reevaluation is done, schools have the right to seek such an evaluation if parents don't consent but must go through due process procedures or mediation to do so.

Mediation. Rather than go through due process, parents and schools can use the more informal mediation process to resolve disputes.

Due process. Parents or the school can initiate a due process hearing to resolve disputes at any stage in the process (from evaluation, planning and placement, and review). Parents must be informed of their rights and the possibilities for free or low-cost legal representation. The due process hearing is similar to a regular court hearing (but less formal) and parents and the school may be represented by attorneys. An entire appeals process is also available.

Stay put. The stay put provision means that if a child is in a program and there is a dispute about moving the child to another program this cannot be done until a placement decision is

> reached; that is, the school cannot unilaterally remove a child from a program (parents, of course, can). Practically, this usually means that when a dispute is under way the child stays where he or she is until the dispute is resolved.

The parents must participate in the IEP meeting and planning process. There are a few tips if you are asked to look at an IEP draft and make recommendations to the parents. It is possible for IEPs to be too short or way too long (the record we've seen is over 100 pages). Too short means not enough detail in terms of an assessment and plan. Too long means that everyone is overwhelmed and can't possibly keep the goals in mind. Goals and objectives should be outlined and measurable. Ways to document progress on these goals should be provided so that if the child is not achieving them, another IEP meeting can be called to reset the plan. Parent advocates who have been through the process (sometimes with additional training) can be helpful to parents just beginning to cope with this.

Special Issues for Young Children

As we mention in Chapter 7 the IDEA also provides a program to support early intervention services in children from birth to 3 years of age. These programs (sometimes called *Birth to Three* as well as *early intervention* services) provide a range of services. The law was intended to provide a very comprehensive program of services. In reality, the degree of sophistication and intensity of these services again varies considerably from state to state and even town to town. Some young children with autism may require and may be entitled to more intense services than are typically provided.

Young children also present special issues for **mainstreaming,** or **inclusion.** It is *not* usual for children younger than age 3 to be in group (school) settings. Sometimes parents have arranged for a home-based instruction program, and a number of intervention programs have a strong home-based component (National Research Council, 2001). **Early intervention services** are, accordingly, often provided in the home, and a 1997 modification of the law included the term *natural environment* to be consistent with this idea.

A different kind of plan is developed for young children. This plan is called the *individualized family service plan (IFSP)*; in contrast to the IEP, it is meant to be oriented toward the family. There is explicit recognition of the importance of the family in the development of very young children and that the family also needs support. So, for the IFSP, there may be specific attention focused on helping siblings or in helping parents learn ways to promote the development of their child.

Finding eligible children is a major concern of this program. The law mandates that an assessment be completed promptly and a meeting with the family to develop the IFSP be developed within 45 days of referral. The IFSP should include a discussion of the child's development, parental concerns, and a discussion of how service will be delivered and progress monitored. Unlike the IEP, the IFSP is reviewed every 6 months. As the child nears his third birthday, a written transition to school-based (preschool) services is required, and the IEP process may begin. The IDEA requires states to ensure that the process is completed by the time the child reaches his or her third birthday. For that reason, many states begin the process when the child is 2½. The variability of programs from state to state and often within states makes it important for parents and health care providers to know what is available locally.

504 Plans and ADA

As we mentioned previously a different law (**section 504** of the **Americans with Disabilities Act [ADA]** of 1973) has to do with public school students with disabilities rather broadly defined. It is designed, similar to an IEP, to help a student with a disability participate more effectively in school with accommodations and modifications of the curriculum. The definition here is much broader than under IDEA and includes children who have a physical or mental impairment that "substantially" causes difficulty, for example, in school learning and participation. This has to be a persistent condition and this section frequently is used or invoked when a child has attentional problems or learning disabilities, for example, to give extra time on tests. Either parents or schools can start the process for a 504 plan. The school considers the documentation of the disability (e.g., from the primary care provider or specialist), any observations from school or parents, the results of their own assessment of the child, as well as the child's academic performance. Outside (independent) evaluations can be done and submitted by parents or requested by school or parents (obviously the parents would have to give consent). A number of safeguards are built in to protect the child. Schools vary considerably in how they do 504 plans. Usually the plan will document the additional services, support, or special accommodations the child will get, who will provide supports, and so on. Typically the 504 plan is much less detailed than the IEP and doesn't include annual goals (important for documenting progress in children with ASDs). As a general rule parents should seek IEP rather than 504 plans.

Issues of Discipline

Behavior problems can lead schools to consider disciplinary actions. This is, as one imagines, more complicated if a child has a disability. Under IDEA, even under section 504 and the ADA, reasonable accommodations may be requested (and such requests should usually be granted); for example, a child with autism who is sensitive to loud noises should not be suspended from school if he has a panic attack and runs out of school during a fire drill. Schools should have appropriate behavioral intervention programs in place; if they don't, they can't suspend the child. If a student has a plan and if problems still occur, the team needs to review the behavior plan. There are very specific issues, including consideration of whether the behavior is a manifestation of the disability that must be considered before a student can be suspended, and lengthy suspensions particularly require careful review under the IDEA. Even if a student is suspended, the school is usually obligated to continue to provide educational services. Suspension is not an excuse for excluding children with disabilities from school service.

For very serious situations (e.g., involving guns or danger to other students), the child can be placed in an alternative setting for up to 45 days, during which time the IEP team will review the IEP and placement. There are special aspects of the stay put provision of the law and specific consideration for situations in which the child's behavior is a danger to self or others. If a student's educational placement is being changed as a result of code-of-conduct violations, there must be a "manifestation determination" in order to determine whether the behavior was a result of the child's disability or of the district's failure to provide an appropriate educational program or an appropriate behavioral intervention.

Issues for Transition of Adolescents and Young Adults

As we discuss in more detail in Chapter 9 transition planning should start in high school. The **transition plan** should be individualized and reflect the strengths and interests of the students and should include opportunities to develop community and work skills. This plan is developed by the IEP team and should include measurable goals with appropriate services to meet the students' need. There should be identification of who is responsible for what. The student should be informed of the goals. A year before the student becomes a legal adult the law requires that the student be notified of this (the age of legal adulthood varies from state to state). We discuss this in more detail in Chapter 9 (the "Suggested Reading" list in that chapter also has some web resources than can be helpful). Note that a different section of the ADA applies to accommodations for students in college and vocational school as well as to the workplace. We talk more about this in Chapter 9.

Private Services

Parents can withdraw their child from a school program they do not believe is appropriate. They can provide home-based instruction along with services such as occupational or speech therapy on a private basis. Schools may be liable for reimbursement of parents' costs if the IEP is found not to be appropriate and if the program provided by the parents was beneficial educationally. Parents should understand that there is no guarantee that they will be reimbursed—only that they can ask for reimbursement.

Insurance-Related Issues

The current crisis in the US health insurance system has an unfortunate impact on the quality and the quantity of care provided to individuals with all kinds of disabilities. Unfortunately, despite the considerable hype in advertisements about various insurance and health maintenance organization (HMO) programs such care often is neither available nor provided.

Parents should look for quality insurance programs. Another unfortunate tactic that insurance companies use is to try to avoid paying for ancillary but important services such as occupational or physical therapy or speech-language services; they may say these should be provided by the schools and not paid for by the insurance company, which may attempt to effectively limit access to more specialized care providers. This is unfortunate because even when primary care providers are very interested, often they need to have the option of asking very experienced specialists for help when problems arise.

Various types of insurance are available. Traditional fee-for-service insurance plans used to be the only thing available. Often such plans had (and still have) very limited coverage for mental health or behavioral problems. Indeed in many states providers of mental health care take no insurance whatsoever! However, various public programs provide health care coverage for families who cannot afford other insurance. These plans provide a basic coverage for those in financial need. Somewhat paradoxically these programs may provide more services to families in need than families with private insurance receive. Again there is some variation from state to state. Usually, the primary care provider must ask for authorization for more specialized services; the range of choices of such services may be more limited than fee for service. Those paying privately do, of course, have a much wider choice of providers. The transition to adulthood presents insurance challenges as well. Current controversies over insurance coverage and revision of the Affordable Care Act may, in the United States, have a major impact.

Coordination Between School and Private Providers

The primary care provider has a very important role in coordination of care. As we have discussed the medical home model is an excellent resource in this regard (Cheak-Zamora & Farmer, 2015). Particularly when multiple care providers are involved there is the potential for either duplication (which is not always bad) or therapies that are in competition. For example, a child might be getting one approach to stimulating vocabulary development in school and a very, very different approach in private speech therapy. Keep in mind that sometimes this can be a good thing, but what is really critical here is to have the two professionals (school and private) have some discussion with each other. This is also very important if they are doing their own assessments. There is some potential for scores to be inflated if the child is unwittingly given the same assessment instrument more than once within a short period of time; this can mislead clinicians about what is actually going on.

ADULT SERVICES

Provision of services (and entitlements to services) varies significantly for adults. Once the student has graduated high school the laws mandating educational services to children no longer apply. For adults going on to vocational school or college there are some protections under the ADA in the United States (e.g., relative to providing reasonable accommodations and supports in college). For adults who continue to need more intensive services, entitlements often are related to whether the person also has an associated intellectual disability (i.e., IQ < 70). The quality and quantity of these vary from state to state. Paradoxically, with more young children identified and given services early in life, fewer adults with ASD will likely qualify for such programs. It is important to look at the broader picture of community services and potential opportunities for the adult to be involved in a job or even a volunteer position within the community. This is an area in which, we hope, things will change in the coming years with the realization of the growing number of adults who continue to need some supports.

SUMMARY

In this chapter, we have reviewed some of the issues involved in getting services for children on the autism spectrum. In the United States, the passage of Public Law 94–142 and its various successors marked a turning point in our approach, as a society, to children with disabilities and resulted in a much greater effort to include children with autism in the lives of schools and communities. One important consequence of this effort has been the general trend toward improved outcome. Despite its many advantages, the IDEA is not perfect. Schools understandably complain about paperwork and lack of funding from the federal government, which has never lived up to its original commitment. Parents complain that the law is not fully implemented and that procedures aren't followed. They also complain that they want the best for the child, not just what is appropriate. Although the schools aren't required to pay for medical treatments, there are some treatment modalities (e.g., speech therapy, physical therapy, and occupational therapy) that clearly fall into a gray zone of being quasi-medical and that the schools are required to provide as related services.

▉ REFERENCES

Cheak-Zamora, N. C., & Farmer, J. E. (2015). The impact of the medical home on access to care for children with autism spectrum disorders. *Journal of Autism & Developmental Disorders, 45*(3), 636–644.

Doehring, P., & Becker-Conttrill, B. (2013). *Autism services across America.* Baltimore, MD: Brookes.

Kohler, F. W., & Strain, P. S. (1999). Maximizing peer-mediated resources integrated preschool classrooms. *Topics in Early Childhood Special Education, 19*(2), 92–102.

Martins, M. P., Harris, S. L., & Handleman, J. S. (2014). Supporting inclusive education. In F. R. Volkmar, S. J. Rogers, R. Paul, & K. A. Pelphrey (Eds.), *Handbook of autism and pervasive developmental disorders* (4th ed., Vol. 2, pp. 858–870). Hoboken, NJ: Wiley.

Mayerson, G. S. (2014). Autism in the courtroom. In F. R. Volkmar, S. J. Rogers, R. Paul, & K. A. Pelphrey (Eds.), *Handbook of autism and pervasive developmental disorders* (4th ed., Vol. 2, pp. 1036–1050). Hoboken, NJ: Wiley.

National Research Council. (2001). *Educating young children with autism.* Washington, DC: National Academies Press.

▉ SUGGESTED READING

Addison, A. (2005). *Unfolding the tent: Advocating for your one-of-a-kind child.* Shawnee Mission, KS: Autism Asperger.

Anderson, W., Chitwood, S., & Hayden, D. (2008). *Negotiating the special education maze: A guide for parents and teachers* (4th ed.). Bethesda, MD: Woodbine House.

Bateman, B., & Herr, C. (2006). *Writing measurable IEP goals and objectives.* Verona, WI: Attainment/IEP Resources.

Cohen, J. (2006). *Guns a' blazing: How parents of children on the autism spectrum and schools can work together without a shot being fired.* Shawnee Mission, KS: Autism Asperger.

Cohen, M. (2009). *A guide to special education advocacy: What parents, clinicians and advocates need to know.* London, UK: Jessica Kingsley.

Dawson, P., & Guare, R. (2009). *Smart but scattered: The revolutionary "executive skills" approach to helping kids reach their potential.* New York, NY: Guilford Press.

Dawson, P., & Guare, R. (2016). *The smart but scattered guide to success: How to use your brain's executive skills to keep up, keep calm, and get organized at work and home.* New York, NY: Guilford Press.

Eason, A., & Whitbread, K. (2006). *IEP and inclusion tips for parents and teachers—handout version.* Verona, WI: Attainment/IEP Resources.

Fouse, B. (1999). *Creating a win-win IEP for students with autism: A how-to manual for parents and educators.* Arlington, TX: Future Horizons.

Graham, J. (2008). *Autism, discrimination and the law: A quick guide for parents, educators and employers.* London, UK: Jessica Kingsley.

Guare, R., & Dawson, P. (2013). *Smart but scattered teens: The revolutionary "executive skills" program for helping teens reach their potential.* New York, NY: Guilford Press.

Hope-West, A. (2010). *Securing appropriate education provisions for children with autism spectrum disorders.* London, UK: Jessica Kingsley

Hyatt-Foley, D., & Foley, M. G. (2002). *Getting services for your child on the autism spectrum.* London, UK: Jessica Kingsley.

Lentz, K. (2004). *Hope and dreams: An IEP guide for parents of children with autism spectrum disorders.* Shawnee Mission, KS: Autism Asperger.

Mandlawitz, M. R. (2005). Educating children with autism: Current legal issues. In F. Volkmar, A. Klin, R. Paul, & D. J. Cohen (Eds.), *Handbook of autism and pervasive developmental disorders* (3rd ed., Vol. 2, pp. 1161–1173). New York: Wiley.

Pierangelo, R., & Giuliani, G. (2007). *Understanding, developing, and writing effective IEPs: A step-by-step guide for educators.* Thousand Oaks, CA: Corwin Press.

Shore, S. (2004). *Ask and tell: Self-advocacy and disclosure for people on the autism spectrum.* Shawnee Mission, KS: Autism Asperger.

Siegel, L. (2005). *The complete IEP guide.* Berkeley, CA: Nolo.

Siegel, L. (2007a). *The complete IEP guide: How to advocate for your special ed child* (5th ed.). Berkeley, CA: Nolo.

Siegel, L. (2007b). *Nolo's IEP guide: Learning disabilities.* Berkeley, CA: Nolo.

Silver Lake Editors. (2004). *Kids and health care: Using insurance, cash, and government programs to make sure your children get the best doctors, hospitals and treatments possible.* Los Angeles, CA: Silver Lake.

Winkelstern, J. A., & Jongsma, A. E. (2001). *The special education treatment planner.* Hoboken, NJ: Wiley.

Wright, P., & Wright, P. (2006). *Wrights law: From emotions to advocacy; The special education survival guide* (2nd ed.). Hartfield, VA: Harbor House Law Press.

Wright, P., & Wright, P. (2007). *Wrights law: Special education law* (2nd ed.). Hartfield, VA: Harbor House Law Press.

CHAPTER 7

Autism in Infants and Preschool Children

In the past, diagnosis often didn't occur until the child was 3 or 4 years of age. There was less awareness of autism on the part of professionals and parents, no screening procedures, and a tendency to write off problems such as language delay, expecting the child to "grow out" of it. Another limitation was, and remains, the heavy reliance on history and a lack of awareness of how autism manifests in very young children. This has changed dramatically. We have better awareness, screening instruments are often used (although see Chapter 3 for a discussion of their uses and limitations), and more evidence-based treatment options are available. There has also been a growing awareness of recurrence risk in siblings and a growing literature on autism as it manifests itself early in life.

Observing babies is complicated because they change so quickly and behavior can vary tremendously. Some behaviors that are perfectly fine at one age may be a warning sign at a later age. For example, some of the simple play that babies do in exploring things with their mouths becomes worrisome if it isn't replaced by more advanced play skills as the child gets older. In infants, there can normally be what appear to be major disconnects, for example, between what the baby seems to want and how good he or she is at getting it. Such abilities develop in the first year of life. Variability in the state (awake-asleep), behaviors, and motivation creates some challenges for assessment (Chawarska, Klin, & Volkmar, 2008).

SIGNS OF AUTISM BEFORE 1 YEAR OF AGE

In most cases parents become concerned as the child fails to develop words or to respond to sounds or seems socially disconnected. Leo Kanner (1943) emphasized this social disconnectedness in his use of the word *autism* in his first report on the condition. Other behaviors that he described in slightly older children, for example, echolalia, motor mannerisms, and stereotypies, require more developmental skills than very young babies can muster. Problems in imitation can include copying motor things (pat-a-cake) or vocal ones (babbling to imitate). Sometimes babies who go on to have clear autism are described as easily startled or "on a high wire act" all the time. When picking up the baby, by 6 months or so he or she may seem to be floppy (low tone) or too stiff (high tone). Often there is no response to calling his or her name between 6 to 12 months.

Looking at all the studies on early development and behavior, there are six groups of behaviors that children with autism don't do nearly as regularly as typically developing children (Chawarska & Volkmar, 2014):

- Showing anticipation of being picked up
- Showing affection toward familiar people
- Showing interest in children or peers other than siblings
- Reaching for a familiar person
- Playing simple interaction games with others
- Being either very difficult (easily upset or hard to soothe) or very passive

Typically developing babies are interested in faces from very early in life, and by 8 or 9 months old they have become so good at looking at them that they readily recognize familiar people and usually become afraid of strangers. Children with autism may not show this. Early work in this area using home movies and videos also show some differences in the first year of life in children with autism. It was found that children who go on to have a diagnosis of autism seemed less likely to look at other people or to smile or vocalize to others and may be less likely to seek out others. As babies get a little older, they start to respond to their own name, but children with autism, by about 8 to 10 months, often do not like to be touched. Some of the unusual sensory behaviors seem to develop a bit later than other behaviors (Chawarska et al., 2008).

Overall, it seems that many infants with autism do display differences in the first months of life. Sometimes parents will notice differences from very early on. More frequently, parents start to notice problems at 6 to 8 months of age, because the child seems not very interested in interaction with them. The infant with autism may still have an interest in the nonsocial world. Failure to respond to his or her name is one of the striking manifestations by the end of the first year of life (and an item frequently included in screening instruments for autism). Symptoms suggestive of autism in the first year of life are summarized in Box 7.1.

BOX 7.1 SYMPTOMS OF AUTISM IN THE FIRST YEAR OF LIFE

Social Symptoms
- Limited ability to anticipate being picked up
- Low frequency of looking at people
- Limited interest in interactional games
- Limited affection toward familiar people
- Content to be left alone

Communication Symptoms
- Poor response to name (doesn't respond when called)
- Does not frequently look at objects held by others

Restricted interests and stereotyped behaviors
- Mouths objects excessively
- Does not like to be touched

Source: Reprinted with permission from Chawarska and Volkmar (2005, p. 230).

SIGNS OF AUTISM BETWEEN 12 AND 36 MONTHS

By about a year of age even more sophisticated social skills start to emerge; for example, joint attention skills are usually starting to develop, and these skills help infants engage with their parents and learn to focus on what is important in the environment. Although we know much about this based on parent reports and looking back at home videos, only now are we starting to collect good information (Mundy & Burnette, 2014).

Even when they are worried early on, it is still typical for parents to start to seek help only after the child turns 1 year of age. Unfortunately months or years often elapse between the time parents are first worried and the child's diagnosis and treatment. Fortunately, parents and health care providers now have increased awareness of autism. All that being said, it still can be hard to diagnose autism in very young infants, and parents often start pursuing assessments after the first birthday. What kinds of concerns trigger this? Common reasons for parents to seek assessment include these issues:

- Speech delay
- Lack of response to speech (worries the child may be deaf)
- Regression or loss of skills or failure to make usual gains in skills
- Unusual behaviors (preoccupations, early repetitive movements)
- Limited interest in playing and interacting with others

Unusual interests and behaviors usually appear sometime after 12 months and before 3 years. These can include staring at fans or spinning things or developing repetitive movements (often of the hands or fingers). After 1 year of age, the kinds of things parents start to notice correspond with the kinds of things we look at in older children in making a diagnosis of autism: problems in social interaction, communication, play, and unusual responses to the environment. Of the behaviors required for a diagnosis, this last category seems to be the one that comes later, sometimes raising problems in diagnosis if a baby has trouble in the other two areas but not the third one yet (Chawarska & Volkmar, 2014).

After 12 months, problems in communication often become more notable. These include delays in development of language and nonverbal means of communication, that is, gestures and eye contact. Young children with autism typically do not use pointing gestures, do not show things to other people, and rarely give objects to others to share or to get help. Typical young children often engage in joint attention, the two-way back-and-forth between people about a third thing, often an object. So if, say, something interesting (or scary) happens, or maybe just something a little new occurs, the typically developing baby will more or less immediately check in with the parents, looking at them to get their take on the situation. Or the child will look at the parent and then look at the thing he or she is concerned about and then back to parent, drawing the parent's attention to it. Toddlers with autism may use their finger to point to something they want but do not usually use eye contact with their parent. The child may not follow if the parent points to something and may have little interest in imitating parents or siblings. The child's preference for being left alone may also be dramatic. The child's emotional response to things may be unusual. The child may seem less sensitive to pain or may start having marked taste sensitivities and unusual food preferences (often refusing to eat new foods).

By 12 to 36 months, research studies often are able to compare toddlers with autism to toddlers with other kinds of problems, such as toddlers whose language is delayed. Children with autism have trouble pointing to show and using gestures. Children with other language problems are able to do these things. As children get a little older, those with autism may not be using imagination in play. Signs of autism between 12 and 36 months are summarized in Box 7.2.

BOX 7.2 SYMPTOMS OF AUTISM: AGES 1 TO 3 YEARS

Social Symptoms
- Abnormal eye contact
- Limited social referencing
- Limited interest in other children
- Limited social smile
- Low frequency of looking at people
- Limited range of facial expression
- Limited sharing of affect or enjoyment
- Little interest in interactive games
- Limited functional play
- No pretend play
- Limited motor imitation

Communication Symptoms
- Low frequency of verbal or nonverbal communication
- Failure to share interest (e.g., through pointing, sharing, giving, showing)
- Poor response to name

- Failure to respond to communicative gestures (pointing, giving, showing)
- Use of other's body as a tool (pulls hand to desired object without making eye contact, as if hand rather than person obtains object)

Restricted Interests and Stereotyped Behaviors
- Hand or finger mannerisms
- Inappropriate use of objects
- Repetitive interest or play
- Unusual sensory behaviors
- Hyper- or hyposensitivity to sounds, texture, tastes, visual stimuli

Source: Reprinted with permission from Chawarska and Volkmar (2005, p. 230).

It is reasonable to ask how certain we are of a diagnosis early in life. The literature on this is fairly clear; by age 3 we can be reasonably certain of a diagnosis, and before that time the issue is often more spectrum versus classical autism. Diagnosis is most stable when made by experienced individuals or teams (Chawarska and Volkmar, 2014). In one of the first follow-up studies of 2-year-olds referred for possible autism, Lord (1996) followed a group of 30 children and found several attributes at age 2 that predicted which children were likely to have autism. These included a lack of several social behaviors (shared enjoyment, interest in other children, social reciprocity, greeting behavior) and use of the other person's body as a tool (Lord, 1996). Other problems included attending to voice, pointing, and understanding of gestures. Some of the repetitive and restricted behaviors also were noted, including unusual hand and finger movement and odd sensory behaviors. Abnormality in two of the behaviors (showing and attending to voice) could be used to classify correctly more than 80% of cases. One of the things that was very helpful about this study was the clarification that some children, at age 2, did not show the unusual finger or hand movements or sensitivities characteristic of autism, but they did start to do so by age 3. In other words, it seemed that some children only gradually developed all the symptoms technically needed for a diagnosis of autism, but did so by 3 years of age. Much less commonly, a child who looked like he had autism as an infant doesn't have it later on (after age 3 years).

Given their problems in social interaction, it is important to know that young children with autism do form attachments to their parents (Rogers, Ozonoff, & Maslin-Cole, 1993). At first, this might seem counterintuitive, given what parents often report as their experience of the child. Interestingly, the process of attachment formation can sometimes also be a bit indiscriminate. For example, the child may develop attachments to unusual objects. In typically developing children, the attachment objects, also called *transitional objects,* are usually soft (teddy bear, blanket) and the actual object is very important. In autism, these objects differ in two respects: They are unusual in that they are typically hard and not soft and may be unusual in other respects (e.g., Wheaties boxes, bundles of sticks, rocks, metal airplanes, fire trucks), and the specific object is not as important as the class of object (any magazine of the same type will do). It may be that the attachments we see in autism are "strategic" rather than "affiliative," that is, that they have to do less with purely social connections.

Are parents always the ones who are first concerned? The answer is no. Often parents, particularly first-time parents, aren't the experts in child development they will become after they have had a child. Parents may not be worried if the child has developed some language. Although parents are often the first ones to be worried, sometimes it is grandparents (who have had a lot of experience) or other family members. Sometimes it is the pediatrician or health care provider (and, as we talk about in the next section, screening for autism is increasingly common). Sometimes it is the day care providers who are worried about autism in a child who seems not to be developing normally. All this reflects the greater awareness of autism and the greater access to information about it.

ASPERGER'S AND THE BROADER AUTISM SPECTRUM

Much less is known about the early development of children with Asperger's and the broader autism spectrum, although some infants with early delays of the type seen in autism clearly develop into the latter category. In Asperger's, most of what we know comes from reports of parents and, in general, is fairly consistent with what Asperger said in the first place, that is, that social difficulties occur in the face of what seems to be good language (but not necessarily communication) skills so parents would tend to be worried much later. The typical time for parents of a child with Asperger's to become concerned is at entry to preschool, when social difficulties become much more noticeable (Volkmar, Klin, & McPartland, 2014). Motor delays are frequent, but parents are typically not very concerned because they see the child as very bright and verbal. In Asperger's, the unusual motor manifestations are less likely to develop early on, and the child is more likely to start exhibiting unusual interests and preoccupations that start to interfere in other ways with the life of the child and family. These interests may include train or bus schedules, the weather, dinosaurs, or astronomy. Sometimes the child is interested in something that originally frightened him. For instance, he may develop an interest in snakes because he is afraid of them. Usually, however, parents are not so worried until the child goes into preschool and they receive a call from a concerned teacher that the child isn't fitting in. Often, the child is interested in being social, but his attempts to make friends put off other children, for example, hugging children he barely knows or engaging them in long discussions about his topic of interest. Sometimes the child will have trouble tolerating changes in the schedule.

SCREENING FOR AUTISM AND FIRST STEPS IN GETTING A DIAGNOSIS AND SERVICE

Various screeners for autism have been developed. Some of these are specific to autism. Others assess development more generally (see Chapter 2). Some are based on parent report, some on observation by a professional, and others use both sources of information (Ibanez, Stone, & Coonrod, 2014). Essentially all of these try to tap into some of the characteristics in autism. At this point, what is critically needed are more objective, physiologically based screenings, for example, on how the child takes in social information. Efforts are under way to develop such techniques. An example of one potential method is shown in the Figure 7.1, which uses eye tracking; other methods may look at things such as listening, processing, or EEG response to social stimuli (Chawarska & Volkmar, 2014; McPartland et al., 2014).

Usually, the first person parents turn to when they have concerns about their child's development is the child's health care provider. As we

FIGURE 7.1   **Eye gaze pattern in a 2-year-old with autism. The image is generated using infrared eye tracking and shows the unusual gaze of a toddler with autism. Rather than looking at any of the characters in the scene, the child focuses on what, to most toddlers (and adults), would be much less relevant details.**

Source: Reprinted with permission from Klin, Jones, Schultz, and Volkmar (2003, p. 350).

discuss in Chapters 2 and 3, the initial assessment should encompass a careful history including family history, review of the pregnancy and delivery, developmental history, and so forth. Specific screeners such as the M-CHAT or others should be used. A thorough review of systems and a physical exam should be performed with an awareness of the genetic conditions, seizures, and other impairments sometimes associated with autism. A family history of autism, particularly in a sibling, also is an important risk indicator. Hearing and vision testing is indicated, and as we have discussed genetic testing should be carefully considered. Keep in mind that the children can "fail" screens for many reasons other than having autism; this is fairly common. In and of itself failing a screen may suggest another problem and require prompt referral for further assessment and diagnostic evaluations.

Diagnostic Assessments

For younger children, obtaining a good assessment can be complicated. Many of the problems associated with autism can interfere with assessment, and difficulties with new people, places, and transitions create further problems. Depending on the family's location a team from an early intervention program may be involved and may make referral for more specialized assessments. The latter can include assessments of communication, developmental skills, motor abilities, and administration of diagnostic assessment instruments (rather than screeners) more specific to autism (Lord et al., 2014; Volkmar, Booth, McPartland, & Wiesner, 2014; Volkmar et al., 2014).

It is important to follow up with families and those providing assessments; there is tremendous potential for diagnosis and service to be delayed if the weakest link in the chain breaks down, that is, parents fail to follow up or an assessment is done but results are not communicated to you. An important function of the medical home (see Chapter 3) for children with ASDs is coordination of care and assurance that all the individuals involved are on the same page and in communication with each other. These days there is additional paperwork required for permission to share information but it is very important.

Keep in mind that it is the observations of the child in the assessment as well as the assessment results themselves that are important. Also keep in mind that more experienced diagnosticians do a better job than those with less experience and that the use of any specific instrument is less important than having a truly experienced clinician involved.

Developmental Tests

For preschool children, developmental tests are often used. These are like traditional IQ tests in many ways, but by avoiding the use of the term *IQ*, there is more emphasis on emerging skills and less stress on long-term prediction. Several different tests can be used; some selected tests are summarized in Table 7.1. Note that these differ in various ways, for example, the mean **standard score** may be 50 (the average) with a standard deviation of 10, and some can include parent report as well as direct assessment. Appendix 2 summarizes aspects of psychological assessment.

TABLE 7.1	FREQUENTLY USED DEVELOPMENTAL ASSESSMENTS

Test	Comments
Mullen Scales of Early Learning (Mullen, 1995)	Individually administered assessment, birth to 5–8 years. Takes 15–60 minutes to administer. Scores in gross and fine motor skills, visual reception (similar to nonverbal learning), and receptive and expressive language. Disentangling nonverbal and verbal abilities is a plus in this population.
Battelle Developmental Inventory, 2nd ed. (Newborg, 2005)	This assessment can be based on structured testing, observation, or interview (structured test is preferred). Addresses skills in multiple areas and frequently used to assess children with potential developmental delays. Can be used from birth to age 7 years 11 months.
Bayley Scales of Infant Toddler Development, 3rd ed. (Bayley, 2006)	A revision of one of the earliest developmental tests. Can be used from 1 to 42 months typically taking 30 to 90 minutes to complete. Skills in multiple areas assessed (language, cognition, social-emotional, motor, and adaptive).

Note: Other tests are available as well. Note that the term developmental tests emphasizes that these are not to be simply treated like IQ tests; the latter scores begin to be more predictive of ultimate school success only as the child enters school (not surprisingly). It is important for professionals and parents to realize that there can be tremendous change over the first years of life—particularly in children with ASDs—and the results should not be taken as a predictor of ultimate outcome.

Delays in development of speech and communication are common in children with autism; these include the skills (babbling, development of typical prosody, "conversational" turn taking) that come before first words are heard. Communication skills develop in typical children in parallel with social skills; for example, at about 9 months of age, typically developing infants start to coordinate eye contact and gestures when they request things (looking at the parent while reaching for an object) and a shared focus of interest becomes important. By contrast, children with ASDs may not make eye contact or do so only in very specific situations. They often don't check in with parents when something interesting happens in the environment (a failure in joint attention). Children with autism may not respond to their own name.

Typically a speech language pathologist will do some aspect of the initial assessment and almost always will be involved once the child starts school.

Some of the same assessment instruments (e.g., measures of understanding or spoken vocabulary) can also be done by a psychologist, but other instruments require the special skills of the speech pathologist. Some of the most frequently used assessment instruments are summarized in Table 7.2.

In addition to formal testing, the speech pathologist will be looking at the entire array of behaviors involved in communication, including the range and types of sounds produced, unusual language features (such as echoed language, pronoun reversal), unusual or idiosyncratic language (word or phrase use that is unique to the individual), and other features seen in

TABLE 7.2 SELECTED SPEECH-COMMUNICATION ASSESSMENTS

Peabody Picture Vocabulary Test, 4th ed. (Dunn & Dunn, 2007)	The test examines understanding of words (single-word vocabulary) in children from age 2 years 6 months through adulthood. This is a well-established, frequently used test. The child is given a word and asked to select it from a panel of pictures.
Expressive One Word Picture Vocabulary Test, 4th ed. (Martin & Brownell, 2011)	This test is used with children age 2 to adult and tests ability to name objects, actions, and concepts. The child is shown a picture and asked to provide a name. The test is well done and is also frequently used.
Rossetti Infant Toddler Language Scale	This test assesses communication (not just vocabulary) in children from birth to age 3. It is a **criterion-referenced test** that looks at verbal and preverbal communication skills. Information comes from direct observation and parental report.
The New Reynell Developmental Language Scale (Edwards Letts, & Sinka, 2011)	This is a revision of previous versions. Used from 2 years to 7 years 5 months, it assesses comprehension and production using play-based materials. Useful in documenting major discrepancies in reception and production (past the level of vocabulary).
Communication and Symbolic Behavior Scales (Wetherby & Prizant, 2002)	This test is designed for infants and young children assessing communication skills and symbolic development. It takes about an hour to complete and includes ratings in a number of different areas.
Clinical Evaluation of Language Fundamentals-Preschool-2 (Wiig, Seecord, & Semel 2006)	This test assesses a range of language skills in preschool children (3 years to 6 years 11 months). It is individually administered; it is less appropriate when severe delays are present.

autism. For children who have some spoken language, a focus on their social use of language (what speech pathologists call ***pragmatics***) will also be included. Often the speech pathologist will use a variety of procedures to see what the child will do to communicate and, if the child is verbal, will try to get a language sample to see what the child will do to ask for help, protest, request, and so forth.

In addition to the results of formal testing, the observations of the occupational therapist, psychologist, or speech pathologist can also add to intervention planning. For example, although the professional may have to give certain items in certain ways to administer the test the right way, there are many opportunities to see how the child approaches tasks, what kinds of things the examiner can do to get the child interested, and ways you can get the child engaged. These kinds of observations often can be used readily to help develop the intervention program. In addition to the various screening and assessment instruments, a range of assessments have been developed specifically for assessment of autism or ASD diagnosis—we will discuss these in more detail in Chapter 8. They include parent report and direct observation instruments. The Autism Diagnostic Observation scale is most frequently used. The use of all these instruments can provide important information that supplements but does not replace the need for careful clinical assessment.

ACCESS TO SERVICES FOR VERY YOUNG CHILDREN

The law in the United States mandates school responsibility for providing a free and appropriate public education (FAPE) for every child, starting when the child is 3. Before that time a different federal law applies to infants and toddlers with disability. Unlike the law for children of school-age, states have a choice to participate in offering early childhood services. Parents can be asked for part of the cost, but families who can't pay still should be able to get services. Once a child is referred to the responsible agency, it should provide an evaluation and develop an individualized family service plan (IFSP) that is similar to the individualized education plan (IEP) developed for school-aged children. We discuss issues of legal entitlements in Chapter 6. As with the subsequent IEP there is a mandate for regular review. Supporting the family is particularly important.

Sadly, early intervention services around the country are quite variable— sometimes from state to state and other times from town to town. Some programs are center-based and others may be home-based. Even when the forms of early intervention differ, the goals are generally the same: minimizing any disruption that autism or another condition has on the child's development and enhancing pathways to learning (National Research Council, 2001).

Toddlers with autism are very good candidates for early intervention. They can be taught using various methods, and it is while they are young that they are most likely to learn new skills. As children turn 3, the school district is obligated to provide services, and in many cases this works well because a more intensive program can be provided and it is easier to coordinate all the services in one setting.

Usually, parents will have let the school district know that they have a child who is 3 or nearly 3 and in need of special preschool services. The early intervention providers should work to coordinate a smooth transfer. Parents must be part of this process and give consent.

PROGRAM CONTENT

As we discuss in Chapter 5, a large body of work has now shown the importance of early diagnosis and intervention for improving long-term outcome. The report from the National Research Council (2001) emphasizes that the evidence for many programs effectiveness is strong. A range of options are available including those based on the applied behavior analysis (ABA) (Harris & Weiss, 2007) approach model (probably the most well-known approach and sometimes referred to as Lovaas treatment after the man who pioneered it) (Lovaas & Smith, 1988). Other programs may focus more on natural settings and target what are thought of as highly critical and important behaviors (that is, pivotal response training programs) (Koegel & Koegel, 2006). Other programs are more developmentally based, giving the child a role in helping set the agenda for what is learned. The Early Start model (Rogers, Dawson, & Vismara, 2012); the Greenspan floortime approach (Greenspan & Wieder, 2009); and SCERTS models (Prizant, Wetherby, Rubin, Laurent, & Rydell, 2004; Wetherby & Woods, 2008) are examples of these approaches. In other cases, programs are what might be called eclectic, picking and choosing based on a range of techniques—one of the best-known examples is the TEACCH statewide autism program in North Carolina (Welterlin, Turner-Brown, Harris, Mesibov, & Delmolino, 2012).

Unfortunately, it is usual for the school to want the child to be in "their" autism program. Sometimes this is like trying to fit a square peg into a round hole! Fortunately, many, probably most, programs work well for most children. But when there is an exception, parents and teachers need to be more creative in thinking about solutions. It is important to remind the parents that the school must program for this child! Good programs should have an explicit focus on teaching communication and social interaction skills, dealing with problem behaviors, fostering social interaction and play, as well as generalization of skills. There also will be a focus on organization and attention, which become increasingly important as the child gets older. The communication part of the program should include all relevant aspects of communication, including understanding (receptive language) and speaking (expressive language) and social language use (pragmatic language). Because communication is also intrinsically social, there is usually a focus on social aspects of language and communication. The kinds of activities that are worked on include imitation of other people's movements or sounds they make, building up vocabulary, using words for objects or actions or both, developing sentences, and then adding the bells and whistles of language, starting with words such as *yes* and *no* and moving to more sophisticated concepts. For children who have trouble with verbal communication, a variety of alternative methods are available, including picture exchange, visual supports, computerized systems, and apps or sign language (Hodgdon, 2011; Mirenda, 2014). As we discussed in Chapter 5, parents sometimes assume that if the therapist wants to use these methods, it means they've given up on the child's talking. In fact, anything that can be done to help the child learn to communicate can help the child eventually learn to speak (Mirenda, 2014).

Self-help skills can be a great source of difficulty for adolescents and adults, and it is important that teaching personal independence and self-sufficiency starts in preschool. Some young children with autism have fairly good motor skills early on; others have delays. As time goes on, motor skills often become much more social (think about how socially related you have to be to play football or baseball or soccer). To foster development of these skills, early intervention often focuses on activities that involve big muscle movements (gross motor skills), such as riding a trike or kicking a ball, as well as more fine motor skills, such as building with blocks, tracing a diamond, or cutting paper with scissors. Both kinds of skills are important. Often, in relation to work on motor problems, there is work on sensory skills. This might focus on helping the child tolerate a greater range of sensations or materials. Often, the physical therapist and particularly the occupational therapist will be involved in sensory and motor interventions.

Toilet Training

Toilet training can present special challenges for the child with autism. For the typically developing child the process is typically completed in toddlerhood, often occurring in girls slightly before boys. This accomplishment builds on three factors: a desire to please the parents, sufficient motor control, and an understanding of what is wanted. If any one of these factors is compromised, the process is more challenging, and this is usually the case in the child with autism. Similar to the typically developing child, consistency of parents and use of a planned, deliberate approach can be helpful. A number of excellent resources are available (Wheeler, 2007). Some of the requirements for and aids to toilet training are summarized in Box 7.3.

BOX 7.3 TOILET TRAINING IN ASD—BASIC ASPECTS

Requirements for Toilet Training
- Understanding what is wanted
- Motivation to do what is wanted
- Motor coordination

Obstacles to Toilet Training in ASDs
- Cognitive problems (may not understand what is wanted)
- Social problems (problems with imitation, problems with body awareness)
- Motor and sensory issues (may interfere)

Approaches to Toilet Training
- Develop a routine, be aware of optimal times

- Develop system for communicating need (words, pictures, object swap)
- Plan clothing ahead of time (to expedite the attempts)
- Use visual schedules and supports
- Identify problem areas (sound of the toilet)
- Think about motor issues (step stool may help child)
- Praise and **reinforcement** for success
- Keep language simple (also use visuals)
- Practice in less familiar environments (encourage generalization)

Source: Reprinted and adapted from Volkmar and Wiesner (2009, pp. 212–213).

Teaching Play and Social Skills

You might think that play is something you wouldn't need to teach, but for children with autism, you'd be wrong. For the typical child, early play involves a lot of exploration of the feeling, color, and smell of objects or the sounds they make. For the child with normal social abilities, this changes dramatically in the second year of life, when play focuses more on the function of things (cars are to roll, cups to drink from). This is then followed by much more complicated imaginative play. Play sets the stage for a number of different developments critical for the growing child. It helps the child learn flexibility: The cup can be a cup, or a bathtub, or a rocket—whatever you want it to be. Play also becomes very social, with children learning to move very quickly in play with roles of people and materials changing rapidly. Among its many other functions, play also helps children develop more sophisticated ways of thinking; it is the beginning of being able to imagine how things could be and to be able to take the world apart and put it right back together, sometimes in very creative ways. Because play is also very symbolic, it is intimately related to language and cognitive development. For the typically developing child then, play opens up whole new worlds and the child learns to seek new experiences from which he or she can learn. For children with autism, there are many challenges for play. They don't much like social interaction. They also don't particularly like new things and the challenges that new things bring.

Children with autism start to exhibit problems in play, often around a year or so of age. In contrast to the developing imaginative play of the typical child, the child with autism may fixate on one aspect of a material—sometimes one that isn't very productive, such as its taste or smell. By age 2 the unusual patterns of play are often very striking, and by age 3 they tend to be very dramatic. Imaginative play does not kick in as usual. Instead, children tend to become fixated on a narrow range of materials, often wanting to play with simple cause-and-effect toys (push a button and something happens), the sort of play behavior more typical of much younger children. Fortunately, it is possible to explicitly teach skills needed for play. The use of typical peers can be very helpful in this regard (Wolfberg & Schuler, 1999).

Preschool programs for young children with ASDs will typically include a very explicit and important focus on teaching a range of social skills such as imitation, joint attention, affective engagement, as well as aspects of communication, play, and learning-to-learn skills. Although programs vary, there are also many commonalities (National Research Council, 2001). Some programs may emphasize use of routines, schedules, and visual support, and others may emphasize peer interaction or incidental teaching. Still others focus on more naturalistic methods, and others focus on discrete trial learning, particularly at the beginning of treatment.

Unfortunately, we still don't know why some children respond better to intervention than others. Sometimes it seems (with the wisdom of hindsight) predictable; for example, the child who was very, very uninterested in other people versus the child who was interested but very odd. It does appear that children who have greater cognitive delay when treatment starts may be less likely to improve, although, of course, they are also starting from a position from where even more catch-up is required. Parents understandably want an opinion about the child's long-term prognosis, but this is inevitably impossible to give. The good news is that there is much potential for change. The bad news is that we don't always know who will change and in what direction. Another major problem for prediction is that in the preschool years, the tests we use to look at cognitive development and language tell us about the child relative to other children the same age but not about the future. The reason for this is that only as the children (of all types) become older do traditional tests of intelligence or cognitive ability start to tap the kinds of skills closely related to school success.

Infants and Preschoolers and Medical Care Issues

As we have emphasized previously, a number of things can be done to support good medical care in this population. The time of initial diagnosis and service provision is a particularly important time for parents to feel supported by the primary care provider and for that provider to assume what likely will be a central long-term role in coordination of information, assessments, and services; the medical home approach has many advantages in this regard (Volkmar, Rowberry, et al., 2014). A number of relatively simple modifications in procedures (see Chapter 3) can make office visits more tolerable for all concerned. Use of visual apps, stories, and so forth can help child and parent feel more at ease. In addition to coordinating the various educational and medical professionals and other service providers involved, the primary care provider will be able to maintain a unique perspective of the individual child in the context of his or her family and community.

Vigilance for associated conditions at the time of initial diagnosis and indeed over the long haul is important—there is an increased risk for the development of a seizure disorder through childhood and well into adolescence if not beyond. As we've noted the vaccine controversies have unfortunately delayed many parents from obtaining appropriate immunizations. Similarly the tendency to avoid dental visits can have a very sad long-term impact on the child's quality of life. Safety concerns in this age group are always a major issue further heightened by the increase for accidents and injury in children with ASDs. Problems with running away (bolting) as children get older and with poor impulse control can result in accidental injury and death (we talk more about safety concerns in Chapter 4).

SUMMARY

In this chapter we reviewed some of what we know about autism and related conditions as they appear in infants and young children. Until recently most of the information on this topic came from either parent memories or the retrospective study of children through videotapes. Most parents of children with autism become concerned about the child's development in the first year or two of life. The earliest features of autism tend to fall into two groups: social engagement and early communication abilities. Although unusual sensory interests and motor behaviors develop, they often develop somewhat later, usually by age 3, but these issues can be preceded by unusual sensory sensitivities that, as Kanner suggested, stand in stark contrast to the child's lack of interest in the social world.

When parents are concerned, the health care provider is usually the initial professional to see the child, conduct an initial assessment, and suggest more extensive testing. Depending on the results of this assessment, services can be provided even before the child is eligible for school-based programming (at age 3). The unusual profiles of strengths and weaknesses in children on the autism spectrum can present some challenges for intervention. It does appear that, on balance, early and more intensive intervention is the most effective. Parents must negotiate the challenges of dealing with two systems: the early intervention system and then the public schools. A range of well-documented programs are available for slightly older children. As interest in early diagnosis of autism increases, there will undoubtedly be more interest in evaluating programs for children under 3 as well. That being said, there are still individual differences, and predicting what will happen to a specific child is often difficult. A major challenge for current research is the development of better tools for screening and assessing children with possible autism or related disorders. Several studies are under way at present in different places around the country, often studying children who are siblings of those with known autism. We hope that this research will lead to earlier and more effective interventions.

■ REFERENCES

Bayley, N. (2006). *Bayley scales of infant and toddler development* (3rd ed.). San Antonio, TX: Harcourt Assessment.

Chawarska, K., Klin, A., & Volkmar, F. R. (2008). *Autism spectrum disorders in infants and toddlers: Diagnosis, assessment, and treatment.* New York, NY: Guilford Press.

Chawarska, K., & Volkmar, F. R. (2005). Autism in infancy and early childhood. In F. Volkmar, A. Klin, R. Paul, & D. J. Cohen (Eds.), *Handbook of autism and pervasive developmental disorders* (3rd ed., Vol. 1, pp. 70–78). New York: Wiley.

Chawarska, K., & Volkmar, F. R. (2014). Autism in infancy and early childhood. In In F. R. Volkmar, S. J. Rogers, R. Paul, & K. A. Pelphrey (Eds.), *Handbook of autism and pervasive developmental disorders* (4th ed., Vol. 1, pp. 223–246). New York: Wiley.

Dunn, L. M., & Dunn, D. M. (2007). *Peabody Picture Vocabulary Test* (4th ed.) (PPVT-4). Minneapolis, MN: NCS Pearson.

Edwards, S., Letts, C., & Sinka, I. (2011). *The New Reynell Developmental Language Scales*. London, UK: GL Assessment Ltd.

Greenspan, S. I., & Wieder, S. (2009). *Engaging autism: Using the floortime approach to help children relate, communicate, and think.* Cambridge, MA: Da Capo Lifelong Books.

Harris, S., & Weiss, M. J. (2007). *Right from the start: Behavioral intervention for young children with autism* (2nd ed.). Bethesda, MD: Woodbine House.

Hodgdon, L. (2011). *Visual strategies for improving communication: Practical supports for school and home.* Troy, MI: QuirkRoberts Publishing.

Ibanez, L. V., Stone, W. L., & Coonrod, E. E. (2014). Screening for autism in young children. In F. R. Volkmar, S. J. Rogers, R. Paul, & K. A. Pelphrey (Eds.), *Handbook of autism and pervasive developmental disorders* (4th ed., Vol. 2, pp. 585–608). New York: Wiley.

Kanner, L. (1943). Autistic disturbances of affective contact. *Nervous Child, 2,* 217–250.

Klin, A., Jones, W., Schultz, R., & Volkmar, F. (2003). The enactive mind from actions to cognition: Lessons from autism. *Philosophical Transactions of the Royal Society,* p. 350.

Koegel, R. L., & Koegel, L. K. (Eds.). (2006). *Pivotal response treatments for autism: Communication, social, & academic development.* Baltimore, MD: Brookes.

Lord, C. (1996). Follow-up of two-year-olds referred for possible autism. *Journal of Child Psychology and Psychiatry, 36*(8), 1065–1076.

Lord, C., Corsello, C., Grzadzinski, R., Volkmar, F. R., Paul, R., Rogers, S. J., & and Pelphrey, K. A. (2014). Diagnostic instruments in autistic spectrum disorders. In F. R. Volkmar, S. J. Rogers, R. Paul, & K. A. Pelphrey (Eds.), *Handbook of autism and pervasive developmental disorders* (4th ed., Vol. 2, pp. 730–771). New York: Wiley.

Lovaas, O., & Smith, T. (1988). Intensive behavioral treatment for young autistic children. In B. B. Lahey & A. E. Kazdin (Eds.), *Advances in clinical child psychology* 11, pp. 285–324). New York, NY: Springer Science + Business Media.

Martin, N. A., & Brownell, R. (2011). *Expressive One-Word Picture Vocabulary Test* (4th ed.). Novato, CA: Academic Therapy.

McPartland, J. C., Tillman, R. M., Yang, D.Y.J., Bernier, R. A., Pelphrey, K. A. Volkmar, F. R., Paul, R., Rogers, S. J., & Pelphrey, K. A. (2014). The social neuroscience of autism spectrum disorder. In F. R. Volkmar, S. J. Rogers, R. Paul, & K. A. Pelphrey (Eds.), *Handbook of autism and pervasive developmental disorders* (4th ed., Vol. 1, pp. 482–496). New York: Wiley.

Mirenda, P. (2014). Augmentative and alternative communication. In In F. R. Volkmar, S. J. Rogers, R. Paul, & K. A. Pelphrey (Eds.), *Handbook of autism and pervasive developmental disorders* (4th ed., Vol. 2, pp. 813–825). New York: Wiley.

Mullen, E. (1995). *Mullen scales of early learning* (AGS ed.). Circle Pines, MN: American Guidance Service.

Mundy, P., & Burnette, C. (2014). Joint attention and neurodevelopmental models of autism. In F. R. Volkmar, S. J. Rogers, R. Paul, & K. A. Pelphrey (Eds.), *Handbook of autism and pervasive developmental disorders* (4th ed., Vol. 2, pp. 650–681). New York: Wiley.

National Research Council. (2001). *Educating young children with autism.* Washington, DC: National Academies Press.

Newborg, J. (2005). *Battelle Developental Inventory* (2nd ed.). Itaska, IL: Riberside.

Prizant, B., Wetherby, A. M., Rubin, E., Laurent, A. C., & Rydell, P. J. (2004). *The SCERTS model: Enhancing communication and socioemotional abilities of children with autism spectrum disorder.* Baltimore, MD: Brookes.

Rogers, S. J., Dawson, G., & Vismara, L. A. (2012). *An early start for your child with autism: Using everyday activities to help kids connect, communicate, and learn.* New York, NY: Guilford Press.

Rogers, S. J., Ozonoff, S., & Maslin-Cole, C. (1993). Developmental aspects of attachment behavior in young children with pervasive developmental disorders. *Journal of the American Academy of Child & Adolescent Psychiatry, 32*(6), 1274–1282.

Volkmar, F. R., Booth, L. L., McPartland, J. C., & Wiesner, L. A. (2014). Clinical evaluation in multidisciplinary settings. In F. R. Volkmar, S. J. Rogers, R. Paul, & K. A. Pelphrey (Eds.), *Handbook of autism and pervasive developmental disorders* (4th ed., Vol. 2, pp. 661–672). New York: Wiley.

Volkmar, F. R., Klin, A., & McPartland, J. C. (2014). *Asperger syndrome: Assessing and treating high-functioning autism spectrum disorders* (pp. 1–42). New York, NY: Guilford Press.

Volkmar, F. R., Rowberry, J., de Vinck-Baroody, O., Gupta, A. R., Leung, J., Meyers, J., Vaswani, N., & Wiesner, L. A. (2014). Medical care in autism and related conditions. In F. R. Volkmar, S. J. Rogers, R. Paul, & K. A. Pelphrey (Eds.), *Handbook of autism and pervasive developmental disorders* (4th ed., Vol. 1, pp. 532–555). New York: Wiley.

Welterlin, A., Turner-Brown, L. M., Harris, S., Mesibov, G., & Delmolino, L. (2012). The home TEACCHing program for toddlers with autism. *Journal of Autism and Developmental Disorders, 42*(9), 1827–1835.

Wetherby, A., & Prizant, P. (2002). *Communication and Symbolic Behavior Scale.* Baltimore, MD: Paul H. Brookes.

Wheeler, M. (2007). *Toilet training for individuals with autism and other developmental issues.* Arlington TX: Future Horizons

Wiig, E. H., Secord, W. A., & Sempel, E. (2006). *Clinical Evaluation of Language Fundamentals–Preschool (2nd. ed.) (CELF P-2).* San Antonio, TX: Harcourt Assessment.

Wolfberg, P. J., & Schuler, A. L. (1999). Fostering peer interaction, imaginative play and spontaneous language children with autism. *Child Language Teaching & Therapy, 15*(1), 41–52.

SUGGESTED READING

Bailey, K. (2008). Supporting families. In K. Chawarska, A. Klin, & F. R. Volkmar (Eds.), *Autism spectrum disorders in infants and toddlers: Diagnosis, assessment, and treatment* (pp. 300–326). New York, NY: Guilford Press.

Baker, J. (2003). *The social skills picture book teaching play, emotion, and communication to children with autism.* Arlington, TX: Future Horizons.

Barbera, M. L., & Rasmussen, T. (2007). *The verbal behavior approach: How to teach children with autism and related disorders.* London, UK: Jessica Kingsley.

Baron-Cohen, S., Allen, J., & Gillberg, C. (1992). Can autism be detected at 18-months? The needle, the haystack, and the CHAT. *British Journal of Psychiatry, 161*(1), 839–843.

Baronet, G. T., Wakeford, L., & David, F. J. (2008). Understanding, assessing, and treating sensory-motor issues. In K. Chawarska, A. Klin, & F. R. Volkmar (Eds.), *Autism spectrum disorders in infants and toddlers: Diagnosis, assessment, and treatment* (pp. 104–140). New York, NY: Guilford Press.

Batts, B. (2010). *Ready, set, potty! Toilet training for children with autism and other developmental disorders.* London, UK: Jessica Kingsley.

Begun, R. W. (Ed.). (1995). *Ready-to-use social skills lessons & activities for grades preK–K.* San Francisco, CA: Jossey-Bass.

Bishop, S. L., Luyster, R., Richler, J., & Lord, C. (2008). Diagnostic assessment. In K. Chawarska, A. Klin, & F. R. Volkmar (Eds.), *Autism spectrum disorders in infants and toddlers: Diagnosis, assessment, and treatment* (pp. 23–49). New York, NY: Guilford Press.

Bondy, A., & Frost, L. (2001). *A picture's worth: PECS and other visual communication strategies in autism.* Bethesda, MD: Woodbine House.

Bretherton, A. V., & Tonger, B. L. (2005). *Preschoolers with autism: An education and skills training programme for parents.* London, UK: Jessica Kingsley.

Brinton, B., Robinson, L. A., & Fujiki, M. (2004). Description of a program for social language intervention: If you can have a conversation, you can have a relationship. *Language, Speech, and Hearing Services in Schools, 35,* 283–290.

Cafiero, J. M. (2005). *Meaningful exchange for people with autism: An introduction to augmenting & alternative communication; Topics in autism.* Bethesda, MD: Woodbine House.

Chawarska, K., & Bearss, K. (2008). Assessment of cognitive and adaptive skills. In K. Chawarska, A. Klin, & F. R. Volkmar (Eds.), *Autism spectrum disorders in infants and toddlers: Diagnosis, assessment, and treatment* (pp. 50–75). New York, NY: Guilford Press.

Chawarska, K., Klin, A., Paul, R., & Volkmar, F. (2007). Autism spectrum disorder in the second year: Stability and change in syndrome expression. *Journal of Child Psychology and Psychiatry and Allied Disciplines, 48*(2), 128–138.

Dawson, G., Meltzoff, A. N., Osterling, J., & Rinaldi, J. (1998). Neuropsychological correlates of early symptoms of autism. *Child Development, 69*(5), 1276–1285.

DiLavore, P. C., Lord, C., & Rutter, M. (1995). Prelinguistic autism diagnostic observation schedule. *Journal of Autism and Developmental Disorders, 25*(4), 355–379.

Eikeseth, S., Smith, T., Jahr, E., & Eldevik, S. (2002). Intensive behavioral treatment at school for 4- to 7-year-old children with autism: A 1-year comparison controlled study. *Behavior Modification, 26*(1), 49–68.

Fein, D., Helt, M., Brennan, L., & Barton, M. (2016). *The activity kit for babies and toddlers at risk: How to use every day routines to build social and communication skills.* New York, NY: Guilford Press.

Goldstein, H. (2002). *Promoting social communication: Children with developmental disabilities from birth to adolescence.* Baltimore, MD: Brookes.

Greenspan, S. I. (2006). *Engaging autism: Helping children relate, communicate and think with the DIR floortime approach.* Cambridge, MA: De Capo Lifelong Books.

Handleman, J. S., & Harris, S. L. (1994, 2001, 2008). *Preschool education programs for children with autism.* Austin, TX: PRO-ED.

Hoskins, B. (1996). *Conversations: A framework for language intervention.* Eau Claire, WI: Thinking Publications.

Jahr, D., Eldevid, S., & Eileseth, S. (2000). Teaching children with autism to initiate and sustain cooperative play. *Research in Developmental Disabilities, 21,* 151–169.

Kasari, C. (2002). Assessing change in early intervention programs for children with autism. *Journal of Autism & Developmental Disorders, 32*(5), 447–461.

Klein, M., Cook, R. E., & Richardson-Gibbs, A. M. (2001). *Strategies for including children with special needs in early childhood settings.* Albany, NY: Delmar.

Klin, A., Chawarska, K., Paul, R., Rubin, E., Morgan, T., Wiesner, L., & Volkmar, F. R. (2004). Autism in a 15-month-old child. *American Journal of Psychiatry, 161*(11), 1981–1988.

Klin, A., Saulnier, C., Chawarska, K., & Volkmar, F. R. (2008). Case studies of infants first evaluated in the second year of life. In K. Chawarska, A. Klin, & F. R. Volkmar (Eds.), *Autism spectrum disorders in infants and toddlers: Diagnosis, assessment, and treatment* (pp. 949–969). New York, NY: Guilford Press.

Koegel, L. K., Koegel, R. L., Fredeen, R. M., & Gengoux, G. W. (2008). Naturalistic behavior approaches to treatment. In K. Chawarska, A. Klin, & F. R. Volkmar (Eds.), *Autism spectrum disorders in infants and toddlers: Diagnosis, assessment, and treatment* (pp. 207–242). New York, NY: Guilford Press.

Lord, C., Shulman, C., & DiLavore, P. (2004). Regression and word loss in autistic spectrum disorders. *Journal of Child Psychology and Psychiatry, 45*(5), 936–955.

Lytel, J. (2008). *Act early against autism: Give your child a fighting chance from the start.* New York, NY: Perigree Trade.

Maestro, S., Muratori, F., Barbieri, F., Casella, C., Cattaneo, V., Cavallaro, M., et al. (2009). Attentional skills during the first 6 months of age in autism spectrum disorder. *Journal of the American Academy of Child and Adolescent Psychiatry, 34*(3), 947–952.

Matson, J. L., & Minshawi, N. F. (2006). *Early intervention for autism spectrum disorders: A critical analysis.* Philadelphia, PA: Elsevier.

Maurice, C., Green, G., & Luce, S. C. (Eds.). (1996). *Behavioral intervention for young children with autism: A manual for parents and professionals.* Austin, TX: PRO-ED.

McClannahan, L. E., & Krantz, P. J. (2005). *Teaching conversation to children with autism: Scripts and script fading.* Bethesda, MD: Woodbine House.

McGinnis, E., & Goldstein, A. P. (1990). *Skillstreaming in early childhood: Teaching prosocial skills to the preschool and kindergarten child.* Champaign, IL: Research Press.

National Research Council. (Ed.). (2009). *Educating children with autism.* Washington, DC: National Academies Press.

Osterling, J. A., & Dawson, G. (1994). Early recognition of children with autism: A study of first birthday home videotapes. *Journal of Autism and Developmental Disorders, 24*(3), 247–257.

Paul, R. (2008). Communication development and assessment. In K. Chawarska, A. Klin, & F. R. Volkmar (Eds.), *Autism spectrum disorders in infants and toddlers: Diagnosis, assessment, and treatment* (pp. 76–103). New York, NY: Guilford Press.

Pepper, J., & Weitzman, E. (2004). *It take two to talk: A practical guide for parents of children with language delay.* Toronto, ON, Canada: The Hanen Centre.

Prizant, B. M., Wetherby, A. M., Rubin, E., Laurent, A., & Rydell, P. (2006). *The SCERTS model: A comprehensive educational approach for children with autism spectrum disorders.* Baltimore, MD: Brookes.

Quill, K. (1995). *Teaching children with autism: Strategies to enhance communication and socialization.* Albany, NY: Delmar.

Quill, K. (2000). *Do watch listen say: Social and communication intervention for children with autism.* Baltimore, MD: Brookes.

Robins, D. L., Fein, D., Barton, M. L., & Green, J. A. (2009). The Modified Checklist for Autism in Toddlers: An initial study investigating the early detection of autism and pervasive developmental disorders. *Journal of Autism and Developmental Disorders, 31,* 131–144.

Siperstein, G., & Richards, E. (2004). *Promoting social success.* Baltimore, MD: Brookes.

Stone, W. L., Ousley, O. Y., Hepburn, S. L., Hogan, K. L., & Brown, C. S. (1999). Patterns of adaptive behavior in very young children with autism. *American Journal on Mental Retardation, 104*(2), 187–199.

Strain, P. S., Kerr, M. M., & Ragand, E. U. (1979). Effects of peer-mediated social initiations and prompting/reinforcement procedures of the social behavior of autistic children. *Journal of Autism and Developmental Disorders, 9,* 41–54.

Volkmar, F. R., & Wiesner, E. A. (2009). *A practical guide to autism: What every parent, family member, and teacher needs to know.* Hoboken, NJ: Wiley.

Weiss, M. J., & Harris, S. L. (2001). *Reaching out, joining in: Teaching social skills to young children with autism.* Bethesda, MD: Woodbine House.

Wetherby, A. M., & Woods, J. (2008). Developmental approaches to treatment. In K. Chawarska, A. Klin, & F. R. Volkmar (Eds.), *Autism spectrum disorders in infants and toddlers: Diagnosis, assessment, and treatment* (pp. 170–206). New York, NY: Guilford Press.

Wetherby, A. M., Yonclas, D. G., & Bryan, A. A. (1989). Communicative profiles of preschool children with handicaps: Implications for early identification. *Journal of Speech and Hearing Disorders, 54*(2), 148–158.

Whalen, C., & Schreibman, L. (2003). Joint attention training for children with autism using behavior modification procedures. *Journal of Child Psychology and Psychiatry and Allied Disciplines, 44*(3), 456–468.

Wheeler, M. (2004). *Toilet training for individuals with autism and related disorders: A comprehensive guide for parents and teachers.* Arlington, TX: Future Horizons.

Wiseman, N. D. (2006). *Could it be autism? A parent's guide to the first signs and next steps.* New York, NY: Broadway Books.

Wolfberg, P. J. (2003). *Peer play and the autism spectrum: The art of guiding children's socialization and imagination. Integrated play groups field manual.* Shawnee Mission, KS: Autism Asperger.

CHAPTER 8

School-Age Children

C hildren with ASDs face new challenges in primary and middle schools. Expectations change based on increased psychological and physical maturity with new prospects for independence and self-directed learning. Transitions within, and often between, schools pose other challenges. A range of options are available—from fully mainstreamed to full-time special ed. Many of the same issues and program considerations relevant to younger children (Chapter 7) continue to apply, although with more emphasis on academics.

By first grade there will start to be major divergences in learning for many children with ASDs. Some will have made substantial progress and others will continue to have significant challenges. We still do not know why some children seem to do better than others, even in what appear to be rather similar and appropriate programs. By about age 6, we can have a much better sense of the child's ability to communicate and his or her verbal abilities over the longer term. Also about this time traditional tests of intelligence begin to be more predictive (this is true for typically developing children as well), although gains and losses in IQ can occur subsequently. Inclusion with peers can be more problematic if difficulties with play, social interaction, unusual interests, and odd behaviors persist and if peers and teachers are unprepared. Probably not unexpected, some of the places where typically developing children have the greatest enjoyment of downtime (e.g., recess, physical education, the cafeteria) can be some of the most stressful for the child with an ASD.

DEVELOPMENT AND BEHAVIOR

As children with autism and Asperger's enter traditional school age they face new challenges. Academic demands increase substantially (and this continues over time). Fewer supports may be provided and the mainstream setting poses some challenges as well as opportunities, particularly in terms of social skills and organization issues. The push for increased independence becomes stronger. Adaptive skills present important challenges, as well as opportunities, for example, when the child can be helped by parents (and teachers) to apply academic skills in community settings. Behavior problems sometimes increase, particularly as the child enters adolescence. Physical management of a larger child may present issues for some parents. What once were seen as "cute" statements on the part of a preschool child can become a source of embarrassment to parents and siblings. In this chapter we'll review some of the challenges and opportunities for the school-age child with ASD.

Social Skills and Style

Research has shown us that difficulties in brain processing of social stimuli pose a major challenge for learning and social interaction. The multiple cues usually present in social interaction are a source of difficulty and affect other aspects of learning (Pierce & Schreibman, 1997). Various social styles are observed; the child may be very isolated and aloof or may be interested but inappropriate. Some children don't seek out others and may actively avoid social contact; they are often the most cognitively impaired. Some children are more passively accepting of social interaction and, for some of the more cognitively able and older individuals, they become "active but odd" (Wing & Gould, 1979), with clear social interest but eccentric styles of engagement, for example, the child is in your face talking about his collection of trains.

For typically developing children, emotional development has proceeded very quickly in pace with gains in social development. By the time they enter school they can reflect on their own feelings and experiences and those of others. Children are easily aware of what makes them, or other people, happy, anxious, or sad and use these feelings and observations to help regulate their behavior. Unfortunately, children with ASDs often have unique and rather idiosyncratic emotional development.

These problems are not necessarily unique to autism; for example, children with learning problems or Down syndrome may also have difficulties in this area. As a practical matter, parents and teachers frequently observe unusual emotional responses. This may take the form of highly idiosyncratic responses of pleasure or displeasure in response to what otherwise seem like trivial events. However, the child might have minimal reaction to what most of us would see as a major life event. When more cognitively able people with autism write about their experience of emotions, they often report feelings of anxiety, fear, and frustration (see Box 8.1). Children may say things (often things that are quite true) that are very hurtful of other people's feelings with little appreciation of this.

BOX 8.1 ANXIETY AND AUTISM: A FIRST-PERSON ACCOUNT

I was living in a world of daydreaming and fear revolving about myself. I had no care about human feelings or other people. I was afraid of everything! I was terrified to go in the water swimming (and of) loud noises; in the dark I had severe, repetitive nightmares and occasionally hearing electronic noises with nightmares. I would wake up so terrified and disoriented I wasn't able to find my way out of the room for a few minutes. It felt like I was being dragged to Hell. I was afraid of simple things such as going into the shower, getting my nails clipped, soap in my eyes, rides in the carnival.

Source: Reprinted with permission from Volkmar and Cohen (1985, p. 49).

There are also differences in the ways children on the autism spectrum show feelings; for example, expressions may be very idiosyncratic. It is likely that the constellation of social difficulties and communication problems, often coupled with some degree of cognitive processing problem, account for these difficulties. Differences in brain processes of social information may also have an impact; for example, differences in face processing may speak to a reduction in the importance of the face as a source of information. The fast pace and multimodal nature of usual social interaction pose further challenges. Some programs have been developed to train emotional recognition and improve responding, although it is not always clear how readily the results translate into real-world settings.

Play

As with other skills, an expected sequence of play usually emerges in typically developing children, going from simple object manipulation to increasingly complex imaginative play, so that by the time they enter school they are capable of very sophisticated and elaborate pretend play and engaging in games with others. Play activities help children learn and foster a range of skills, such as self-regulation, language, and memory. Given their multiple areas of challenge, it is not surprising that children with ASDs come into primary school settings without these skills. As younger children, they are less interested in play, particularly social play, and their play may consist of repetitive action rather than more dramatic imagination. By school-age, many children with ASDs will have acquired at least some play skills. These can be supported and expanded on in school programs.

Various techniques have been used to enhance play skills. These include teacher-directed and peer-focused efforts (we'll talk more about the use of peers shortly). Behavioral reinforcement techniques can be used to increase interactive play, for example, by reinforcing contact and a wider range and use of play materials. For some children, more basic skills, such as joint attention or basic language skills, need to be taught. Modeling play can be effective. For some students, providing scripts is helpful. Using the child's specific motivations (e.g., toys that are of greatest interest to the child) may help. Peers can be highly effective as play teachers, particularly if they are given some structure and guidance (Carter, Cushing, & Kennedy, 2009).

Language and Communication

Problems in communication are universal for children with ASDs. In the past, as many as 50% of children with strictly diagnosed autism were largely nonverbal at the time they entered school; with earlier detection and intervention, that number has now been significantly reduced—maybe to 30%. As with other areas, the range of levels of function is broad. Some students may come into first grade with minimal language. Others—those with Asperger's—may have amazing vocabularies but still have problems with communication. Minimally verbal students may have problems with some of the basic social aspects of communication, for example, joint attention or understanding simple gestures. It is clear that having at least some language by the time of school entry is a significant indicator of better prognosis. That being said, even in students with minimal language, further gains are possible and desirable. In general, improved language levels will strongly relate to better social skills, fewer behavior problems, and ultimately more personal independence and self-sufficiency.

Verbal children may have language that is unusual in various ways. These include a number of different problems, including echolalia, pronoun reversals, unusual speech intonation and volume (what speech pathologists call *register*), and problems in social language use. Echolalia, the repetition of speech, is seen in typically developing very young children. It is common for verbal individuals with ASDs but is not always seen. It can be immediate (repeating something just heard or said) or remote (something said days, weeks, or months ago—including on TV or radio). Early on in the history of autism, echolalia was viewed as something bad and something to be eliminated. Several different lines of work have changed this view. As noted, normally developing infants echo language as they are starting to speak, and many different, adaptive functions of echoing have been identified, for example, in trying to keep a conversation going or to remember something. Echolalia is also viewed now as one manifestation of a more general problem in learning, with a tendency for many children with ASDs to learn language in whole chunks rather than in terms of single words. As children with ASDs learn more complex language, echolalia tends to decrease. An intermediate step in this process occurs when the child starts to transform some part of the echoed speech, that is, changing it a bit so it is not totally echoed (this is termed *mitigated echolalia*) and is a sign that the child's language is progressing.

Problems with pronoun use were first noted by Kanner in his original description of autism. Errors in use of personal pronouns (particularly I-you pronoun reversal) have long been described as characteristic of verbal children with ASDs. Among typically developing children, pronoun use becomes reasonably well established by age 2 to 3. Pronouns are complicated because the nature of the pronoun changes depending on context (e.g., if I have a red pen, it is *my* red pen, but if I give it to Mary, it is *her* red pen). The tendency to echo also may contribute to pronoun problems; for example, if the child repeats the last pronoun heard, it will often be incorrect. Pronoun problems may be more frequent in autism than in Asperger's. When pronoun problems occur, they can be a source of confusion—sometimes because the child's language otherwise seems well organized.

Difficulties with prosody, the musical aspect of speech and register, are also frequent in more-able, verbal children with ASDs. Prosody may be quite impaired, so the child talks in a robot-like, or monotonic, voice. Prosody helps in conversation by indicating, among other things, areas of special importance and emphasis. In ASDs, there may be some inflection of speech, but the inflection pattern may not correspond to ordinary use (e.g., atypical words are inflected). Problems in register mean that in contrast to most of us, who use hundreds of different voice volumes, the child with an ASD has only one—often loud. Prosody has been the focus of relatively little study, but there is limited research available, for example, the work of our colleague Rhea Paul (Paul, Augustyn, Klin, & Volkmar, 2005).

Difficulties in the social use of language, termed *pragmatics,* are areas of great difficulty for more cognitively able students with ASDs. These problems include difficulties with carrying on a conversation, for example, only wanting to talk about one thing and not allowing the conversational partner a turn. Some of the difficulties may reflect the social problem of putting oneself in the other person's place (e.g., in starting a conversation in the middle as opposed to the beginning). A particular area of difficulty results from the subtle combinations of language features, such as discrepancies between word use and tone, as in sarcasm. Humor, irony, ambiguous language, and figurative language may pose great obstacles to communication. Myles, Trautman, and Schelvan (2004) provide a very helpful list of figurative speech phrases and idioms that can be explicitly taught. Seemingly simple tasks that involve politeness may be a problem. For example, a man with autism who once worked for one of us doing copying was left a paper with a yellow note on top asking him if he could make three copies; the paper was returned with the word *yes* written on the note—but no copies.

A final area of challenge can be in the ability of the child to generate narrative language, that is, tell a story. Typically, a story will have a beginning, middle, and end. There are some basic—culturally determined—rules (e.g., about characters, plot, feeling, etc.). Generating narratives can be an area of challenge for the child with ASD. If you find a book with pictures (but no words) and ask the child with an ASD to tell the story, he or she may focus on only one element and not get the big picture. The significance of difficulties in this area relates, among other things, to the importance of people being able to generate their own internal narratives, for example, to recall the events of the day and plan and organize their lives. These difficulties can be seen in older and more-able children as they struggle in English class with novels or short stories that focus on feelings and nuances of communication and interaction with less emphasis on generation of facts. Various approaches can be used to help children, including explicit focus on identification of relevant plot and narrative aspects, for instance, *who* is involved, *where* are they, *what* are they doing, *when* are they doing it, and *why* are they doing it? Some computer resources devoted to storytelling and narrative (e.g., the Storybook Weaver program) can be used for children to work on developing their own narrative abilities.

Different strategies can be used to facilitate communication in children with ASDs. For children with limited verbal language, an emphasis on communication, broadly defined, is indicated. Behavioral techniques can be used to increase word use. As discussed previously, for children with limited or no words, picture or object exchange or other augmentative communication aids may be helpful. For the verbal child with an ASD, a host of intervention techniques are available and must be tailored to the specific needs of the child. Often, there is an early emphasis on vocabulary building, but it is important not to neglect issues of generalization and developing more complex language. For the most cognitively able students, particularly those with Asperger's, the child may have a tremendous vocabulary but rather poor communication skills. The child's speech may be oddly inflected and pedantic with a rather "professorial" aspect (a major problem for peers). For this group, there should be a strong emphasis on the explicit teaching of conversational rules, with many opportunities for practice and critique coupled with a strong social skills–acquisition program. Language and social skills are intimately related. Often, but not always, gains in both areas proceed in tandem. For some children, even major gains in language abilities may not be associated with similar social gains, such as the ability to put oneself in the other person's place (theory of mind). Poor social judgment coupled with **rigidity** and **resistance to change** and an emphasis on telling the truth can lead to some complicated situations. Fortunately, when given appropriate supports, children with ASDs can become more communicative, and often teachers and parents discover that the child has a lot to say.

SENSORY AND BEHAVIORAL ISSUES

Stereotyped and repetitive behaviors are frequent in school-aged children. These tend to be somewhat more common in students with lower levels of cognitive ability. For more-able children, the unusual behaviors may take the form of intense, often unusual interests or preoccupations; for instance, the child may be fixated on the weather channel or train, bus, or TV schedules. These unusual behaviors may also be observed along with unusual sensory responses.

Observations of children over time often reveal some change. For example, early repetitive behavior may start in a rather simple fashion but come to be much more complicated. Unusual rigidity and difficulties dealing with new situations are common. Some studies have suggested that these unusual behaviors, particularly the more common stereotyped movements, become less common as children move into adolescence, although some individuals will retain these into adulthood. Occasionally, the rigidity and repetitive nature of some of the behaviors exhibited is taken to suggest the presence of obsessive-compulsive disorder. However, the more traditional stereotyped movements seen in children with autism are usually less complex than those of obsessive-compulsive disorder. For more cognitively able children, another differentiation is that children with obsessive- compulsive disorder do not usually *like* their preoccupation—that is, they would like *not* to be so preoccupied; this is not the same in more-able children with Asperger's, who usually like their special interest.

It is important to note that unusual sensory responses and stereotyped behaviors are seen in a range of developmental disorders, including intellectual disability (see Chapter 3). When they are present, however, they can present significant obstacles for intervention. Behavioral methods (Chapter 10) and drug treatments (Chapter 11) can be used very effectively. As with other areas, there is always a need to balance potential benefits and risks. Unusual behaviors and sensory responses that interfere with the child's learning are ones that appropriately might be targeted either by medication or behavioral intervention. There is some evidence that, when carefully done, these interventions can significantly enhance the child's learning.

GENDER DIFFERENCES

More boys than girls usually have autism and ASDs—with rates three to four times higher in boys. Among individuals with Asperger's disorder, the rate may be much higher—with boys outnumbering girls 20 or more to 1. This has, unfortunately, meant that information on girls with ASDs is generally rather limited. For example, researchers have sometimes excluded girls from participation in research studies. There are some suggestions of differences in presentation. For girls with autism, as a group, there are often more severe cognitive problems. When girls with autism or ASDs are higher functioning, there are some suggestions of differences in how they present; for example, girls in general may be more concerned about the impression they make on peers. Girls with autism and Asperger's may have even more trouble fitting in socially than boys. However, they may have fewer behavior problems and the degree of the social difficulties may be somewhat less. By middle school, girls with ASDs may be more anxious than boys and stressed by social demands. However, girls may also have stronger play and communication skills and may be less prone to attentional problems than boys (Nichols, Moravick, & Tetenbaum, 2009). They also may face special challenges in terms of personal safety and sexuality. It is important that parents and teachers think about the special problems that girls with ASDs face. Various theories have tried to account for differences between boys and girls. British researcher Simon Baron-Cohen (2003) has suggested that perhaps these differences relate to sex differences in the brain. However, some of the differences in clinical presentation of autism and Asperger's in girls may relate to more general sex differences. Regardless of its cause, the fact that girls less commonly have ASD makes for some challenges in school programs; for example, girls in special ed class settings are likely to be significantly outnumbered by boys, and opportunities for interaction with other, typically developing girls may be limited.

SCHOOL-RELATED ISSUES

School presents many challenges for the child with an ASD. These include the complicated learning environment as well as the social-communication, emotional, and academic challenges intrinsic to the school experience. Differences in response to situations and contexts become much more important, and the child has, for the first time, to become much more differentiated in his or her behavior and responses. There are many more expectations for self-directed learning, and organization usually comes from within the child as opposed to external structure. Problems with social interaction and communication can have a negative impact on peer interaction. For the more cognitively able student, this may be combined with a growing awareness of being isolated and feeling different.

Some students with ASDs will do well academically, particularly in more "fact-based" areas and most particularly those in which they have a special interest or ability. Other children will have variable kinds and degrees of learning difficulties. Some children reach school-age but are nonverbal or largely nonverbal, and, accordingly, traditional academic subjects hold little interest for them. In such cases, increasing communication skills and participating in structured learning situations are relevant goals.

Teachers and others often take children's language skill as a measure of their overall ability; for children who are typically developing, this is often reasonable. However, for children with ASDs, there are some pitfalls. Children with more classical autism presentations may have much less well-developed verbal than nonverbal abilities, and there is a danger that schools will program *only* to the lower verbal skills. Conversely, students with Asperger's may have much better verbal skills but areas of great difficulty with other kinds of tasks; therefore, teachers may not realize the severity of the social problems in this group. It must be emphasized that appropriate supports be provided given the individual's specific needs. *Reaching and Teaching the Child with Autism Spectrum Disorder* by Mackenzie (2008) discusses these issues in some detail.

ACADEMICS AND CURRICULUM

Several considerations arise in thinking about objectives for the academic program. Students with ASDs present teachers with some unusual challenges. It is important that the objectives spelled out for students in their individualized education plan (IEP) and in their classroom settings be developmentally appropriate. These objectives also have to be realistically placed within the broader context of the curriculum. What is appropriate will vary considerably from child to child. Sometimes the regular program, often with some modification, may meet the child's needs. At other times, a smaller teaching setting will be more helpful. As we have noted, the profiles of relative strengths and weakness can and will vary considerably from one child to another; accordingly, there is not a simple one-size-fits-all approach (Tsatsanis, 2004). Although cognitive profiles are of some help in thinking about the most appropriate teaching strategies and goals, other issues—for example, behavior problems, social difficulties, sensory issues, and difficulties with transitions and change—may also need to be considered. Difficulties with attention and organization, combined with a lack of social attention, pose other problems. When medications are given to help with associated problems, side effects can complicate teaching. The age of the student may also be relevant; for instance, activities or materials that are appropriate for much younger children might attract the interest of the child with an ASD, but there is a risk of typical peers reacting negatively.

Goals targeted will usually include social interaction skills and expanding communication, as well as more traditional academic goals (see Kluth, 2003, for a discussion of teaching procedures and strategies). Fostering other skills, such as leisure time and adaptive skills, is also important. Some of the general areas that are addressed in the IEP for a school-aged child are listed in Box 8.2. Keep in mind that this is a general list and the IEP must be tailored to the individual student; also keep in mind, as we've discussed, that the IEP needs to strike a sensible balance—having some short-, medium-, and longer-term (vision) goals along with objective data to monitor progress. Continued communication with parents is important.

BOX 8.2 AREAS TO CONSIDER ADDRESSING IN THE IEP FOR SCHOOL-AGE CHILD

Social Skills and Social Difficulties
- Social skills teaching methods
- Understanding social cues and emotions
- Appropriate social responding, initiation
- Explicit teaching regarding social problem-solving
- Teaching social routines

Increase Self-Awareness and Self-Advocacy
- Increasing awareness of feelings and emotions
- Using appropriate strategies for anxiety and problem situations
- Teach self-advocacy and strategies for seeking assistance
- Learning when to ask for help—for example, even learning a sign for "help" can substantially reduce behavior problems

Communication and Language Skills

- Using augmentative communication if appropriate
- Increasing complexity of spoken and written communication
- Understanding social language: nonverbal cues, prosody, voice volume
- Conversational and pragmatic skills
- Starting and stopping a conversation
- Responding to cues
- Learning figurative and nonliteral language

Organizational Skills

- Visual, written organizers such as schedules, lists, color codes
- Working independently for longer periods
- Management of materials and tasks (including self-correction)
- Keyboarding (as appropriate) and computer resources
- Use computer and online resources to help with organization

Behavioral and Sensory Issues

- Address specific behavior problems or sensory issues
- Increase flexibility and ability to deal with transitions
- Use OT supports to address sensory problems

Source: Reprinted with permission from Volkmar and Wiesner (2009, pp. 243–244).

There are a number of ways to support learning. These must be tailored to the needs of the individual student. They can range from simple organizational aids (written or visual schedules) to much more technologically sophisticated procedures (computers, personal digital assistants, text-to-speech programs, etc.). For some students, there is a genuine pull toward computer-based technology—it is predictable and rule governed, the information load can be tailored to the student, and it can combine auditory and visual information in very interesting ways. Moore (2002) makes a number of suggestions for assisting with organizational issues; for example, color coding can help all students in the classroom. Technological supports have become increasingly sophisticated; the speech pathologist and occupational therapist can often be helpful in thinking about use of assistive technologies (see Chapter 6). Computer-assisted instruction can be helpful in a host of ways. Students who have difficulty in writing may profit from the use of organization software (e.g., Kidspiration, www .inspiration.com), and if the child can use a laptop, the potential for other aids (spelling and grammar checking) is also present. For some students, speech recognition software may be useful; this turns the student's spoken words into text and may be particularly helpful for students with fine motor problems. In thinking about such systems, any difficulties the student has with the flow of speech should be considered; for example, some systems can accommodate students whose speech is slower because of articulation problems. The occupational therapist may be helpful in thinking about approaches to writing problems and a range of alternatives from more sophisticated computer programs to much simpler interventions, such as using a slant board to assist in handwriting (Myles, 2005). In this regard, it is important to note that the value of some of the simplest things—visual schedules, preteaching, use of lists and checklists, charts, and so forth—should not be underestimated. Technology is certainly not a replacement for effective instruction.

Whenever possible the special interests and motivations of the student with an ASD should be used; Kluth and Schwarz (2008) give some good examples of this. Often, considerable "incidental" teaching can occur in the topic of special interest or fascination. This isn't always easy to do, but even when it isn't, giving the student the opportunity to spend some time on an area of special interest can be used as a reward and motivator. Challenges for children with ASDs—particularly those whose verbal skills are less advanced than nonverbal and other abilities—include difficulties in auditory processing. Spoken language is fast-paced and ephemeral (in contrast to pictures and the written word). Teachers should plan, in such situations, to give extra time for processing, provide relevant visual supports (outlines, checklists), and keep their language simple and direct (Myles & Adreon, 2001). For more cognitively able students who have trouble with the pace of the class, the use of written notes (e.g., from another student) or even tape recordings of class lectures and discussion may be very helpful. Moore (2002) has some very useful suggestions, including various possibilities for assisting students with note-taking strategies. Scott, Clark, and Brady (2000) give an excellent review of a range of educational supports.

Teachers should also be aware that although small groups can be good learning environments for students with ASDs, group work needs to be carefully monitored. The student with an ASD will often need support ahead of time, such as reviewing key concepts, terms, and goals, with written or visual supports available if needed as well. First and foremost, the teacher and then other students (we hope modeling the teacher's behavior) should show consideration and respect for the student with an ASD; for example, if the student makes an off-topic comment, the teacher can help redirect the conversation to the topic at hand. We'll talk more about ways to help peers shortly.

Some children on the autism spectrum have an early—and sometimes very precocious—interest in iconic symbols, including letters and numbers. Some of these children become early readers, occasionally even what has been termed *hyperlexic* readers (very advanced reading skills for the child's chronological age). In contrast to spoken language, written language is static and, for many children, much easier to master. As previously noted, it is important for teachers and parents to understand that reading decoding (literally sounding out words) may be much higher—misleadingly higher—than the child's actual understanding.

Several steps can be taken to encourage literacy. These include availability of books and word processing programs, giving children time for reading, and encouraging reading and related literacy skills. Some of the available computer programs (e.g., Living Books) can be highly motivating to students. The reading program should be sure to include an emphasis on strengthening comprehension skills. It is important that teachers keep in mind the possibility that students with ASDs will do well with comprehension of basic facts but may miss other key aspects of stories relating to emotions, intentions, and the like. For testing purposes, teachers may wish to consider ways to minimize the burden of additional language processing; for example, as opposed to open-ended questions, multiple choice, yes-no, and fill-in-the-blank questions may more accurately reflect the student's ability to understand the information conveyed.

Spelling can be quite challenging for students with ASDs. This is particularly true for the English language, which borrows heavily from other languages and has a complex set of rules. Students can use a range of different strategies, and it is important to understand the sources of errors in an attempt to provide remediation (Attwood, 1998). Computers can be used to help teach and, when appropriate, to help students spell-check their work. Peer tutoring can also be used. Sometimes spelling or some other area may be such a difficult homework task that it becomes all-consuming, and the student with ASD is spending all his homework time stuck on it, for example, working on spelling to the exclusion of everything else. When this happens, modification to the rules can be helpful, such as using a visual timer to give the student a set amount of time to focus on spelling—at the end of the time, he is done regardless of where he is on the spelling list. Myles and Adreon (2001) provide an excellent discussion of homework-related issues.

Mathematical abilities are highly variable. Basic math concepts may present tremendous challenges for some students, and other students may be years ahead of their classmates. Some individuals can engage in prodigious savant skills (e.g., calendar calculation) (Thioux, Stark, Klaiman, & Schultz, 2006). Others are interested in certain types of equations or areas of mathematics. Visual cues and multisensory approaches (e.g., TouchMath) may be helpful. Some children are very good at understanding the basic math facts because of their strengths in rote memorization; the same students may not have nearly as good an understanding of the underlying principles. Peer tutoring and use of concrete materials (e.g., money) can be helpful. As with other skills, generalization is important.

TEACHING PROCEDURES AND PROGRAMS

We discuss specific teaching procedures extensively in Chapter 6 and listed some of the many potential resources and programs teachers can appropriately use in work with children on the autism spectrum. These programs have many areas of similarities and some areas of difference. Most are strongly behaviorally based using procedures such as discrete trial and pivotal response training and work with teaching functional routines. Others have a stronger developmental component in which following the child's motivation becomes more important. It is important that the curriculum be appropriate to the child's level of ability, considering the child's developmental levels and chronological age, and, to the extent possible, specific interests and motivations. Curricular materials and teaching strategies need to be carefully considered. Pivotal response procedures can, for example, be used for various purposes. There are advantages to using various strategies and teaching materials approaches, for example, for enhancing generalization of skills (see Arick, Krug, Fullerton, Loos, & Falco, 2005, for a discussion). For school-aged children, sensory issues may need to be addressed to enhance learning. Teaching approaches (e.g., use of visual materials, provision of organization aids, and supports) need to be adapted for the individual student. As children progress through school, academic demands become more challenging, with greater expectations in abstract thinking and self-organization. This can lead to attentional and behavioral difficulties, and teachers should be careful to monitor students to be sure that what appears to be a lack of attention does not, in fact, reflect greater cognitive challenge; accordingly, periodic assessment should be accomplished.

As noted in Chapter 6, various models of instruction and curricula have been developed. For example, the Support and Treatment for Autism and Related Disorders (STAR) program provides a range of training and teaching materials useful in developing individualized behavioral treatment programs for children and their families. It makes use of a number of different methods (e.g., discrete trial, pivotal response training, picture exchange, verbal behavior, and other behavioral procedures). The website (www.starautismprogram.com) provides additional information and links to training and other materials, including DVDs. This program has the great advantage of providing detailed lesson plans along with teaching materials and data systems, including curriculum-based assessments in a number of relevant areas such as functional routines, receptive and expressive language, and so forth. The data system helps monitor progress and can be used to help document progress as specified in the IEP. Other programs may use the Treatment and Education of Autistic and Related Communication Handicapped Children (TEACCH) method. This approach, based at the University of North Carolina at Chapel Hill, was begun by Eric Schopler and continues under the direction of the Gary Mesibov. The approach draws on a number of different methodologies in development of individualized programs for students and their families. It includes careful attention to teaching methods, the structure of the learning environment, and use of visual and other supports in teaching. Materials and information on training are provided on the TEACCH website (www.teacch.com). Some excellent summaries of the range of behavioral and curriculum approaches useful to teachers are available (e.g., Hall, 2008).

Programs such as TEACCH emphasize the importance of careful consideration of the classroom and classroom structure for learning. For example, placement of the child with an ASD at the front of the class (to be near the teacher) may be appropriate. Classroom rules, schedules, and so forth can be prominently displayed at the front of the room. Moore (2002) makes a number of suggestions for helping the child with Asperger's syndrome, and many of these would apply to other students on the autism spectrum as well. Attention to physical aspects of the classroom environment may reveal specific factors or distracters that need to be addressed, for example, moving the child to an area where he has an opportunity for reduced exposure to extraneous stimuli. For children who must move from one classroom to another, the possibility of moving just before the bell rings may be helpful. Use of visual supports and clear directions is also helpful. Instructions should be considered relative to the child's language level. For students—particularly those with Asperger's—who have handwriting problems, or for students whose anxiety interferes, modified test taking may be appropriate; for example, taking a test in the library or a quiet area or using a different format (oral versus written examination) or doing the test in several shorter periods can be considered. Depending on the material changes in format of the test (e.g., true-false or multiple choice), there may be better choices for assessing knowledge than open-ended tests (see Moore, 2002). Grades can sometimes be a source of anxiety, and the teacher and student can often work together to develop a straightforward way of giving feedback with explicit guidelines about how grades are calculated.

Mainstreaming and Peer Preparation

Students with ASDs are increasingly included in mainstream settings. Early diagnosis and more intensive intervention have resulted in many children with ASDs being ready to be fully included by the time they reach first grade. For others, even the opportunity to spend part of the day in a mainstream setting can provide important opportunities for positive peer interaction and academic success (see Handleman, Harris, & Martins, 2005, for a detailed discussion, and Myles, 2005, for strategies specific to students with Asperger's syndrome).

Various terms are used, more or less interchangeably to describe mainstream educational opportunities (e.g., *inclusive classrooms, inclusion,* or *integration*). Various models of mainstreaming have been developed. For example, at times children, particularly younger children, may be in a special ed classroom where there are some typically developing peers. In general, the inclusion refers to any time the child with an ASD is with typically developing peers within school. Many variations in inclusion are possible. The child with an ASD may be included in some classes and not others. Specific strategies can be used in particular situations; for example, the peer-assisted learning strategies (PALS) method has been used in work on math and reading (see Utley & Mortweek, 1997). The most cognitively able students with ASDs (e.g., those with Asperger's) may be most readily included in academic classes, and special services can be provided at less structured times when the child is more likely to have difficulty (e.g., lunch, recess, PE). In some instances, peer buddy systems and other supports may be used appropriately at such times to support inclusion of the child with an ASD. Networks of support can be created in several ways, such as using the **Circle of Friends** approach (Schlieder, 2007). A range of peer support procedures is available (see Carter et al., 2009). Adaptive PE can also be helpful.

For children with ASDs who have greater cognitive and behavioral challenges, inclusion may occur only in very specific contexts in which high levels of adult support can be provided. Although many mainstream procedures have been based on work with younger children, there has been an increasing focus on school-aged children, and it is clear that the typically developing peer can be a wonderful model for the school-aged child with an ASD. Indeed, peers can be highly effective teachers and supporters, although some degree of training and support is needed if peers are to be effective; that is, just having the child with an ASD in the classroom is not of itself sufficient (Carter et al., 2009). Several programs have used typical peers of elementary or junior high school–age to increase social contacts and peer relationships (e.g., Haring & Breen, 1992; Morrison, Kamps, Garcia, & Parker, 2001). In one study, Pierce and Schreibman (1997) were able to train elementary school–aged peers in a modified version of pivotal response training (PRT) with notable success.

Various considerations go into selecting peers to work with the child with an ASD, such as the level of disability that the child with an ASD exhibits, the motivation and interest of the typical peer, the degree of supervision and support that the typical peer needs, and so forth. Carter and colleagues (2009) have summarized some of the pros and cons of different approaches for recruiting peers into programs, such as identification of peers to be mentors, teacher recommendations, classroom announcements, and so forth. Peers may need some minimal training but they may benefit from this work. Peers can be assigned as peer buddies or can participate in social skills groups. For younger and less socially advanced students with ASDs, preteaching, social scripts, and other supports may be of help. Another approach has used videotape review of social interaction with typical peers for teaching social skills (Thiemann & Goldstein, 2009). There are many different activities that can incorporate peer support, from walking with the student from one class to another to helping with homework, reviewing lessons and course content, sharing materials, and helping with communication, to name just a few (see Carter et al., 2009).

Peer supports can be particularly helpful at what are some of the most challenging times of the day for students with ASDs—notably, lunch, recess, transitions from one classroom to another, and PE. PE can be particularly challenging for students with ASDs; for example, changing clothes can take longer than for other students; the social back-and-forth in the locker room may be very confusing; and team sports can be very challenging, given the combination of organizational, motor, and social skill requirements. Adaptive PE can be used when appropriate with specially trained teachers who work with students in smaller settings.

Teachers and school staff members should also keep in mind the more general importance of providing information to the entire student body about disabilities. This can take a more general and generic approach in the beginning, for example, encouraging discussion of ways people cope with difficulties and disabilities, having students participate in activities that help them understand the challenges disabilities present, and using videotapes and a class or school discussion section to present information and encourage an atmosphere of mutual tolerance and respect. Various specific resources relevant to autism, Asperger's, and related disorders are now available, including some excellent videos and children's books. All students will know someone with a disability (even if it is as minor a disability as wearing glasses). We have fond memories of attending one of our daughter's second-grade classes and doing an in-service on disability in general, including having children practice how it feels to be a child with vision impairment (with a blindfold on and a cane to try to get around), using a wheelchair, or using crutches. Box 8.3 provides some good sources of information about peer help.

BOX 8.3 PEER INFORMATION AND RESOURCES

Amenta, C. A. (1992). *Russell is extra special: A book about autism for children.* New York, NY: Magination Press.

Cook, J., & Hartman, C. (2008). *My mouth is a volcano!.* Chattanooga, TN: National Center for Youth Issues.

Donlon, L. (2007). *The other kid: A draw it out guidebook for kids dealing with a special needs sibling.* Coral Springs, FL: Llumina Press.

Gosselin, K. (2002). *Taking seizure disorders to school: A story about epilepsy.* Hawthorne, NY: JayJo Books.

Hoopmann, K. (2001a). *Blue bottle mystery: An Asperger adventure.* Philadelphia, PA: Jessica Kingsley.

Hoopmann, K. (2001b). *Of mice and aliens: An Asperger adventure.* Philadelphia, PA: Jessica Kingsley.

Hoopmann, K. (2002). *Lisa and the lacemaker: An Asperger adventure.* Philadelphia, PA: Jessica Kingsley.

Hoopmann, K. (2003). *Haze.* Philadelphia, PA: Jessica Kingsley.

Keating-Velasco, J. L. (2007). *A is for autism, F is for friend: A kid's book for making friends with a child who has autism.* Shawnee Mission, KS: Autism Asperger.

Source: Reprinted with permission from Volkmar and Wiesner (2009, pp. 250–251).

In addition to peer preparation, the classroom teacher will benefit from training in methods to support inclusion. The teacher needs to consider the role of the peers, the nature of the activities, support for the peers, and the needs of the child with an ASD. Picking activities that are fun and motivating will increase the interests of typical peers and the student with an ASD. The teacher should also consider the physical arrangements of the room and have plans in place, in advance, for dealing with behavioral issues. In general, the goal should be for the teacher to be a background presence and facilitator once activities are under way with, as much as possible, interaction and feedback coming from the students interacting with each other. It must be emphasized that peers need preparation and support, particularly in the early phases of the process.

Discussion of peer and teacher support strategies also raises an important issue: providing enough but not too much support. Readily available supports, such as peers, are much less intrusive and often more effective than other supports (e.g., paraprofessionals). Aides and other paraprofessionals have an important role but, as with students and teachers, they need preparation for their role. They are present in the classroom to facilitate the accommodation of the student(s) with special needs but must maintain a careful balance, for example, in encouraging peer interaction and increasing levels of autonomy and independence for the student with ASD. Having a paraprofessional who sticks like glue to the student with an ASD can be off-putting to peers. They should always keep in mind the overall goal of fostering classroom inclusiveness and participation and think about how their intervention can help the student become more independent. There are some good books written specifically for the child with an ASD that may be helpful as well (see Box 8.4).

BOX 8.4 INFORMATION FOR CHILDREN WITH ASDS

Cook, J., & Hartman, C. (2008). *My mouth is a volcano!* Chattanooga, TN: National Center for Youth Issues.

Coulter Video: www.coultervideo.com/Coulter

Larson, E. M. (2006). *I am utterly unique: Celebrating the strengths of children with Asperger syndrome and high-functioning autism.* Shawnee Mission, KS: Autism Asperger.

Lears, L. (2002). *Becky the brave: A story about epilepsy.* Morton Grove, IL: Albert Whitman.

Ludwig, T., & Manning, M. J. (2006). *Sorry!* Berkeley, CA: Tricycle Press.

Naylor, P. R. (1994). *King of the playground.* New York, NY: Aladdin Paperbacks.

Strachan, J., & Schnurr, R. G. (1999). *Asperger's huh? A child's perspective.* Gloucester, ON, Canada: Anisor Publishing.

Source: Reprinted with permission from Volkmar and Wiesner (2009, pp. 243–244).

BULLYING AND TEASING

Unfortunately, one of the issues that comes about with exposing children on the autism spectrum to typically developing peers is the potential for teasing or bullying to occur. Although the data on this topic are in some ways limited, it is fairly clear that children with ASDs—probably particularly those with Asperger's and high-functioning autism—are more likely to be bullied than their typically developing peers. The higher-functioning individuals with ASDs are also, unfortunately, the ones who have greater potential for subsequent problems with self-esteem given their higher cognitive abilities. Given that these are the individuals most likely to be mainstreamed, there clearly is potential for significant trouble.

Some of the factors that predispose children with ASDs to teasing and bullying include their difficulties in reading social cues and in dealing with the fast pace of social interaction. Unusual interests may make them stand out from peers and be perceived as profoundly uncool. Language issues may be a problem—difficulties with more sophisticated language and figures of speech may lead to confusion. The child with an ASD may say something not intended to be funny and feels bad when laughed at.

Bullying can be verbal or physical. It can also be either very overt or much more subtle, for example, involving exclusion or isolation from a group. It can take the form of malicious gossip. There can sometimes be a fine line in deciding what bullying is or isn't (e.g., the teacher who uses sarcasm or ridicule). Bullying can be an isolated instance but can also be ongoing and frequent. As Heinrichs (2003) notes, bullying types vary with the developmental level of the child so that younger children are more likely to exhibit physical or verbal aggression toward same-sex peers, whereas in early adolescence social and other kinds of bullying become more common and affect same-sex and opposite-sex peers.

Factors that seem to increase the potential for being bullied include social isolation and social awkwardness. Difficulties with language use in general and social language use (pragmatics) in particular are also risk factors. Individuals with ASDs have trouble understanding more sophisticated forms of humor and this, along with idiosyncratic communication styles, contributes to risk for being bullied. Social eccentricity, social isolation, and what appears to be self-centeredness likely also contribute to this problem. One study (Little, 2002) found that children with Asperger's or the

nonverbal learning disability (NLD) profile had a fourfold increase in bullying. Bullying leads to stress and symptoms of stress. Bullying may also precipitate aggression as well as depression and symptoms of anxiety. In his original description of the condition that now bears his name, Hans Asperger commented on the potential for these problems.

Although definitions of bullying vary somewhat, they almost all involve some sense of one student's having power over another one. As Attwood (2008) notes, bullying is more likely to occur in situations when adults are not closely monitoring things (e.g., hallways, recess, sports arenas, or gyms). Bullying can also happen outside of school, for example, on the neighborhood playground or even with siblings. As noted, teachers and other adults in authority can sometimes use sarcasm to the point that this becomes bullying. Attwood (2008) also comments on a problem that we've seen fairly frequently—overly trusting children on the autism spectrum can be set up by other students who use the child's desire for friendship and acceptance as a path to getting them to engage in inappropriate behaviors, for example, the boy who pulls the fire alarm on a dare at the suggestion of a peer who says he's "chicken" otherwise.

Unfortunately, some of the same problems that contribute to bullying in the first place also make it less likely that the more-able child with an ASD will report the bullying. The child may be afraid of retaliation or payback, he may not understand the motivation of the bullying, and he doesn't often think about asking adults for help. As a result, sometimes teacher and parent awareness of bullying emerges only when the child comes into treatment for symptoms of anxiety or depression (Attwood, 2008). Sometimes children will start having major meltdowns over seemingly trivial things, and it may emerge that the child has been under considerable stress because of bullying. It is important for parents and teachers to be alert for signs of possible bullying. It is also important that the school environment be one that discourages bullying.

Preventing bullying requires a broad-based approach with staff members and teacher training, explicit discussion and class rules against bullying, monitoring and intervention when bullying occurs, and promotion of social competence for all involved (including the bully). Zero tolerance of bullying might seem to be a good solution, but it carries its own problems; for example, it potentially discourages reporting (Heinrichs, 2003). Having an explicit discussion with all students and an established school code of conduct can be helpful. Explicit teaching on how to get help is important (for the victim and observer). An effective bullying-prevention program will also include sensible strategies for helping students being bullied and those who bully (sometimes there is overlap of the two groups). Finally, as Heinrichs points out, it is important to help the student with an ASD understand the differences between normal peer conflicts and bullying. These clarifications can be particularly helpful to more-able students with ASDs who have trouble disentangling the normal ups and downs of social relationships from bullying. Various resources to prevent and deal with bullying are provided by Heinrichs (2003) and Dubin and Carley (2007).

Summary

In this chapter we've talked about some of the issues that affect school-age children and their families. In some ways this age group is the one we know the most about, at least in terms of research. There are many opportunities for positive growth and behavior change in this age group. However, behavioral management issues can also become much more important. Parents and teachers should pay attention to academic and nonacademic skills. There is the potential for children to learn skills in isolation, and the family has a critically important role in helping children learn to generalize skills. Parents and teachers should also be alert to the potential for problems with bullying in this age group.

REFERENCES

Arick, J. R., Krug, D. A., Fullerton, A., Loos, L., & Falco, R. (2005). School-based programs. In F. Volkmar, A. Klin, R. Paul, & D. J. Cohen (Eds.), *Handbook of autism and pervasive developmental disorders* (3rd ed., Vol. 2, pp. 1003–1028). New York: Wiley.

Attwood, T. (1998). *Asperger's syndrome: A guide for parents and professionals.* London, UK: Jessica Kingsley.

Attwood, T. (2008). *The complete guide to Asperger's syndrome.* London, UK: Jessica Kingsley.

Baron-Cohen, S. (2003). *The essential difference: Male and female brains and the truth about autism.* New York, NY: Basic Books.

Carter, E. W., Cushing, L. S., & Kennedy, C. H. (2009). *Peer support strategies for improving all student's social lives and learning.* Baltimore, MD: Brookes.

Dubin, N., & Carley, M. J. (2007). *Asperger syndrome and bullying: Strategies and solutions.* London, UK: Jessica Kingsley.

Hall, L. J. (2008). *Autism spectrum disorders: From theory to practice.* Upper Saddle River, NJ: Prentice Hall.

Handleman, J. S., Harris, S. L., & Martins, M. (2005). Helping children with autism enter the mainstream. In F. Volkmar, A. Klin, R. Paul, & D. J. Cohen (Eds.), *Handbook of autism and pervasive developmental disorders* (3rd ed., Vol. 2, pp. 1029–1042). New York: Wiley.

Haring, T. G., & Breen, C. G. (1992). A peer-mediated social network intervention to enhance the social integration of persons with moderate and severe disabilities. *Journal of Applied Behavior Analysis, 25,* 319–333.

Heinrichs, R. (2003). *Perfect targets: Asperger syndrome and bullying—practical solutions for surviving the social world.* Shawnee Mission, KS: Autism Asperger.

Kluth, P. (2003). *You're going to love this kid: Teaching students with autism in the inclusive classroom.* Baltimore, MD: Brookes.

Kluth, P., & Schwarz, P. (2008). *Just give him the whale: 20 ways to use fascinations, areas of expertise and strengths to support students with autism.* Baltimore, MD: Brookes.

Little, L. (2002). Middle-class mothers' perceptions of peer and sibling victimization among children with Asperger's syndrome and nonverbal learning disorders. *Issues in Comprehensive Pediatric Nursing, 25,* 43–57.

Mackenzie, H. (2008). *Reaching and teaching the child with autism spectrum disorder: Using learning preferences and strengths.* London, UK: Jessica Kingsley.

Moore, S. T. (2002). *Asperger syndrome and the elementary school experience: Practical solutions for academic & social difficulties.* Shawnee Mission, KS: Autism Asperger.

Morrison, L., Kamps, D., Garcia, J., & Parker, D. (2001). Peer mediation and monitoring strategies to improve initiations and social skills for students with autism. *Journal of Positive Behavior Interventions, 3,* 237–250.

Myles, B. S. (2005). *Children and youth with Asperger syndrome: Strategies for success in inclusive settings.* Thousand Oaks, CA: Corwin Press.

Myles, B. S., & Adreon, D. (2001). *Asperger syndrome and adolescence: Practical solutions for school success.* Shawnee Mission, KS: Autism Asperger.

Myles, B. S., Trautman, M. L., & Schelvan, R. L. (2004). *The hidden curriculum: Practical solutions for understanding unstated rules in social situations.* Shawnee Mission, KS: Autism Asperger.

Nichols, S., Moravick, G., & Tetenbaum, S. P. (2009). *Girls growing up on the autism spectrum.* London, UK: Jessica Kingsley.

Paul, R., Augustyn, A, Klin, A., & Volkmar, F. R. (2005). Perception and production of prosody by speakers with autism spectrum disorders. *Journal of Autism and Developmental Disorders, 35*(2), 205–220.

Pierce, K., & Schreibman, L. (1997). Using peer trainers to promote social behavior in autism: Are they effective at enhancing multiple social modalities? *Focus on Autism & Other Developmental Disabilities, 12,* 207–298.

Schlieder, M. (2007). *With open arms: Creating school communities of support for kids with social challenges using Circle of Friends, extracurricular activities, and learning teams.* Shawnee Mission, KS: Autism Asperger.

Scott, J., Clark, C., & Brady, M. (2000). *Students with autism: Characteristics and instruction programming*. San Diego, CA: Singular.

Thiemann, K. S., & Goldstein, H. (2009). Social stories, written text cues, and video feedback: Effects on social communication of children with autism. *Journal of Applied Behavior Analysis, 34,* 425–446.

Thioux, M., Stark, D. E., Klaiman, C., & Schultz, R. T. (2006). The day of the week when you were born in 700 ms: Calendar computation in an autistic savant. *Journal of Experimental Psychology: Human Perception and Performance, 32*(5), 9955–9968.

Tsatsanis, K. D. (2004). Heterogeneity in learning type in Asperger syndrome and high-functioning autism. *Topics in Language Disorders, 24*(4), 260–270.

Utley, C. A., & Mortweek, S. L. (1997). Peer-mediated instruction and intervention. *Focus on Exceptional Children, 29*(5), 9–24.

Volkmar, F., & Cohen, D. (1985). The experience of infantile autism: A first person account by Tony W. *Journal of Autism and Developmental Disorders, 15,* 47–54.

Volkmar, F. R., & Wiesner, L. (2009). *A practical guide to autism*. Hoboken, NJ: John Wiley.

Wing, L., & Gould, J. (1979). Severe impairments of social interaction and associated abnormalities. *Journal of Autism and Developmental Disorders, 9*(9), 11–29.

▪ SUGGESTED READING

Aarons, M., & Gittens, T. (1998). *Autism: A social skills approach for children and adolescents*. Bradwell Abbey, Milton Keynes, UK: Speechmark.

Adreon, D., & Stella, J. (2001). Transition to middle and high school: Increasing the success of students with Asperger's syndrome. *Intervention in School and Clinic, 36,* 266–271.

Aspy, R., Grossman, B., & Mesibov, G. B. (2007). *The Ziggurat model: A framework for designing comprehensive interventions for individuals with high-functioning autism and Asperger syndrome*. Shawnee Mission, KS: Autism Asperger.

Baker, J. (2001). *Social skills picture book: Teaching play, emotion, and communication to children with autism*. Arlington, TX: Future Horizons.

Baron-Cohen, S. (2008). *Autism and Asperger syndrome (the facts)*. New York, NY: Oxford University Press.

Bishop, B. (2003). *My friend with autism: A coloring book for peers and siblings*. Arlington, TX: Future Horizons.

Brock, S. E., Jimerson, S. R., & Hansen, R. L. (2006). *Identifying, assessing, and treating autism at school*. New York, NY: Springer.

Buron, K. D. (2007). *A 5 is against the law! Social boundaries straight up*. Shawnee Mission, KS: Autism Asperger.

Buron, K. D., & Curtis, M. (2004). *Incredible 5-point scale: Assisting students with autism spectrum disorders in understanding social interactions and controlling their emotional responses*. Shawnee Mission, KS: Autism Asperger.

Burrows, E. L., & Wagner, S. J. (2004). *Understanding Asperger's syndrome: Fast facts-a guide for teachers and educators to address the needs of the student.* Arlington, TX: Future Horizons.

Carter, E. W. (2008). *Peer support strategies for improving all students' social lives and learning.* Baltimore, MD: Brookes.

Carter, M., & Santomoura, J. (2004). *Space travelers: An interactive program for developing social understanding, social competence and social skills for students with AS, autism and other social cognitive challenges.* Shawnee Mission, KS: Autism Asperger.

Cook, J., & Hartman, C. (2008). *My mouth is a volcano!* Chattanooga, TN: National Center for Youth Issues.

Coulter, D. (Producer/Director). (2000). *Asperger syndrome: Success in the mainstream classroom* [DVD]. Winston Salem, NC: Coulter Video.

Coulter, D. (Producer/Director). (2006a). *Intricate minds: Understanding classmates with Asperger syndrome* [DVD]. Winston Salem, NC: Coulter Video.

Coulter, D. (Producer/Director). (2006b). *Intricate minds II: Understanding elementary school classmates with Asperger syndrome* [DVD]. Winston Salem, NC: Coulter Video.

Coulter, D. (Producer/Director). (2006c). *Intricate minds III: Understanding elementary school classmates who think differently* [DVD]. Winston Salem, NC: Coulter Video.

Crary, E., & Casebolt, P. (1990). *Pick up your socks … and other skills growing children need.* Seattle, WA: Parenting Press.

Dunn, M. A. (2005). *S.O.S. Social skills in our schools: A social skills program for children with pervasive developmental disorders, including high-functioning autism and Asperger syndrome, and their typical peers.* Shawnee Mission, KS: Autism Asperger.

Edwards, A. (2001). *Taking autism to school.* Hawthorne, NY: JayJo Books.

Ernsperger, L. (2002). *Keys to success for teaching students with autism.* Arlington, TX: Future Horizons.

Faherty, C., & Mesibov, G. B. (2000). *Asperger's: What does it mean to me?* Arlington, TX: Future Horizons.

Fein, D., & Dunn, M. (2007). *Autism in your classroom: A general educator's guide to students with autism spectrum disorders.* Bethesda, MD: Woodbine House.

Flowers, T. (1996). *Reaching the child with autism through art: Practical, "fun" activities to enhance motor skills and improve tactile and concept awareness.* Arlington, TX: Future Horizons.

Grandin, T., & Barron, S. (2006). *The unwritten rules of social relationships: Decoding social mysteries through the unique perspectives of autism.* Arlington, TX: Future Horizons.

Gray, C. (2000). *The new social story book.* Arlington, TX: Future Horizons.

Gutstein, S. E. (2001). *Autism Asperger's: Solving the relationship puzzle—a new developmental program that opens the door to lifelong social and emotional growth.* Arlington, TX: Future Horizons.

Heflin, L. J., & Alaimo, D. F. (2007). *Students with autism spectrum disorders: Effective instructional practices.* Upper Saddle River, NJ: Pearson.

Hobson, P. (2005). Autism and emotion. In F. Volkmar, A. Klin, R. Paul, & D. J. Cohen (Eds.), *Handbook of autism and pervasive developmental disorders* (3rd ed., Vol. 1, pp. 406–424). New York: Wiley.

Howlin, P. (1998). *Children with autism and Asperger syndrome: A guide for practitioners and careers*. Hoboken, NJ: Wiley.

Jaffe, A., & Gardner, L. (2006). *My book of feelings: How to control and react to the size of your emotions*. Shawnee Mission, KS: Autism Asperger.

Kluth, P., & Chandler-Olcott, K. (2008). *"A land we can share": Teaching literacy to students with autism*. Baltimore, MD: Brookes.

Koegel, R. L., & Koegel, L. K. (1995). *Teaching children with autism: Strategies for initiating positive interactions and improving learning opportunities*. Baltimore, MD: Brookes.

Koegel, R. L., Koegel, L. K., & Brookman, L. I. (2003). Empirically supported pivotal response interventions for children with autism. In A. E. Kazdin & J. R. Weisz (Eds.), *Evidence-based psychotherapies for children and adolescents* (pp. 341–357). New York, NY: Guilford Press.

Koegel, L. K., & LaZebnik, C. (2009). *Growing up on the spectrum*. New York, NY: Penguin Books.

Larson, E. M. (2006). *I am utterly unique: Celebrating the strengths of children with Asperger syndrome and high-functioning autism*. Shawnee Mission, KS: Autism Asperger.

Ludwig, T. (2006). *Just kidding*. Berkeley, CA: Tricycle Press.

McClannahan, L. E., & Krantz, P. J. (2005). *Teaching conversation to children with autism: Scripts and script fading*. Bethesda, MD: Woodbine House.

McKinnon, K., & Kremps, J. L. (2005). *Social skills solutions: A hands-on manual for teaching social skills to children with autism*. New York: DRL Books.

Myles, B. S. (2001). *Asperger syndrome and sensory issues: Practical solutions for making sense of the world*. Shawnee Mission, KS: Autism Asperger.

Myles, B. S., & Southwick, J. (1999). *Asperger syndrome and difficult moments: Practical solutions for tantrums, rage, and meltdowns*. Shawnee Mission, KS: Autism Asperger.

Naylor, P. R. (1994). *King of the playground*. New York: Aladdin Paperbacks.

Ozonoff, S., Dawson, G., & McPartland, J. (2002). *A parent's guide to Asperger syndrome and high-functioning autism: How to meet the challenges and help your child thrive*. New York, NY: Guilford Press.

Pierce, K., & Schreibman, L. (1997). Multiple peer use of pivotal response training to increase social behaviors of classmates with autism: Results from trained and untrained peers. *Journal of Applied Behavioral Analysis, 30*(9), 957–960.

Quill, K. (1995). *Teaching children with autism: Strategies to enhance communication and socialization*. New York, NY: Delmar.

Silverman, S., & Weinfeld, R. (2007). *School success for kids with Asperger's syndrome: A practical guide for parents and teachers*. Waco, TX: Prufrock Press.

Small, M., & Kontente, L. (2003). *Everyday solutions: A practical guide for families of children with autism spectrum disorder*. Shawnee Mission, KS: Autism Asperger.

Strachan, J., & Schnurr, R. G. (1999). *Asperger's huh? A child's perspective*. Gloucester, ON, Canada: Anisor.

Strong, C. J., & North, K. H. (1996). *The magic of stories*. Eau Claire, WI: Thinking Publications.

Tsatsanis, K. D., Foley, C., & Donehower, C. (2004). Contemporary outcome research and programming guidelines for Asperger's syndrome and high functioning autism. *Topics in Language Disorders, 24*(4), 249–259.

Vicker, B. (2007). *Sharing information about your child with autism spectrum disorder: What do respite or alternative caregivers need to know?* Shawnee Mission, KS: Autism Asperger.

Weber, J. D. (2000). *Children with Fragile X syndrome: A parents' guide*. Bethesda, MD: Woodbine House.

Winter, M. (2003). *Asperger syndrome: What teachers need to know*. London, UK: Jessica Kingsley.

CHAPTER 9

Adolescents and Adults

A dolescence can present challenges for children and parents alike and can be a time for positive or, sometimes, negative change. Although the issues vary with levels of cognitive and communicative ability, changes in the body, sexual maturation, and emotions present challenges. This is also a time when transition planning should start—for some individuals this may mean going to college or vocational school—with all the changes entailed in being independent. For other individuals, the goal may be living apart from parents, in a setting where some level of supervision is provided. Sometimes adults will live at home with their parents but have a job, perhaps with support, in the daytime. For others, there may be an option for a group home with **supported employment.** Medical care presents special challenges for this population—research is very limited, knowledge among providers of adult services is often similarly limited, insurance coverage is spotty, and supports can be few and far between. Paradoxically it can be the higher cognitively functioning individuals who are at greatest risk, because states provide adult services only to those with lower intellectual levels. Fortunately with better outcomes and increased knowledge, this may start to change (Burke & Stoddart, 2014; Volkmar, Reichow, & McPartland, 2014; Volkmar et al., 2014).

ADOLESCENCE

The increase in the child's size in adolescence can make behavior management more challenging; for example, aggressive or self-injurious behavior can be more difficult to physically manage. As with other times in the individual's life, the primary care provider should be alert to any potential physical contributions to increased problems; for example, dental problems (especially emergent wisdom teeth) and ear infections can trigger more or new-onset self-injury in nonverbal individuals. New-onset seizure disorders sometimes occur. For socially isolated adolescents, particularly those who are on certain behavior-related medications, obesity may start.

The number of children who improve in communication, social skills, and behavior during adolescence varies from study to study and also depends on how improvement is defined, but it seems to be between 40% and maybe 80% of cases. In some cases, the improvement is very significant, and sometimes the person, as a young adult, may even seem to "lose" the diagnosis of autism, although some associated difficulties (social anxiety and awkwardness, mood problems, and so forth) can persist (Fein et al., 2013). In perhaps 10% or so of cases children seem to take a downturn in adolescence. This can be associated with new medical problems, such as seizures.

Sometimes children who make major gains also develop a sense of being different and of wanting to fit in. These children can be excellent candidates for psychotherapy or counseling; they are also potentially at increased risk for anxiety or depression (Lugnegard, Hallerback, & Gillberg, 2011). Sadly, it is these most cognitively able children who usually will receive the least amount of services in school. They can benefit from explicit teaching of social skills and from participation in thoughtfully selected community activities in which they can have a chance to generalize skills. Indeed, many activities can be therapeutic without being psychotherapy! At times psychotherapy or medications can be helpful (Wood et al., 2015).

Sexuality

Sexuality poses a complicated set of issues for typically developing children, much less those with some developmental vulnerability. Parents are commonly worried about sexual development. Behavior or emotional problems can intensify, often some months before the first signs of sexual development are detected. As with other adolescents, monitoring physical growth and stages of adolescence is important. Of course puberty is driven by biology and not developmental status. The transitions and changes of puberty can be much more difficult for children with ASDs.

When possible, attempts can be made to educate about puberty and body changes—this is more challenging for nonverbal individuals but even there some good resources are available (see the "Suggested Reading" list at the end of this chapter).

Because of social isolation, adolescents with ASD may have less access to the sources of information that are usually available (e.g., siblings and peers); limited teaching may occur in school. Accordingly it is important for the primary care provider to be able to assist the adolescent and be open to discussion of these topics and help students find other helpful resources, for example, support groups for teens with ASD. Some adolescents with autism will have strong sexual feelings; others won't. Some children, particularly higher-functioning children, may be very motivated to have a girlfriend or boyfriend, and sometimes this extra motivation helps the child make important gains. It is important to realize that sexual feelings are very much tied up with feelings about relationships—given the problems with social skills, this is very complicated for the adolescent with an ASD, and explicit teaching (e.g., about what is and isn't appropriate) is usually needed. Unfortunately, one of the prime sources of information available to typically developing children, (i.e., their peers), is not so readily available to the child with an ASD. The child's learning difficulties and adults anxiety may pose further challenges in addressing this topic! With better outcomes and increased social skills some of the socially and cognitively able individuals have increasingly been able to engage in long-term relationships and some have now married.

In helping the person learn to develop relationships, keep in mind that care providers should make the learning experience as positive as possible, teaching what to do, as well as what not to do. Carefully monitored experience is helpful starting with peer activities and learning about how to fit in with peers (in terms of clothes, appearance, and music). Teaching the difference between what we think and what we say (Lorimer, Simpson, Myles, & Ganz, 2002; Myles, 2004) and what is done in public versus private is important. Explicit teaching about distance, touching, and so on is essential. A social skills group with other teenagers can be a big help.

For some individuals masturbation can be a source of embarrassment to parents and siblings. Explicit teaching about what is done where is helpful—this can be done even with more cognitively challenged students. For parents, inappropriate sexual contact is often a concern, and teaching about boundaries and appropriate behavior on the part of others should be a priority. A number of programs and curriculums are available (see the "Suggested Reading" list at the end of the chapter). These programs can help to teach about levels of intimacy in a very explicit way.

Both girls and boys should be prepared (as much as possible) for puberty. For girls this can include teaching about onset of their period and self-care. Some girls will be able to manage on their own with the help of their caregivers, but others may require more direct supervision or help during their periods. For girls with more limited communication skills, cramps may be a cause of behavior change; cramps are often treated with NSAIDs or, in some cases, birth control pills. As much as possible girls should also be prepared for their first gynecological exam—as long as no other problems have arisen, that often can be put off until age 18 or even 20.

For boys the onset of puberty includes erections and wet dreams (both of which can be very confusing) as well as growth changes and more muscle mass. For verbal boys explicit teaching again is helpful and can be reassuring. When puberty has its onset, examination of the genitals provides a time for teaching as well. Both boys and girls should be offered the HPV immunization.

As adolescents become young adults, they may need to find new health care providers. Some pediatricians may be willing to continue to care for adolescents or young adults with an ASD into their 20s. As they reach their 30s, or earlier with some doctors, parents will need to find an internist or family physician to take care of them. The main reason parents will eventually need to switch to an internist or family practice physician is that as the adolescent or young adult with an ASD grows older, the individual may develop the same kinds of medical problems that other older people get. For example, adults with autism are subject to all adult-related medical conditions, such as high blood pressure, high cholesterol, heart disease, and so on. Pediatricians become uncomfortable in dealing with medical problems such as hypertension that are much less common in childhood.

The need for birth control can arise in various contexts, for example, if an adolescent is in a longer-term relationship. As with other adolescents sexual activity brings potential risks of sexually transmitted disease, and part of the primary care provider's task is to be available to the individual and his or her family. And for other young people, issues of gender identity emerge in childhood or adolescence.

High School: Challenges and Opportunities

High school presents a range of challenges: the need for higher levels of social skills and more complex executive functioning (e.g., as the child has a greater role in monitoring assignments, moves from one class to another, and so forth). Academic demands can be greater—a challenge for less cognitively able students. Even for the most able there is a critical need for parents, schools, and care providers to focus on adaptive skills—that is, taking skills out into the real world. The physical environment of high schools can be challenging. Demands for self-care and personal hygiene are high; adolescents are often meticulous (even when they sport a studied non-meticulous look) about appearance, cleanliness, and so forth. Issues of peer acceptance loom large. Many students will still have an IEP, and goals for social learning as well as adaptive, organizational, and executive skills can be explicitly addressed in that plan. Depending on the needs of the individual, services in high school can be provided up to age 21. Also, it is important to realize that as part of the IEP process, vocational and other assessments can be requested.

Unfortunately as many as 70% of children with ASDs experience some aspects of bullying (Cappadocia, Weiss, & Pepler, 2012). The flip side, inappropriate pursuit of other students—either as friends or romantic partners—is sometimes seen. This can be a major source of legal difficulty. Teaching appropriate social behaviors and appropriate boundaries is critical.

Transition from High School

An increasing number of students with ASDs are moving on to college or vocational school after high school. A number of special programs around the country also offer transitional supports for these students with explicit teaching about the skills needed for attending college and living independently. The students and parents must understand that college attendance is not a right. Rather, the applicable law has to do with nondiscrimination for students with disabilities. This means (1) students must self-identify as having some disability to the college disability office (parents can't do this) and provide necessary documentation and (2) the college or vocational school must make appropriate accommodations based on documented need (e.g., tutors, extra time for tests, etc.). In contrast to elementary and high school, students with inappropriate behavior can rapidly be terminated from programs. A host of supports, fortunately, are available, although these can vary from school to school; support can come from the learning disabilities office, tutors and peer mentors, as well as therapists (Cappadocia et al., 2012).

As students (and parents) think about appropriate jobs, they should have a realistic awareness of strengths and weaknesses and the degree to which potential jobs might be a good fit given these (Lawer, Brusilovskiy, Salzer, & Mandell, 2009). Independent living skills should be explicitly taught and an excellent array technological support is available, for example, use of IPads or IPods for organizational support (Kellems & Morningstar, 2012).

Moving to Adulthood

The first outcome studies of autism were not very encouraging, with maybe 5% or so of children becoming self-sufficient adults, but this began to change with the mandates for education as well as more sophisticated and effective treatments (Howlin, Volkmar, Paul, Rogers, & Pelphrey, 2014). Several factors appear to be important in predicting ultimate outcome. One is the presence of truly communicative speech (by about age 5), another is nonverbal cognitive ability in the normal range, and yet another is the person's capacity for self-sufficiency and independence. Some work has tried to refine early predictive factors; for example, vocabulary size has been thought to be a good predictor of outcome, although this is controversial. Family involvement is critical in teaching real-world adaptive skills (capacities for personal self-sufficiency and independence). Many late adolescents now will have good cognitive abilities but poor real-life skills.

Mental Health and Medical Issues

As is true for other adolescents some individuals develop new mental health problems. For more cognitively able individuals, these most often include increased difficulties with depression and anxiety problems. For some of these individuals the awareness of being or feeling "different" can motivate change on the one hand but also contribute to mental health problems on the other hand (Ghaziuddin, 2005). There may also be higher rates of anxiety and depression in family members, suggesting some increased genetic risk (Rutter & Thapar, 2014).

Safety issues can continue to be a concern for adolescents and adults. Driving (for the more cognitively able) can be an option but calls for an extraordinary range of skills including social awareness, multitasking (executive functioning), and constant awareness of the environment—all things that can be a challenge for the student with ASD (Huang, Kao, Curry, & Durbin, 2012). Poor social judgment can lead to involvement in risk-taking or dangerous situations, and for those with anxiety or mood problems self-medicating with alcohol or drugs may also be a problem (Palmqvist, Edman, & Bolte, 2014).

Adult Living and Occupational Issues

As for all of us the major challenge for adulthood is independent function. Even when learning and behavior problems make this less likely, the overall goal should be to help the individual attain as much self-sufficiency and independence as possible. For more and more individuals, adult independence is possible and, although challenges remain, more resources are available to help individuals reach this goal. Unfortunately, there is considerable variability from state to state in what is actually available. There are some federal supports for vocational training for students who have substantial handicaps to employment and who can benefit from vocational services. Typically, state departments of vocational services (sometimes called the *Department of Vocational Rehabilitation* or *DVR*) are the agencies mandated to provide these. If adults qualify, a plan for employment—similar to the IEP—can be developed. Various other federal and sometimes state laws can apply. These have to do with discrimination against individuals with disabilities. At the federal level, the Americans with Disabilities Act of 1990 is often most relevant. It prohibits discrimination based on disability. This act applies in a range of settings, including most private employers, colleges, public accommodations, and so forth.

Community resources often lag behind what we need to help adolescents and adults enter the workforce. It is important for everyone concerned to realize that there are no mandates or rights relative to adult employment, unlike the right to a free and appropriate education in the United States. Some parents take matters into their own hands and have developed a range of potential vocational opportunities—this varies tremendously by region. Transition planning is mandated for children with disabilities as part of a student's IEP beginning no later than his or her 16th birthday, and the high school–aged student should be included in this process. Sadly, even the best planning is of little benefit if few opportunities and supports are available. Family supports are important as are community resources.

In general, jobs that deemphasize social skills (to the extent possible) often work best. The marked variability in social, communicative, and cognitive abilities poses significant problems for securing employment. Individual interests and their strengths and vulnerabilities always should be taken into account. The range of adult options includes these choices:

- *Sheltered employment.* This used to be the most common job placement for adults with cognitive or mental disability, but the work was often repetitive with few opportunities for community engagement.

- *Secured employment.* The individual is supported in the community in the least restrictive setting. This requires considerable planning but can work out very well if supports are available; for example, one very disabled adult with autism whom we know walks every day to a diner where he works loading dishwashers—he returns home every evening to his family.

- *Supported employment.* In this approach, employment is combined with ongoing support (e.g., a job coach). More extensive support is provided initially and then gradually reduced; sometimes small groups of disabled adults can work together. However, continued support is often needed, even at a low level, and the move to decrease supports should not be too fast. Other factors, such as engagement of the other workers, are important. This might take the form of bussing tables at a fast-food restaurant or bagging groceries.

- *Independent (competitive) employment.* Typically individuals find jobs that line up with their strengths—for example, computer programming, Internet sales, and so on; social requirements tend to be minimal. For some individuals with high cognitive abilities, advanced degrees can be obtained, and work in a range of settings is possible. Again, often such jobs play to the special interests and abilities of the person, for example, in areas such as astronomy, cartography, mathematics, chemistry, and computer science (Keel, Mesibov, & Woods, 1997).

Individuals with ASDs can be extremely conscientious workers. Clear expectations and routines still often seem to be important, and life management skills still may need to be a focus of intervention.

As with vocational programs, an increasing number of potential living arrangements are available. These include living with family, living semi-independently, and living truly independently. Semi-independent options include group homes and supported apartments (with various levels of support from staff members). A number of transitional programs have grown up around the country that specialize in helping to teach independent living skills to foster as much personal self-sufficiency as possible in adulthood. The hope is for adults with autism to live as independently as possible. It is important that supports be flexible and consider the needs of the individual. Life satisfaction in adulthood appears to be strongly related to participation in activities in the family and community (Schmidt et al., 2015).

An increasing number of adults, particularly the higher cognitively functioning, are able to marry and have families. This seems to be more common in Asperger's disorder than in autism, although even in autism this is observed (Szatmari, Bartolucci, Bremmer, Bond, & Rich, 1989). Family history studies sometimes have revealed family members who had married but who also appeared to have problems on the autism spectrum. Several accounts of these experiences are now available and listed in the "Suggested Reading" list at the end of the chapter; in addition, books outlining specific support and coping strategies for couples are now available. Although the literature on work with older adults is limited, there are some resources available (Lawson, 2015).

Government Benefits

This is an area that seems to be in a state of flux at the present. As adolescents become adults, most no longer can remain on their parents' insurance plans. As a result, most move to state-supported programs. At times this can complicate finding specialist services. Sometimes eligibility requirement also complicate getting coverage.

Two major US federally supported programs exist that provide additional support for individuals with disabilities who can't support themselves. These programs are called **Supplemental Security Income (SSI)** and **Social**

Security Disability Insurance (SSDI). The SSI program (www.ssa.gov/ssi) provides a basic payment to individuals or couples every month. The amount paid is reduced by the amount the person earns as income. The program is designed for people who cannot bring in substantial income or what is called *substantial gainful activity,* which means they can't engage in work.

Legal Issues for Adults

There is a significant risk for adults with ASD to have involvement in the legal system (Woodbury-Smith, 2014). For the less cognitively able this may have to do with poorly informed police arresting an adult who has had a behavioral meltdown or who has been the victim of a crime. For the more cognitively able the lack of social judgment and tendency to rigidity can cause trouble, such as the high school student who explicitly comments on a girl's breast or who stops in the middle of the street when the walk sign switches to "don't walk." There is a tiny amount of literature (almost all based on case reports) suggesting that individuals with Asperger's may be at increased risk for legal or criminal justice involvement. Sometimes adolescents are set up by peers or others to engage in some illegal activity. In general, our experience is that adults on the autism spectrum are more likely to be victims than to victimize others.

For those who continue to need support as adults, parents should be reminded that their children typically automatically assume legal and societal responsibility for themselves unless some special provision is made. Unless that happens, individuals become independent as they reach the legal age of adulthood—usually 18 years old. Parents of less cognitively able children (and sometime those with moreable children) just assume that they can continue to make decisions for the individual as he or she becomes an adult, but this is not the case. Depending on the situation, parents (or brothers and sisters or other family members) may wish to become guardians as the person with autism becomes a legal adult. Procedures and issues vary somewhat from state to state. There are different levels of guardianship—this may involve all kinds of decisions about the person, or it may be much more limited (e.g., to financial issues). A person who is a guardian of property can make investments for the person. Depending on how the guardianship is done, this individual can make all decisions including living arrangements, medical treatments, and so forth. Typically, some—often very formal—legal proceeding is (rightfully) involved in this. Because laws vary from state to state, it is very important for parents to talk with a knowledgeable lawyer. It is also important for parents to discuss long-term planning issues with other siblings or family members or others they wish involved in long-term planning and care.

Estate planning should begin once anyone has a child—this should include provision for care and custody of any minor children and also guidance for disposition of life insurance, trusts, and so forth. The temptation to delay planning is enormous. Unfortunately, so are the risks of not doing so. Simply leaving money, property, or other assets to a child in a will may not be the best approach. Even setting up a special trust account in the child's name may simply result in it going to the state if the child needs care as an adult. There are several ways to approach the problem. Some states now have special needs trusts that allow the person (the trustee in charge of the trust) to use funds to benefit the designated person. As long as there is no specific legal requirement for the money to be spent for a special purpose on behalf of the individual, it may be relatively safe from being taken.

Medical Care Issues

Many of the same considerations in medical care for children remain quite relevant to adolescents and adults with ASD. Obviously as they age these individuals are just as much at risk for the usual range of common adult medical conditions, for example, hypertension, obesity, and so forth; however, for various reasons they may be at even higher risk. For example, commonly used behavior-modifying or seizure medications can have their own risks; similarly, increased rates of obesity may predispose to other problems. Finally, as Burke and Stoddart (2014) point out, the fragmentation of the many systems of care involved further contributes to risk.

Unfortunately, information on medical problems in adolescents and adults is quite limited. Resources on aging in populations with ASD are almost nonexistent at this time. Clearly needs and challenges vary depending on the individual—his or her levels of adaptive, cognitive, and communicative functioning as well as family and community supports. More communicative and cognitively able individuals can participate actively in their own care; issues become more complex for the more challenged individuals who remain dependent on family members or others to advocate for them. These issues can be reflected in insurance coverage in which, paradoxically, individuals who function at higher levels may have more difficulty obtaining insurance. With some modifications the medical home model can continue to be useful (Connell, Souders, & Kerns, 2016). An awareness of the special needs of these individuals on the part of primary care providers is also essential.

SUMMARY

As a result of earlier detection more individuals with autism and related conditions are growing up, doing well, and achieving some degree of personal independence or semi-independence. More are going on to college or vocational school, and with appropriate training they can enter the workforce. Unfortunately, knowledge regarding this population is rather limited. We do know that challenges for obtaining high-quality medical care exist—particularly as these individuals transition to health care providers with less experience in dealing with adults with developmental disabilities such as ASD.

Adolescence presents the same set of challenges to students with ASD as to typically developing students. The primary care provider can be a good source of information and help adolescents and young adults obtain information and, if needed, additional support as they cope with issues of sexuality, privacy, intimacy, and social norms. With support, some individuals are able to achieve reasonable adult independence, and a small number achieve optimal outcomes—in the technical sense of no longer meeting usual criteria for an ASD diagnosis. However, issues concerning anxiety and depression as well as life satisfaction can remain. Even with early detection and intervention not all students do well, and a significant number remain in need of intensive care throughout their lives. Somewhat paradoxically it is the more cognitively able students who often have the least entitlements as adults to services.

The overall improvement in outcome in ASDs represents the combination of several factors: better (and earlier) diagnosis, early and more appropriate intervention, and (possibly) expanded definitions of autism. A number of adult vocational options, ranging from college to supported employment, are available, and more and more are living independently. Even when adults aren't fully independent, they can live rewarding and fulfilling lives.

It is important for parents to be aware of the changes in entitlements that come with age, particularly in the transition from school-age (through age 21), when education is a right, to older ages, when entitlements to services can vary dramatically from state to state and when, for many problems, the applicable set of laws relates to the mandate not to discriminate based on disability. In college, technical, vocational, and other programs, it is essential that the program be informed—usually by the student—of any special needs related to disability.

For more and more adults, independent living is now possible, and many individuals, particularly the most cognitively able, are involved in family life—sometimes having long-term relationships and families of their own. Even when this is not possible, the goal should be as much independence and self-sufficiency as possible. Planning for adulthood starts many years in advance. In addition to cognitive and language abilities, self-care skills (see Chapter 6) are critical. For many adults, there is a significant gap between overall cognitive ability and capacities for adult independence and self-sufficiency.

Medical problems such as obesity and subsequent diabetes and hypertension are probably more common in the more isolated and sedentary population of adults (Grondhuis & Aman, 2014). Mental health problems are also relatively common and supports (psychotherapeutic and pharmacologic) can be made available. As interest in this age group increases, more knowledge regarding best practices will become available. Current practice guidelines likely will be expanded as this knowledge accumulates (McClure, 2014; NICE, 2012).

▧ REFERENCES

Burke, L., & Stoddart, K. P. (2014). Medical and health problems in adults with high-functioning autism and Asperger syndrome. In F. R. Volkmar, B. Reichow, & J. C. McPartland (Eds.), *Adolescents and adults with autism spectrum disorders*. New York, NY: Springer Science + Business Media.

Cappadocia, M. C., Weiss, J. A., & Pepler, D. (2012). Bullying experiences among children and youth with autism spectrum disorders. *Journal of Autism & Developmental Disorders, 42*(2), 266–277.

Connell, J. E., Souders, M. C., & Kerns, C. M. (2016). The adult medical home. In E. Giarelli & K. M. Fisher (Eds.), *Integrated health care for people with autism spectrum disorder* (pp. 158–172). Springfield, IL: Charles C. Thomas.

Fein, D., Barton, M., Eigsti, I.-M., Kelley, E., Naigles, L., Schultz, R. T., & Tyson, K. (2013). Optimal outcome in individuals with a history of autism. *Journal of Child Psychology and Psychiatry, 54*(2), 195–205.

Ghaziuddin, M. (2005). *Mental health aspects of autism and Asperger's syndrome.* London, UK: Jessica Kingsley.

Grondhuis, S. N., & Aman, M. G. (2014). Overweight and obesity in youth with developmental disabilities: A call to action. *Journal of Intellectual Disability Research, 58*(9), 787–799.

Howlin, P., Volkmar, F. R., Paul, R., Rogers, S. J., & Pelphrey, K. A. (2014). Outcomes in adults with autism spectrum disorders. In F. R. Volkmar, S. J. Rogers, R. Paul, & K. A. Pelphrey (Eds.), *Handbook of autism and pervasive developmental disorders* (4th ed., Vol. 1, pp. 97–116). Hoboken, NJ: Wiley.

Huang, P., Kao, T., Curry, A. E., & Durbin, D. R. (2012). Factors associated with driving in teens with autism spectrum disorders. *Journal of Developmental & Behavioral Pediatrics, 33*(1), 70–74.

Keel, J. H., Mesibov, G. B., & Woods, A. V. (1997). TEACCH-supported employment program. *Journal of Autism & Developmental Disorders, 27*(1), 3–9.

Kellems, R. O., & Morningstar, M. E. (2012). Using video modeling delivered through iPods to teach vocational tasks to young adults with autism spectrum disorders. *Career Development and Transition for Exceptional Individuals, 35*(3), 155–167.

Lawer, L., Brusilovskiy, E., Salzer, M. S., & Mandell, D. S. (2009). Use of vocational rehabilitative services among adults with autism. *Journal of Autism and Developmental Disorders, 39*(3), 487–494.

Lawson, W. (2015). *Older adults and autism spectrum conditions.* London, UK: Jessica Kingsley.

Lorimer, P. A., Simpson, R. L., Myles, B. S., & Ganz, J. B. (2002). The use of social stories as a preventative behavioral intervention in a home setting with a child with autism. *Journal of Positive Behavior Interventions, 4*(1), 53–60.

Lugnegard, T., Hallerback, M. U., & Gillberg, C. (2011). Psychiatric comorbidity in young adults with a clinical diagnosis of Asperger syndrome. *Research in Developmental Disabilities, 32(5),* 1910–1917.

McClure, I. (2014). Developing and implementing practice guidelines. In F. R. Volkmar, S. J. Rogers, R. Paul, & K. A. Pelphrey (Eds.), *Handbook of autism and pervasive developmental disorders* (4th ed., Vol. 2, pp. 1014–1035). Hoboken, NJ: Wiley.

Myles, B. S. (2004). Review of Asperger syndrome and psychotherapy: Understanding Asperger perspectives. *American Journal of Psychotherapy, 58*(3), 365–366.

NICE. (2012). Autism spectrum disorder in adults: Diagnosis and management. Retrieved from http://www.nice.org.uk/guidance/cg142/chapter/1-recommendations

Palmqvist, M., Edman, G., & Bolte, S. (2014). Screening for substance use disorders in neurodevelopmental disorders: A clinical routine? *European Child & Adolescent Psychiatry, 23*(5), 365–368.

Rutter, M., & Thapar, A. (2014). Genetics of autism spectrum disorders. In F. R. Volkmar, S. J. Rogers, R. Paul, & K. A. Pelphrey (Eds.), *Handbook of autism and pervasive developmental disorders* (4th ed., Vol. 1, pp. 411–423). Hoboken, NJ: Wiley.

Schmidt, L., Kirchner, J. Strunz, S., Brozus, J., Ritter, K., Roepke S., & Dziobek, I. (2015). Psychosocial functioning and life satisfaction in adults with autism spectrum disorder without intellectual impairment. *Journal of Clinical Psychology, 71*(12), 1259–1268.

Szatmari, P., Bartolucci, G., Bremner, R., Bond, S., & Rich, S. (1989). A follow-up study of high-functioning autistic children. *Journal of Autism & Developmental Disorders, 19*(2), 213–225.

Volkmar, F., Reichow, B., & McPartland, J. (2014). *Adolescents and adults with autism spectrum disorders.* New York, NY: Springer.

Volkmar, F. R., Rowberry, J., de Vinck-Baroody, O., Gupta, A. R., Leung, J., Meyers, J., Vaswani, N., & Wiesner, L. A. (2014). Medical care in autism and related conditions. In F. R. Volkmar, S. J. Rogers, R. Paul, & K. A. Pelphrey (Eds.), *Handbook of autism and pervasive developmental disorders* (4th ed., Vol. 1, pp. 532–535). Hoboken, NJ: Wiley.

Wood, J. J., Ehrenreich-May, J., Alessandri, M., Fujii, C., Renno, P., Laugeson, E., Piacentini, J. C., De Nadai, A. S., Arnold, E., Lewin, A. B., Murphy, T. K., & Storch, E. A. (2015). Cognitive behavioral therapy for early adolescents with autism spectrum disorders and clinical anxiety: A randomized, controlled trial. *Behavior Therapy, 46*(1) 7–19.

Woodbury-Smith, M. (2014). Unlawful behaviors in adolescents and adults with autism spectrum disorders. In F. R. Volkmar, B. Reichow, & J. C. McPartland (Eds.), *Adolescents and adults with autism spectrum disorders* (pp. 269–281). New York, NY: Springer Science + Business Media.

▓ SUGGESTED READING

Antony, P. J., & Shore, S. M. (2015). *We do belong.* London, UK: Jessica Kingsley.

Aston, M. C. (2009). *The Asperger couple's workbook: Practical advice and activities for couples and counsellors.* London, UK: Jessica Kingsley.

Attwood, T. (2004). *Exploring feelings: Cognitive behavior therapy to manage anxiety.* Arlington, TX: Future Horizons.

Attwood, S. (2008). *Making sense of sex: A forthright guide to puberty, sex and relationships for people with Asperger's syndrome.* London, UK: Jessica Kingsley.

Baker, J. (2003). *Social skills training for children and adolescents with Asperger syndrome and social-communications problems.* Shawnee Mission, KS: Autism Asperger.

Baker, J. (2006). *Preparing for life: The complete guide for transitioning to adulthood for those with autism and Asperger's syndrome.* Arlington, TX: Future Horizons.

Bashe, P. R., Kirby, B. L., Baron-Cohen, S., & Attwood, T. (2005). *The OASIS guide to Asperger syndrome: Completely revised and updated; Advice, support, insight, and inspiration.* New York, NY: Crown Publishing.

Bellini, S. (2006). *Building social relationships: A systematic approach to teaching social interaction skills to children and adolescents with autism spectrum disorders and other social difficulties.* Shawnee Mission, KS: Autism Asperger.

Bentley, K., & Attwood, T. (2007). *Alone together: Making an Asperger marriage work.* London, UK: Jessica Kingsley.

Bissonnette, B. (2014). *Helping adults with Asperger's syndrome get & stay hired: Career coaching strategies for professionals and parents of adults on the autism spectrum.* London, UK: Jessica Kingsley.

Buron, K. D. (2007). *A 5 is against the law! Social boundaries: Straight up! An honest guide for teens and young adults.* Shawnee Mission, KS: Autism Asperger.

Bruey, C. T., & Urban, M. B. (2009). *The autism transition guide: Planning the journey from school to adult life.* Bethesda, MD: Woodbine House.

Coulter, D. (Producer/Director). (2001). *Asperger syndrome: Transition to college and work* [DVD]. Winston-Salem, NC: Coulter Video.

Coulter, D. (Producer/Director). (2006). *Intricate minds: Understanding classmates with Asperger syndrome* [DVD]. Winston-Salem, NC: Coulter Video.

Coyne, P., Nyberg, C., & Vandenburg, M. L. (1999). *Developing leisure time skills for persons with autism: A practical approach for home, school and community.* Arlington, TX: Future Horizons.

Debbaudt, D. (2002). *Autism, advocates, and law enforcement professionals: Recognizing and reducing risk situations for people with autism spectrum disorders.* London, UK: Jessica Kingsley.

Duncan, M., & Myles, B. S. (2008). *The hidden curriculum 2009 one-a-day calendar: Items for understanding unstated rules in social situations.* Shawnee Mission, KS: Autism Asperger.

Edwards, D. (2008). *Providing practical support for people with autism spectrum disorders: Supported living in the community.* London, UK: Jessica Kingsley.

Fegan, L., Rauch, A., & McCarthy, W. (1993). *Sexuality and people with intellectual disability* (2nd ed.). Baltimore, MD: Brookes.

Fullerton, A., Stratton, J., Coyne, P., & Gray, C. (1996). *Higher functioning adolescents and young adults with autism: A teacher's guide.* Austin, TX: PRO-ED.

Gaus, V. O. (2007). *Cognitive-behavioral therapy for adult Asperger syndrome.* New York, NY: Guilford Press.

Getzel, E. E., & Wehman, P. (Eds.). (2005). *Going to college.* Baltimore. MD: Brookes.

Guare, R., Dawson, P., & Guare, C. (2013). *Smart but scattered teens.* New York, NY: Guilford Press.

Harpur, J., Lawlor, M., & Fitzgerald, M. (2004). *Succeeding in college with Asperger syndrome.* London, UK: Jessica Kingsley.

Henault, I., & Attwood, T. (2005). *Asperger's syndrome and sexuality: From adolescence through adulthood.* London, UK: Jessica Kingsley.

Hingsburger, D. (1995). *Just say know! Understanding and reducing the risk of sexual victimization of people with developmental disabilities.* Barrie, ON, Canada: Diverse City Press.

Hollins, S., & Downer, J. (2000). *Keeping healthy down below.* London, UK: Gaskell and St. George's Hospital Medical School.

Hollins, S., & Perez, W. (2000). *Looking after my breasts*. London, UK: Gaskell and St. George's Hospital Medical School.

Howlin, P. (2004). *Autism and Asperger syndrome: Preparing for adulthood* (2nd ed.). London, UK: Routledge.

Howlin, P. (2014). Outcomes in autism spectrum disorder. In F. R. Volkmar, S. J. Rogers, R. Paul, & K. A. Pelphrey (Eds.), *Handbook of autism and pervasive developmental disorders* (4th ed., Vol. 1, pp. 201–220). Hoboken, NJ: Wiley.

Hoyt, P. R., & Pollock, C. M. (2003). *Special people, special planning*. Orlando, FL: Legacy Planning Partners.

Jackson, L., & Attwood, T. (2002). *Freaks, geeks and Asperger syndrome: A user guide to adolescence*. London, UK: Jessica Kingsley.

Kellems, R. O. (2012). Using video modeling delivered through iPods to teach vocational tasks to young adults with autism spectrum disorders (ASD). *Dissertation Abstracts International Section A: Humanities and Social Sciences, 73*(2-A), 575.

Korin, E. S. H. (2007). *Asperger syndrome: An owner's manual for older adolescents and adults: What you, your parents and friends, and your employer need to know*. Shawnee Mission, KS: Autism Asperger.

Korpi, M. (2007). *Guiding parent's teenager with special needs through transition from school to adult life: Tools for parents*. London, UK: Jessica Kingsley.

McAfee, J., & Attwood, T. (2001). *Navigating the social world: A curriculum for individuals with Asperger's syndrome, high-functioning autism and related disorders*. Arlington, TX: Future Horizons.

Myles, B. S., & Adreon, D. (2001). *Asperger syndrome and adolescence: Practical solutions for school success*. Shawnee Mission, KS: Autism Asperger.

Myles, B. S., Trautman, M. L., & Schelvan, R. L. (2004). *The hidden curriculum: Practical solutions for understanding unstated rules in social situations*. Shawnee Mission, KS: Autism Asperger.

Nadeau, K. G. (1994). *Survival guide for college students with ADD or LD*. Washington, DC: Magination Press.

Newport, J., & Newport, M. (2002). *Autism, Asperger's and sexuality: Puberty and beyond*. Arlington, TX: Future Horizons.

Patrick, N. J. (2008). *Social skills for teenagers and adults with Asperger syndrome: A practical guide to day-to-day life*. London, UK: Jessica Kingsley.

Perry, N. (2009). *Adults on the autism spectrum leave the nest: Achieving supported independence*. London, UK: Jessica Kingsley.

Shore, S. (2003). *Beyond the wall: Personal experience with autism and Asperger syndrome* (2nd ed.). Shawnee Mission, KS: Autism Asperger.

Sicile-Kira, C. (2006). *Adolescents on the autism spectrum: A parent's guide to the cognitive, social, physical, and transition needs of teenagers with autism spectrum disorders*. New York, NY: Penguin.

Silverman, S., & Weinfeld, R. (2007). *School success for kids with Asperger's syndrome: A practical guide for parents and teachers*. Waco, TX: Prufrock Press.

Smith, M. D., Belcher, R. G., & Juhrs, P. D. (1995). *A guide to successful employment for individuals with autism*. Baltimore, MD: Brookes.

Stanford, A. (2002). *Asperger syndrome and long-term relationships.* London, UK: Jessica Kingsley.

Stevens, B. (2002). *The ABC's of special needs planning made easy.* Phoenix, AZ: Stevens Group.

Taymans, J. M., & West, L. L. (2000). *Unlocking potential: College and other choices for people with LD and AD/HD.* Bethesda, MD: Woodbine House.

Tincani, M., & Bondy, A. (2014). *Autism spectrum disorders in adolescents and adults: Evidence-based and promising interventions.* New York, NY: Guilford Press.

Urgolo Huckvale, M., & Van Riper, I. (Eds.). (2016). *Nature and needs of individuals with autism spectrum disorders and other severe disabilities: A resource for preparation programs and caregivers.* Baltimore, MD: Rowman & Littlefield.

Vermeulen, P. (2000). *I am special: Introducing young people to their autistic spectrum disorder.* London, UK: Jessica Kingsley.

Wall, K. (2007). *Education and care for adolescents and adults with autism: A guide for professionals and careers.* Los Angeles, CA: Sage Publications.

Wehman, P., Smith, M. D., & Schall, C. (2008). *Autism & the transition to adulthood: Success beyond the classroom.* Baltimore, MD: Brookes.

Willey, L. (1999). *Pretending to be normal: Living with Asperger's syndrome.* London, UK: Jessica Kingsley.

Wolf, L. E., Brown, J. T., & Bork, G.R.K. (2009). *Students with Asperger syndrome: A guide for college personnel.* Shawnee Mission, KS: Autism Asperger.

Wrobel, M. (2003). *Taking care of myself: A hygiene, puberty and personal curriculum for young people with autism.* Arlington, TX: Future Horizons.

▓ WEB-BASED RESOURCES

- National Clearinghouse on Postsecondary Education for Individuals with Disabilities provides information about educational support services, procedures, and opportunities at a variety of postsecondary entities. www.heath.gwu.edu

- National Center for Learning Disabilities provides information about transition, including checklists for various ages. http://www.ncld.org/

- Postsecondary Innovative Transition Technology (POST-ITT) provides a technology-based tool to help with transition planning.

- National Center on Secondary Education and Transition (NCSET; www.ncset.org) focuses on secondary education and transition.

- http://ncset.org/tacommunities/transition/default.asp

- National Dissemination Center for Children with Disabilities (NICHCY) includes information about the basics of student involvement, person–centered planning, and materials for students. http://www.parentcenterhub.org/nichcy-gone/

- Website Videos and materials available from James Stanfield Company (P.O. Box 41058, Santa Barbara, CA 93140; 800-421-6534, www.stansfield.com)

CHAPTER 10

Behavioral and Psychiatric Problems

Issues and Interventions

Behavioral difficulties in ASD can take many forms and can be uncommon or frequent. These include repetitive movements such as hand mannerisms, finger or hand flapping, or complicated whole-body movements such as rocking (see Table 10.1). Sometimes these include major tantrums or self-injurious behaviors such as head banging. The child may pursue very unusual interests; for example, she may line up toys or dolls rather than play with them and not tolerate disruption. Behavioral problems tend to change over time, often becoming most problematic in the early and middle teenage years. Sometimes behaviors persist over time, but what was slightly problematic behavior in a 3-year-old can become much more so in a 13-year-old! In this chapter, we discuss some of these behavioral problems and emotional difficulties seen in ASDs. When the problem is affecting a particular child, a specialist in behavioral difficulties is often needed. For purposes of this chapter, we group problem behaviors and emotional problems into several broad categories that include the most common kinds of behaviors you might see within each category. Then we discuss some general aspects of interventions. Near the end of the chapter, we also talk about mental health issues and conditions, particularly those seen in the more cognitively able individuals on the autism spectrum. Specific medications and aspects of drug treatment are discussed in Chapter 11.

TABLE 10.1   COMMON BEHAVIORAL AND MOOD PROBLEMS IN AUTISM SPECTRUM CONDITIONS

Type of Behaviors	Specific Examples
Stereotyped behaviors	• Body rocking
	• Hand or finger flicking
	• Other repetitive behaviors
Self-injury and aggression	• Injury to self or others; property destruction
Problems with rigidity and **perseveration**	• Resistance to change
	• Perseveration, compulsiveness
	• Unusual interests
Overactivity and problems with attention	• High activity levels
	• Difficulties with attention
	• Impulsivity
	• Running or bolting
Mood problems	• Depression
	• Anxiety
	• Bipolar disorders (mania)

Source: Reprinted with permission from Volkmar and Wiesner (2009, p. 424).

In an ideal world, there would be a simple one-to-one correspondence between a behavioral or emotional difficulty and a treatment. Unfortunately, things are a lot more complicated. It can be hard to apply usual diagnostic categories when individuals are very cognitively delayed. Second, people sometimes do not recognize the other difficulties or disorders that are present, or they mistakenly assume that having autism somehow protects you from other problems. That is, the diagnosis of autism or Asperger's disorder overshadows an awareness of other difficulties, such as anxiety or depression. Even the most cognitively able children can have meltdowns, and these can be approached behaviorally as well.

More than one problem can be present, for example, problems with attention may go along with problems with stereotyped behaviors. It is important to decide which problems are the ones to focus on, as well as what the benefits and potential risks of treatments are. The same problem behavior is often the product of several different factors.

BEHAVIORAL INTERVENTIONS: AN OVERVIEW

Behavioral and educational interventions are usually the first line of treatment for the behavior problems observed in ASD and are based on intervention principles from applied behavior analysis (ABA) (Powers, Palmieri, Egan, Rohrer, Nulty, & Forte, 2014). These are well-established treatments with a strong evidence base (Volkmar et al., 2014). The assumptions of ABA are that, similar to other children, those with an ASD learn through experience. Accordingly, the events that precede behavioral difficulties (the antecedents) and those that follow them (the consequences) are important. The antecedents are the things that set off the behavior in the first place. For example, if parents ask the child to stop body rocking and put away her toys and this leads to a tantrum, you have a pretty good idea that the child does not want to stop her body rocking or put away her toys. If the response to the tantrum is to let the child continue to body rock, you've given a pretty strong message (the consequence) that the child doesn't need to listen.

There are many different approaches to dealing with behavior problems; the "Suggested Reading" list at the end of the chapter provides some basic information. Because parents (and sometimes teachers) find themselves coping with a lot of things at the same time, it is not always easy to step back and get the big picture on behavior problems. There are some general principles to keep in mind. First, don't pay attention to the child only when problem behaviors are present. Second, to encourage desired behavior be sure to acknowledge and praise those behaviors specifically. Put another way, one of the tricks of dealing with problem behaviors is to have a vision of the kinds of positive behaviors you want to have replace them. Third, look for regularities in behavior. For example, does the problem behavior occur in only one setting? Following one activity? Look at what goes before and what follows the behavior: Is the behavior being (unintentionally) rewarded (reinforced)? This assessment approach is sometimes referred to as doing an *ABC analysis* (antecedent-behavior-consequence) (Matson, Turygin, Beighley, Rieske, Tureck, & Matson, 2012).

Often the solution to decreasing a behavior is to get the child to increase good behaviors to replace it; for example, if we are trying to eliminate or reduce a problem behavior, we ought to have something we want to happen instead. All those working with the individual can be careful observers. Sometimes behaviors are noted that serve as warning signs and provide a clue for intervention, such as giving the child something else to do or giving the child a better strategy to use for communicating his needs (e.g., picture exchange to indicate wants in a nonverbal person). This is particularly important for nonverbal individuals.

Sometimes simple adjustments in the child's environment (e.g., moving from a more disorganized environment to a simpler, structured one) can make for a major change. Children with ASDs respond well to structure, predictability, and consistency, and it is important to be sure that the environment is not contributing to the child's problems. The function of the behavior is also important; for example, if it is attention seeking then planned ignoring might help. Keep in mind you want to praise, reward, and reinforce desired behaviors.

Sometimes problems will arise because the child is trying to avoid work or other activities. Unfortunately, if parents give in, this tells the child about how to get out of work! Rather they should get the child to engage for a short time in the activity initially, then praise her and let her do something else for a while.

Some sensory behaviors can be addressed by helping the child find more appropriate ways to engage in the behavior (Baranek, Little, Diane, D'Ausderau, & Sabatos-DeVito, 2014). Occupational therapists can help. For individuals with major communication difficulties problem behaviors may well have a communicative function, for example, if the child can't say no or stop, the problem behavior does it for them. We should try to minimize communication difficulties in dealing with problem behaviors. Parents should keep language simple and exact. For nonverbal individuals some basic ways to communicate no or yes can be useful, such as a help card to ask for help rather than screaming to ask for help or some basic other signs. The speech-language pathologist should be able to suggest strategies or communication methods to help with this and may be able to collaborate with the school psychologist or a behavior specialist on ways to do this. Primary care providers can help parents by telling them there are options and help the treatment team be in good communication with each other, such as if a help card is working at school parents should use it at home. Table 10.2 summarizes some of the common mistakes in dealing with behavior problems.

TABLE 10.2   COMMON MISTAKES IN DEALING WITH BEHAVIOR PROBLEMS

Problem	Solution
Making language too complicated	Keep language simple and to the point; do not resort to complicated terms such as "would you" or "could you" and so on; these seem polite but are complex and confusing.
Focusing only on the negative	This sends a strong message that what you want is negative! Focus instead on what is desired. If you want to have the person stop doing something then give some alternative.
Time pressure	Give sufficient time and visual supports, if needed, to help the individual process; moving too quickly disorganizes the person.
Complex humor (sarcasm, irony)	Keep humor simple; sarcasm and irony are very complicated to understand.
Figurative language	Saying "it's raining cats and dogs" may be taken literally.
Ambiguity	Ambiguity can be very difficult to cope with. Keep things explicit and straightforward. Avoid things with unpredictable ends or time components.
Inconsistency	Introduce change gradually and in gradual ways; major changes and inconsistences are very disruptive to learning.
Unintentional reinforcement of behavior	Be careful that you are not actually reinforcing a problem behavior; for example, is your attention to screaming increasing the behavior because the individual gets more attention?

TYPES OF BEHAVIORAL DIFFICULTIES

Behavioral difficulties in autism and related conditions can take many different forms, but generally fall into several, sometimes overlapping, categories. Occasionally, the individual exhibits so many difficulties that it is hard to sort out exactly what is going on. This is one of the reasons that an outside consultant (a behavioral psychologist or behavior specialist) can be helpful, for example, in coming up with a plan on what behaviors to prioritize.

Stereotyped Behaviors and Agitation and Irritability

Stereotyped behaviors are apparently purposeless, repetitive movements common in young children with autism and related conditions (although not as common in Asperger's disorder). They often seem to emerge around ages 2 to 3 and can include body rocking, finger flicking, toe walking, and other complex, whole-body movements. Stereotyped movements are also sometimes referred to as **self-stimulation** (note this is not the same thing as masturbation in this context, although the latter can indeed be an issue at times).

Stereotyped movements are often associated with other behavior problems such as self-injury, aggression, behavioral rigidity, and difficulties with change. Occasionally similar behaviors (body rocking and sometimes head banging) are seen in typical infants but disappear as the child ages. Typically developing school- and high school–age children may also engage in mild levels of self-stimulatory movements, such as moving their legs rapidly while taking a test, because this helps them feel less anxious. Unusual movements such as **tics** can be seen in other conditions, for example, in Tourette's syndrome. Tics differ from stereotyped behaviors in that they tend to occur in bouts, involve the head and neck (particularly early on), and the child doesn't seem to enjoy engaging in them. Thus, they tend not to involve the hands or finger flicking or the whirling or twirling seen more frequently in children with ASDs. Movement problems may also be seen in other disorders (e.g., sometimes following strep infections); occasionally, it can be difficult to disentangle the nature of the movements. This is one of the reasons it is good to have a specialist such as an experienced psychiatrist or neurologist involved if the child is making seemingly purposeless movements, particularly if you are unsure of the diagnosis—inquire about recent infections (e.g., strep) or family history of tics or exposure to drugs that might be associated with unusual movements (Scahill, Tillberg, & Martin, 2014).

Repetitive, stereotyped movements vary over the short and long term. Often, they seem to increase after about age 3, then may increase in frequency or intensity (or both) again around 5 or 6 years of age, then decrease, only to return again around the onset of puberty, often some months before the first physical signs of puberty. These behaviors can show up at times when the child is bored or stressed, as well as overstimulated or anxious.

They may also seem to serve as a preferred mode of activity for the child, almost like relaxation.

Parents and teachers often ask us when we would intervene with these behaviors and often are eager to try medications. These behaviors are often more difficult for parents to manage effectively when the child is in more public settings, and parents and siblings are often quite distressed by these behaviors. Teachers may find that the behaviors interfere with engaging the child in the educational program. Fortunately, although these behaviors are difficult to entirely eliminate, many children can be helped to decrease them. The decision to pursue treatment should include consideration of whether the behavior really interferes with the child's or the family's life or the classroom in some important way. Low levels of such behavior are often easier to live with, and parents and others can work to confine the behaviors to certain places or contexts. Occasionally, giving the child the opportunity to engage in these behaviors can itself be used as a reward for appropriate behavior. With occasional exceptions (e.g., when the behavior is putting the child in some danger), we would not generally recommend medications as a first step.

It is also clear that movement and vigorous physical activity can help reduce stereotyped behaviors (Sowa & Meulenbroek, 2012). Children who engage in high levels of spinning or twirling can benefit from regular exercise. Even getting the child up for short periods in the classroom to engage in vigorous movement such as stretching, jumping, or bouncing can help. Sometimes one of the problems with more-inclusive classroom settings is that opportunities for physical movement and vigorous activity are limited to gym and recess (places where children with autism often need the most supervision and where, because of social isolation, they may not get as much exercise as other children). In addition, children are generally encouraged to stay seated in the regular classroom setting. If movement seems to help, some modification in the program to allow for periodic breaks for movement and other physical activity can be useful.

Occasionally, children engage in auditory self-stimulation, for example, by spending long periods of time humming or making noises. This sometimes happens when the child is overly stimulated (particularly by noises and sounds), and a look at the environment may help clarify what is going on. For children who are overly responsive to sounds, various devices are available, ranging from simple earplugs to music (an iPhone or other smartphone) and those that produce white noise or certain sounds (such as the sound of the ocean or of rain falling). Pharmacological interventions (discussed in Chapter 11) can also be effective in helping reduce levels of these behaviors.

Aggression and Self-Injury

These behaviors involve either self-inflicted injury or injury to others and are among the most difficult and problematic behaviors for parents, teachers, and professionals to deal with. Fortunately, this problem is not that common, and, even when it occurs, there are a number of potential interventions. Aggression and self-injury often occur along with other problems (such as stereotyped movements, rigidity, or perseveration).

Self-injury can take many different forms, including head banging, pinching oneself, pulling out hair, poking the eye, biting the hand or arm, and so forth. Aggression against others may include biting, scratching, or hitting. Behavior that is destructive to property is also often associated with this category of difficulties. Self-injurious behavior can be extremely distressing for parents and teachers to see. It is not common until school-age although occasionally it occurs in younger children with autism.

The sudden onset of self-injurious behavior, particularly head banging, should prompt medical examination because such behavior may be a way for a child who does not have words to communicate about her physical pain. Infected ears are particularly likely culprits in younger children; in adolescents who are nonverbal and who start head banging for the first time, dental problems, such as impacted wisdom teeth, are sometimes to blame. This is another important reason for the child to have regular dental care! Children who start to poke their eyes may have some physical problem or occasionally even a visual difficulty that they can't complain about in words.

Aggression toward others is often (but not always) provoked in some way, for example, because the child is interrupted or asked to do something more challenging. Because of the unusual interests and preoccupations, it may be hard to know what sets off these behaviors. Similarly, the unusual ways that the person who is verbal talks may sometimes make it difficult to understand what gets the behavior going. Similar to self-injury, aggression can be a major problem for parents as well as teachers and school staff members. It may take the form of biting, hitting, kicking, scratching, or head butting.

Again, a careful analysis of what seems to set off the behavior is very important. For example, is it a response to frustration, an escape behavior, or the child's way of saying, "No, I don't want to do this"? In analyzing the behavior, it is also important to look at the context in which the behavior occurs. For example, is it only at school? Only with some care providers? Only during some activities or situations? Only at certain times of the day? Often, this information gives important clues as to why the behavior may be happening and what you can do about it. Turn yourself into a reporter or a detective and ask the basic *wh* questions: *who, what, where, when,* and *why.* The parents of one 8-year-old boy with autism called one of us complaining that their child needed medication to decrease his aggression. Discussion with the parents made it clear that this was a new behavior following a recent change in the child's bus route and driver. The new route (itself a potential problem) was much longer, there was no longer a bus monitor, and there was a new student on board who screamed during the bus ride. The child, who was very sensitive to loud sounds and greatly annoyed by the screaming student, reacted by trying to bite him. In this case, some modifications in the bus arrangements and giving the boy an MP3 player to listen to resulted in a quick change in the behavior.

As our example illustrates and as with other behavioral difficulties, a good analysis of potential causes and consequences of the behavior is very important. Did the head banging or self-injury start after the child entered a new classroom or after some aspect of her program was changed? Does the self-injury occur only during downtimes or with certain people or situations? Is it related to levels of environmental stimulation (either too much or too little)? Some children head bang only at night, and others will engage in this behavior only in very specific situations. For other children it may be a more general problem seen in many different situations and contexts.

If the behavior is potentially very dangerous, medications may be used more quickly. For example, occasionally children with autism will bite themselves to the point of causing significant injury and may need medications to help change the behavior. Even when medications are used, it is important to try to understand what sets off, and keeps up, the behavior. In such cases, a comprehensive functional assessment including all involved in the child's care is essential and part of the treatment planning process.

Some of the same medicines used for treating stereotyped behaviors can be used for treating aggression. Again, behavioral methods are, generally, the first things to try, and again, the exception has to do with dangerous behaviors.

Rigidity and Perseverative Behaviors

Unusual interests, ritualistic and compulsive behaviors, and problems with transitions are frequent in children with ASDs. For example, a child may be preoccupied with turning lights on and off, opening and closing doors, or feeling water run out of faucets. Some children may hoard objects or place them in very specific ways or places (and become upset if anyone changes them).

Although sometimes hard to measure, these behaviors can be sources of great difficulty for higher-functioning children. Children with Asperger's syndrome can spend inordinate amounts of time pursuing more facts in relation to their topic of interest (Myles & Smith, 2007). Typical kinds of interests in children with Asperger's include time, geology, astronomy, dinosaurs, and snakes. Some of the more unusual interests we've seen have included deep fat fryers, telegraph pole line insulators, disasters, and the names, dates of birth, and home addresses of every member of Congress!

Sometimes lower-functioning children with autism who otherwise seem to have very short attention spans can spend seemingly endless time on their particular fixation. Regardless of the child's level of functioning, these special interests are a problem if the child spends so much time on them that they actually interfere with her functioning in other areas.

Unfortunately, by being so fixated on a particular object or topic, the child also avoids being exposed to new situations and learning new things. Teaching staff members and parents may find themselves going to great lengths not to provoke the child and allow too much time for the child to pursue his or her interest at the expense of time for learning.

The difficulties that children with autism have in dealing with change really speak to their problems with social information processing as well as their tendency to learn things in whole chunks (what psychologists call *gestalt learning*) rather than breaking things down into bits. As long as things stay exactly the same, the child doesn't have to deal with the complexity posed by change. This problem also speaks to the difficulties children with autism have in getting the big picture of social interaction. That is, social interaction presents many significant obstacles if you have trouble dealing with any change, because meaning is always changing, depending on who is talking and what that person is talking about. Furthermore, the multiple competing cues in interaction (tone of voice, facial expression, gesture, and content of words), which provide important meaning for the rest of us, are potential sources of confusion and disorganization for children with ASDs.

Sometimes, particularly for higher-functioning children, special interests and preoccupations can be put to good use. For example, a child with Asperger's disorder who was interested in astronomy led the discussion of space and planets in his fifth-grade class. Similarly, another child who was interested in chess was able to work as a chess teacher for his peers. Unfortunately, finding a good use for special interests is not always so easily done—particularly when the interest is more esoteric.

Various strategies can be used to help deal with resistance to change. For children who do not have much spoken language (Hodgdon, 1999; see http://usevisualstrategies.com). This is one aspect of the more general approach to using concrete visual materials to help the child be more communicative or organized. A small camera and notebook or cards can be used to help the child see what came before, what is happening now, and what is going to happen in the future. These visual schedules can be placed on refrigerators at home or on bulletin boards in the classroom, and the student's attention can periodically be drawn to them. An ever-increasing number of apps are available to help with schedules, transitions, times, and so on. The "Suggested Reading" list at the end of this chapter provides other good resources.

A second strategy entails helping the child tolerate change through a more gradual process. Again, an entire body of work based on learning theory can be used to introduce change gradually. You can try planned change or planned surprises and have times when you give the child the choice among three secret surprises, which can be put on the back of an index card. The child gets to pick one, not knowing what it is, of course. In the beginning it helps to make all the choices ones the child will like. Help the child work with time and organization skills (see Chapter 5). Depending on the child's level of ability, these can range from use of simple visual supports to lists (for children who can read) and organizers and more sophisticated computer software devices. Another approach is to make the behavior more functional, that is, by helping the child use his or her interest in a more normal or typical way. The idea is that by helping the child learn to use behaviors in more productive ways he or she can be helped to be more functional in daily life.

Other strategies are available for verbal individuals and are especially effective for children with Asperger's syndrome (Volkmar, Klin, & McPartland, 2014). These can include use of the following:

- Scripts and verbal routines (basically a canned set of verbalized guidelines a child can use to talk herself through specific situations)

- Social Stories (prewritten stories children can review to help them practice and rehearse strategies for dealing with potentially problematic situations; see Chapter 6)

- Provide rules (e.g., you must always ask before you take something) that are simple, functional, and can be written down for children who read

Behavioral approaches can be helpful with more-able children as well. For example, many higher-functioning individuals have difficulty dealing with novelty, because this makes them anxious. In addition they may have trouble in recognizing that something is new and in realizing that they are anxious. Explicit teaching and counseling can be quite helpful for these children.

A related issue has to do with compulsive and ritualistic behaviors. The child may have to go through a set series of actions or behaviors when engaging in some activity.

Some ritualistic or compulsive behaviors have some similarity to those seen in obsessive-compulsive disorder (OCD), a condition in which people are troubled by obsessions (things they can't stop thinking about, such as the thought that they are bad) and compulsions (the need to do an activity over and over, such as washing the hands because of a fear that they are dirty). Some degree of obsessiveness and compulsiveness is perfectly normal and can be adaptive. It is not normal, however, if the child is washing her hands for 50 minutes at a time (often to the point where they are bleeding) or is so troubled by doing something bad that she is essentially immobilized.

The similarities of more typical OCD-type behaviors to some of those seen in autism (the rigidity and tendency to repeat things) are very interesting, and some of the same drug treatments for these behaviors are used for OCD and autism. A major point of difference is that often children (or adolescents and adults) with OCD will tell you that they don't like having to engage in the behaviors. By contrast, individuals with ASDs often find their compulsive behaviors are not distressing and, if anything, they are sources of comfort and pleasure.

Various medications may be helpful with this set of problems (see Chapter 11). The most frequently used medications are the selective serotonin reuptake inhibitors (SSRIs). The particular advantage of these medications is that they target the rigidity and compulsiveness as well as the anxiety involved in dealing with change. Sometimes these behaviors respond to other medications as well.

Attention and Overactivity

Problems with attention, overactivity, and hyperactivity are fairly common in children with ASDs. These problems may include difficulties with listening, disorganization, high levels of activity, and impulsiveness. The child may be restless and on the go more or less all the time. Difficulties with not listening and impulsive behavior can be the source of much trouble, such as bolting into the street. For children with emerging language or no language, it is important to realize that at least some of the difficulties may relate to difficulties with language and communication (Mayes, Calhoun, & Molitoris, 2012). For higher cognitively functioning children the attentional problems (and to some extent hyperactivity) may suggest attention deficit hyperactivity disorder (ADHD). The question as to whether to formally diagnose ADHD in children with ASDs remains somewhat complicated.

In evaluating attention problems, one of the first questions to ask is whether the child's difficulties with activity and attention are seen in all situations or only at school. If they occur only at school, it is then worth asking if these difficulties are seen in every class or setting or only in some. If only in school and only in some settings, it would be worth paying careful attention to what is going on. For example:

- Are the language (or social-communication) demands for the child too high?
- Is the academic material over his or her head?
- Can the classroom environment be modified to help the child be more organized?

- Can visual supports or augmentative communication systems or other strategies be used to help the child have a more predictable learning environment? For example, can a review of a schedule or preteaching be helpful?

- Does the child start the day doing well and then seem to lose it as time goes on? (If so, fatigue may be a factor.)

- Do different approaches seem to be helpful (giving the child periods for activity interspersed with schoolwork)?

- What rewards motivate the child? What will the child work for?

- Is the classroom overstimulating (what can be fine for the typical child can be a real disaster for a child with marked auditory or visual sensitivities)?

If the problems with attention or overactivity seem to be happening in all parts of the child's life, some of the same considerations will apply. For instance, there should be a functional assessment and consideration of measures (such as visual cues) to help the child be more organized. For the more-able child with Asperger's or high-functioning autism or PDD, other organizational aids may be helpful. A behavioral program may be helpful in school and home settings, with consistent record keeping and attention to the child's behavior coupled with a system of rewards and positive supports. This effort should involve parents and teachers so that the system can be applied consistently across the child's day.

A number of different treatments have been used over the years to help children with attentional problems. The most commonly used medicines (in all children) are the stimulants (amphetamines and methylphenidate). Some children, particularly more classically autistic children, may respond to these medicines by becoming more disorganized and active. (This does not always happen, and even when it does, the medicine is out of the system fairly quickly!) A range of drugs is sometimes used as well and are discussed in Chapter 11.

MENTAL HEALTH ISSUES AND BEHAVIOR PROBLEMS

Particularly for more verbal and cognitively able individuals, behavior problems are frequently seen in the context of additional mental health problems, for example, the child with Asperger's who is highly anxious or depressed or the more-able student with autism who is rigid and compulsive. This phenomenon of having more than one disorder at a time is called **comorbidity**. This issue comes up with reference to thinking about behavioral problems and medications (and we talk about this again in Chapter 11 with special reference to drug treatments). Comorbidity has special importance when we think that behavior problems are coming about because of some other difficulties with anxiety or attention or depression (Volkmar, Reichow, & McPartland, 2014). It makes sense that many of the same treatments (behavioral, counseling, and drug treatments) that work in non-autistic children might work for emotional problems in individuals with ASDs. Unfortunately, until recently, this area has been a relatively neglected topic for research (Volkmar, Reichow, et al., 2014).

Fortunately, this situation is beginning to change. Within the field of autism, particularly as individuals have become older, it is clear that many people can profit from very focused, counseling-type psychotherapies (Volkmar, Reichow, et al., 2014). Often, the explicit verbal teaching and focused problem-solving so helpful to students with Asperger's (Myles, 2004) verges into psychotherapy. The boundaries of teaching, counseling, and psychotherapy can be blurry, but these approaches can sometimes be very, very helpful to students with associated behavior problems. There are some excellent papers that address some of these issues (Attwood, 2003), specifically, the behavioral difficulties, social problems, and difficulties with mood and anxiety so often found in older children and adolescents.

Within the psychotherapy field itself there have been some important advances. One approach, called *cognitive behavior therapy (CBT)*, is grounded in research done in cognitive and behavioral psychology. CBT refers to different treatments used for a range of problems, including mood and anxiety disorders. These approaches focus on the cognitive and behavioral sides of things and have a number of advantages over older psychotherapies in that they tend to be brief, focused, and time limited. Some have been adapted for people with ASD. For example, the objective may be to help the individual understand why he or she becomes anxious and how anxiety can be identified and dealt with in more appropriate ways (Wood et al., 2015). There now have been some scientifically well-controlled studies in people with ASD showing that CBT methods works well in helping children cope with and reduce levels of anxiety.

What are the limitations of these methods? It is important to realize that one of the reasons psychotherapy (and, by extension, many forms of counseling) got a bad reputation in the autism world was the early focus on blaming parents and attempting to cure the child with autism. Even now, when our perspectives have changed dramatically, there is some potential for people to overly focus on some condition as causing, explaining, or excusing bad behavior. The excusing part is a particular source of disagreement with schools. Sometimes there is, of course, truth in the observation that the child acted out because he was stressed or anxious or depressed. However, other children without ASDs also become anxious and depressed and stressed. For many children, an explicit focus on problem behavior will lead parents and teachers to a straightforward behavioral assessment and intervention. However, particularly for more-able students, a broader view of the troubles may lead to other kinds of intervention. When CBT or other talking-type therapies are explored, it is important that teachers and parents (and the individual) not lose sight of the behavioral difficulties. Also, it is important for therapists to keep in mind that usual short-term intervention models (for example, the individual comes to a group for 6 to 10 weeks and then is finished) may be less applicable. In our experience (and one of us has seen a handful of patients, off and on, for several decades), a model in which people on the autism spectrum tap into services when they need them may be most appropriate.

Integrating Behavioral and Medical Treatments

Although behavioral and educational interventions are typically tried first, medications also play an important role. Sometimes behavioral interventions alone don't do the trick. Other times there may be a real emergency (such as when a child is seriously injuring herself by head banging). Medicines and behavioral procedures can be used together, often very effectively. We discuss this issue in much more detail in Chapter 11.

There are several times in the life of a child with autism when medications are more likely to be considered. Generally, very young children are least likely to receive medications. Usually, their behavioral difficulties are pretty minimal, and it is much easier to physically manage an out-of-control 2-year-old than an out-of-control 12-year-old. The time before and when children enter puberty is often when behavioral difficulties arise. We are not sure why this is, although the various changes they experience in their bodies and changes in hormone levels probably are part of the picture. For some children, particularly higher-functioning children, the advent of adolescence also means that the child is more aware of being different, in some important ways, from other children. They may be able to talk about feeling anxious and may also talk about feelings of depression, sometimes serious symptoms of depression. Fortunately, we have fairly effective treatments for depression in terms of drug and behavioral options. Even more important, the desire to fit in really spurs remarkable growth in some children.

Case Examples

The following three case examples show how behavioral techniques were used effectively.

Case 1: Willy Willy was a 9-year-old boy with autism. He had some words, but generally his expressive speech was rather limited. He understood language to a greater degree than he actually used it. Cognitive testing with him had consistently shown that he was functioning overall in the moderate range of intellectual disability, with a full-scale **intelligence quotient (IQ)** of about 50, although his nonverbal abilities were higher (close to 70). The problem with bolting and running out of the classroom had started in the fall when Willy was enrolled in a new classroom setting. He previously had not had many behavior problems. As part of the understandable attempt to provide him with greater access to peers, he was being mainstreamed for the mornings (for the most part), spending most of his afternoon in special education or getting his various specials. Staffing in the morning included a regular education teacher along with a paraprofessional (mostly for Willy, but also for one other student with special needs). The special education teacher consulted with the regular ed teacher but only periodically. The bolting was almost entirely confined to the morning setting. The regular ed teacher had tried several things, including trying to reason with Willy, and then, at the suggestion of the speech pathologist, gave Willy a written schedule and made some other accommodations for him. Despite these changes, by the middle of October, he was running or bolting about 15 times a day on average. A behaviorally

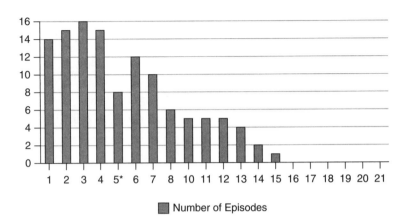

Number of Episodes

FIGURE 10.1   **Bolting and running behavioral data from Willy. Data represented for consecutive school days and indicate changes in behavior procedures.**

Source: Reprinted from Volkmar and Wiesner (2009, p. 443).

trained psychologist was asked to consult and spent some time observing Willy at various points during his day and in his various classroom settings. She also spoke to Willy's parents, who were as mystified as his regular ed teacher because Willy did not generally have a problem with bolting or running at home.

The psychologist noticed two different factors that seemed to contribute to the behavioral difficulties, and she recommended two different interventions. In the first 4 days of observation, the psychologist realized that the bolting or running business had turned into a fairly exciting and dramatic game for Willy. He would carefully wait for his moment, then bolt, precipitating yelling, screaming, and general upset. He was smiling a good part of the time and seemed to enjoy the run-and-chase activities (see Figure 10.1).

The psychologist's first recommendation was to arrange for the school guard to be available in the immediate area (but outside the classroom on day 5), and she had asked him to be on the alert for Willy and to calmly and matter-of-factly escort him back to class. The teacher and paraprofessional were instructed when Willy bolted to not engage in the run-and-chase game but to generally ignore this behavior. The system was in place for alerting the school guard, who indeed would meet Willy in the hall and redirect him back to the classroom.

On the first day this was instituted as a procedure Willy had 14 episodes of bolting. For the next 2 days, it appeared that Willy was testing the limits, but by day 8 it did appear that the behavior had been markedly reduced but still persisted at lower levels. The next recommendation resulted after further observations. In keeping track of episodes, the psychologist realized that these were now almost always confined to a situation (reading group) when Willy was most challenged. Accordingly, she arranged for Willy to spend this time in a quiet area away from the main group, where he worked with his paraprofessional for most of the time, rejoining the class only at the end. Willy's bolting quickly dropped to zero.

Case 2: Johnny   Johnny was a 6-year-old with Asperger's who had begun attending a new primary school. He was quite verbal but also very socially disabled. Although motorically clumsy, he was fascinated with the furnace and the basement of his school (which is where the furnace was located). He quickly developed a habit of sneaking away (whenever the teacher's back was turned). After a search, he was invariably found in the furnace room in the basement. Attempts to reason with him were not successful. A brief medication trial with a stimulant led to agitation and irritability and was quickly discontinued. The custodian, whose room was next to the furnace, was understandably annoyed by all the trouble Johnny created.

In this case the consultant's recommendation was to try to use, to the extent possible, Johnny's motivations and interest in a positive way. Accordingly, a token reward system was instituted. When he stayed through an entire class without sneaking away, he received a red poker chip. When he had six chips (and there were six classes during the day), he was able, at the end of the day, to have a prearranged 10-minute meeting with the janitor (Mr. Bob) at the furnace area, who would demonstrate different aspects of the furnace, talk about furnaces, and so on. This turned out to be highly motivating for Johnny, and, somewhat paradoxically, Mr. Bob developed a real friendship with him (after all, they shared an interest in the furnace).

The predictability meant that the janitor's life was not constantly disrupted and, in the end, Mr. Bob became a real advocate for Johnny at school and he began to serve as the "safe address" for Johnny. For example, if Johnny felt himself getting anxious or starting to feel overwhelmed he could always ask for a pass to see Mr. Bob, who would then ask him what was going on before he returned him to his classroom. At the end of the day, Mr. Bob would check with the teacher to be sure she or he knew about Johnny's trouble.

In this instance it was possible to rapidly address the problem behavior. More important, what seemed like a simple subsequent step (having Mr. Bob serve as Johnny's safe address in school) was actually a fairly sophisticated technique in that it (1) disrupted the behavior and (2) encouraged self-observation. Rather than losing it (for reasons he often was unaware of), Johnny was encouraged to substitute a more appropriate behavior (seeking his adult friend), which prevented or disrupted blowups and got a sympathetic adult involved in the process of monitoring Johnny's behavior.

Case 3: Carla Carla was a 12-year-old girl with Asperger's. She had (for many years) a preoccupation with small creatures—and was now focused on the various kinds of protozoans.

Her nonverbal problem-solving skills were in the average range, and her verbal skills were in the superior range. Her social skills were more like those of a typically developing 4-year-old. She had a strong desire to have friends but rather limited abilities to make and actually keep friends. Her anxiety was a major problem for her—any kind of pressure (a test, assignment, upcoming school special event) would be the source of tremendous anxiety, and behavioral upset regularly followed. Her parents began to dread special days in school because they knew she would be highly anxious and extremely difficult for the day or two before the event.

The school psychologist recommended a local clinical psychologist who was interested in CBT and was able to secure some training in working with children on the autism spectrum. He and Carla worked together for a period of several months. They outlined very specific issues in the first two sessions. These included stress identification and stress management, learned relaxation techniques, increased awareness of the experience of anxiety, and a series of homework to help Carla focus on using specific techniques to reduce anxiety. This effort met with considerable success in reducing acute anxiety levels, although Carla and the therapist realized it had done little to work on her desire for more friends in her peer group. They agreed to continue individual work focused on this issue, and Carla began to attend a social skills group. In this case, a more cognitively able child could use some of the strategies provided by CBT to focus on acquiring specific problem-solving skills and strategies (Wood et al., 2015).

As is sometimes the case, having helped Carla become more able to cope with her anxiety, she was then aware of other issues, particularly peer relationships, and she and her family chose to pursue further, focused work on this topic.

SUMMARY

In this chapter, we described some of the more common behavior problems that children with ASDs exhibit. Again, we emphasize that many children with autism do not have these problems. Sometimes problems come up at certain times in life or in certain situations (the start of a new school, adolescence), and sometimes they go away on their own. It is important to realize that behavioral interventions can be very effective. Occasionally, problem behaviors are unwittingly encouraged by teachers or parents. It is important that parents and teachers be aware of their own effect on the child and the potential, for good or ill, of significant behavioral effects. Thinking about interventions requires a careful look at the entire situation, including the child's environment and a detailed analysis of when, where, and why the behaviors seem to be occurring. The good news is that many problem behaviors can be managed effectively.

REFERENCES

Attwood, T. (2003). Frameworks for behavioral intervention. *Child & Adolescent Psychiatric Clinics of North America, 12,* 65–86.

Baranek, G. T., Little, L. M., Diane, P., D'Ausderau, K. K., & Sabatos-DeVito, M. G. (2014). Sensory features in autism spectrum disorders. In F. R. Volkmar, S. J. Rogers, R. Paul, & K. A. Pelphrey (Eds.), *Handbook of autism and pervasive developmental disorders* (4th ed., Vol. 1, pp. 378–407). Hoboken, NJ: Wiley.

Hodgdon, L. (1999). *Solving behavior problems in autism: Improving communication with visual strategies.* Troy, MI: QuirkRoberts.

Matson, J. L., Turygin, N. C., Beighley, J., Rieske, R., Tureck, K., & Matson, M. L. (2012). Applied behavior analysis in autism spectrum disorders: Recent developments, strengths, and pitfalls. *Research in Autism Spectrum Disorders, 6*(1), 144–150.

Mayes, S. D., Calhoun, S. L., Mayes, R. D., & Molitoris, S. (2012). Autism and ADHD: Overlapping and discriminating symptoms. *Research in Autism Spectrum Disorders, 6*(1), 277–285.

Myles, B. S. (2004). Review of Asperger syndrome and psychotherapy: Understanding Asperger perspectives. *American Journal of Psychotherapy, 58*(3), 365–366.

Myles, B. S., & Smith, S. (2007). Understanding the special interests of individuals with Asperger syndrome: Introduction to the special series. *Focus on Autism and Other Developmental Disabilities, 22*(2), 66.

Powers, M. D., Palmieri, M. J., Egan, S. M., Rohrer, J. L., Nulty, E. C., & Forte, S. (2014). Behavioral assessment of individuals with autism: Current practice and future directions. In F. R. Volkmar, S. J. Rogers, R. Paul, & K. A. Pelphrey (Eds.), *Handbook of autism and pervasive developmental disorders* (4th ed., Vol. 2, pp. 695–736). Hoboken, NJ: Wiley.

Scahill, L., Tillberg, C. S., & Martin, A. (2014). Psychopharmacology. In F. R. Volkmar, S. J. Rogers, R. Paul, & K. A. Pelphrey (Eds.), *Handbook of autism and pervasive developmental disorders* (4th ed., Vol. 2, pp. 556–579). Hoboken, NJ: Wiley.

Sowa, M., & Meulenbroek, R. (2012). Effects of physical exercise on autism spectrum disorders: A meta-analysis. *Research in Autism Spectrum Disorders, 6*(1), 46–57.

Volkmar, F. R., Klin, A., & McPartland, J. C. (Eds.). (2014). Treatment and intervention guidelines for Asperger syndrome. *Asperger syndrome: Assessing and treating high-functioning autism spectrum disorders* (2nd ed., pp. 143–178). New York, NY: Guilford Press.

Volkmar, F. R., Reichow, B., & McPartland, J. C. (2014). Adolescents and adults with autism spectrum disorders. *Adolescents and adults with autism spectrum disorders* (pp. xv, 337). New York, NY: Springer Science + Business Media.

Volkmar, F., Siegel, M., Woodbury-Smith, M., King, B., McCracken, J., State, M., & the American Academy of and Child and Adolescent Psychiatry (AACAP) Committee on Quality Issues (CQI). (2014). Practice parameter for the assessment and treatment of children and adolescents with autism spectrum disorder. Erratum. *Journal of the American Academy of Child and Adolescent Psychiatry, 53*(8), 931.

Volkmar, F., & Wiesner, L. (2009). *A practical guide to autism.* Hoboken NJ: Wiley.

Wood, J. J., Ehrenreich-May, J., Alessandri, M., Fujii, C., Renno, P., Laugeson, E., et al. (2015). Cognitive behavioral therapy for early adolescents with autism spectrum disorders and clinical anxiety: A randomized, controlled trial. *Behavior Therapy, 46*(1), 7–19.

SUGGESTED READING

Attwood, T. (2004). *Exploring feelings: Cognitive behavior therapy to manage anxiety.* Arlington, TX: Future Horizons.

Bailey, J., & Bruch, M. (2006). *How to think like a behavior analyst.* Mahwah, NJ: Erlbaum.

Bauminger, N. (2002). The facilitation of social-emotional understanding and social interaction in high-functioning children with autism: Intervention outcomes. *Journal of Autism and Developmental Disorders, 32*(4), 283–298.

Bauminger, N. (2007). Brief report: Group social-multimodal intervention for HFASD. *Journal of Autism and Developmental Disorders, 37*(8), 1605–1615.

Bauminger, N., Shulman, C., & Agam, G. (2004). The link between perceptions of self and of social relationships in high-functioning children with autism. *Journal of Developmental and Physical Disabilities, 16*(2), 193–214.

Buron, K. D., & Myles, B. S. (2004). *When my autism gets too big! A relaxation book for children with autism spectrum disorders.* Shawnee Mission, KS: Autism Asperger.

Cardon, T. A. (2004). *Let's talk emotions: Helping children with social cognitive deficits including AS, HFA, and NVLD learn to understand and express empathy and emotions.* Shawnee Mission, KS: Autism Asperger.

Clements, J., & Zarkowska, E. (2000). *Behavioural concerns and autism spectrum disorders: Explanations and strategies for change.* London, UK: Jessica Kingsley.

Cooper, J. O., Heron, T. E., & Heward, W. L. (2007). *Applied behavior analysis* (2nd ed.). Upper Saddle River, NJ: Prentice Hall.

Dubin, N. (2009). *Asperger syndrome and anxiety: A guide to successful stress management.* London, UK: Jessica Kingsley.

Evans, K., & Dubowski, J. (2001). *Art therapy with children on the autistic spectrum: Beyond words.* London, UK: Jessica Kingsley.

Fletcher, R., Loschen, E., Stavrakaki, C., & First, M. (2007). *Diagnostic manual—intellectual disability (DM-ID): A textbook of diagnosis of mental disorders in persons with intellectual disability.* Kingston, NY: NADD Press.

Fouse, B., & Wheeler, M. (1997). *A treasure chest of behavioral strategies for individuals with autism.* Arlington, TX: Future Horizons.

Gaus, V. O. (2007). *Cognitive-behavioral therapy for adult Asperger syndrome.* New York, NY: Guilford Press.

Ghaziuddin, M. (2005). *Mental health aspects of autism and Asperger syndrome.* London, UK: Jessica Kingsley.

Glasberg, B. A. (2006). *Functional behavior assessment for people with autism: Making sense of seemingly senseless behavior.* Bethesda, MD: Woodbine House.

Grandin, T., & Barron, S. (2005). *The unwritten rules of social relationships: Decoding social mysteries through the unique perspectives of autism.* Arlington, TX: Future Horizons.

Harpur, J., Lawlor, M., & Fitzgerald, M. (2006). *Succeeding with interventions for Asperger syndrome adolescents: A guide to communication and socialization in interaction therapy.* London, UK: Jessica Kingsley.

Huebner, D. (2006). *What to do when you worry too much: A kid's guide to overcoming anxiety.* Washington, DC: Magination Press.

Jacobsen, P. (2003). *Asperger syndrome and psychotherapy: Understanding Asperger perspectives.* London, UK: Jessica Kingsley.

Kearney, A. J. (2007). *Understanding applied behavior analysis: An introduction to ABA for parents, teachers, and other professionals.* London, UK: Jessica Kingsley.

Leaf, R., McEachin, J., & Harsh, J. D. (1999). *A work in progress: Behavior management strategies & a curriculum for intensive behavioral treatment of autism.* New York, NY: DRL Books.

Leaf, R., Taubman, M., & McEachin, J. (2008). *It's time for school! Building quality ABA educational programs for students with autism spectrum disorders.* New York, NY: DRL Books.

Lean, R., McEachin, J., & Harsh, J. D. (1991). *A work in progress: Behavior management strategies and a curriculum for intensive behavioral treatment of autism.* New York: DRI Books.

Luiselli, J. K., Russo, D. C., Christian, W. P., & Wilczynski, S. M. (2008). *Effective practices for children with autism: Educational and behavior support interventions that work.* New York: Oxford University Press.

Maurice, C. M., Green, G., & Luce, S. L. (Eds.). (1996). *Behavioral intervention for young children with autism: A manual for parents and professionals.* Austin, TX: PRO-ED.

Miller-Kuhaneck, H. (2004). *Autism: A comprehensive occupational therapy approach* (2nd ed.). Bethesda, MD: American Occupational Therapy Association.

Moyes, R. A. (2002). *Addressing the challenging behavior of children with high functioning autism/Asperger syndrome in the classroom.* London, UK: Jessica Kingsley.

Myles, B. S. (2001). *Asperger syndrome and sensory issues: Practical solutions for making sense of the world.* Shawnee Mission, KS: Autism Asperger.

Myles, B. S. (2003). Behavioral forms of stress management for individuals with Asperger syndrome. *Child and Adolescent Psychiatric Clinics of North America, 12*(1), 123–141.

Myles, B. S., Adreon, D., & Gitilitz, D. (2006). *Simple strategies that work! Helpful hints for all educators of students with Asperger syndrome, high-functioning autism, and related disabilities.* Shawnee Mission, KS: Autism Asperger.

Myles, B. S., & Southwick, J. (2005). *Asperger syndrome and difficult moments: Practical solutions for tantrums, rage and meltdowns.* Shawnee Mission, KS: Autism Asperger.

Myles, B. S., Trautman, M. L., & Schelvan, R. L. (2004). *The hidden curriculum: Practical solutions for understanding unstated rules in social situations.* Shawnee Mission, KS: Autism Asperger.

O'Donohue, W. T., & Fisher, J. E. (2009). *General principles and empirically supported techniques of cognitive behavior therapy.* Hoboken, NJ: Wiley.

O'Neill, R. E., Horner, R. H., Albin, R. Q., Storey, K., & Sprague, J. R. (1997). *Functional assessment and program development for problem behavior: A practical handbook.* Pacific Grove, CA: Brooks/Cole.

Paxton, K., & Estay, I. A. (2007). *Counseling people on the autism spectrum: A practical manual.* London, UK: Jessica Kingsley.

Powers, M. D. (2005). Behavioral assessment of individuals with autism: A functional ecological approach. In F. Volkmar, A. Klin, R. Paul, & D. J. Cohen (Eds.), *Handbook of autism and pervasive developmental disorders* (4th ed., Vol. 2, pp. 817–830). New York: Wiley.

Prior, M. (Ed.). (2003). *Learning and behavior problems in Asperger syndrome.* New York, NY: Guilford Press.

Richman, S. (2001). *Raising a child with autism: A guide to applied behavior analysis for parents.* London, UK: Jessica Kingsley.

Richman, S. (2006). *Encouraging appropriate behavior for children on the autism spectrum: Frequently asked questions.* London, UK: Jessica Kingsley.

Riddle, M. A. (1987). Individual and parental psychotherapy in autism. In D. J. Cohen & A. Donnellan (Eds.), *Handbook of autism and pervasive developmental disorders* (pp. 528–544). New York: Wiley.

Savner, J., & Myles, B. S. (2000). *Making visual supports work in the home and community: Strategies for individuals with autism and Asperger syndrome.* Shawnee Mission, KS: Autism Asperger.

Sze, K. M., & Wood, J. J. (2007). Cognitive behavioral treatment of comorbid anxiety disorders and social difficulties in children with high-functioning autism: A case report. *Journal of Contemporary Psychotherapy, 37*(3), 133–143.

Weiss, M. J., & McBride, K. (2008). *Practical solutions for educating children with high-functioning autism and Asperger syndrome.* Shawnee Mission, KS: Autism Asperger.

Wood, J. J., Drahota, A., Sze, K., Har, K., Chiu, A., Langer, D. A., et al. (2009). Cognitive behavioral therapy for anxiety in children with autism spectrum disorders: A randomized controlled trial. *Journal of Child Psychology and Psychiatry, 50*(3), 224–234.

CHAPTER 11

Considering Medications for Behavior and Mental Health Problems

A t present there is no medication that specifically addresses the core social difficulties in autism. However, medications are playing a growing and promising role in treating some of the behaviors and problems that often go along with autism. In some cases, drugs can help reduce difficulties with anxiety, moodiness, irritability, hyperactivity, aggression, or stereotyped behaviors. This can often help children be more amenable to educational and other interventions. In this chapter, we will discuss some of the medications more frequently used in treating challenging behaviors and mental health problems in individuals with ASDs. A discussion of all the medicines would fill this book (and has filled several others listed in the "Suggested Reading" list at the end of the chapter). Accordingly this is a highly selective discussion.

MENTAL HEALTH ISSUES IN AUTISM

In the past, many people thought that having a chronic condition such as autism (or any developmental disorder) almost seemed to "protect" the individual from other disorders; in fact, this is not at all true. We now realize that having a problem such as ASD makes it even more likely that the person will have other difficulties, for example, problems with anxiety or mood. There are many issues in disentangling the complicated effects autism has on behavior and emotional problems, that is, in deciding whether the difficulty is really part of having autism or is something separate. There are also marked differences around the world in how these problems are thought of. In the United States, there has been a tendency to equate symptoms with disorder; that is, if a child with autism has trouble with feeling moody or sad, he often will be diagnosed with a form of depression. Around the world additional diagnoses are given less quickly. This is very complex when the individual with ASD has trouble communicating. As a result, it is sometimes hard to know when a symptom or symptoms really become another disorder. We do know that there are higher-than-expected rates of anxiety and mood problems in family members of people with autism. These issues also vary with age.

In younger children and those with less spoken language, some of the most frequent problems have to do with irritability, tantrums, and sometimes self-injury. Sometimes these problems also seem related to difficulties in focusing on or in tolerating change. It remains unclear how we ought to best think about these problems, but some medications can be very helpful (and so can behavioral treatments). For older and more able individuals (who communicate with words), issues with depression and anxiety and, sometimes, trouble with change and rigid behavior patterns become more predominant.

Individuals with ASD (and particularly adolescents and young adults) seem to have an increased risk for depression. This is particularly true among higher cognitively functioning individuals who may, as time goes on, have an increasing sense of being isolated and may feel that they are missing out on many things their typically developing peers enjoy. Research also suggests that there may be a genetic basis for some increased vulnerability for depression and anxiety problems, given increased rates in the families of children with ASD.

More verbal children sometimes talk directly about feeling depressed. Occasionally they may feel irritable rather than depressed. Other children seem to get more agitated and upset when depressed. Not surprisingly, depression can be difficult to diagnose in younger children with developmental problems and in older children who have significant communication problems.

Occasionally, children with ASD have periods of depression and then go back to "normal" before becoming somewhat high and "hyper." It has been suggested that perhaps they have bipolar disorder. The final word is not yet in on whether some children with ASD are more likely to have bipolar disorder, although marked swings in mood combined with major changes in behavior suggest that this might be considered. It is always important to look at the big picture, because, for example, some of the medicines used to treat depression can cause children to be agitated if they actually have bipolar disorder, not depression.

Recurrent difficulties with anxiety can also be seen in children with ASDs. These may include high levels of anxiety as well as more specific anxiety problems, for example, in social situations or around specific activities. Sometimes the problem is with panic attacks. Children with better language skills often can talk about some of the symptoms of anxiety, but even when children do not have good language, the individual may look anxious. Sometimes the difficulties with anxiety lead to other problems, such as self-injury, aggression, or stereotyped movements.

Some research suggests that anxiety may be part and parcel of the autism spectrum disorders. Other work suggests that it may come about as a result of repeated frustration and negative experiences. Higher cognitive functioning children with ASDs often complain about feeling socially isolated and victimized. Trouble processing social information (itself the hallmark of ASDs) almost certainly will lead to anxiety because one can never really envision what will happen. Some work from our group indicates that in some situations maybe 90% of the social-affective information in interaction is lost to the individual on the autism spectrum. Clearly, growing awareness of difficulties in dealing with peers and social situations may lead to a vicious cycle in which anxiety increases and leads to further isolation and so on.

For typically developing individuals, counseling or psychotherapy can often be helpful. This is sometimes true for children with ASDs, although usually the therapist has to be more structured in his or her interaction with the person than would be typical and also has to be more problem focused (that is, more like a teacher in some respects). Various behavioral techniques can also be used, particularly for anxiety difficulties. These include teaching the child how to relax through methods such as biofeedback, visual imagery, and relaxation training. There are effective behavioral treatments for anxiety and depression (see Chapter 10). There are also a number of interventions to put into place relative to teaching social and coping skills (see Chapter 5).

Effective drug treatments for depression include the more traditional antidepressants as well as the more recently developed selective serotonin reuptake inhibitors (SSRIs). Other agents for anxiety problems include minor tranquilizers and buspirone as well as the SSRIs, and some of the alpha-adrenergic agonist medications. Careful monitoring is again important. Side effects can include a kind of behavioral disinhibition—that is, the child becomes more agitated, not less. For children with mood swings, various medications are available. These are often referred to as mood stabilizers.

WHEN TO USE MEDICATION

In Chapter 10, we discussed the various kinds of behavioral and emotional difficulties common in children with autism and related conditions, and we discussed some of the problems that behavioral interventions can help with. In this chapter, we consider how medicines are sometimes used in treatment. In thinking about whether to try medication to help the child, there are several things to consider:

- Are there alternatives to medication, and have these been given a (good) try?
- Are there any physical problems or changes in the child's life that may have contributed to the problem?
- How serious is the problem; for example, does it jeopardize the child's education, or does it put him or others at risk of harm?
- Is it possible that addressing the problem may improve the child's feelings or adjustment to his intervention program?
- When did the behavior or problem start? How long does it last?
- How severe is it?
- What makes it worse (or better)?
- Does it happen in some places and not others?
- Is this a long-standing problem or worsening of a long-standing problem, or is it really a new problem?
- Is the problem getting better or worse?
- How is it changing over time?

As discussed in Chapter 10, a careful behavioral assessment may be worthwhile. There is no reason that medications can't be used with behavioral interventions (in some ways, these often work quite well together), but once you start doing multiple interventions simultaneously, it gets more difficult to understand why things change; that is, it is hard to know which intervention (or combination) is responsible for the improvement.

Depending on the specifics of the situation, it may make the most sense to try behavioral interventions first and then move to medications if these are not successful or only partly successful. Exceptions would be for problems that are more serious, such as those that pose some risk of serious physical injury to the child or others. For example, an adolescent girl who engages in dangerous self-injurious behavior might well be appropriately treated with medication even to the point of slight sedation. In weighing the risks and benefits of the medication, the risks of slight sedation might well be worth the benefit of preventing serious self-injury. However, drug interventions may be less effective than behavioral ones for infrequent behaviors that are less intense and that seem to come up only in certain places or at certain times.

Often, children with ASDs have more than one emotional or behavioral problem. In such cases, it is sometimes possible to choose a medication that may target both problems. For example, the SSRIs may target anxiety and depression. But, in many cases, it may be necessary to choose one target problem at a time to focus on, because the effects of the medication may be relatively narrower.

Medications can be combined with behavioral and educational approaches to produce more lasting benefit particularly if good data are kept. The use of medications always requires a careful balancing act between risk and benefit and a consideration of all the causes of the behavioral difficulties.

The variety of medications used to treat children with autism and related conditions is growing. Some medications have been used more frequently and have been carefully studied in a scientific way so we know a fair amount about them. For other medications, the information available is based on a small number of children treated with the medication, children treated non-blindly, or involving only one or a few cases.

Ruling Out Pain as a Cause

Sometimes behavioral troubles arise because a child is in pain. This is most common in children with limited communication skills. For example, a child who previously had not had self-injurious behavior might one day start to hit the side of his head. Before beginning medications to control his self-injurious behavior, it would be important to look in his ears and mouth to be sure that an ear infection, sore throat, impacted tooth, or some other medical or dental problem has not triggered the self-injury.

Medication Fads and Off-Label Uses

Often, when a new medicine is first proposed for autism, there is great enthusiasm for it. Usually, early uncontrolled reports make it appear to be helpful, with few side effects. An example of such a medication was fenfluramine, which initially, according to a few case reports, seemed to produce significant and dramatic improvements in children with autism. Unfortunately, this turned out not to be the case over time and it had significant side effects. For new medications, it may make sense to wait until the results of well-conducted clinical trials are available. This can be a major problem when parents understandably ask about something they have heard praised on TV!

Off-label use of medicines is very common; possibly 50% or more of medicines used in pediatrics are given for off-label uses. This is a real problem in pediatrics in general, and in autism in particular, and reflects difficulties in doing research on children, particularly children with disabilities, as well as a lack of incentives or requirements for testing medications in these populations. Thus, given the lack of research on medications for children with autism, it is often the case that the medicines being used are off label. In contrast to off-label uses, in 2006 the FDA approved the use of risperidone for the treatment of tantrums, aggression, and self-injury in children with autism.

AUTISM AND RELATED CONDITIONS

The following sections provide some basic information on the major classes or groups of medication sometimes used in treatment of individuals with ASDs. Each section has a short description of what we know about how the medication works and what it seems most useful for. The most common adverse effects of the medications are discussed, and we give some examples of medications in this group. Please remember that this is a selective and not an exhaustive list of medications. Also keep in mind that we provide only a short description of some of the more common side effects and that many others are possible.

With a few notable exceptions (discussed further on), most of the information available to us on medications for treating behavior problems is, unfortunately, rather limited. Mostly, we are relying on case reports and studies of series of cases rather than on well-controlled, double-blind studies. Fortunately, more research is now being done on these medicines, and new knowledge will be coming out at an increasingly rapid pace. So, for example, based on a body of research, the FDA has approved Risperidone and aripriprazole for the irritability that can be very problematic for individuals on the autism spectrum. Although the information we provide here is up-to-date at the time of our writing, keep in mind that new studies are always being conducted and information may change.

Major Tranquilizers (Typical and Atypical Neuroleptic Medications)

The medications most often prescribed to treat irritability in autism are called *major tranquilizers*. There is probably more research on them than on any other class of drugs. Some newer, "second-generation" antipsychotics have been developed in recent years and lack some of the side effects of the older major tranquilizers. These medicines are often used when individuals have significant problems with self-injury, stereotyped behaviors, aggression, and irritability. They are sometimes used for high levels of activity or behavioral rigidity associated with irritability.

The antipsychotics seem to have a major effect on the brain systems that involve dopamine and act to block the effects of dopamine in the brain. They also have effects on other systems in the brain. These various effects account for the desired—or positive—effects, as well as some of the adverse effects, of medication. Dopamine appears to be involved in some way in certain behavior problems in autism, for example, the self-injurious behavior and stereotyped or purposeless repetitive movements. Sometimes low doses of antipsychotics effectively increase the attention span of children with autism and help them to learn more effectively, although this is not usually why antipsychotics are prescribed for children with autism.

Usually, a low dose is started and gradually increased. The effects of the medicine can be relatively rapid. Occasionally, a higher dose may be used to start. This is mostly done in emergency situations. Because the newer second-generation medications are now used most frequently, we'll discuss them first and then review the older agents—the latter are now much less frequently used but still occasionally encountered.

Second-Generation Antipsychotics

Second-generation antipsychotics (see Table 11.1) have attracted much attention because of their greatly reduced risk of a side effect called *tardive dyskinesia*. This term literally means a slow-to-develop movement disorder and is a side effect that occurred more frequently with the first generation of these drugs. These newer medicines, sometimes called *atypical antipsychotics,* also seem to be more effective in helping with the social withdrawal and lack of motivation in adults with schizophrenia (which may or may not have much to do with the social problems in autism). Additionally, these medicines seem to help with agitation, temper tantrums, aggressiveness, self-injury, high activity levels, and impulsivity—the same problems that the older first-generation neuroleptics were used for. One large,

TABLE 11.1   SELECTED SECOND-GENERATION ATYPICAL ANTIPSYCHOTICS

Generic Name	Brand Name	Typical Range of Dose
Risperidone	Risperdal	0.5–3.0 mg/day
Quetiapine	Seroquel	50–300 mg/day
Olanzapine	Zyprexa	5–20 mg/day
Ziprasidone	Geodon	20–100 mg/day
Aripiprazole	Abilify	2–15 mg/day

Note: Dose ranges are approximate; other medications are available in this category. Potential side effects include weight gain (varies with medicine), sedation, movement problems, and possibly diabetes, among others. Note that in this and subsequent tables pediatric doses are generally given; current prescribing information should always be verified independently by practitioners.
Source: Adapted and reprinted with permission from Volkmar and Wiesner (2009, p. 465).

double-blind, placebo-controlled study of these medications has shown them to be effective in children with autism.

The atypical neuroleptics have largely replaced the older, first-generation medications. Still, there is a variety of side effects, which can include sedation, movement problems, weight gain (with the possible exception of ziprasidone), changes in the ECG, and possibly diabetes.

One of the first drugs in this group, clozapine, can have some major side effects, including reducing the white blood count. Consequently, it is not used as frequently as the others and has not been as intensively studied in autism.

Another of these medicines, risperidone, has been very well studied and is now approved by the FDA for the treatment of aggression, tantrums, and self-injury in children with autism ages 5 to 17 years. One of the studies that contributed to approval of risperidone was a trial by the Research Units on Pediatric Psychopharmacology (RUPP) Autism Network (RUPP, 2002). In this study, children with autism and serious behavioral problems were randomly assigned to an 8-week double-blind trial of either risperidone or a placebo. The children in the risperidone group had a large and significant reduction in these serious behaviors and were more likely to be rated as much or very much improved by clinicians who did not know whether the child was on the active medicine or a placebo. There were some minor side effects of risperidone (fatigue, drooling, drowsiness), most of which passed quickly. The major side effect was weight gain (2.7 kg or almost 6 pounds on average) in the 8-week trial.

In a second part of the study, children were followed over time in an open-label study (i.e., there was no longer any attempt to keep up the double-blind part of the study). Children who responded well to risperidone continued to do so at a low to medium dose level. After 6 months, children were then randomly assigned to a discontinuation trial (some children stayed on the active medicine; others gradually switched over to a placebo). As with the first phase of the study, the discontinuation was double-blinded. Only a few children tapered off the medicine successfully; most had the return of behavioral difficulties and went back on the risperidone. The response to risperidone in this study was larger than the response to the first-generation antipsychotics in older studies. Although there were many fewer side effects overall, weight gain emerged as a common problem. It is worth noting that sometimes weight gain could be substantial, and it may not be easy to lose the extra weight even after the medicine is stopped.

There have been studies of other atypical antipsychotics as well, although they have not been as well studied as risperidone. In particular, olanzapine has shown some potential to reduce irritability, aggressiveness, overactivity, and obsessiveness in open trials, but weight gain seems to be an even bigger problem. Some parents don't mind the weight gain (particularly if their child is on the thin side). However, substantial weight gain can be a problem for many children with autism, who may not get enough exercise anyway.

First-Generation Antipsychotics

These medicines were the first to be developed. They were often used for treatment of severe behavioral difficulties, such as aggression and self-injury, as well as agitation and stereotyped movements. Some of these medicines have been studied in controlled, double-blind trials in autism (see Scahill, Tillberg, & Martin, 2014).

A few trials have followed children for several months. Improvements have been documented in areas such as agitation, withdrawal, and self-stimulatory movement. Many children respond well to these medicines.

In general, children should be prescribed the lowest possible dose of these medications, because some of the side effects occur more often at higher doses. Sedation is a common problem and can be mistakenly viewed as a positive response. That is, the child is no longer causing much trouble; however, the child may also not be doing much learning!

There are a number of medicines in this group. Haloperidol (Haldol) is one of the more potent members of this group and is the most well studied in children with autism. It can be effective in reducing high levels of activity, agitation, and stereotyped or self-injurious behavior. Studies of Haldol have demonstrated that it works quite well in children affected with moderate to severe autism (Scahill et al., 2014). Significant behavioral improvement may occur at relatively low doses. Side effects are observed but are not usually common at low doses. When effective, usually there are periodic attempts to lower the dose of medication. It is important that such a drug holiday be planned to ensure that children receive the lowest effective dose of medication. At very low doses, haloperidol is not usually very sedating, but at higher doses, it can be.

Another medicine sometimes used in treating children with autism is chlorpromazine (Thorazine). Thorazine is a low-potency antipsychotic; that is, a higher dose needs to be taken to achieve the same effects as with a high-potency medication such as Haldol. For example, about 100 mg of Thorazine equals about 1 mg of Haldol in terms of effectiveness. Thorazine is much more sedating than Haldol. This can be a benefit for some children; however, sedation is often a problem, but sometimes this can be avoided by giving a larger dose before bedtime, when it may help the child get to sleep.

In between Haldol and Thorazine, there are a number of other medications (see Table 11.2). These tend to be intermediate in terms of potency and their side effect profile. Some of these medicines come as capsules or tablets and some are available in liquid form; this can be important if the child has trouble taking pills.

Side effects of the first generation of antipsychotics include various neurological abnormalities as well as sedation. These symptoms can include stiffness in arms or legs, shaking of the fingers or hands, restlessness (akathisia), stiffness of the neck, and unusual movements of the head and eyes. These problems often appear in the first weeks or with dose increase. These neurological adverse effects are called *dystonias* (muscle stiffness) and *dyskinesia* (disordered movements). These can sometimes also be seen when the medicine is discontinued or reduced (withdrawal dyskinesia).

TABLE 11.2   SELECTED FIRST-GENERATION ANTIPSYCHOTIC MEDICATIONS

Generic Name	Brand Name	Typical Range of Dose
Haloperidol*	Haldol	0.5–3 mg/day
Thiothixene	Navane	1–20 mg/day
Chlopromazine**	Thorazine	50–400 mg/day

Note: Dose ranges are approximate. Liquid forms (which may be easier to give and provide a range of dosing options) are also often available. Many similar drugs are available. Possible side effects include sedation, movement problems, restlessness, allergic reactions, and dry mouth, among others.
*Least sedating and most potent but with the most motor side effects
**Most sedating and less potent with fewer motor side effects
Source: Adapted and reprinted with permission from Volkmar and Wiesner (2009, p. 468).

The restlessness and some of the motor movements associated with these medications can be treated with other medications such as benztropine (Cogentin) or diphenhydramine (Benadryl), which can be given along with the major tranquilizers. Often these agents are used routinely to try to prevent any of the acute movement problems.

Rarely, the serious movement problem called *tardive dyskinesia* occurs. This movement disorder usually develops after months or even years of treatment, but sometimes more quickly. It takes the form of various involuntary movements of the body extremities and can be confusing because at times it resembles the kinds of motor mannerisms frequently seen in autism. It is important to note that reducing the dose of medication may seem to make the tardive dyskinesia even worse.

Because tardive dyskinesia is sometimes irreversible, doctors should screen for it when they begin treatment with antipsychotics and as they follow a child who is treated over time. That way, if there are early signs suggesting tardive dyskinesia, the medicine can be stopped. There are specific rating scales that doctors and nurses can use to monitor the unusual movements sometimes associated with these medications.

Occasionally, when a medication is discontinued or reduced, withdrawal dyskinesias occur; that is, the child begins to exhibit some unusual movements. These usually persist for only a few weeks but may be disturbing to parents and children. Adolescents and adults appear to be more likely to have these than young children. The risk of withdrawal dyskinesia increases if the medication is stopped abruptly rather than being slowly tapered.

Other side effects sometimes observed in first-generation antipsychotics include true allergic reactions (not just motor side effects). These can be a serious medical problem. As a group, these medicines tend to have anticholinergic side effects such as dry mouth, constipation, and so forth. Liver and kidney functions should be monitored. Some of the medicines in this group have a tendency to increase the likelihood of seizures in children with epilepsy (Chapter 4). Thus, their use should be considered carefully in a child with a seizure disorder. Furthermore, many of these medications can cause some degree of weight gain. Finally, individuals taking these medications (especially in high doses) need to be careful not to become too hot. A rare condition (malignant hyperthermia) can occur in children whose temperature increases dramatically. Children on these medications should be encouraged to drink a lot of fluids, particularly in the summer. Again, it's important to keep in mind that adverse effects are often dose related although they can occur at low doses.

MEDICATIONS FOR ATTENTIONAL PROBLEMS

Stimulant medications are used very widely in the United States for treatment of attention deficit hyperactivity disorder (ADHD). It appears that these medicines work by increasing levels of a brain messenger chemical called *dopamine*. (Note that this is different from antipsychotics, which block dopamine in the brain.) Stimulants help the child to focus, attend, and be less restless. These medicines are very effective in individuals with ADHD, probably helping about 75% of those diagnosed with the disorder (see Table 11.3). There are also some nonstimulant medications used to treat attentional problems, although the stimulants are still the most widely used.

The many different types of stimulant medications differ from each other in several ways. Some are longer acting than others. They may have a range of side effects, which include in children with ADHD irritability, occasional worsening of hyperactivity, sleep problems, and decreased appetite. Occasionally, children have problems with dizziness and sometimes seem to become more moody or agitated. Children taking these medications sometimes develop tics, although the significance of this has been debated. Other side effects can include other habit problems (picking their skin) or, more rarely, hallucinations, particularly with higher doses. Stimulant medications are among the more commonly used in children with ASDs for the same reason they are used in children with ADHD: to help increase attention and decrease hyperactivity and decrease impulsivity.

Until recently, there were few studies of stimulant medications in children with ASDs. The few studies that were done included only small numbers of children. As is often the case, results of these small studies don't agree simply because the samples were not comparable. The RUPP Autism Network completed a large-scale trial using three different doses of methylphenidate (Ritalin) and placebo (RUPP, 2002). The trial used a so-called crossover design so that each child took the low dose, the medium dose, the high dose, and placebo in alternating weeks. Results showed that each active dose was better than the placebo, but only about

TABLE 11.3   SELECTED MEDICATIONS FOR TREATMENT OF ADHD

Generic	Brand Name	Typical Range of Dose
Methylphenidate Derivatives*		
Methylphenidate	Ritalin	2.5–60 mg/day
	Ritalin LA	10–60 mg/day
	Concerta	18–72 mg/day
	Focalin	2.5–20 mg/day
	Focalin XR	5–30 mg/day
Amphetamine Derivatives		
Dextroamphetamine	Dexedrine	10–40 mg/day
Amphetamine mixture	Adderall	2.5–40 mg/day
	Adderall XR	5–20 mg/day
	Vyvanse	30–70 mg/day
Nonstimulants		
Atomoxetine*	Strattera	Start 0.5 mg/kg/0 max–1.2 mg/k/day
Guanficine*	Tenex	Start at 0.5 mg HS; increase to 1.5 mg/day
Extended Release	Intuniv	1–7 mg/day

Note: Dose is adjusted based on a child's weight and clinical response. Except for Strattera, Tenex, and Intuniv, the medications listed are stimulants and controlled substances. Possible side effects vary with the agent and the individual. Some of the more common include headache, abdominal pain, decreased appetite with possible poor growth, difficulty falling asleep, and behavior changes. Sometimes activation with restlessness, increased activity, and irritability can occur. There are many other less common but more serious possible adverse reactions that need to be watched for.
*Nonstimulant medication
Source: Adapted and reprinted with permission from Volkmar and Wiesner (2009, p. 470).

50% of the children showed improvement. This rate of positive response was much lower than the positive response rate of 75% in children with ADHD only. The adverse events were similar to what we see in children with ADHD but were more common in the children with ASDs. The RUPP group looked closely in order to identify which subjects were more likely to show a positive response. There is some evidence that children with normal or near normal intelligence quotient (IQ) are more likely to show a positive response. But no other subgroups (e.g., autism, Asperger's, or PDD-NOS) were more or less likely to show a positive response to methylphenidate. Although stimulant medication can help to reduce hyperactivity and improve attention, these medications may not help with other problems, such as anxiety, depression, or compulsive routines or rigidities. Then the question arises of the worthiness of adding a second medicine to deal with those problems as well.

When stimulant medications do work, they should be monitored over time. Given the medications' potential to decrease appetite, monitor the child's height and weight every 4 to 6 months or so. If there are problems with growth and weight gain, you can try lowering the dose, using drug holidays, or switching to a different class of medicine. Medications such as atomoxetine (Strattera) or guanfacine (Tenex) and extended release guanfacine (Intuniv) can also be used to treat hyperactivity. As the child grows older (and if the medicine is still needed), the dose can be adjusted. It is also important to make sure the child still really needs the medication by occasionally having a drug holiday—planned periods off medication to reevaluate the benefit. These trials off medication should be done in close collaboration with the primary care provider or mental health clinician.

Antidepressants and Selective Serotonin Reuptake Inhibitors

Antidepressants and the chemically related SSRIs were originally developed for the treatment of depression and obsessive-compulsive disorder (OCD). There are several antidepressant medications on the market (see Table 11.4). The most common types are the SSRIs, which inhibit reuptake of the neurotransmitter serotonin increasing the level of serotonin in the brain. SSRIs are quite selective in how they act on serotonin; that is, they have little, if any, effect on other brain chemical systems such as norepinephrine and dopamine. There is also one medicine in the group (clomipramine [Anafranil]) that is less selective but still a potent reuptake inhibitor of serotonin (technically an SRI rather than an SSRI). Because SSRIs are used more frequently, we'll discuss them first.

SSRIs have attracted much interest for use with individuals with ASDs based on the assumption that these medicines could help in treating the prominent behavioral rigidity, ritualistic behaviors, and rituals commonly seen.

A number of studies, not always well controlled, have evaluated how well SSRIs work in autism. Early studies have been encouraging, but research is ongoing. There seems to be a lot of variability in how individuals with

TABLE 11.4 SELECTED ANTIDEPRESSANTS AND SEROTONIN REUPTAKE INHIBITOR MEDICATIONS

Generic Name	Brand Name	Typical Range of Dose	Purpose
Clomipramine	Anafranil	25–200 mg/day*	Depression/OCD/Anxiety
Fluoxetine	Prozac	5–200 mg/day**	Depression/OCD/Anxiety
Citalopram	Celexa	10–40 mg/day***	Depression/OCD/Anxiety
Fluvoxamine	Luvox	50–200 mg/day***	Depression/OCD/Anxiety
Paroxetine	Paxil	10–50 mg/day***	Depression/OCD/Anxiety
Sertraline	Zoloft	50–200 mg/day***	Depression/OCD/Anxiety
Escitalopran	Lexapro	10–20 mg/day**	Depression/Anxiety
Venlafaxine	Effexor	150–300 mg/day***	Depression
Bupropion	Wellbutrin	150–300 mg/day***	Depression
Mirtazaphine	Remeron	7.5–15 mg/day***	Depression

Note: Dose ranges are approximate. Approval for specific ages varies. Many other medicines are available in this category. Beneficial effects may take a period of time (weeks) to develop.

Liquid forms (which may be easier to give and provide a range of dosing options) are available for some of these medications. Some medications also have long-acting forms. Needs for ECG and blood tests vary. Side effects vary with medication and can include activation (restless and increased activity and irritability), dry mouth, constipation, and heart (cardiac) effects.

*Traditional antidepressants

**Selective serotonin reuptake inhibitors

***Newer antidepressant/SSRI with different chemical structure than the older medicines

Source: Adapted and reprinted with permission from Volkmar and Wiesner (2009, p. 472).

autism respond. Some children respond well to a lower dose than a slightly higher dose, others to one of these medicines but not another. It does seem that adolescents and children who are nearing adolescence respond better than younger children.

More recent studies have not always been so positive. The earlier studies were small and the clinical target(s) for the medicine not always so clear. A recent federally funded study with a large sample of children (5 to 17 years of age) was conducted at six different medical centers. One of the SSRIs was studied in terms of its effects on repetitive behaviors and other symptoms. In this placebo-controlled study, after 16 weeks the group treated with the SSRI was no better than the placebo group but did have more adverse effects: sleep problems, overactivity, talkativeness, and impulsivity (this combination of adverse effects is often called *activation* and is sometimes seen with SSRI treatment). The results of this study have challenged the widespread use of SSRIs, although, clearly, other conditions such as depression or clear-cut OCD might be improved.

Because of the variable response in children with ASDs, the first SSRI you try might not be the most effective one. It might take a relatively long time (weeks) to get the dose to a reasonable level and determine how effective the medication is. When stopping these medications, they generally should be tapered gradually. Treatment with clomipramine requires an ECG before and during treatments as well as blood tests for drug levels. The antidepressant bupropion (sold as Wellbutrin, Zyban, and Budeprion) should not be used in individuals with seizure disorder.

Another important consideration with the use of the drugs is the possibility of drug interaction. This can happen several different ways. For example, fluoxetine (Prozac) and citalopram (Celexa) can slow down the metabolism of other medications; this can actually result in an increase in levels of medicines (e.g., risperidone) and may increase the likelihood of adverse effects. To deal with this possibility, clinicians usually move even more slowly than usual if combining medications. Because high levels of clomipramine can be toxic, it is important to be very careful. Commonly used medications such as erythromycin or even grapefruit juice can retard the metabolism of clomipramine and cause levels to rise. The important point is that all the prescribing care providers need to be aware of the medicines the individual is taking and to warn about possible drug interactions.

Mood Stabilizers

The classic example of a mood disorder is manic-depressive illness or bipolar disorder. Individuals with bipolar disorder have major swings in mood. For instance, they may have periods, weeks to months, of serious depression followed by periods of having a normal mood and then by periods of elation and mania. The adult forms of the mood disorders are more straightforward to diagnose than the forms seen in children. In children, irritability, overactivity, and aggressive behaviors may signal a mood disorder or reflect severe disruptive behavior.

There has been some speculation that mood disorders may be increased in children and adolescents with PDD. These issues are somewhat

TABLE 11.5   SELECTED MOOD STABILIZERS

Generic Name	Brand Name
Divalproex	Depakote
Valproic acid	Depakote
Carbamazepine	Tegretol
Lamotrigine	Lamictal
Lithium compounds	Eskalith
	Lithobid

Note: All these medicines require careful monitoring for side effects, including sedation or agitation, changes in the blood count, liver, thyroid, and kidneys. Dose of these medicines depends on blood level and side effects. Potential side effects for these and other medications should be reviewed carefully with the doctor who prescribes the medicine.

Source: Adapted and reprinted with permission from Volkmar and Wiesner (2009, p. 474).

controversial, given that, for example, irritability and overactivity are often seen in children with PDD.

In strictly diagnosed autism, the general response to mood stabilizers is not usually positive. However, these medications may be helpful if the child has symptoms suggesting that an additional diagnosis of bipolar disorder or other mood disorder is justified, particularly if there is a family history of mood disorders. Patients with cyclical patterns of mood problems and irritability associated with insomnia and overactivity may also be candidates for mood stabilizers.

Medications used to treat mood disorders (see Table 11.5) include lithium (now used much less frequently) and some of the same agents used to treat seizures—these are now the more commonly used. The precise way these medicines work is not known. Lithium is probably the most well known of the mood stabilizers used with adults, although anticonvulsants are more frequently used now and are more likely to be used in children. Blood levels are regularly monitored. For the health care provider inexperienced with these agents we strongly advise consultation with someone who is. The balance of side effects and benefit is often a complex one to manage.

There are some studies of anticonvulsants for mood problems in children with autism, but these are mostly reports of single or a few cases and tend not to be of the most rigorous quality. More research is clearly needed.

Some of the medicines used to deal with cycles in mood associated with overactivity and insomnia include carbamazepine and valproic acid and also sometimes lamotrigine. In children with ASDs, problems that have reportedly improved on such mood stabilizers include mood problems, impulsivity, and aggression. Be alert for drug interactions. Before using these agents liver, kidney, and thyroid functions must be assessed.

Side effects of mood stabilizers can include sedation, changes in the blood count, and liver toxicity. Lithium can affect thyroid and kidney function and lead to a fair amount of weight gain over time. Because of concerns about lithium's side effects, it is used less often than some of the other mood stabilizers.

MEDICINES TO REDUCE ANXIETY

Children with ASDs can have problems with anxiety. Sometimes this seems similar to the kinds of anxiety that others of us experience in confronting frightening or stressful situations. At other times, the anxiety may take unusual forms; for example, it might be more related to difficulties in dealing with new situations or certain problem situations.

The agents used in treating anxiety problems for typically developing children, adolescents, and adults can sometimes be used successfully in treating serious anxiety problems in children with ASDs (see Table 11.6). However, as we will discuss shortly, there has not been much research on using these medicines in autism. In addition, sometimes the same medicines can cause individuals to be more agitated and disorganized.

Benzodiazepines

The benzodiazepines have been very widely used in adults and typically developing children to help deal with anxiety specific to situations, for example, before the person goes for dental work. They have not been as well studied in children, and even less so for children with ASDs. Common benzodiazepines include diazepam (Valium) and lorazepam (Ativan).

Occasionally, children, including those with developmental problems, become somewhat more agitated on these medicines (this is called *paradoxical agitation*). If, for example, the dentist suggests these medications to help calm the child during a dental procedure, parents may want to try a test dose at home first to judge the child's response. There are some alternatives

TABLE 11.6 SELECTED ANTIANXIETY MEDICATIONS

Generic Name	Brand Name	Typical Range of Dose
Benzodiazepines		
Diazepam	Valium	2–10 mg/day
Lorazepam	Ativan	0.5–2 mg/day
Clonazepam	Klonopin	0.25–2 mg/day
Beta Blockers		
Propranolol	Inderal	10–120 mg/day
Nadolol	Corgard	20–200 mg/day

Note: Dose ranges are approximate. Approval for specific ages varies. Other medicines are also available. Side effects include sedation and agitation. Beta blockers should be carefully monitored and should not be stopped abruptly. They also may make asthma worse.

for sedation when these medicines don't work. For instance, occasionally Benadryl works well in some children.

The benzodiazepines are potentially habit forming and should not be used in an open-ended way. However, if these medications do work for the child, they can be valuable when used on an occasional basis for situations you know will make the child very anxious.

Beta Blockers

Another group of medicines called *beta blockers* are sometimes used for children with autism and related conditions. These medicines were originally used as antihypertensives but are sometimes used to deal with anxiety and irritability. There have been some open-label studies and case reports of beta blockers in the treatment of anxiety in individuals with ASDs.

These medicines have a number of potential side effects, and it is important to weigh the pros and cons seriously before starting them. Side effects can include low blood pressure and problems with heart rate. These medicines can also make asthma worse.

Alpha-Adrenergic Agonists

Another group of medicines that were first used to lower blood pressure are sometimes used to treat behavioral problems. These medicines, called *alpha-adrenergic agonists,* work through a different system than beta blockers and can help in the treatment of tics. For some children, they can also improve problems with overactivity. They are sometimes recommended for children with autism, particularly for children who are hyperactive and impulsive. The data on using these drugs for ASDs are limited, but they are commonly used in children with other conditions such as Tourette's syndrome and ADHD.

These medicines are also used to control blood pressure, so they can cause hypotension and lower heart rates. Occasionally, children may develop what is called *orthostatic hypotension,* or low blood pressure when standing up, which can cause dizziness. In addition, these agents can cause sedation, either at the start or over the long term. If sedation is a problem, the medication can be given mostly at night to help with sleep. Some children may fall asleep without difficulty but may wake up during the night. This can usually be handled by adjusting the dose. It is particularly important that they be given as prescribed and tapered off slowly if they are discontinued. (Blood pressure can rapidly increase if these agents are stopped too quickly.) Sometimes tolerance to the medicine seems to develop.

Opiate Blockers

There has been some speculation that some of the self-injurious behaviors in autism may induce the release of opiate-like compounds in the brain. Thus perhaps the same medicines that are used to block the effects of externally produced opiates might also serve to undercut this effect and therefore eliminate or reduce the behavior. A small number of studies have raised the possibility that individuals with autism have higher natural levels of endorphins (the opiate-like compounds the body naturally produces). If so, it could be that self-injury is, paradoxically, an attempt by the child to make himself feel better.

Two different drugs that are ordinarily used to help people with opiate drug overdose problems have been used in children with ASDs: naloxone (Narcan) and naltrexone (Trexan). Naltrexone has been more extensively studied in autism. Initial studies tended to be small case reports. Initial results were encouraging but larger-scale double-blind studies have not shown the same positive picture. Now most of the apparent benefit appears to be in reducing hyperactivity. At present, these agents do not seem to have major usefulness in children with autism.

COMBINING MEDICATIONS

Children with ASDs often end up being given more than one medicine for their various emotional or behavioral problems. This practice, referred to as polypharmacy, is complex. Sometimes two medicines are given because one is controlling side effects of the other. Sometimes a second medicine is added after a first one seems to work a bit but not as much as is wanted. Occasionally, taking two medicines together may mean that a lower dose of each can be used. Sometimes one medicine, which acts more quickly, may be given while a longer-acting medicine is being introduced. Sometimes two conditions are really present and using two medications to treat them makes sense. These are just some of the possible reasons for giving more than one medicine at a time. Some of the issues and complexities in considering treatment of comorbid conditions are summarized in Box 11.1.

BOX 11.1 COMORBIDITY

- Comorbidity refers to the simultaneous presence of more than one condition.
- In the past often the presence of autism or associated intellectual disability (mental retardation) masked the presence of multiple problems (this is referred to as *diagnostic overshadowing*).
- In ASDs the most common associations of problems or conditions include
  - In younger (school-age) children: attentional problems and irritability
  - In adolescents and young adults: anxiety and depression (these are also often associated in the general population)

Occasionally, we have seen children with autism on many different medicines at the same time (the record for us is about 10) with the idea that each medicine is treating a different thing—anxiety, depression, attention, and so forth. In these situations, the child's behavior often deteriorates and it is impossible to figure out why and what to change. In general, with some exceptions, it probably makes sense to start with one medicine.

New and Developing Agents

A small, but growing literature on new approaches to drug treatment has emerged (see Scahill et al., 2014). There are many obstacles to research in this area—the general complexity of clinical trials compounded by the difficulties of doing research in children with disabilities and the complexities of autism. A further major problem has been the lack of good and reliable measures of change for assessment of core features. One of the exceptions in this area has been the use of a reliable and well-validated scale for OCD; this has generally not suggested major changes in autism. The adaption of approaches to assess other symptoms, such as attentional problems, anxiety, and mood disorders, is critically needed as are new approaches to assessing the core social difficulties of autism. New approaches to measuring change that are more brain-based (e.g., fMRI and EEG approaches) may hold some hope in this regard.

One of the interesting agents currently being evaluated (along with related agents) is oxytocin. This nine–amino acid peptide has a well-established role in animals in aspects of mother-infant attachment and pair bonding. Use of a single dose delivered intransally has been shown to increase social attention in typically developing adults. This work has now been extended to adults and youth with ASD with small and transient significant improvement on social tasks (Anagnostou et al., 2014; Guastella et al., 2010).

A variety of other agents have been assessed; these target rather different putative CNS mechanisms: (1) N-acetylcysteine, an amino acid supplement used as an antioxidant in the treatment of acetaminophen overdose and thought to reduce glutamate transmission (Hardan et al., 2012); (2) Arbaclofen, a GABA-B receptor agonist (Erikson et al., 2011); (3) MGluR antagonists (metabotropic glutamate receptor antagonists), being assessed in Fragile X syndrome (Jacquemont et al., 2011); (4) case reports have also appeared regarding the use of intranasal ketamine in adults for treatment of severe depression; and (5) the nicotine patch for treatment of adolescents with autism and aggressive behavior (Van Schalkwyk, Lewis, Qayyum, Koslosky, Picciotto, & Volkmar, 2015).

Summary

Although many gaps remain, our knowledge of drug treatments in autism and related disorders has increased dramatically in recent years. Although no medicine has, as yet, been shown to really improve the core difficulties of autism, medicines have been shown to help with some of its very problematic symptoms. Medicines can be very effective in dealing with agitation, hyperactivity, anxiety, aggression, depression, and some aspects of obsessions and compulsions. Some of the new agents currently under development offer considerable promise.

In thinking about medications for behavioral problems, always weigh the potential benefits and potential side effects. You should think about drug treatments if problems are quite severe, if they limit the child's opportunities to participate in his or her educational program or community activities, or if they negatively affect his or her quality of life (or the quality of the family's life). For some medicines, side effects are pretty minimal, and, depending on the situation, you might consider using these medicines for a problem that is less severe or interfering. For more serious behavioral problems that warrant more potent medication, you may want to track the behavior for a period of time in order to gauge severity and to help determine if the medication is actually making a difference.

It can be extremely helpful for school staff members to collect data when a new drug (or any intervention) is tried to see whether there is a difference in behavior at school. You may also want to use some rating scales or checklists as a way of monitoring the medicine (including potential side effects).

One of the exciting, but as yet unrealized, possibilities is that in the future, as we discover more about what really causes autism, we may be able to develop much better treatments that target the core difficulties. In the meantime, we now have a number of medicines that often can be helpful.

REFERENCES

Anagnostou, E., Soorya, L., Brian, J., Dupuis, A., Mankad, D., Smile, S., & Jacob, S. (2014). Intranasal oxytocin in the treatment of autism spectrum disorders: A review of literature and early safety and efficacy data in youth. *Brain Research, 1580,* 188–198.

Guastella, A. J., Einfeld, S. L., Gray, K. M., Rinehart, N. J., Tonge, B. J., Lambert, T. J., & Hickie, I. B. (2010). Intranasal oxytocin improves emotion recognition for youth with autism spectrum disorders. *Biological Psychiatry, 67*(7), 692–694.

Hardan, A. Y., Fung, L. K., Libove, R. A., Obukhanych, T. V., Nair, S., Herzenberg, L. A., Frazier, T. W., & Tirouvanziam, R. (2012). A randomized controlled pilot trial of oral N-acetylcysteine in children with autism. *Biological Psychiatry, 71*(11), 956–961.

Jacquemont, S., Curie, A., des Portes, V., Torrioli, M. G., Berry-Kravis, E., Hagerman, R. J., Ramos, F. J., Cornish, K., He, Y., Paulding, C., Neri, G., Chen, F., Hadjikhani, N., Martinet, D., Meyer, J., Beckmann, J. S., Delange, K., Brun, A., Bussy, G., Gasparini, F., Hilse, T., Floesser, A., Branson, J., Bilbe, G., Johns, D., & Gomez-Mancilla, B. (2011). Epigenetic modification of the FMR1 gene in Fragile X syndrome is associated with differential response to the mGluR5 antagonist AFQ056. *Science Translational Medicine, 3*(64), 64ra1.

Research Units in Pediatric Psychopharmacology (RUPP). (2002). Risperidone in children with autism and serious behavioral problems. *New England Journal of Medicine, 347,* 314–321.

Scahill, L., Tillberg, C. S., & Martin, A. (2014). Psychopharmacology. In F. R. Volkmar, S. J. Rogers, R. Paul, & K. A. Pelphrey (Eds.), *Handbook of autism and pervasive developmental disorders* (4th ed., Vol. 2, pp. 556–579). Hoboken, NJ: Wiley.

Van Schalkwyk, G. I., Lewis, A. S., Qayyum, Z., Koslosky, K., Picciotto, M. R., & Volkmar, F. R. (2015). Reduction of aggressive episodes after repeated transdermal nicotine administration in a hospitalized adolescent with autism spectrum disorder. *Journal of Autism and Developmental Disorders, 45,* 3061–3066.

Volkmar, F., & Wiesner, L. (2009). *A practical guide to autism.* Hoboken, NJ: Wiley.

Werry, J. S., & Aman, M. G. (1999). *Practitioner's guide to psychoactive drugs for children and adolescents* (2nd ed.). New York, NY: Plenum Press.

▪ SUGGESTED READING

Blumer, J. L. (1999). Off-label uses of drugs in children. *Pediatrics, 104*(3 Suppl), 598–602.

Connor, D. F., & Meltzer, B. M. (2006). *Pediatric psychopharmacology—Fast facts.* New York, NY: Norton.

Dulcan, M. K. (2006). *Helping parents, youth, and teachers understand medications for behavioral and emotional problems: A resource book on medication information handouts* (3rd ed.). Washington, DC: American Psychiatric Press.

Erickson, C. A., Veenstra-Vanderweele, J. M., Melmed, R. D., McCracken, J. T., Ginsberg, L. D., Sikich, L., Scahill, L., Cherubini, P., Zarevics, M., Walton-Bowen, K., Carpenter, R. L., Bear, M. F., Wang, P. P., & King, B. H. (2014). STX209 (arbaclofen) for autism spectrum disorders: An 8-week open-label study. *Journal of Autism & Developmental Disorders, 44*(4), 958–964.

Green, W. H. (2006). *Child and adolescent clinical psychopharmacology.* Philadelphia, PA: Lippincott.

Kennedy, D. (2002). *The ADHD autism connection.* Colorado Springs, CO: Random House.

King, B., Hollander, E. Sikich, L., Marcaken, J., Scahill, L., et al. (2009). Lack of efficacy of citalopram in children with autism spectrum disorders and high levels of repetitive behavior. *Archives of General Psychiatry, 66*(6), 583–590.

Kutcher, S. (Ed.). (2002). *Practical child and adolescent psychopharmacology.* Cambridge, UK: Cambridge University Press.

Martin, A., Scahill, L., Charney, D. S., & Leckman, J. F. (2003). *Pediatric psychopharmacology.* Oxford, UK: Oxford University Press.

McCracken, J. T., McGough, J., Shah, B., Cronin, P., Hong, D., Aman, M. G., et al. (2002). Risperidone in children with autism and serious behavioral problems. *New England Journal of Medicine, 347*(5), 314–321.

Posey, D. J., Erickson, C. A., Stigler, K. A., & McDougle, C. J. (2006). The use of selective serotonin reuptake inhibitors in autism and related disorders. *Journal of Child and Adolescent Psychopharmacology, 16,* 181–186.

Tinsley, M., & Hendrickx, S. (2008). *Asperger syndrome and alcohol: Drinking to cope?* Philadelphia, PA: Jessica Kingsley.

Towbin, K. E. (2003). Strategies for pharmacologic treatment of high functioning autism and Asperger syndrome. *Child and Adolescent Psychiatric Clinics of North America, 12,* 23–45.

Tsai, L. K. (2001). *Taking the mystery out of medication in autism/Asperger syndrome: A guide for parents and non-medical professionals.* Arlington, TX: Future Horizons.

Volkmar, F. (2009). Commentary: Citalopram treatment in children with autism spectrum disorders and high levels of repetitive behaviors. *Archives of General Psychiatry, 66*(6), 581–582.

Wilens, T. E. (2008). *Straight talk about psychiatric medications for kids* (3rd ed.). New York, NY: Guilford Press.

Wink, L. K., O'Melia, A. M., Shaffer, R. C., Pedapati, E., Friedmann, K., Schaefer, T., & Erickson, C. A. (2014). Intranasal ketamine treatment in an adult with autism spectrum disorder. *Journal of Clinical Psychiatry, 75*(8), 835–836.

Considering Complementary and Alternative Treatments

Many different complementary and alternative treatments have been suggested and used for individuals with ASDs. These treatments may be complementary (treatments undertaken in combination with evidence-based treatments) or alternative (undertaken instead of more conventional treatments). They are often referred to as **complementary and alternative medicine (CAM).** Another way to refer to this group of treatments is as nonestablished. Sometimes there is a fine line between established and nonestablished treatments; occasionally, as research is done, treatments move from alternative to mainstream. At other times, promising treatments don't pan out. Indeed a review by the El Dib, Atallah, & Andriolo (2007). Cochrane collaboration suggested that of all treatments surveyed 44% likely were helpful, 7% were likely harmful, and the benefits of 49% unclear! The "Suggested Reading" list at the end of the chapter includes some Internet resources on CAM as well as books and scientific papers that may be of interest and some that may be of help to parents. As in other chapters we have tried to cite only a few of the most relevant references in the text. There are a handful of excellent resources available (e.g., Jacobson, Foxx, & Mulick, 2005; Smith, Oakes, & Selver, 2014).

It is important to be aware that families frequently use CAM treatments (Perrin, Coury, Hyman, Cole, Reynolds, & Clemons, 2012). Patients often pick up subtle, or not so subtle, opinions of medical professionals on alternative treatments and as a result may not be as forthcoming about their use of them. Our own general stance is that (1) we want to know what parents are trying and (2) with two important exceptions, we are nonjudgmental and willing to talk about them. The exceptions are in the case of treatments that have clear risks and side effects or when parents so doggedly pursue an alternative program that they forego established and proven treatments to the detriment of their child.

Another issue arises given the tremendous explosion of information (some good and a lot bad) on the Internet. Typing the word *autism* into a search engine gets you millions on millions of hits. Unfortunately even in the top 100 downloads about one-third of sites either promise a magical cure or are selling something. To complicate life even more, the valuable growth of research, with more than 3,100 peer-reviewed scientific papers in 2015 alone, presents its own problems for someone who wants to be current with the field! Fortunately a growing body of work on evidence-based treatments has begun to appear and some excellent resources (see the "Suggested Reading" list at the end of the chapter) are available. Parents also, of course, may have less understanding of the role of peer review, the importance of replication, and understanding what kinds of studies give the best evidence. Also the fact that a website is in the "top 100" means very little (Reichow, Naples, Steinhoff, Halpern, & Volkmar, 2012)!

In talking about treatments with parents we should encourage them to become educated consumers. They need to understand that extravagant claims are often made based on scanty, dubious, or nonexistent data. They also should understand that the goal of peer review is not to ban discussion but rather to inject some element of quality control into what gets published. Parents can be confused because someone might say a treatment was presented at a conference or mentioned in newspaper or media reports—but of course there is not the same quality review there and some parents may not understand that. Even if a treatment is reported in a peer-reviewed journal it needs to be replicated in other places and with different samples before it becomes standard treatment. In addition, even good studies that are done may never appear in peer-reviewed journals—particularly if results are negative.

In the most rigorous kinds of studies, there is some attempt to control for the important effects of just being in a study (the placebo effect). This placebo effect can be surprisingly large—even in a condition such as autism. And to complicate things further, even a reputable journal can make serious mistakes (witness the vaccine controversy set off by a single study, now withdrawn, published in the *Lancet* [Offit, 2008]). Finally, parents should understand that initial reports on effective treatments tend to be more positive than later ones reflecting all the difficulties in moving treatments from research centers to real-world settings.

TALKING WITH PARENTS ABOUT COMPLEMENTARY AND ALTERNATIVE TREATMENTS

If parents are exploring alternative or other less-conventional treatments here are some questions for them to keep in mind.

Do the Claims Make Sense?

What are the claims being made? Usually the more dramatic and flamboyant they are, the less likely they are to be true. Is there some attempt at providing a scientific explanation for the treatment? If so, does it make much sense? This can be one of the hardest things for nonprofessionals to figure out.

What Is the Evidence?

If advocates for the treatment claim they have evidence in favor of the treatment, ask to see copies of this evidence. Be very wary if parents are told it is "going to be published," or are simply given a list of testimonials, or told that the people doing the treatment are too busy curing autism to show that the treatment works. Testimonials and case reports are very difficult to interpret.

Who Was Involved in the Study?

Sometimes it isn't clear that the children who are "cured" had autism in the first place or at times parents seek out a treatment only when the child is at his or her worst (and just at a point where things likely will then change for the better even without treatment).

How Reputable Is the Publisher of the Study?

If a study is published it is good to help parents understand how reputable the journal is. Some publishers will publish almost anything if they think it will sell and chapters in books or books themselves may not have had any independent peer review.

There are some important warning signs that suggest that a treatment should be avoided. If the treatment is supposed to treat all aspects of autism or cure everyone, it is not very likely it works. Parents should pay particular attention to the costs of the treatment—the obvious cost in dollars but also hidden costs in their time and that of the child. Also be wary if treatment proponents explain that when it doesn't work, it is because the parents or other people did not do it "quite right."

Box 12.1 summarizes some of the issues in considering new treatments.

BOX 12.1 EVALUATING NEW THERAPIES

- What is the quality of the evidence? Word-of-mouth, case report, or a more controlled scientific study? Watch out for claims not based on solid, scientific information.

- Has a paper on the work been published in a peer-reviewed journal? If not, why not? If so, what is the quality of the science in the paper? If people tell you a treatment can't be scientifically proven to work, it is best avoided.

- Has the finding been replicated by another group? If not, be wary.

- Can the treatment be proven wrong? If it can't, it is a matter of faith, not science! It is perfectly fine, of course, to have faith and to hope for good things to happen. This is not, of course, a matter for science or scientific investigation. Keep in mind that often the way we establish that treatments don't work is by having multiple negative studies.

- What are the costs (financial and time) of the treatment? Be careful of treatments if they have a lot of upfront costs! Also be very wary if treatments consume a lot of child or parent time, particularly when this is done at the expense of other treatments known to work.

- Who is the treatment designed to help? Treatments usually won't work for everyone. A claim that every single child is helped should arouse skepticism.

- What is the treatment supposed to do? Is there a theory behind the treatment? Is the theory a scientifically reputable one?

- Who doesn't the treatment work for? No treatment works the same for everyone.
- What are the side effects? All treatments have side effects. Are the potential side effects worth the potential benefits?
- How are people trained to do the treatment? Is there some way to be sure that the training was adequate?

Source: Adapted and reprinted with permission from Volkmar and Wiesner (2009, p. 529).

We emphasize that simply talking to parents about these treatments does *not* mean we are recommending them. As health care professionals we help parents (and teachers) to become better informed and sensible consumers, but they should also find out what the potential risks as well as promised benefits are. We now have a large body of evidence showing that educational interventions make a very big difference indeed for children with ASDs and that outcome, for many but sadly not all children, has improved with earlier diagnosis and treatment.

AN OVERVIEW OF COMPLEMENTARY AND ALTERNATIVE TREATMENTS

Treatments of all kinds have been suggested to help children (and adults) with ASD. It is impossible to list all that have been proposed but in this section we will review some of those usually of interest to parents. To simplify the presentation we organize this discussion based on the types of treatments proposed.

Sensory Treatments

A number of treatments aimed at improving how children deal with sensory input have been proposed. Some of these treatments are also advocated for children with other disorders, such as learning disabilities. Auditory training methods have been proposed given the unusual sound sensitivities that children with autism often exhibit. The underlying idea is to target and improve listening and auditory processing. Several different versions of auditory treatments exist. The most common forms are based on the idea that first you identify the sound frequencies that children are overly sensitive (or not sensitive enough) to and then train them to better tolerate these sounds. Supporting evidence for auditory training and auditory treatments is based on testimonials, not really evidence.

Other auditory treatments are designed to improve auditory processing. These therapies focus on helping children process the sounds produced in speech or in helping children understand the connection between written and spoken language (phonics). Sometimes these problems are thought to be the result of what are termed *central auditory processing* problems. The theory is that even though hearing is normal, the child has trouble processing language and more complex auditory information, which results in, among other things, problems with reading and spelling. There is some work on how this alleged condition might be diagnosed and treated—for example, by improving listening to material, improving **auditory memory,** and assisting listening skills. The basic idea behind the concept remains controversial, because there seem to be problems with the definition and theory of the problem and with how the various approaches suggested for improving such skills really differ from other approaches to improving listening and attention. At the present time these treatments cannot yet be regarded as established.

The visual modality is often emphasized in intervention programs because children on the autism spectrum tend to be better visual learners (unlike the spoken word, the written word or any symbol or icon is static). Obvious problems with vision should, of course be addressed. In addition some proposed treatments involve the use of special prism glasses or glasses with colored lenses designed to improve attention and processing in some way—evidence for these is generally lacking. Other kinds of vision therapies may involve rapid eye movement training with the goal of helping the child better process visual information, but again, there is no solid evidence for effectiveness.

Learning-Focused Visual-Auditory Therapies

Other programs exist that emphasize the combination of auditory and visual (and other) processing abilities in tasks such as reading. Often these programs build on older systems of intervention—some of which have been well studied in children with dyslexia (not usually autism). One of the oldest of these is the Orton-Gillingham method, which was developed in the 1930s and emphasizes integration of auditory, visual, and tactile cues in a phonics-based approach to reading. Modern approaches include Letterland, which attempts to provide a more meaningful context to phonics.

Another tool emphasizing improved listening and attending skills is Fast ForWord, a computer-based program administered by professionals specifically trained in the method. Fast ForWord emphasizes specific exercises, games, and other activities that are thought to help children understand spoken language and help them to more readily understand the relationship between spoken and written language. Again, there is an important kernel of truth here because we know that many children with autism, in particular, have much stronger interest in written letters and numbers than in spoken ones.

Several papers have been published on these treatments. They currently exist in a bit of a gray area with not quite enough evidence to be regarded as established. There is no question that organizational aids, visual supports, and other procedures can be helpful in learning. Similarly, the Lindamood-Bell intervention is concerned with sounding out words and comprehending language. Variants of this approach focus on math and other skills.

Motor and Body-Manipulation Treatments

A number of therapies focus on motor or sometimes sensory-motor skills. One of the more common of these approaches is called *sensory integration (SI) therapy*, which was first developed by Jean Ayres many years ago. Techniques from this approach are frequently used by occupational therapists to help the child develop greater awareness of his or her body and to tolerate different kinds of sensory input. Frequently, various tests or assessments will be done to demonstrate areas in which the child has difficulty. A related approach aims to decrease the child's sensory problems through brushing of the body (this is usually one piece of an entire program of interventions). Although these approaches are very commonly used, the amount of research on them is, unfortunately, very small. Sometimes techniques can be of great help to an individual child but these treatments cannot yet be regarded as firmly evidence-based (although more studies are becoming available—see the "Suggested Reading" list at the end of this chapter).

A number of other programs focus on motor or **sensoro-motor skills.** Again many of these were first developed for children with dyslexia or other learning problems. The Miller method aims to help the child build a sense of bodily awareness and then use this awareness to build other skills. One aspect of this approach is the use of various platforms that force the child to balance and solve problems. Controlled studies are lacking, and most of the support for this method comes from case studies and testimonials.

Over the years, a number of different therapies that involve some kind of manipulation of the body have sprung up. There have been claims for "nerve realignment" (on the basis of manipulation of the back), as well as for various other therapies that involve the child's "relearning" skills correctly—for example, by teaching the child to crawl or walk in the proper way. These therapies have no independent verification, and it is a far stretch to believe that some of them could possibly work.

In recent years, one of the more popular of these "body" therapies, at least in some areas of the United States, has involved holding. The holding therapy approach comes out of the view of a famous ethologist who had the fundamental notion that you can help children with autism connect with others by holding onto them until they realize that they are connected with other people (the ones doing the holding). This typically involves sessions in which one holds the child (who struggles initially at being held) until he stops fighting the holding. As you might imagine, many children with autism do *not* like to be held, and so fights can ensue over the holding. There is not good scientific information supporting this (Zappella, 1998).

Some years ago another treatment, called *patterning,* suggested that children should relearn skills. It was based on work with children who had suffered brain injuries and the idea was that the child needed to relearn tasks in correct ways and sequences. This treatment required considerable time and effort on the part of families and others, and systematic research failed to show benefit.

Other body therapies have been proposed as well. For example, at least one study has shown some improvement in imitation and social skills in young children with autism who received massages several times a week as compared to children who were only held (Escalona, Field, Singer-Strunck, Cullen, & Hartshorn, 2001). There are also several studies that have shown that regular aerobic exercise for children with autism results in lower levels of some maladaptive behaviors (Sowa & Meulenbroek, 2012).

You may hear about a range of other treatments, including cranial-sacral therapy, Feldenkrais, reflexology, and similar treatments. These treatments often involve light pressure, massage, or sometimes work on body movements. Although each of these has its own theory, there is no solid scientific data that these treatments are of help in autism. These treatments may, however, be of benefit for another reason—if they reduce the individual's anxiety level. Indeed, many nonspecific activities that involve relaxation may help children with behavior problems.

Diet and Nutritional Interventions

Nutrition is as important for children with autism as it is for other children. Sometimes the diet of a child with an ASD is complicated because of the child's marked food preferences. Occasionally children with autism, similar to other children, have trouble with certain kinds of foods, such as lactose, and have to avoid them. Children with autism may also be more likely to eat nonfood items such as dirt, clay, or paper. Obviously, addressing these nutritional issues can help children with autism lead healthier lives. Some claims have been made that modifications in diet can lead to improvements in behavior, communication skills, or even cognitive functioning.

Unfortunately, although there is much interest in the effects of diet on autism, the quality of the scientific information available to address such claims is not very high, and substantive research is generally lacking. Claims for dietary treatments may invoke any of several factors, including food sensitivities, response to artificial flavors or colors, sensitivity to wheat- and gluten-containing products, or allergies to some food or other substance. Occasionally very complex diets are suggested—sometimes after a prolonged period of fasting or with a diet so limited that certain vitamin deficiencies can develop (or sometimes the converse, with massive administration of vitamins leading to other problems) (Arnold, Hyman, Mooney, & Kirby, 2003).

Most of the evidence in favor of these claims is based on single case reports or, at times, grouped case reports. Controlled scientific studies with groups of cases are not yet widely available. Many different types of dietary treatments have been proposed. We can discuss only some of them here. For each of these diets we provide a brief summary of the basic idea of the diet and what is involved. The primary care physician should be sure that dietary intake is adequate, which is important particularly for children who are unusually picky or when major dietary changes are introduced as potential treatments.

Feingold Diet This diet was quite popular in the 1970s. The idea (proposed by Dr. Ben Feingold) was that artificial additives (food colorings, preservatives, and artificial flavors and other ingredients) caused attentional difficulties and hyperactivity. The original diet proposed eliminating all non-natural ingredients and was not particularly risky in terms of the child's health. A few parents of children with autism and related disorders investigated the diet because their child also had difficulties with hyperactivity. There have been some attempts to combine the Feingold diet with the gluten-free–casein-free diet (see the next section). There is some serious scientific work on this diet and the results are mixed—and most apply to children with attention deficit disorder, not autism.

Gluten-Free–Casein-Free (GFCF) Diet Some children and adults in the general population are sensitive to gluten or casein. At present, however, there is limited solid evidence to suggest that these sensitivities are any more common in children with ASDs than in other children. Advocates of this diet have differing recommendations regarding the length of time you are supposed to try it to determine whether it helps (a couple of months seems to be the most frequent recommendation).

The evidence for the GFCF diet is largely case reports and anecdotes. Often this diet is tried in combination with other interventions, complicating the task of figuring out exactly why changes might be observed. There is a slight risk of inadequate nutrition with specialized diets, so it is important to monitor growth and nutritional status. Children can have celiac disease, which means they cannot tolerate gluten. Celiac disease and casein allergy can be tested for. Sensitivity to gluten in people without celiac disease also exists. The only test for this is a trial of a gluten-free diet. One relatively small controlled study has been done, and in this study no effects of this diet were observed in children with autism (Hyman et al., 2015).

Anti-Yeast Diets The idea behind this diet is that yeast infection, sometimes acquired at the time of vaginal birth, causes autism. The diet consists of having children avoid food that contains yeast or fermented foods, perhaps combined with medications used in treatment of yeast infections. Although dramatic claims have been made, the treatment is unproven.

In summary the data, generally, supporting the use of any of those diets is highly limited—there is some suggestion that children with ADHD might respond to some dietary interventions, and of course dietary interventions are used in other contexts (e.g., obesity, sometimes for seizures). Although we haven't seen many children who we thought were helped (over and above that people may be paying more attention to dietary treatments) we've not seen people made much worse, with the exception that sometimes parents become so fixated on the diet that other interventions are slighted.

Vitamin and Minerals It has long been suggested that high **megadose vitamin therapy** might improve functioning in autism; this is one aspect of the DAN (Defeat Autism Now) protocol. Usually high doses of Vitamin B6 and magnesium are involved, sometimes with large doses of other vitamins and minerals as well. Again data are mostly case reports or poorly controlled studies. Although probably generally innocuous, occasionally very high doses of vitamins can lead to difficulties.

OFF-LABEL DRUG TREATMENTS AND MEDICAL PROCEDURES

As discussed in Chapter 11 some medicines now have been FDA approved specifically for autism. Other medications used for disorders such as anxiety or ADHD can be combined with these autism drugs, when appropriate. There are also many drug treatments for ASD that are controversial or alternative given the lack of solid supportive data (much less approval). We can summarize some of these briefly.

Secretin is a peptide hormone involved in water homeostasis. It is widely used in tests of pancreatic functioning. Back in 2007 it was claimed that its use markedly improved functioning in autism. This was highlighted on a TV program and quickly a black market developed. Subsequently several different, well-controlled double-blind studies conclusively showed that it didn't work any better than a placebo.

Anticonvulsant medications are, of course, used in treating seizure disorders, and they are also used in treatment of some psychiatric and other conditions. The use of anticonvulsants for children without seizures or other clear indication is more controversial. Similarly, steroids are sometimes used for good reason, but sometimes they have been given following a period of regression. Steroids can lead to activation, which can be mistaken as substantive clinical improvement.

Another controversial area is use of antibiotics long term to treat putative infections (from bacteria, viruses, or yeast). Advocates of antifungal treatments suggest that the child acquired this infection at birth (even if the mother can't be shown to have had a yeast infection). High-potency antibiotics have been used to treat putative chronic Lyme disease and others.

Chelation treatment (of various types) is sometimes proposed to treat for presumed high levels of mercury or lead. This therapy binds the lead (which is then excreted). Clearly the deleterious effects of high lead levels on children's development is well known and treatment guidelines are well established. There is some clear risk to chelation with at least one death associated with it. In the absence of demonstrated, documented abnormalities, however, there is no reason to conduct chelation therapy.

Other Interventions

Facilitated communication (sometimes called *FC*) is an unusual treatment in that it has now been clearly proven not to work. This is rather an accomplishment, because it usually is much easier to show that a treatment works rather than that it doesn't. Now uncommonly used, in this treatment a facilitator holds the hand of the child with his or her index finger pointed out, steadying the hand. This way the child can allegedly type out words or sentences on a computer keyboard or communicate by picking out letters of the alphabet—for example, on a board or other communication device. Early claims for demonstration of remarkably high levels of cognitive and communication abilities with this support attracted considerable interest. However, this was puzzling because, unlike children with cerebral palsy or serious motor problems, children with autism usually do not have difficulties using their hands and the levels of what was allegedly communicated were very sophisticated—often much higher than expected given either the child's apparent cognitive abilities or IQ.

This technique took a while to catch on in the United States. Surprisingly brighter (and verbal) children with autism were said to be able to facilitate more effectively than they could talk—leading to the notion that you often had to ignore what the child actually said and really pay attention only to the FC. One of the first ominous warning signs about FC was that it was quickly apparent that the people doing the facilitating were reluctant to have the method validated. Very often the child who was allegedly communicating was not even looking at the keyboard. (Those of you who type can try to do this and will see that it is very difficult for even a good typist to do without occasional glancing at the keyboard.) Sometimes the claim was made that attempting to test the child would ruin her trust in the facilitator (again, somewhat odd, given that we know that children with autism often have a hard time in forming relationships anyway). Research, and for that matter the legal system, put an end to FC. It is important to note that this does not mean children with autism can't use a keyboard or can't use communicative devices. This does not mean that individuals with autism can't be helped by keyboards and so on. It does mean we have to be sure the communication is coming from the child.

The Options method grew out of the experience of two parents in dealing with their child with autism. In a series of books, Barry Kaufman describes how he and his wife spent long periods of time trying to follow their son's lead and reconnect with him. This method is expensive because of the training required and the amount of time expended. Some aspects of its philosophy are also controversial (the suggestion, for example, that a good part of the cause of autism is psychological). There are no solid scientific data to back it up, with most of the available support being anecdotal.

A range of other activities and therapies is frequently used for children with ASD but lack a strong research base, for example, art therapy and music therapy. Clearly activities can be enjoyable and therapeutic even when not therapy as such are not clearly evidenced base. Art therapists have training in counseling as well as in art therapy. Music therapists use simple, or more complicated, musical activities for a similar purpose. As with art therapy there are training programs available. Similar approaches are based on dance or movement associated with music and drama. The literature supporting these activities as treatments is mostly anecdotal so far, but it is growing, and better controlled and sophisticated research is needed. These can be valuable activities particularly with experienced therapists who employ a developmental approach (moving from simple to more complex) and respect the special issues involved in autism. It is important to emphasize that activities can be therapeutic without being conventional therapies!

Pets can be wonderful companions and can encourage independence and increase motivation. Sometimes animals are used to improve the lives of individuals in a group home or residential facility. Other animals may be present specifically to provide supports to an individual with a disability and may be certified as service animals. In some situations service animals, usually dogs, or therapeutic horseback riding (hippotherapy) is clearly viewed as beneficial. Similarly horses provide a special example of animal or pet therapy. Hippotherapy has been widely used for children with movement problems as one part of a therapeutic program that encourages better motor and postural control. The benefit is not as much riding as the child's ability to adapt to the horse and be involved in the activity. Therapeutic riding requires an actual riding ability. There is a small amount of research work on pet therapy and hippotherapy (Carlisle, 2015; Gabriels et al., 2012).

The development of stem cell technology, particularly the more recent ability to use a patient's own skin or blood to develop stem cell lines, has considerable scientific interest. It also has been recommended to improve brain functioning and development. Unfortunately the data behind these claims are very minimal, and they can have some risk for the child, for example, through allergic reaction or even because the process that produces stem cells can increase their risk of becoming other problems.

Hyperbaric oxygen therapy has several legitimate medical indications, for example, facilitating wound healing if there is poor circulation or to treat carbon monoxide poisoning. There have been claims that this procedure can be used for children with various developmental disabilities but data are lacking. There are also some important medical risks (e.g., seizures). A few studies have started to appear on this treatment with, at best, mixed results (Bent, Bertoglio, Ashwood, Nemeth, & Hendren, 2012; Rossignol, 2007).

Transcranial magnetic stimulation (TMS) uses a magnetic field generator that can be used noninvasively to stimulate specific brain regions. It has been used diagnostically in relation to a number of conditions, including ALS, stroke, and multiple sclerosis. It has been used clinically for migraines as well as for treatment-resistant depression and pain. There is some, apparently slight, risk. It has also been used in childhood-onset psychiatric conditions such as Tourette's syndrome (in relation to the motor movements); work in autism is limited at present essentially to case reports (Casanova et al., 2014).

SUMMARY

Sometimes a fine line exists between accepted and unconventional treatments. At other times it is clear treatments have been shown not to work or may even pose some risk. Medical professionals probably underestimate how frequently such treatments are used, so it is important for the primary care provider to ask about them and also be prepared to hear about them (often parents get the strong nonverbal message that doctors don't want to talk about them). It is important to help the parent be a well-informed consumer. We suggest helping parents be aware of hidden as well as more obvious costs. Obviously therapies, which pose some risk, are of great concern. Sometimes parents will devote many months or years to the pursuit of a "cure" through some unconventional treatment program without simultaneously pursuing treatments that do work.

Care providers (and parents) should be appropriately skeptical of highly dramatic accounts of "cures" and "miracles" in the media or treatments that are promised to work or are very expensive but don't have a strong evidence base.

▪ REFERENCES

Arnold, G. L., Hyman, S. L., Mooney, R. A., & Kirby, R. S. (2003). Plasma amino acids profiles in children with autism: Potential risk of nutritional deficiencies. *Journal of Autism and Developmental Disorders, 33*(4), 449–454.

Bent, S., Bertoglio, K., Ashwood, P. Nemeth, E., & Hendren, R. L. (2012). Brief report: Hyperbaric oxygen therapy (HBOT) in children with autism spectrum disorder; A clinical trial. *Journal of Autism and Developmental Disorders, 42*(6), 1127–1132.

Carlisle, G. K. (2015). The social skills and attachment to dogs of children with autism spectrum disorder. *Journal of Autism and Developmental Disorders, 45*(5), 1137–1145.

Casanova, M. F., Hensley, M. K., Sokhadze, E. M., El-Baz, A. S., Wang, Y., Li, X., & Sears, L. (2014). Effects of weekly low-frequency rTMS on autonomic measures in children with autism spectrum disorder. *Frontiers in Human Neuroscience, 8*(Oct.), 851–858.

El Dib, R. P., Atallah, A. N., & Andriolo, R. B. (2007). Mapping the Cochrane evidence for decision making in health care. *Journal of Evaluation in Clinical Practice, 13*(4), 689–962.

Escalona, A., Field, T., Singer-Strunck, R., Cullen, C., & Hartshorn, K. (2001). Brief report: Improvements in the behavior of children with autism following massage therapy. *Journal of Autism and Developmental Disorders, 31*(5), 513–516.

Gabriels, R. L., Agnew, J. A., Holt, K. D., Shoffner, A., Zhaoxing, P., Ruzzano, S., et al. (2012). Pilot study measuring the effects of therapeutic horseback riding on school-age children and adolescents with autism spectrum disorders. *Research in Autism Spectrum Disorders, 6*(2), 578–588.

Hyman, S. L., Stewart, P. A., Foley, J., Cain, U., Peck, R., Morris, D. D., et al. (2015). The gluten-free/casein-free diet: A double-blind challenge trial in children with autism. *Journal of Autism and Developmental Disorders,* doi:10.1007/s10803-015-2564-9.

Jacobson, J. W., Foxx, R. M., & Mulick, J. A. (Eds.). (2005). *Controversial therapies for developmental disabilities: Fad, fashion and science in professional practice.* Mahwah, NJ: Erlbaum.

Offit, P. (2008). *Autism's false prophets.* New York, NY: Columbia University Press.

Perrin, J. M., Coury, D. L., Hyman, S. L., Cole, L., Reynolds, A. M., & Clemons, T. (2012). Complementary and alternative medicine use in a large pediatric autism sample. *Pediatrics, 130*(Suppl 2), S77–S82.

Reichow, B., Naples, A., Steinhoff, T., Halpern, J., & Volkmar, F. R. (2012). Brief report: Consistency of search engine rankings for autism websites. *Journal of Autism and Developmental Disorders, 42*(6), 1275–1279.

Rossignol, D. A. (2007). Hyperbaric oxygen therapy might improve certain pathophysiological findings in autism. *Medical Hypotheses, 68*(6), 1208–1227.

Smith, T., Oakes, L., & Selver, K. (2014). Alternative treatments. In F. R. Volkmar, S. J. Rogers, R. Paul, & K. A. Pelphrey (Eds.), *Handbook of autism and pervasive developmental disorders* (4th ed., Vol. 2, pp. 1051–1069). Hoboken, NJ: Wiley.

Sowa, M., & Meulenbroek, R. (2012). Effects of physical exercise on autism spectrum disorders: A meta-analysis. *Research in Autism Spectrum Disorders, 6*(1), 46–57.

Volkmar, F., & Wiesner, L. (2009). *A practical guide to autism.* Hoboken, NJ: Wiley.

Zappella, M. (1998). Holding has grown old. *European Child & Adolescent Psychiatry, 7*(2), 119–121.

▪ SUGGESTED READING

Committee on Children with Disabilities. (2001). American Academy of Pediatrics: Counseling families who choose complementary and alternative medicine for their child with chronic illness or disability. *Pediatrics, 107*(3), 598–601.

Coniglio, S. J., Lewis, J. D., Lang, C., Burns, T. G., Subhani-Siddique, R., Weintraub, A., et al. (2001). A randomized, double-blind, placebo-controlled trial of single-dose intravenous secretin as treatment for children with autism. *Journal of Pediatrics, 138,* 649–655.

Dawson, G., & Watling, R. (2000). Interventions to facilitate auditory, visual, and motor integration in autism: A review of the evidence. *Journal of Autism and Developmental Disabilities, 3,* 415–421.

Elder, J. H., Shankar, M., Shuster, J., Theriaque, D., Burns, S., & Sherrill, L. (2006). The gluten-free, casein-free diet in autism: Results of a preliminary double blind clinical trial. *Journal of Autism and Developmental Disorders, 36,* 413–420.

Findling, R. L., Maxwell, K., Scotese-Wojtila, L., Huang, J., Yamashita, T., & Wiznitzer, M. (1997). High-dose pyridoxine and magnesium administration in children with autistic disorder: An absence of salutary effects in a double blind, placebo-controlled study. *Journal of Autism and Developmental Disorders, 27,* 467–478.

Finn, P., Bothe, A. K., & Bramlett, R. E. (2005). Science and pseudoscience in communication disorders: Criteria and applications. *American Journal of Speech-Language Pathology, 14,* 172–186.

Hansen, R. L., & Ozonoff, S. (2003). Alternative theories: Assessment and therapy options. In S. Ozonoff, S. J. Rogers, & R. L. Hendren (Eds.), *Autism spectrum disorders: A research review for practitioners.* Washington, DC: American Psychiatric Press.

Hanson, E., Kalish, L. A., et al. (2007). Use of complementary and alternative medicine among children diagnosed with autism spectrum disorder. *Journal of Autism and Developmental Disorders, 37*(4), 628–636.

Harrington, J., Rosen, L., Garnecho, A., & Patrick, P. (2006). Parental perceptions and use of complementary and alternative medicine practices for children with autistic spectrum disorders in private practice. *Journal of Developmental and Behavioral Pediatrics, 27*(2), S156–S161.

Horvath, K., Stefanatos, G., Sokolski, K. N., Wachtel, R., Nabors, L., & Tildon, J. T. (1998). Improved social and language skills after secretin administration in patients with autistic spectrum disorders. *Journal of the Association for Academic Minority Physicians, 9,* 9–15.

Hyman, S. L., & Levy, S. E. (2005). Introduction: Novel therapies in developmental disabilities, hope, reason, and evidence. *Mental Retardation & Developmental Disabilities Research Reviews, 11*(2), 107–109.

Institute of Medicine. (2004). *Immunization safety review: Vaccines and autism.* Washington, DC: National Academies Press.

Joint Commission Resources. (2000). A practical system for evidence grading. *Joint Commission Journal on Quality Improvement, 26,* 700–712.

Kane, K. (2006, Jan. 6). Death of 5-year-old boy linked to controversial chelation therapy. *Pittsburgh Post-Gazette.* Retrieved January 30, 2006, from www.postgazette.com/pg/06006/633541.stm

Kay, S., & Vyse, S. (2005). Helping parents separate the wheat from the chaff: Putting autism treatments to the test. In J. W. Jacobson & R. M. Foxx (Eds.), *Fads, dubious and improbable treatments for developmental disabilities* (pp. 265–277). Mahwah, NJ: Erlbaum.

Kurtz, L. A. (2008). *Understanding controversial therapies for children with autism, attention deficit disorder & other learning disabilities.* Philadelphia, PA: Jessica Kingsley.

Lawler, C. P., Croen, L. A., Grether, J. K., & Van de Water, J. (2004). Identifying environmental contributions to autism: Provocative clues and false leads. *Mental Retardation and Developmental Disabilities Research Reviews, 10,* 292–302.

Levy, S. E., & Hyman, S. L. (2005). Novel treatments for autistic spectrum disorders. *Mental Retardation and Developmental Disabilities Research Reviews, 11,* 131–142.

Millward, C., Ferriter, M., Calver, S., & Connell-Jones, G. (2004). Gluten and casein free diets for autistic spectrum disorder. *Cochrane Database of Systematic Reviews, 3,* 1–14.

Mostert, M. P. (2001). Facilitated communication since 1995: A review of published studies. *Journal of Autism and Developmental Disorders, 31,* 287–313.

Newsom, C., & Hovanitz, C. A. (2005). The nature and value of empirically validated interventions. In J. W. Jacobson & R. M. Foxx (Eds.), *Fads, dubious and improbable treatments for developmental disabilities* (pp. 31–44). Mahwah, NJ: Erlbaum.

Owley, T., McMahon, W., Cook, E. H., Laulhere, T. M., South, M., Mays, L. Z., et al. (2001). Multi-site, double-blind, placebo-controlled trial of porcine secretin in autism. *Journal of the American Academy of Child and Adolescent Psychiatry, 40,* 1293–1299.

Park, R. (2000). *Voodoo science: The road from foolishness to fraud.* Oxford, UK: Oxford University Press.

Politi, P., Cena, H., Comelli, M., Marrone, G., Allegri, C., Emanuele, E., et al. (2008). Behavioral effects of omega-3 fatty acid supplementation in young adults with severe autism: An open label study. *Archives of Medical Research, 39*(7), 682–685.

Rawstron, J. A., Burley, C. D., & Eldeer, M. J. (2005). A systematic review of the applicability and efficacy of eye exercises. *Journal of Pediatric Ophthalmology and Strabismus, 42,* 82–88.

Roberts, W., Weaver, L., Brian, J., Bryson, S., Emelianova, S., Griffiths, A. M., MacKinnon, B., et al. (2001). Repeated doses of porcine secretin in the treatment of autism: A randomized, placebo-controlled trial. *Pediatrics, 107,* E71.

Rogers, S. J., & Ozonoff, S. (2005). What do we know about sensory dysfunction in autism? A critical review of the empirical evidence. *Journal of Child Psychology and Psychiatry, 46,* 1255–1268.

Sandler, A. D., & Bodfish, J. W. (2000). Placebo effects in autism: Lessons from secretin. *Journal of Developmental and Behavioral Pediatrics, 21,* 347–350.

Sandler, A. D., Sutton, K. A., DeWeese, J., Girardi, M. A., Sheppard, V., & Bodfish, J. W. (1999). Lack of benefit of a single dose of synthetic human secretin in the treatment of autism and pervasive developmental disorder. *New England Journal of Medicine, 341,* 1801–1806.

Shapiro, A. K., & Shapiro, E. (1997). *The powerful placebo.* Baltimore, MD: Johns Hopkins University Press.

Smith, T., Mruzek, D., & Mozingo, D. (2005). Sensory integrative therapy. In J. W. Jacobson & R. M. Foxx (Eds.), *Fads, dubious and improbable treatments for developmental disabilities* (pp. 311–350). Mahwah, NJ: Erlbaum.

Tolbert, L., Haigler, T., Waits, M. M., & Dennis, T. (1993). Brief report: Lack of response in an autistic population to a low dose clinical trial of pyridoxine plus magnesium. *Journal of Autism and Developmental Disabilities, 23,* 193–199.

Volkmar, F. R. (1999). Editorial: Lessons from secretin. *New England Journal of Medicine, 341,* 1842–1844.

Volkmar, F. R., Cook, E. H., Jr., Pomeroy, J., Realmuto, G., Tanguay, P., & the Work Group on Quality Issues. (1999). Practice parameters for the assessment and treatment of children, adolescents, and adults with autism and other pervasive developmental disorders. *American Academy of Child and Adolescent Psychiatry Working Group on Quality Issues Journal of the American Academy of Child and Adolescent Psychiatry, 38*(12 Suppl), 32S–54S. [Published erratum appears in *Journal of the American Academy of Child and Adolescent Psychiatry, 39*(2000) (7), 938.]

Watling, R., Deitz, J., Kanny, E. M., & McLaughlin, J. F. (1999). Current practice of occupational therapy for children with autism. *American Journal of Occupational Therapy, 53,* 489–497.

CHAPTER 13

Supporting Families

A ll parents want to maximize the potential of their child. The old tendency, in the 1950s, to blame parents and basically ignore siblings of children with ASDs has dramatically changed. Increasingly we've recognized that family involvement is an essential part of implementing effective treatment. Parents, siblings, and other family members may need support in their own right (Fiske, Pepa, & Harris, 2014; Harris & Glasberg, 2012). In contrast to teachers and classmates, family members stay the course for the child with ASD (as often do many primary care providers). In this chapter, we discuss some of the issues for families of having a child with ASD. This includes the role of parents and other family members, the special issues posed for siblings, how parents and family members can effectively communicate with each other, and how members of the extended family can be involved. Finally, we touch on some aspects of long-term planning and legal issues. A number of excellent parent resources are available; some are provided at the end of this chapter in the "Suggested Reading" list.

CHALLENGES AND STRESSES

By including the family in treatment planning and care for the child with ASD, it is clear that the most important considerations are the strengths and vulnerabilities of the individual with an ASD and of the family members. Some of these are obvious; others much less so. For example, potential areas of strengths include higher levels of cognitive and communicative ability in the individual with autism, good educational programs, and greater resources available to parents and families. Somewhat less obvious are potential supports from extended family and friends, community resources and attitudes, parental (and family) ability to cope, and willingness to tackle problems. Areas of vulnerability are more or less obvious. Children with lower levels of cognitive ability and limited communication skills present more challenges for parents, siblings, and schools. School supports can be variable, ranging from great to marginally adequate or poor. Parents with few resources—be they educational, financial, or family supports—also have more difficulty in coping. Sometimes one parent is much more able than the other to tackle these issues; this creates its own tensions and stresses that we discuss shortly. Finally, sometimes it is important to emphasize that every family is unique—things that might be horribly difficult for one family to deal with turn out to be much easier for other families.

There are some obvious stresses for the couple and the marriage. These occur, in different ways, as the child develops—everything from getting a diagnosis, implementing treatment, monitoring programs, and thinking about the transition to adulthood! Parents may have feelings of guilt or responsibility or deal with the problem with denial and a tendency toward isolation. However, some parents focus on the tasks at hand and are open to support from family members, other parents, care providers, and the broader community. Some parents have an experience of severe loss and grief for the idealized child that they didn't get.

Paradoxically, some of the things that might seem to be (and are) potential areas of strength can also be stresses for families. So, for example, the combination of a normal, often beautiful, physical appearance and some areas of strength or ability can easily lead the unknowing observer to assume the child is developing normally and that problem behaviors are a result of poor parenting of a difficult child. Transitions in school programs are frequently stressful—this can occur at any point in the child's development. Some transitions (particularly to more complex social and physical environments such as junior and senior high school) are often very stressful. Difficulties in generalization can lead to unexpected problems. Sometimes the child adamantly refuses to engage in a behavior that parents know perfectly well he or she is capable of—often because some small (to typically developing people) issue has fundamentally changed the perception of the situation on the part of the child with an ASD. Unusual patterns of communication can be sources of distress and embarrassment to parents and, particularly, to siblings. This can lead to social isolation of the family and child.

Services from the array of educators and professionals can be helpful. However, particularly as more professionals are involved there can be a lack of coordination—something that the primary care provider can help to remedy.

Parents can be asked to choose from among a sometimes dizzying array of possible therapies—some of which have empirical support and others of which don't (see Chapter 12). Again as primary care providers become involved they can help parents make sense of competing claims and demands for time (and often money).

SUPPORT FROM EDUCATORS AND OTHERS

Educators, health, and mental health professionals can be a great support to families. This can take different forms (Fiske, 2017; Marcus, Kunce, & Schopler, 2005) and is summarized in Box 13.1.

BOX 13.1 SUPPORTS FOR THE PARENTS AND FAMILY

- *Educational supports.* Provide parents and family members with relevant information about the child and his or her needs.
- *Learning supports.* Learn to support the child's learning, for example, in generalization of skills from school to home and community settings.
- *Behavioral supports.* Learn to apply behavioral approaches in encouraging desired behaviors and discouraging problem behaviors.
- *Social skills supports.* Parents and siblings can learn to help children have more positive family relationships and engage in more sophisticated interpersonal behaviors and play skills.
- *Cognitive skills.* Parents and other family members can systematically encourage problem-solving skills, self-monitoring, and other approaches that facilitate learning.
- *Emotional-affective supports.* Parents and siblings can learn to encourage more sophisticated and integrated emotional responses, coping strategies, more appropriate communication of feelings, and develop more sophisticated coping strategies.

- *Instrumental.* Professionals can help parents and family members access services available in communities, including parent support networks, babysitters, **respite care,** financial supports, and so forth.
- *Technological supports.* Use any of an increasingly vast array of technological supports (going from very low to very high tech) that can help organize the child with ASD.
- *Advocacy.* Parents can learn to be more effective as advocates for their children in schools and other settings.

Source: Adapted from Table 42.1 in Marcus et al. (2005, pp. 1062–1063).

The nature of stress varies with age and developmental level of the child. For parents of younger children who need constant supervision, fatigue can be a big problem. Basic safety concerns, sleep, eating and feeding issues can loom large. These problems can affect the couple individually, their marriage, and indeed the entire family. Parents should be encouraged to make time for each other and with their other children. For school-age children, sometimes behavior problems decrease but problems with schools and after-school and community activities become greater. Siblings may need help in coping, particularly as they must explain a sibling's behavior to peers. Although there's usually less day-to-day involvement with the child's school program as the child moves into school-age there are issues about academic progress, behavioral interventions, special supports, and inclusive settings that may need some degree of parent involvement. As we discuss in Chapter 9, adolescence and young adulthood bring all the usual challenges and more. Some children make gains during this time, although a smaller number may lose skills. Possibilities for post–high school placement and vocation begin to loom larger and issues of long-term care sometimes become a concern. As we have noted, adulthood brings its own challenges.

Marital Issues

Of all the potential supports parents have available to them, usually the most important resource is each other. Parents have to support each other as well as support other children and members of the extended family and friends.

Although fathers are much more involved in the lives of children than was true in past decades, it often is mothers who spend much of their time on the front line in dealing with the needs of the child with an ASD. The father is frequently called in when the mother needs backup. Often, parents take somewhat different paths in dealing with their feelings about a child with a disability of any kind. We occasionally see one parent in deep denial about the child's problems and the other parent is unrealistically glum about the child's future.

Parents can be helped to take their own time and path to dealing with the recognition of the degree to which the child needs support, although obviously not at the expense of the child's treatment. Sometimes a mother or father will have had a brother or sister with a problem or know someone else who did, and this may profoundly color their own take on the situation. Parents can be encouraged to talk with each other about their own feelings, and if needed a support person or group may be indicated (Fiske et al., 2014).

Parents have different ways of coping. Some move into a getting-information mode. Others become more depressed or angry. Others throw themselves into their occupation. Occasionally, parents deny the reality of the child's problem. For others, there are opportunities to enjoy and take pleasure in the child's successes. Problems are most likely to arise when parents are constantly denying their own emotions—this will mean that they can't effectively communicate with their spouse and often the emotion then leaks out in other, sometimes very inappropriate, ways.

Support for parents and family members can come from various sources: the primary care provider, schools, parent groups, community and faith-based organizations. Sometimes just attending parent meetings and hearing that other people have gone through similar situations is important. Parents should avail themselves of family resources—a friend, older niece or nephew who can be trusted to babysit, or an aunt or uncle who may be willing to stay with the child for a weekend. Grandparents can be even more effective as caregivers and babysitters, particularly for younger children.

Developing a sense of humor won't hurt either. Parents have endless stories to tell. We recall one parent who came up to us at a conference to tell us how well her teenage son was doing. He had gotten very interested in social skills development and was indeed doing much better, although he had to learn to sort out some of the language he learned from the typical peers. His mother laughingly reported how he had come across one of his old teachers in a shopping mall and ran up to greet her, saying loudly, "Hi, Mrs. Smith. I am so happy to see you. How ya doing, you old whore!"

SINGLE-PARENT FAMILIES AND DIVORCE

Single parents raising a child with an ASD face the same stresses as other parents, although without the potential benefit of having someone to share the responsibilities and experiences with. Sometimes a marriage that was already in trouble is pushed over the edge by the addition of a child with a disability. Sometimes single mothers (or fathers) will choose to have a child without being married. It can be very helpful to single parents to have someone to talk with: a family member, friend, therapist, or social worker. When divorce does occur (as it frequently does in the United States) both parents should be in good communication with each other regarding their children. This can be hard when divorces are bitter, and some of the worst family situations can arise in this context. A professional (sometimes mandated by the court) can help. The worst situation in a divorce occurs when the child becomes an object of contention rather than an individual who needs help.

GRANDPARENTS AND FAMILY MEMBERS

Grandparents, aunts, uncles, and other family members can be invaluable resources and sources of support for parents and children with ASDs. As is true for parents, having good and continuing communication is important. In some ways, one of the benefits of our electronic age is the potential for staying in close touch, even when living some distance away from each other.

SIBLINGS

Siblings have unique relationships with each other. In contrast to relations with other children, those of siblings are lifelong. They are continuous, and unlike many child relationships, siblings (except for twins) are of different ages. As with parents, siblings have myriad ways of dealing with a brother or sister who has some difficulty. What are the best ways for parents to talk to siblings about the brother's or sister's difficulties? In general, providing age-appropriate information for the siblings is the best way to go. This means neither overwhelming the child nor giving insufficient information. Fortunately, children are very good, in general, at asking questions. Keep things at the child's level. Children may wonder if they have somehow caused the sibling's trouble. They may be angry at the time the sibling with special needs takes from the family and may talk about their own feelings and reactions. Several excellent books are available, and sibling support groups are increasingly available (see Box 13.2).

BOX 13.2 BOOKS FOR SIBLINGS

For Younger Children

Amenta, C. A. (1992). *Russell is extra special: A book about autism for children.* New York, NY: Magination Press.

Bodenheimer, C. (1979). *Everybody is a person: A book for brothers and sisters of autistic kids.* Syracuse, NY: Jowonio/The Learning Place.

Cassette, M. (2006) *My sister Katie: My 6-year-old's view on her sister's autism.* Central Milton Keynes, UK: Authorhouse.

Cook, J., & Hartman, C. (2008). *My mouth is a volcano!* Chattanooga, TN: National Center for Youth Issues.

Donlon, L. (2007). *The other kid: A draw-it-out guidebook for kids dealing with a special needs sibling.* Coral Springs, FL: Llumina Press.

Donlon, L. (2008). *El otro niño: Una guia para niños que tienen un hermano o una hermana especial* (Spanish ed.). Bethpage, NY: Llumina.

Dwight, L. (2005). *Brothers and sisters.* New York, NY: Star Bright Books.

Gold, P. (1976). *Please don't say hello.* New York, NY: Human Sciences Press.

Gorrod, L., & Carger, B. (2003). *My brother is different: A book for young children who have a brother or sister with autism.* London, UK: National Autism Society.

Lears, L. (1998). *Ian's walk: A story about autism.* Morton Grove, IL: Albert Whitman.

Meyer, D., & Gallagher, D. (2005). *The sibling slam book: What it's really like to have a brother or sister with special needs.* Bethesda, MD: Woodbine House.

Meyer, D., & Pillo, C. (1997). *Views from our shoes: Growing up with a brother or sister with special needs.* Bethesda, MD: Woodbine House.

Parker, R. (1974). *He's your brother.* Nashville, TN: Thomas Nelson.

Peralta, S. (2002). *All about my brother.* Shawnee Mission, KS: Autism Asperger.

Phalon, A. C. (2005). *Me, my brother, and autism.* Charleston, SC: BookSurge.

Spence, E. (1977). *The devil hole.* New York, NY: Lothrop, Lee, and Shepard.

Thompson, M. (1996). *Andy and his yellow frisbee.* Bethesda, MD: Woodbine House.

Werlin, N. (1994). *Are you alone on purpose?* New York, NY: Houghton Mifflin.

For Older Children and Adolescents

Band, E., & Hect, E. (2001). *Autism through a sister's eye.* Arlington, TX: Future Horizons.

Barnill, A. C. (2007). *At home in the land of Oz: Autism, my sister, and me.* London, UK: Jessica Kingsley.

Bleach, F. (2002). *Everybody is different.* Shawnee Mission, KS: Autism Asperger.

Cook, J., & Hartman, C. (2008). *My mouth is a volcano!* Chattanooga, TN: National Center for Youth Issues.

Donlon, L. (2007). *The other kid: A draw it out guidebook for kids dealing with a special needs sibling.* Coral Springs, FL: Llumina Press.

Feiges, L. S., & Weiss, M. J. (2004). *Sibling stories: Reflections on life with a brother or sister on the autism spectrum.* Shawnee Mission, KS: Autism Asperger.

Hale, N. (2004). *Oh brother! Growing up with a special needs sibling.* New York, NY: Magination Press.

Hoopmann, K. (2001a). *Blue bottle mystery: An Asperger adventure.* Philadelphia, PA: Jessica Kingsley.

Hoopmann, K. (2001b). *Of mice and aliens: An Asperger adventure.* Philadelphia, PA: Jessica Kingsley.

Johnson, J.B., & Van Rensselaer, A. (2010). *Siblings: The autism spectrum through our eyes.* Philadelphia, PA: Jessica Kingsley.

Thompson, M. (1996). *Andy and his yellow frisbee.* Bethesda, MD: Woodbine House.

Hoopmann, K. (2002). *Lisa and the lacemaker: An Asperger adventure.* Philadelphia, PA: Jessica Kingsley.

Hoopmann, K. (2003). *Haze.* Philadelphia, PA: Jessica Kingsley.

Keating-Velasco, J. L. (2007). *A is for autism, F is for friend: A kid's book for making friends with a child who has autism.* Shawnee Mission, KS: Autism Asperger.

Shally, C., & Herrnington, D. (2007). *Since we're friends: An autism picture book.* Shawnee Mission, KS: Awaken Specialty Press.

Source: Adapted and reprinted with permission from Volkmar and Wiesner (2009, pp. 560–561).

Some sibs are embarrassed by their brother or sister with ASD; others assume a more parental role fairly quickly (even when they are younger). Parents should make every effort to talk with the typically developing sibling and keep lines of communication open. Having a sibling with a disability may have a very important impact (positive or negative) on the life of the typical brother or sister. Box 13.3 summarizes one sibling's experience of his older brother with severe autism.

BOX 13.3 ONE SIBLING'S EXPERIENCE OF AUTISM

My brother was diagnosed as autistic in 1974 … as a "classic case" of childhood autism. He was 3 and a half years old. I was a year younger…. From that early age, I was consumed by a self-imposed sense of responsibility for my brother's safety and well-being….

I began trying to figure my brother out. I was wrought with questions. What does he want? What does he feel? Why does he not seem to love me? My brother had a complete inability to understand social conventions, matched by my inability to understand him.... He refused to make eye contact with me or anyone else for that matter. I learned to not take offense at it.... He broke anything and everything he could get his hands on.... He had pica and ate Play-Doh, among other things.... He ate staples. I learned to berate him without guilt because I drew the line at his health and well-being.... My brother emerged as one of my greatest teachers—through whom I learned responsibility, accountability, patience, stamina, self-discipline, and unconditional love.... My brother lived at home and attended a day school. From the beginning, my parents had made a conscious decision to keep him with the family during a time when the norm was to gravitate toward institutionalization.... This decision proved to be the single most significant force affecting my upbringing—one with long-lasting implications. I have always agreed with the decision for as long as I recall.... Family trips were a vacation from the everyday life at home, but never from the responsibility surrounding the care of my brother. He was a full-time job. At 9 years old ... Disney World was exciting but not fun to me. I remember constantly looking over my shoulder to make sure my brother was following.... I had heard stories of autistic children getting lost in crowds and recovered by police.... My saddest moments revolved around my brother's disinterest in most activities and the rest of the family's lack of involvement as a result. My happiest times were when we found a ride that my brother would enjoy—a ride that we could get on together.... Eventually, I left for college. Siblings who do plan to leave home to pursue higher learning generally fall into one of two schools of thought. Many attend relatively close to home for the obvious purpose of being near the family and the subsequent ability to continue helping the autistic sibling.... The second mind-set takes an opposite approach ... by attending school far away ... I chose the first option. Our plans for maintaining the direct connection with my brother were changed dramatically when my family was transferred halfway across the country in August, due to my father's work.... I missed my brother tremendously. At the same time, though, I realized something that I had never felt before. I no longer looked over my shoulder after several months when out shopping or walking through large crowds. I was able to walk freely without the pressing fear of losing my brother. I also seemed to have much more time on my hands. There was no pressing feeling of need to occupy my brother with learning or activities. I never mentioned this to any of my friends at school. I assumed they would not have understood. I was probably right.... As I contemplated career decisions years before, I always viewed them within the context of my brother's future. How would I be able to help him best in the years to come?... I have been fortunate to know that neither one of my parents ever assumed that I would be completely responsible for my brother's well-being. That in itself removes an otherwise immense pressure. It has been my unspoken desire to oversee my brother's future. Why would I not do that as an adult, when I had already assumed that responsibility as a 4-year-old?

Source: Adapted and reprinted with permission from Konidaris (2005, pp. 1265–1275).

Older children may do quite a bit of the child-rearing. Girls may do this more than boys, but that is certainly not always the case. Harris and Glasberg (2012) have produced an excellent book on siblings of children with autism that summarizes many of the steps parents can take to help siblings. For younger children, there can be confusion about what caused the autism in the first place. Children should be encouraged to ask questions and talk about their experience. Probably the most frequent mistake parents make is in not talking enough to siblings about their experience. It helps to be sensible about this—giving enough, but not too much, information. Also moving from a more general discussion of various kinds of difficulties to a more specific discussion of ASD as a social learning disability may help. Once children start looking, they quickly will realize that many of us have disabilities of various types and all of us have things we are stronger at and things we are weaker at.

How parents cope with the diagnosis of an ASD in their child will also have an impact on how the siblings react. What siblings are told may influence what they feel comfortable saying to their peers in the neighborhood, at school, and at home. Problems will vary over time. Some siblings will cope easily for long periods of time and then have some very particular problem, for example, the child who has done very well but suddenly, in adolescence, doesn't want to have potential girlfriends meet his older brother. Others will be fairly comfortable in talking to their friends about a brother's or sister's problems and handle things rather calmly and straightforwardly.

FAMILY ENGAGEMENT, GENERALIZATION, AND LIFE IN THE COMMUNITY

Children with ASDs have major problems in learning, particularly learning that involves social learning and generalization of skills across settings. Over the past two decades, there has been a growing appreciation on the part of educators and other professionals of the important role that parents, siblings, and others can have in addressing this problem of generalization for the child with an ASD. Parents and siblings can be with the child in church or at the synagogue or mosque, the grocery store, and in the park. The focus at home and in the community should not be concerned so much with teaching cognitive and other skills in isolation but in helping the child learn to apply these skills at home and in the community (Matson, Hattier, & Belva, 2012; Palmen, Didden, & Lang, 2012). A number of supports can be used; these range from work on functional routines using visual supports to help with written schedules, organizers, and so forth (see the "Suggested Reading" list for resources).

Community activities (with supports) should be encouraged for the child with ASD and his or her family. This can range from religious activities, Boy or Girl Scouts, clubs, art or music classes, and so on. For music, the Suzuki method is particularly good, because it is strongly developmental, rule governed, and highly respectful of the child. For other children, music or art therapy may be helpful. Sports and leisure time activities should take into account the child's needs and vulnerabilities. Team sports can be more challenging than more solitary or dyadic activities; for example, swimming, martial arts, or tennis may be better choices than baseball or soccer. Even getting the child to participate in family hikes and other activities that involve some exercise can be helpful.

Exercise has been shown to be associated with improved behavior in several studies. The "Suggested Reading" list offers books about leisure activities, some of which can be enjoyed by all members of the family. Leisure activities also involve opportunities for socialization and for practicing other daily living skills. Parents should be encouraged to explore potential extracurricular activities at school. Help parents keep in mind that experiences can be therapeutic (in the broader sense) without being therapy (in the narrower sense).

SUMMARY

In this chapter, we talked about the impact that having a child with autism can have on parents and families. Having a child with autism can put stresses on the marriage and family. This is true for having typically developing children as well, but children on the autism spectrum have additional challenges and so do parents and family members. Concerns about long-term outcome, planning for the future, and dealing with behavioral issues can all pose stresses. Other issues arise over time as siblings get older. Who will care for the sibling with an ASD as their parents get older and cannot manage it all on their own? What impact will this have on a future spouse of theirs? Will the sibling with an ASD come to live with them? Will they be able to manage as well as their parents have done? Who will provide the financial support that is needed over the years? And perhaps most concerning of all, will they have a child of their own with an ASD? These are all legitimate questions, some of which we can address now and some of which we'll be able to better address over the next several years.

Clearly, talking to siblings in an age-appropriate manner can be enormously helpful. Sometimes meeting with other siblings of children with ASDs can be of benefit. There are now more and more groups providing sibling support, some specifically for siblings of children and adults with ASDs, and some for siblings of children and adults with other chronic disorders with and without intellectual disabilities. We have listed a few websites and books on these topics in the "Suggested Reading" list at the end of the chapter. The Sibling Support Project (www.siblingsupport.org) has been around for many years and has been very helpful for many people of different ages.

Parents and family members can and should take genuine pleasure in the accomplishments of the child with an ASD. It is important that parents feel positive about their ability to parent the child with an ASD along with their other children. It is important that siblings not feel left out or neglected. They will have their own reactions to a brother or sister with an ASD, and these may change over time. There is not a single right way to be an effective parent. From the point of view of the couple and family, it is important to carve out time for each other and the rest of the family and still be a good parent to a child with an ASD.

Families should feel free to use other supports whenever they can. These supports can include relatives and friends. Other parents and parent and sibling support groups can provide useful information and ways to connect with other people having similar experiences and facing similar problems. Teachers and school personnel also may be sources of valuable information and support.

Siblings will have different feelings and experiences. Even as very young children, they may well pick up on the fact that a brother or sister is different. Parents should be honest about these differences without overwhelming the sibling with too much information. Parents should also be aware that siblings can have different reactions over time, including negative ones. By the time children are in school, the typically developing brother or sister may cultivate any of (or many of) a number of reactions, ranging from trying to deny the reality of the brother's or sister's problems to becoming caretakers of the child, to being resentful of the sibling who receives more attention. As with other things, children are often guided by their parents (even when they protest that they are not), so if parents can model openness, tolerance, and a willingness to communicate, things will tend to go best over the long haul.

The challenges and problems families face will change over time, depending on the specifics of the situation and family and age and level of the child with an ASD. Families will work best when parents can have good communication with each other and with family members.

▓ REFERENCES

Fiske, K. E. (2017). *Autism and the family*. New York, NY: Norton.

Fiske, K. E., Pepa, L., & Harris, S. L. (2014). Supporting parents, siblings, and grandparents of individuals with autism spectrum disorders. In F. R. Volkmar, S. J. Rogers, R. Paul, & K. A. Pelphrey (Eds.), *Handbook of autism and pervasive developmental disorders* (4th ed., Vol. 2, pp. 932–948). Hoboken, NJ: Wiley.

Harris, S. L., & Glasberg, B. A. (2012). *Siblings of children with autism: A guide for families* (3rd ed.). Bethesda, MD: Woodbine House.

Konidaris, J. B. (2005). A sibling's perspective on autism. In F. Volkmar, A. Klin, R. Paul, & D. J. Cohen (Eds.), *Handbook of autism and pervasive developmental disorders* (3rd ed., Vol. 2, pp. 1265–1275). New York: Wiley.

Marcus, L. M., Kunce, L. J., & Schopler, R. (2005). Working with families. In F. Volkmar, A. Klin, R. Paul, & D. J. Cohen (Eds.), *Handbook of autism and pervasive developmental disorders* (3rd ed., Vol. 2, pp. 1055–1086). New York: Wiley.

Matson, J. L., Hattier, M. A., & Belva, B. (2012). Treating adaptive living skills of persons with autism using applied behavior analysis: A review. *Research in Autism Spectrum Disorders, 6*(1), 271–276.

Palmen, A., Didden, R., & Lang, R. (2012). A systematic review of behavioral intervention research on adaptive skill building in high-functioning young adults with autism spectrum disorder. *Research in Autism Spectrum Disorders, 6*(2), 602–617.

Volkmar, F., & Wiesner, L. (2009). *A practical guide to autism.* Hoboken, NJ: Wiley.

SUGGESTED READING

Adams, S. (2009). *A book about what autism can be like.* London, UK: Jessica Kingsley.

Anderson, S. R., Jablonski, A. L., Knapp, V. M., & Thomeer, M. L. (2007). *Self-help skills for people with autism: A systematic teaching approach.* Bethesda, MD: Woodbine House.

Andron, L. (Ed.). (2001). *Our journey through high-functioning autism & Asperger syndrome: A roadmap.* Philadelphia, PA: Jessica Kingsley.

Bauer, A. (2005). *A wild ride up the cupboards.* New York, NY: Scribner.

Bolick, T. (2004). *Asperger syndrome and young children: Building skills for the real world.* Gloucester, MA: Fair Winds Press.

Bondy, A., & Frost, L. (2008). *Autism 24/7: A family guide to learning at home and in the community.* Bethesda, MD: Woodbine House.

Boyd, B. (2003). *Parenting a child with Asperger syndrome.* London, UK: Jessica Kingsley.

Brereton, A. V., & Tonge, B. (2009). *Pre-schoolers with autism: An education and skills training programme for parents; Manual for parents.* London, UK: Jessica Kingsley.

Brill, M. T. (2001). *Keys to parenting the child with autism* (2nd ed.). Hauppauge, NY: Barron's Educational Series.

Calinescu, M. (2009). *Matthew's enigma: A father's portrait of his autistic son.* Bloomington, IN: Indiana University Press.

Cohen, J. (2002). *The Asperger parent: How to raise a child with Asperger syndrome and maintain your sense of humor.* Shawnee Mission, KS: Autism Asperger.

Coulter, D. (Producer/Director). (2004). *Asperger syndrome for dad: Becoming an even better father to your child with Asperger syndrome* [DVD]. Winston Salem, NC: Coulter Video.

Coulter, D. (Producer/Director). (2007). *Understanding brothers and sisters with Asperger syndrome* [DVD]. Winston Salem, NC: Coulter Video.

Coyne, P. (1999). *Developing leisure time skills for persons with autism: A practical approach for home, school and community.* Arlington, TX: Future Horizons.

Coyne, P. (2004). *Supporting individuals with autism spectrum disorder in recreation.* Champaign, IL: Sagamore.

Cumberland, D. L., & Mills, B. E. (2010). *Siblings and autism.* London, UK: Jessica Kingsley.

Dillon, K. (1995). *Living with autism: The parents' stories.* Boone, NC: Parkway.

Durand, V. M., & Hieneman, M. (2008). *Helping parents with challenging children: Positive family intervention; Facilitator guide.* Oxford, UK: Oxford University Press.

Elder, J. (2005). *Different like me: My book of autism heroes.* Philadelphia, PA: Jessica Kingsley.

Exkorn, K. (2005). *The autism sourcebook: Everything you need to know about diagnosis, treatment, coping, and healing.* New York, NY: Regan Books.

Fawcett, H., & Baskin, A. (2006). *More than a mom: Living a full and balanced life when your child has special needs.* Bethesda, MD: Woodbine House.

Frender, S., & Schiffmiller, R. (2007). *Brotherly feelings: Me, my emotions, and my brother with Asperger's syndrome.* London, UK: Jessica Kingsley.

Haddon, M. (2003). *The curious incident of the dog in the nighttime.* New York, NY: Doubleday.

Harris, S. L. (1994). *Siblings of children with autism: A guide for families.* Bethesda, MD: Woodbine House.

Harris, S. L., & Glasberg, B. A. (2003). *Siblings of children with autism: A guide for families* (2nd ed.). Bethesda, MD: Woodbine House.

Johnson, J., & Van Rensselaer, A. (2010). *The autism spectrum through our eyes.* London, UK: Jessica Kingsley.

Johnson, J., & Van Rensselaer, A. (2008). *Families of adults with autism: Stories and advice for the next generation.* London, UK: Jessica Kingsley.

Kelly, A. B., Garnett, M. S., Attwood, T., & Peterson, C. (2008). Autism spectrum symptomatology in children: The impact of family and peer relationships. *Journal of Abnormal Child Psychology, 36,* 1069–1081.

Kranowitz, C. S. (1995). *101 activities for kids in tight spaces.* New York, NY: St. Martin's Griffin Press.

Larson, E. M. (2006). *I am utterly unique: Celebrating the strengths of children with Asperger syndrome and high-functioning autism.* Shawnee Mission, KS: Autism Asperger.

Leventhal-Belfer, L., & Coe, C. (2004). *Asperger syndrome in young children.* London, UK: Jessica Kingsley.

Lobato, D. J. (1990). *Brothers, sisters, and special needs: Information and activities for helping young siblings of children with chronic illnesses and developmental disabilities* (Foreword by Eunice Kennedy Shriver). Baltimore, MD: Brookes.

Loomis, J. W. (2014). Supporting adult independence in the community for individuals with high-functioning autism spectrum disorders. In F. R. Volkmar,

S. J. Rogers, R. Paul, & K. A. Pelphrey (Eds.), *Handbook of autism and pervasive developmental disorders* (4th ed., Vol. 2, pp. 949–968). Hoboken, NJ: Wiley.

Luchsinger, D. F. (2007). *Playing by the rules: A story about autism.* Bethesda, MD: Woodbine House.

Marcus, L. J., Kunce, L. J., & Schopler, E. (2005). Working with families. In F. Volkmar, A. Klin, R. Paul, & D. J. Cohen (Eds.), *Handbook of autism and pervasive developmental disorders* (3rd ed., Vol. 2, pp. 1055–1086). New York: Wiley.

Marshak, L. E., & Prezant, F. B. (2007). *Married with special-needs children: A couples' guide to keeping connected.* Bethesda, MD: Woodbine House.

Martin, E. P. (1999). *Dear Charlie, a grandfather's love letter: A guide for living your life with autism.* Arlington, TX: Future Horizons.

Meyer, D., & Vadasy, P. (1996). *Living with a brother or sister with special needs: A book for sibs* (2nd ed.). Seattle, WA: University of Washington Press.

Miller, N., & Sammons, C. (1999). *Everybody's different: Understanding and changing our reactions to disabilities.* Baltimore, MD: Brookes.

Moor, J. (2008). *Playing, laughing and learning with children on the autism spectrum: A practical resource of play ideas for parents and careers* (2nd ed.). London, UK: Jessica Kingsley.

Moore, C. (2006). *George & Sam: Two boys, one family, and autism.* New York, NY: St. Martin's Press.

Naseef, R. A. (2001). *Special children, challenged parents: The struggles and rewards of raising a child with a disability.* Baltimore, MD: Brookes.

Nadworth, J. W., & Haddad, C. R. (2007). *The special needs planning guide: How to prepare for every stage of your child's life.* Baltimore, MD: Brookes.

Newman, S. (2002). *Small steps forward: Using games and activities to help your preschool child with special needs.* London, UK: Jessica Kingsley.

O'Brien, M., & Daggett, J. A. (2006). *Beyond the autism diagnosis: A professional's guide to helping families.* Baltimore, MD: Brookes.

Ozonoff, S., Dawson, G., & McPartland, J. (2002). *A parent's guide to Asperger syndrome & high-functioning autism.* New York, NY: Guilford Press.

Richman, S. (2001). *Raising a child with autism: A guide to applied behavior analysis for parents.* London, UK: Jessica Kingsley.

Schopler, E. (1995). *Parent survival manual: A guide to crisis resolution in autism and related developmental disorders.* New York, NY: Plenum Press.

Senator, S. (2005). *Making peace with autism: One family's story of struggle, discovery, and unexpected gifts.* Boston, MA: Trumpeter.

Sicile-Kira, C. (2006). *Adolescents on the autism spectrum: A parent's guide to the cognitive, social, physical, and transition needs of teenagers with autism spectrum disorders.* New York, NY: Penguin.

Siegel, B., & Silverstein, S. (1994). *What about me? Growing up with a developmentally disabled sibling.* Cambridge, MA: Perseus.

Sohn, A., & Grayson, C. (2005). *Parenting your Asperger child: Individualized solutions for teaching your child practical skills.* New York, NY: Perigee Trade.

Sonders, S. A. (2003). *Giggle time—establishing the social connection: A program to develop the communication skills of children with autism, Asperger syndrome and PDD.* London, UK: Jessica Kingsley.

Spilsbury, L. (2001). *What does it mean to have autism.* Chicago, IL: Heinemann Library.

Starr Campito, J. (2007). *Supportive parenting: Becoming an advocate for your child with special needs.* London, UK: Jessica Kingsley.

Stewart, K. (2002). *Helping a child with nonverbal learning disorder or Asperger's syndrome: A parent's guide.* Oakland, CA: New Harbinger.

Tammet, D. (2006). *Born on a blue day: Inside the extraordinary mind of an autistic savant.* New York, NY: Free Press.

Twoy, R., Connolly, P. M., & Novak, J. M. (2007). Coping strategies used by parents of children with autism. *Journal of the American Academy of Nurse Practitioners, 19*(5), 251–260.

Vicker, B., & Lieberman, L. A. (2007). *Sharing information about your child with autism spectrum disorder.* Shawnee Mission, KS: Autism Asperger.

Welton, J. (2003). *Can I tell you about Asperger syndrome? A guide for friends and family.* Philadelphia, PA: Jessica Kingsley.

Wheatley, T. (2005). *My sad is all gone: A family's triumph over violent autism.* Lancaster, OH: Lucky Press.

Whiteman, N. J. (2007). *Building a joyful life with your child who has special needs.* London, UK: Jessica Kingsley.

Zysk, V., & Notbohm, E. (2004). *1001 great ideas for teaching and raising children with autism spectrum disorders.* Arlington, TX: Future Horizons.

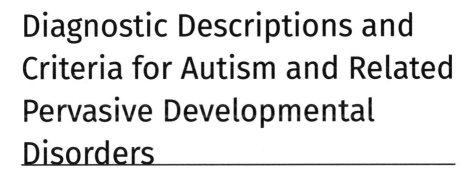

Diagnostic Descriptions and Criteria for Autism and Related Pervasive Developmental Disorders

F84.0 Childhood autism

A. Abnormal or impaired development is evident before the age of 3 years in at least one of the following areas:
    1. receptive or expressive language as used in social communication;
    2. the development of selective social attachments or of reciprocal social interaction;
    3. functional or symbolic play.

B. A total of at least six symptoms from (1), (2), and (3) must be present, with at least two from (1) and at least one from each of (2) and (3).
    1. Qualitative impairments in social interaction are manifest in at least two of the following areas:
        a. failure adequately to use eye-to-eye gaze, facial expression, body postures, and gestures to regulate social interaction;

Source: World Health Organization. (2003). Geneva, Switzerland: Author. Reprinted with permission.

    b. failure to develop (in a manner appropriate to mental age, and despite ample opportunities) peer relationships that involve a mutual sharing of interests, activities, and emotions;

    c. lack of socio-emotional reciprocity as shown by an impaired or deviant response to other people's emotions; or lack of modulation of behaviour according to social context; or a weak integration of social, emotional, and communicative behaviours;

    d. lack of spontaneous seeking to share enjoyment, interests, or achievements with other people (e.g., a lack of showing, bringing, or pointing out to other people objects of interest to the individual).

2. Qualitative abnormalities communication as manifest in at least one of the following areas:

    a. delay in, or total lack of, development of spoken language that is *not* accompanied by an attempt to compensate through the use of gestures or mime as an alternative mode of communication (often preceded by a lack of communicative babbling);

    b. relative failure to initiate or sustain conversational interchange (at whatever level of language skill is present), in which there is reciprocal responsiveness to the communications of the other person;

    c. stereotyped and repetitive use of language or idiosyncratic use of words or phrases;

    d. lack of varied spontaneous make-believe play or (when young) social imitative play.

3. Restricted, repetitive, and stereotyped patterns of behaviour, interests, and activities are manifested in at least one of the following:

    a. an encompassing preoccupation with one or more stereotyped and restricted patterns of interest that are abnormal in content or focus; or one or more interests that are abnormal in their intensity and circumscribed nature, though not in their content or focus;

    b. apparently compulsive adherence to specific, nonfunctional routines or rituals;

c. stereotyped and repetitive motor mannerisms that involve either hand or finger flapping or twisting or complex whole-body movements;

d. preoccupations with part-objects or nonfunctional elements of play materials (such as their odor, the feel of their surface, or the noise or vibration they generate).

C. The clinical picture is not attributable to the other varieties of pervasive developmental disorders; specific development disorder of receptive language (F80.2) with secondary socio-emotional problems, **reactive attachment disorder** (F94.1), or disinhibited attachment disorder (F94.2); mental retardation (F70–F72) with some associated emotional or behavioural disorders; schizophrenia (F20.–) of unusually early onset; and Rett's syndrome (F84.12).

F84.1 Atypical autism

A. Abnormal or impaired development is evident at or after the age of 3 years (criteria as for autism except for age of manifestation).

B. There are qualitative abnormalities in reciprocal social interaction or in communication; or restricted, repetitive, and stereotyped patterns of behaviour, interests, and activities. (Criteria as for autism except that it is unnecessary to meet the criteria for number of areas of abnormality.)

C. The disorder does not meet the diagnostic criteria for autism (F84.0).
Autism maybe atypical in either age of onset (F84.10) or symptomatology (F84.11); the two types are differentiated with a fifth character for research purposes. Syndromes that are typical in both respects should be coded F84.12.

F84.10 Atypicality in age of onset

A. The disorder does not meet criterion A for autism (F84.0); that is, abnormal or impaired development is evident only at or after age 3 years.

B. The disorder meets criteria B and C for autism (F84.0).

F84.11 Atypicality in symptomatology

A. The disorder meets criterion A for autism (F84.0); that is, abnormal or impaired development is evident before age 3 years.

B. There are qualitative abnormalities in reciprocal social interactions or in communication, or restricted, repetitive, and stereotyped patterns of behaviour, interests, and activities. (Criteria as for autism except that it is unnecessary to meet the criteria for number of areas of abnormality.)

C. The disorder meets criterion C for autism (F84.0).

D. The disorder does not fully meet criterion B for autism (F84.0).

F84.12 Atypicality in both age of onset and symptomatology

A. The disorder does not meet criterion A for autism (F84.0); that is, abnormal or impaired development is evident only at or after age 3 years.

B. There are qualitative abnormalities in reciprocal social interactions or in communication, or restricted, repetitive, and stereotyped patterns of behaviour, interests, and activities. (Criteria as for autism except that it is unnecessary to meet the criteria for number of areas of abnormality.)

C. The disorder meets criterion C for autism (F84.0).

D. The disorder does not fully meet criterion B for autism (F84.0).

F84.2 Rett's syndrome

A. Apparently normal prenatal and perinatal period *and* apparently normal psychomotor development through the first 6 months *and* normal head circumference at birth.

B. Deceleration of head growth between 5 months and 4 years *and* loss of acquired purposeful hand skills between 6 and 30 months of age that is associated with concurrent communication dysfunction and impaired social interactions *and* the appearance of poorly coordinated/unstable gait and/or trunk movements.

C. Development of severely impaired expressive and receptive language, together with severe psychomotor retardation.

D. Stereotyped midline hand movements (such as hand wringing or "hand washing") with an onset at or after the time that purposeful hand movements are lost.

F84.3 Other childhood disintegrative disorder

A. Development is apparently normal development up to the age of at least 2 years. The presence of normal age-appropriate skills in communication, social relationships, play, and adaptive behaviour at age 2 years or later is required for diagnosis.

B. There is a definite loss of previously acquired skills at about the time of onset of the disorder. The diagnosis requires a clinically significant loss of skills (and not just a failure to use them in certain situations) in at least two out of the following areas:
    1. expressive or receptive language;
    2. play;
    3. social skills or adaptive behaviour;
    4. bowel or bladder control;
    5. motor skills.

C. Qualitatively abnormal social functioning, manifest in at least two of the following areas:
    1. qualitative abnormalities in reciprocal social interaction (of the type defined for autism);
    2. qualitative abnormalities in communication (of the type defined for autism);
    3. restricted, repetitive, and stereotyped patterns of behaviour, interests, and activities including motor stereotypies and mannerisms;
    4. a general loss of interest in objects and in the environment.

D. The disorder is not attributable to the other varieties of pervasive developmental disorder; acquired aphasia with epilepsy (F80.6); elective mutism (F94.0); Rett's syndrome (F84.2); or schizophrenia (F20.–).

F84.5 Asperger's syndrome

A. A lack of any clinically significant general delay in spoken or receptive language or cognitive development. Diagnosis requires that single words should have developed by 2 years of age or earlier and that communicative phrases be used by 3 years of age or earlier. Self-help skills, adaptive behaviour, and curiosity about the environment during the first 3 years should be at a level consistent with normal intellectual development. However, motor milestones may be somewhat delayed and motor clumsiness is usual (although not a necessary diagnostic feature). Isolated special skills, often related to abnormal preoccupations, are common, but are not required for diagnosis.

B. Qualitative abnormalities in reciprocal social interaction (criteria as for autism).

C. An unusually intense circumscribed interest or restricted, repetitive, and stereotyped patterns of behaviour, interests, and activities (criteria as for autism; however, it would be less usual for these to include either motor mannerisms or preoccupations with part-objects or non-functional elements of play materials).

D. The disorder is not attributable to the other varieties of pervasive developmental disorder: simple schizophrenia (F20.6); schizotypal disorder (F21); obsessive-compulsive disorder (F42.–); anankastic personality disorder (F60.5); reactive and disinhibited attachment disorders of childhood (F94.1 and F94.2, respectively).

F84.8 Other pervasive developmental disorders

F84.9 Pervasive developmental disorder, unspecified

This is a residual diagnostic category that should be used for disorders that fit the general description for pervasive developmental disorders but in which a lack of adequate information, or contradictory findings, means that the criteria for any of the other F84 codes cannot be met.

Understanding School and Specialist Assessment

I t is common for schools to conduct independent assessments of the child; often parents may also pursue assessment from providers or interdisciplinary teams. In both situations usually a relatively long narrative report will result. Given that individuals from a number of different medical and nonmedical specialists are involved, it is ideal if the team provides a unified, coherent report integrating findings and observations. Less helpful is a series of tests conducted in isolation with little interpretation. In this appendix we provide a short overview to reading and understanding assessment reports. If you feel comfortable already you may well not need to review this information. But if you are unfamiliar with the issues, a quick review may be helpful. The end of this appendix has a list of some reading materials that may be of interest as well.

UNDERSTANDING TEST RESULTS

Typically, a number of instruments (tests) are used to assess the child's abilities in various areas. With the exception of autism screening and diagnostic tests (in which different issues apply) the results for standard testing are provided based on scoring of the individual relative to the standardization sample used to develop the tests (i.e., the "normal" population). Keep in mind that although numbers are important, observations of the child or adult during the testing can be just as informative. In addition, particularly for children with ASDs the interpretation of the results is critical. For example, a child may have a very isolated area of strength with many other areas of weakness. In such cases parents may understandably want to focus on this strength—sometimes at the expense of not paying attention to the areas in which the child needs help. As with everything else, knowing that the examiner(s) has (have) considerable experience is important—it is the less-experienced people who often leap to conclusions or make recommendations that move past what the assessment results provide. Parents should be encouraged to ask questions about reports and have them explained in a way that they can understand. It also is hard for parents (who sometimes are encouraged to watch assessments either by video monitor or one-way mirror) to understand that the examiners have a set of rules to follow in administering the assessment. Violation of these rules makes results impossible to compare to the national or standardization sample—this can be very frustrating for parents who say, quite rightly, that "if you had asked the question a different way he'd have known the answer"—they are right but so is the person who did the test! The point with autism is that often children know things in isolation and their lack of flexibility can make it difficult for them to generalize knowledge—something itself that is important to know and work on. Examiners face a number of challenges when working with individuals with ASDs (see Appendix Box 2.1), so having experienced examiners is very helpful.

APPENDIX BOX 2.1 CHALLENGES FOR ASSESSMENT IN AUTISM

- There is a tremendous range of variability in levels of function (within and between children).
- There is great variability in functioning across settings.
- Behavioral problems may complicate assessment.
- Lack of social interest makes it hard to get the child's cooperation.

Standardized scores can be presented in several ways but in all cases there will be a mean (population average) and **standard deviation** (a measure of the variation around the mean). For many tests of intelligence,

achievement tests, and communication assessments, standard scores provide the best way to compare scores for the child and relative to other children or individuals.

Originally, standard scores such as IQ were computed by taking the child's **age-equivalent score (mental age)** and dividing it by the child's actual chronological age and then multiplying the result by 100. Thus, a child with a mental age of 3 years and an actual age of 5 years would have been said to have an IQ of 60 ($\frac{3}{5}$ × 100). Nowadays, tests are developed and standardized in more sophisticated ways, but the general idea is the same. The distribution of standard scores falls on the famous (or infamous) bell-shaped curve. The average score will be in the middle, with other scores around it. For many IQ tests, the average or mean score in the general population is 100. That is, about 50% of people would score above 100, and 50% would score below it. These tests usually have a standard deviation (measure of how the scores scatter around the average) of about 15. This means that most people taking the test will score within 15 points above to 15 points below the mean, or between 85 and 115. Only about 3% of people will score more than 30 points (two standard deviations) above or below the mean. That is, only about 3% of people would have scores of 70 or below. Some tests will have different means and standard deviations, for example, some tests use T scores, in which the mean is 50 and the standard deviation is 10.

In the general population it is common to have many of the individual's scores cluster around the same number, although in individuals with ASDs this is often *not* the case, because there can be a great deal of scatter in the range of skills that IQ tests tap into for these children. The scatter itself is often informative because it tells us much more about strengths and weaknesses. When there is great scatter within an IQ test often an overall score is not reported because it is rather misleading given the child's variability.

Test results can be presented in other ways as well. For example, age-equivalent scores are the easiest to understand but are often less so because they are more likely to fluctuate than standard scores (performance on one or two items may increase or decrease the age-equivalent score more dramatically than it does the standard score). **Percentile scores** may also be reported and provide a score based on what percentage of scores are lower; for example, an 85th percentile score means the person scored higher than 85% of the people who take the test.

The person doing the assessment will be alert to specific problem behaviors that are important either because they help with the issue of diagnosis or because they are important areas for intervention. For example, aggression, self-injury, or stereotyped behaviors may be helped through behavioral (**behavior modification**) or pharmacological (drug) intervention. Similarly, within the constraints of doing the test in the standard way, the examiner has some flexibility, for example, do verbal cues work? Do visual cues help? Does the child need frequent breaks and movement to help stay on task? What kinds of tasks present the greatest difficulty? All this information based on observation during the assessment can be a very informative part of the report and one that is tremendously helpful in the classroom.

PSYCHOLOGICAL ASSESSMENT

This part of the assessment evaluates several aspects, such as establishing children's overall levels of cognitive ability (intelligence quotient [IQ]), as well as describing their profiles of strengths and weaknesses. Any number of tests may be used. Usually, this testing will include, at a minimum, a test of cognitive ability or intelligence and some assessment of adaptive skills (the ability to translate what you know into real-world settings), as well as observation of the child and discussion with you. Observation of the child should be part of the assessment process—giving a psychological test is only one part of a broader assessment. This is important because individuals with autism are quite variable in their behavior. Usually, for most of the assessment, the examiners will be working in a very structured way with the child in an effort to get the best possible performance within the limits of the test or assessment of what they are doing. They do this by setting up a friendly but not overly stimulating environment and picking materials and tests that will be appropriate to the child's needs. As previously discussed, there is both a science and an art to doing assessment with children with autism.

For some portions of the time with the child, the examiner must decide to pull back a bit to give the child more opportunities for less-structured interaction. The examiner may also need to decide what the right pace of the assessment is—this again depends on the child; some children respond better to a rather rapid pace, and others like to take things slow and easy.

The different types of skills assessed on developmental and intelligence tests usually will include more and fewer verbal tasks, some that involve memory, and so forth.

In classical autism, particularly in younger children, nonverbal skills are usually much advanced over more verbal abilities. That is, it is common for a child to have a much higher nonverbal IQ. A child's nonverbal abilities might be, say, at a level corresponding to IQ 75 or 80 (standard score), whereas his verbal abilities might be at the IQ 40 level. For higher-functioning children with autism, this gap is usually not as great but may still be there to some extent. There is some indication that this situation is reversed in Asperger's syndrome, in which verbal skills are better than nonverbal skills.

There are many different intelligence tests available. The specific test or tests chosen will depend on several factors, for example, how much language is required (either to understand or respond), how much the test requires transitions and shifting, the social demands of the test, and how important speed of performance is. Generally, children with autism do best on tests that require less language and social engagement and fewer shifts and transitions. Because IQ tests can vary widely in how much they emphasize these factors, it is possible that the same child could get very different results on different tests. Thus, it is important that the psychologist choose the tests carefully, keeping in mind the specific circumstances and needs of the child. The choice of test (or tests) is up to the psychologist, who may try to start with something he or she thinks will be easier or more interesting to the child. Sometimes what seem to be minor differences in tests (more or less verbal tests) can actually result in major changes for a child with autism; thus, it is important that the psychologist have some experience in working with children with autism and be aware of the range of IQ tests available. Some of the more frequently used tests are listed in Appendix Table 2.1.

For younger children, tests of cognitive ability are usually referred to as developmental tests; these tests provide information on the child's functioning in different areas relative to other children of the same age. The distinction between developmental and intelligence tests is a somewhat arbitrary one and reflects, in part, the fact that results of tests of cognitive development and intelligence become more stable about the time the child is of traditional school age.

APPENDIX TABLE 2.1 **SELECTED TESTS OF INTELLIGENCE AND DEVELOPMENT**

Test Name	Comment
Wechsler Intelligence Scales; Wechsler Preschool and Primary Scale of Intelligence, 3rd ed. (WPPSI-IV, 2012); Wechsler Intelligence Scale for Children, 5th ed. (WISC-V, 2015), Wechsler Adult Intelligence Scale, 4th ed. (WAIS-IV, 2008)	Excellent series of tests covering preschool (about age 4) to adulthood; assesses a range of cognitive abilities. Some tasks are timed, which is a challenge for many children with autism and related conditions (this actually may help document need for untimed tests). Typical profiles of ability are seen in autism and Asperger's disorder.
Stanford Binet Intelligence Scale, 5th ed. (SB5) (Roid, 2003)	Excellent test; can be used with somewhat younger children. Wide age range. Nonverbal scale may underestimate abilities in ASDs.
Kaufmann Assessment Battery for Children, 2nd ed. (KABC-II) (Kaufman & Kaufman, 2004)	Excellent test; can be used from 3 to 18 years of age. Some language is needed (but not much). Somewhat more flexible for children with autism. Many of the materials interest children with ASDs. Language demands minimized and good sensitivity to possible cultural bias.
Leiter International Performance Scale, 3rd ed. (Leiter-3) (Roid & Miller, et al, 2013)	A test originally developed for deaf children, recently revised. Provides assessment of nonverbal cognitive ability. Can be used for children with no expressive speech. Some teaching is allowed. Limitations include no verbal tasks.
Mullen Scales of Early Learning	Can be used with very young children. Provides scores in nonverbal problem-solving, receptive and expressive language, and gross and fine motor skills. Scores from such developmental tests are usually less predictive of later abilities.
Differential Ability Scales, 2nd ed. (DAS-II) (Elliott, 2007)	Well-done test; covers wide range of ages and taps a number of different skills (not just overall IQ). Early years scales can provide an IQ for low-functioning children younger than 9 years old.

Note: Many other tests are available, and tests are constantly revised and reissued.

A range of other tests may be used by the psychologist to assess other skills. For example, adaptive functioning (adaptive skills) is a concept distinct from IQ and refers to the ability of the individual to use what he or she knows in real-world settings. This is critical in autism, because it is not at all uncommon for the child to know something in school but not to be able to generalize it to other settings. For example, we have an adolescent patient with Asperger's syndrome who has a verbal IQ of 140 (genius level), one of whose major preoccupations is solving very complex mathematical equations. But this same patient cannot walk into McDonald's and get a cheeseburger and change! The latter skill—translating his mathematical ability into the real world—is what adaptive skills are all about.

Given the major challenges individuals on the autism spectrum have with generalization, the **Vineland Adaptive Behavior Scales** assess capacities for self-sufficiency in several different domains of functioning in the areas of communication (receptive, expressive, and written skills); daily living (personal, domestic, and community skills); socialization (interpersonal, play-leisure time, and coping skills); as well as motor skills (gross and fine) in younger children. Several versions of this instrument are available, and it is the most widely used assessment for adaptive skills, although other instruments are also available. With the more detailed Vineland assessment, it is possible to develop a set of goals specific to the child for work in classroom and nonclassroom settings. Other assessed areas include achievement abilities (i.e., what has the child actually learned in academic areas relative to other children in contrast to the child's ability to work more generally in solving new problems). Particularly for individuals with ASD some aspects of **neuropsychological testing** can be important, for example, for executive functioning—to see how well organized the person is in forward planning and problem-solving. **Personality tests** and **projective tests** are sometimes used, particularly in older individuals (adolescents and adults) with autism and particularly those with Asperger's disorder. These tests can be used to document problems in thinking and reality testing, but they are not routinely done.

SPEECH-LANGUAGE-COMMUNICATION ASSESSMENTS

Difficulties in communication are one of the central features of autism and a main focus of intervention. This is true even for higher-functioning individuals with autism and Asperger's disorder who have significant problems in the social use of language, even when they have good vocabularies. Typically developing children are quite communicative well before they begin to say words. In children with autism spectrum difficulties, these skills do not develop in the same way, so, for example, early (preverbal) methods of communicating, such as reaching and pointing to show something to someone else, may be quite delayed.

When children with autism do speak, their speech is remarkable in a number of ways. Often the speech pathologist will note that prosody (musical aspects) of speech may be markedly off so that the child speaks in a somewhat robotic (what speech-language pathologists call *monotonic*) way. Or the child's register (what speech pathologists call *volume*) may be uniformly loud across settings and situations. Use of pronouns (which are constantly shifting relative to who is speaking and being referred to) is an area of difficulty for many children with autism, who often reverse pronouns, saying, for example, *you* instead of *I*. Another very common characteristic is echolalia—repeating the same word or phrase over and over—such as saying "wanna cookie, wanna cookie, wanna cookie," having been asked, "Do you want a cookie?" Echolalia tends to persist over time, unlike in typically developing children when it gradually diminishes as the child becomes a more effective and sophisticated communicator. For the more-able person with autism, difficulties in keeping up a conversation and in responding to more sophisticated language (e.g., humor, irony, sarcasm) may present significant obstacles. These are what speech-language pathologists refer to as *pragmatic* aspects (social aspects) of language.

It is important to realize that problems in communication do not exist in isolation. Rather, these difficulties have a major impact on the child's social, organizational, and problem-solving skills. For example, children who do communicate verbally may rely on very idiosyncratic communication, which further contributes to social difficulties. For example, the child may say "the mailman is coming" anytime something unexpected happens, because she remembers once when the mailman came unexpectedly early. Her parents may understand what this phrase means, but most people would not.

Speech-communication assessments are important for all children with autism and related conditions, regardless of their level of functioning. For example, for children who are mute, an assessment of *comprehension* skills can be very appropriate. **Speech–language pathologists (SLPs)** are concerned with broader aspects of communication and not just speech, so they might, for example, consider ways in which a child who is not yet speaking could be helped to communicate through some other means.

The communication assessment should include several components. As was true for psychological assessment, the choice of tests and assessment procedures must reflect an awareness of the child's unique circumstances. For example, the SLP may be interested in assessing the child's ability to produce sounds and words if it seems as if this is an area of specific difficulty. Various **standardized tests** of vocabulary (receptive vocabulary—what the child understands—and expressive vocabulary—what she can say) are available, as are more sophisticated tests that look at exactly how language is used. For very young children, fewer assessment instruments are available. Instead, observation of social functioning (such as during play) may augment the results obtained with more standardized tests. Scores are much like those derived from psychological assessments; and again test types, ages tested, format of test, and so forth vary (see appendix table 2.2).

Depending on the child's age and ability to communicate, the SLP will assess different, usually multiple, areas. These include measures of preverbal communication, single-word vocabulary (receptive and expressive), as well as actual language use. There often is a significant gap between single-word vocabulary and the ability to use words regularly in conversation. As we mentioned, sometimes the assessment will include evaluation of specific problems such as articulation depending on the special needs of the child. Evaluation of the child's ability to use language socially should always be included.

The kinds of tests used are quite varied. Some of them rely on parental report of the child's skills, whereas others are based on assessment of the child by the SLP. Some assessment measures have been developed specifically for children with autism and related disorders or communication delays; often these employ a more play-based format, as is appropriate to younger children and those with more restricted communication skills. For example, the Communication and Symbolic Behavior Scales (CSBS) looks at language and the development of symbolic abilities in a play-based setting. It is used for children whose communication skills are between 6 and 24 months (the child can actually be up to 6 years of age), and it also includes a caregiver questionnaire. It provides a range of scores in different areas.

APPENDIX TABLE 2.2   **FREQUENTLY USED SPEECH-LANGUAGE-COMMUNICATION ASSESSMENTS**

Name	Comment
Peabody Picture Vocabulary Test, 4th ed. (PPVT-4) (Dunn & Dunn, 2007)	Measures receptive vocabulary (what the child understands). This score may underestimate child's actual language ability. Age range 2½–90 years.
Expressive One Word Picture Vocabulary Test, 4th ed. (EOWPVT) (Martin & Brownell, 2011)	Measures naming ability (what the child can label). Again, may overestimate child's actual language ability. Age range 2–80+ years.
Reynell Developmental Language Scales, US ed. (Reynell & Gerber, 1990)	For 3 years–7 years, 6 months; provides measures of actual language use. Scores often lower than when single-word vocabulary assessed. Provides scores for verbal comprehension and expressive language. Materials attractive to children.
Preschool Language Scale-4 (PLS-4) (Zimmerman, Steiner, & Pond, 2002)	Assesses receptive and expressive language; frequently used in schools. A direct assessment. Good instrument for younger children. Age range 2 weeks–<7 years.
Comprehensive Assessment of Spoken Language (CASL) (Carrow-Woolfolk, 1999)	Used from ages 3 to 21; only a verbal or nonverbal (pointing) response required (no reading or writing ability expected); test of various language abilities, including pragmatic ability (social language use) and figurative language.
Clinical Evaluation of Language Fundamentals, 5th ed. (CELF-5) (Wiig, Semel, & Secord, 2013)	Used for children from 3 to 21 (two versions). Assesses various language skills related to school requirements. Useful for older and higher-functioning children.
Test of Language Competence (TLC) (Wiig & Secord, 1989)	Focuses on more complex aspects of language (e.g., ambiguity, figurative language, abstract language); ages 5–18.

Note: Many other tests are available.

For children who are not yet using words, the SLP is interested in the building blocks of language, including social interaction, play, and other behaviors with a strong communicative aspect. The goals include understanding what the child comprehends about communication with others (use of gestures and words) and whether he or she understands communicative intent (the reasons for communicating) and the means for communicating (behaviors, words, vocalization, gestures). The SLP will also be interested in learning how effective and persistent the child is as a communicator. For instance, does he persist in trying to communicate when the other person does not understand, or does he use more or less conventional ways to communicate? In addition, the reasons why the child communicates will be noted. That is, does she communicate only to get things, to protest, or to engage other people? The social quality, as well as the rate of communications, is also important. For example, does the child pair his communication with eye contact or gestures? The SLP will listen to whatever sounds the child does make.

When children are able to combine words, a different range of assessment tools becomes available. It becomes somewhat easier to assess the child's ability to understand receptive and expressive language and relationships between words. Specific tests are chosen based on the child's age and level of language. For this group of children, sometimes one needs to make compromises or accommodations to get information that is helpful for purposes of diagnosis and treatment planning. For example, if the child is older but has limited language, the SLP may choose to use a test originally developed for younger children. Or, if the child has specific issues that complicate giving the test the usual way, some accommodation may be made. These changes might include repeating instructions, using reinforcement, or giving additional cues to the child. When these strategies are used, it does complicate scoring and interpretation of the test but may give valuable information for treatment.

In addition to doing formal testing, the SLP will also usually include a period of play so that he or she can record a language sample. The latter, usually audio- or videotaped, can be used after the assessment to analyze the level and sophistication of the child's spontaneous language.

For older children and those with better language (including children with Asperger's disorder) the usual tests of vocabulary levels and language abilities may tend to be much higher than the child's actual communication ability and thus may mislead school staff members. For such children, the assessment should focus on more complicated aspects of language, including social uses of language, such as understanding humor and nonliteral language (for example, "His eyes were bigger than his stomach"). For these children, often the results of the Vineland assessment are more informative than many of the more usual language measures. For individuals who do speak, the SLP will often pay special attention to the child's ability to modulate or moderate his or her tone of voice and volume as relevant to the specific topic or place.

OT and PT Assessments

Occupational and physical therapists may be involved either as members of the assessment team or in the school-based intervention program. Physical therapists are concerned with the child's ability to engage in gross motor (large muscle) movements, and occupational therapists are often more concerned with fine motor (hand) movements. They also may be needed to help assess the child if she has major sensory challenges. These specialists can provide input to classroom teachers as well as to parents on ways to help cope with and understand challenging behaviors, as well as motor difficulties, such as with writing and unusual sensitivities. Some selected tests of motor development or sensory-motor skills are listed in Appendix Table 2.3.

Putting It All Together

Because of health insurance issues, geographical location, and other factors, parents unfortunately do not always have that much choice when selecting a team to assess their child. If possible, try to connect with people who have worked together previously and who have considerable experience in diagnosing autism and related conditions. Other parents and often school staff members will be able to give you good information about qualified professionals. Often, the primary health care provider is the person who provides an initial referral to a team and then helps you obtain local services and resources. You can help parents obtain local services and resources; this person may be able to direct parents to experienced people. Sometimes the school will have a well-functioning and experienced assessment team,

APPENDIX TABLE 2.3   MOTOR AND SENSORY-MOTOR TESTS

Name	Format and Comment
Sensory Experiences Questionnaire (SEQ) (Baranek, David, Poe, Stone, & Watson, 2006)	Thirty-five items; targets children with autism (2–12 years); focuses on frequency of unusual sensory experiences.
Evaluation of Sensory Processing (ESP) (Parham & Ecker, 2002)	Used in children 2–12 years; 76 items on a 5-point scale.
Sensory Profile (Dunn, 2014)	Normed on a large sample of children (ages birth–15); scales for caregivers and teachers focus on unusual sensory responses.
Toddler Infant Motor Evaluation (TIME) (Miller & Roid, 1994)	Covers birth to 47 months; focuses on several domains based on rating of observed motor behaviors; requires considerable training.
Test of Visual Motor Integration (VMI) (Beery, Buktenica, & Beary 2010)	Widely used and well-standardized individually administered instrument (includes adults); used for ages 2 through adulthood; assesses visual perception and motor coordination; easily done by a trained evaluator; useful in documenting fine-motor and visual-motor delays.
Peabody Developmental Motor Scales, 2nd ed. (PDMS-2) (Folio & Fewell, 2000)	Norm-references scores for fine- and gross-motor abilities; birth to age 5.

because it is increasingly the case that school-based professionals (psychologists, speech pathologists, occupational and physical therapists) are more familiar with autism.

The best of the interdisciplinary teams work well together. Unfortunately, others don't. Sometimes parents and schools end up getting a plethora of individual reports with little integration and a report that lacks a single view of the child. Sometimes we've seen separate reports from six or seven different professionals working in the same group but with little apparent awareness of each other's findings. This usually happens when the team members work as individuals rather than as a group. Ideally, what is desired is a single, sensible, and realistic view of the child.

At the risk of overstating what we hope is now obvious, reports, whether from a team or an individual care provider, should be made to be understandable. Results should be translatable into programs for the person on the autism spectrum. For example, when we write reports, we tell parents that every one of the numbered points in our recommendations is something that might well be included in the child's IEP. Primary care providers can be helpful in helping parents understand test results and in helping them coordinate input from various sources. This becomes particularly true if the child or adolescent or adult has a medical problem that needs to be included in planning as well. Having a specific contact person—often the school nurse, psychologist, or social worker at the school or intervention program—can be helpful.

▩ REFERENCES

Baranek, G. T., David, F. J., Poe, M., Stone, W., & Watson, L. R. (2006). Sensory Experiences Questionnaire: Discriminating response patterns in young children with autism, developmental delays, and typical development. *Journal of Child Psychology and Psychiatry, 47(6),* 591–601.

Beery, K. E., & Buktenica, N. A. (1997). *Developmental test of visual-motor integration (VMI).* Parsippany, NJ: Modern Curriculum Press.

Carrow-Wollfolk, E. (1999). *Comprehensive assessment of spoken language (CASL).* Circle Pines, MN: American Guidance Service.

Dunn, W. (1999). *Sensory Profile.* San Antonio, TX: Psychological Corporation.

Dun, W. (2014). *Sensory Profile 2™.* San Antonio, TX: Pearson.

Dunn, L. M., & Dunn, L. M. (2007). *The Peabody picture vocabulary test (3rd ed.).* Circle Pines, MN: American Guidance Service.

Elliot, S. D. (2007). *Differential ability scales (2nd ed.).* San Antonio, TX: Harcourt Assessment.

Folio, M. R., & Fewell, R. R. (1983). *Peabody developmental motor scales and activity cards (PDMS).* Itasca, IL: Riverside.

Kaufman, A. S., & Kaufman, N. L. (2004). *Kaufman assessment battery for children (2nd ed.).* Circle Pines, MN: American Guidance Service.

Martin, N.A., & Brownell, R. (2011). *Expressive One-Word Picture Vocabulary Test, (4th ed.).* Austin, TX. Pro-Ed Publishing.

Miller, L.G., & Roid, G.H. (1994). *The T.I.M.E. Toddler and Infant Motor Evaluation.* San Antonio, TX. Therapy Skill Builders.

Mullen, E. M. (1995). *The Mullen scales of early learning.* Circle Pines, MN: American Guidance Service.

Parham, L. D., & Ecker, C. L. (2002) Evaluation of sensory processing. In A. Bundy, S. Lane, & E. Murray (Eds.), *Sensory integration: Theory and practice (2nd ed., pp. 194–196).* Philadelphia: Davis.

Reynell, J., & Gruber, C. (1990). *Reynell Developmental Language Scales-U.S. Edition.* Los Angeles: Western Psychological Services.

Roid, G.H., & Miller, L.K (2013). *Leiter International Performance Scale, (3rd ed., Leiter-3).* Torrance, CA: Western Psychological Services.

Roid, G. H. (2003). *Stanford Binet Intelligence Scales (5th ed).* Itasca, IL: Riverside.

Wiig, E. H., & Secord, W. (1989). *Test of language competence.* New York: Psychological Corporation.

Weschler, D. (2008). *Wechsler Adult Intelligence Scale (4th ed., WAIS-IV).* San Bloomington, MN: Pearson.

Weschler, D. (2014). *Wechsler Intelligence Scale for Children (5th ed., WISC-V)* Bloomington, MN: Pearson.

Weschler, D. (2012). *Wechsler Preschool and Primary Scale of Intelligence™ (4th ed., WPPSI-IV).* Bloomington, MN: Pearson.

Wiig, E. H., Semel, E., & Secord, W. A. (2013). *Clinical Evaluation of Language Fundamentals (5th ed., CELF-5).* Bloomington, MN: NCS Pearson.

Zimmerman, I. L., Steiner, V. G., & Pond, R. E. (2002*). Preschool Language Scale-4.* San Antonio, TX: Psychological Corporation.

▦ SUGGESTED READING

Baranek, G. T., Little, L. M., Parham, L. D., Ausderau, K. K., & Sabatos-DeVito, M. G. (2014). Sensory features in autism spectrum disorders. In F. R. Volkmar, S. J. Rogers, R. Paul, & K. A. Pelphrey (Eds.), *Handbook of autism and pervasive developmental disorders* (4th ed., Vol. 2, pp. 378–407). Hoboken, NJ: Wiley.

Goldstein, S., Naglieri, J. A., & Ozonoff, S. (2009). *Assessment of autism spectrum disorders* (pp. xiv, 384). New York, NY: Guilford Press.

Hogan, T. P. (2002). *Psychological testing: A practical introduction.* Hoboken, NJ: Wiley.

Paul, R. & Wilson, K. P. (2009). Assessing speech, language, and communication in autism spectrum disorders. In S. Goldstein, J. A. Naglieri, & S. Ozonoff (Eds.), *Assessment of autism spectrum disorders* (pp 171–208). New York, NY: Guilford Press.

Schaaf, R. C., Benevides, T. W., Kelly, D., & Mailloux-Maggio, Z. (2012). Occupational therapy and sensory integration for children with autism: A feasibility, safety, acceptability and fidelity study. *Autism, 16*(3), 321–327.

Tager-Flusberg, H., Paul, R., & Lord, C. (2014). Language and communication in autism. In F. R. Volkmar, S. J. Rogers, R. Paul, & K. A. Pelphrey (Eds.), *Handbook of autism and pervasive developmental disorders* (4th ed., Vol. 1, pp. 335–364). Hoboken, NJ: Wiley.

Tsatsanis, K. D., Powell, K., Volkmar, F. R., Paul, R., Rogers, S. J., & Pelphrey, K. A. (2014). Neuropsychological characteristics of autism spectrum disorders. In F. R. Volkmar, S. J. Rogers, R. Paul, & K. A. Pelphrey (Eds.), *Handbook of autism and pervasive developmental disorders* (4th ed., Vol. 1, pp. 302–331). Hoboken, NJ: Wiley.

Volkmar, F. R., Booth, L. L., McPartland, J. C., & Wiesner, L. A. (2014). Clinical evaluation in multidisciplinary settings. In F. R. Volkmar, S. J. Rogers, R. Paul, & K. A. Pelphrey (Eds.), *Handbook of autism and pervasive developmental disorders* (4th ed., Vol. 2, pp. 661–672). Hoboken, NJ: Wiley.

Volkmar, F. R., Rowberry, J., Vinck-Baroody, O. D., Gupta, A. R., Leung, J., Meyers, J., Vaswani, N., & Wiesner, L. A. (2014). Medical care in autism and related conditions. In F. R. Volkmar, S. J. Rogers, R. Paul, & K. A. Pelphrey (Eds.), *Handbook of autism and pervasive developmental disorders* (4th ed., Vol. 1, pp. 532–535). Hoboken, NJ: Wiley.

Wodrich, D.L.E. (1997). *Children's psychological testing: A guide for nonpsychologists.* Baltimore, MD: Brookes.

Glossary

ABA *See* Applied behavior analysis.

Accommodations Adaptations of the environment, format, or situation made to suit the need of the student.

Achievement tests Unlike IQ tests, achievement tests are less concerned with how able the person is and more with how he or she uses his or her ability to learn, for example, as applied in math or reading. In addition to standard scores, percentiles, and age equivalent scores, these tests also often give grade-equivalent scores. These tests are often given in schools—they may be given to groups of children.

ADA *See* Americans With Disabilities Act.

Adaptive behavior (functioning) The ability to adjust to new environments, tasks, objects, and people and to apply new skills to those situations.

Age-equivalent score This test result compare the individual's ability to what would be typical for a person of a specific age. For example, an age-equivalent score of 5 years 2 months might be

computed based on a child's ability. The meaning of the score varies depending on the child's age (the same 5 year 2 month score would mean very different things if the child were 5 or 10 years of age).

Americans with Disabilities Act The comprehensive civil rights law passed in 1990 that prohibits discrimination against people with disabilities in employment, public service, public accommodation, and telecommunications. Often referred to as *ADA*.

Applied behavior analysis (ABA) A behavioral science that uses researched-based, highly structured teaching procedures to develop skills in individuals. An emphasis is placed on modifying behavior in a precisely measurable manner using repeated trials.

Auditory memory Recalling what is heard.

Autism A form of pervasive developmental disorder characterized by difficulties in social interaction and language

Note: In this Glossary we are intentionally over-inclusive of terms that may be less familiar to some health care providers.

acquisition and use, as well as odd or unusual mannerisms, behaviors, and habits.

Autism Behavior Checklist (ABC) Screening instrument for autism.

Autism Diagnostic Interview–Revised (ADI-R) Diagnostic and assessment instrument for autism. Focuses on relevant diagnostic (historical) information; typically done with parents. This instrument requires extensive training.

Autism Diagnostic Observation Schedule (ADOS) Diagnostic and assessment instrument for autism. An assessment done with the individual (preschool child to adult) with probes. Designed to elicit behaviors that suggest the individual is on the autism spectrum. Various versions are available (depending on language ability of the individual). This instrument requires extensive training.

Autism spectrum disorders The new term used in *DSM-5* to refer to autism and related conditions. The definition provided there is somewhat more appropriate for classical autism.

Autistic disorder The term for autism used in the *Diagnostic and Statistical Manual of Mental Disorders.*

Autistic savant A person with autism who has an unusual ability, for example, drawing, calendar calculation, memory, and so forth.

Behavior modification Use of positive and negative reinforcements to change behavior.

Childhood autism Same meaning as autistic disorder or infantile autism.

Childhood Autism Rating Scale, 2nd ed. (CARS-2) Diagnostic and assessment instrument for autism. Widely used in schools and easy to learn; gives individual score on a 15-point scale based on assessment and examination with scores on each scale ranging from 0 (normal) to 4 (very autistic).

Childhood disintegrative disorder (CDD) A rare form of pervasive developmental disorder in which a child, who has developed typically in early childhood, begins to display autistic-like characteristics. By definition, development is normal until age 2 years. The usual time of onset is between ages 3 and 4 years.

Circle of Friends Peer-based social skills groups.

Clinical Evaluation of Language Fundamentals, 5th ed. (CELF-5) Test of language and communication skills. Frequently used in schools by speech pathologists.

Comorbidity Refers to having more than one problem, for example, autism *and* an anxiety disorder. This becomes more frequent as individuals with autism enter adolescence and adulthood.

Complementary and alternative medicine (CAM) A diverse group of medical and health care practices and products whose effectiveness is not considered established and evidence-based.

Comprehensive Assessment of Spoken Language (CASL) Test of language and communication skills.

Criterion-referenced test A test of this kind is not used to compare people to each other; rather the comparison is to a specific criterion or standard to demonstrate mastery of some task or skill. A driving test is an example.

Daily living skills Skills needed for everyday life, for example, shopping, using the phone, dressing appropriately for weather, self-care skills.

Denver model A developmentally based information system developed by Sally Rogers for young children with autism. It focuses on encouraging skills based on a developmentally oriented curriculum in a range of settings and is regarded evidence-based.

Department of Vocational Rehabilitation (DVR) Departments in each state required by the Vocational Rehabilitation Act of 1973 to correct the problems of discrimination against people with disabilities.

***Diagnostic and Statistical Manual of Mental Disorders*, 5th ed. (*DSM-5*)** Manual published by the American Psychiatric Association to provide guidelines to diagnose mental disorders.

Differential Ability Scales, 2nd ed. (DAS-II) Test of intelligence.

Discrete trial teaching An instructional technique that is part of applied behavior analysis. This technique involves four steps: (1) presenting a cue or stimulus to the learner; (2) obtaining the learner's response; (3) providing a positive consequence (reinforcer) or correction; and (4) a brief 3- to 5-second break until the next teaching trial is provided. *See* Applied behavior analysis.

Due process hearings Hearings to decide whether an individualized education plan meets the requirements of the Individuals With Disabilities Education Act.

Early intervention services Provided to infants and young children before they become eligible for school-based services.

Echolalia A parrot-like repetition of phrases or words just heard (immediate echolalia) or heard hours, days, weeks, or even months before (delayed echolalia). Also called *repetitive speech*.

Estate planning The process of planning for passing along one's assets to others (often one's children).

Evaluation of Sensory Processing (ESP) Test of sensory processing.

Executive functioning Includes a range of abilities such as planning, forward thinking, inhibition, working memory, cognitive flexibility, all of which are necessary for organization and effective problem-solving.

Expressive One Word Picture Vocabulary Test (EOWPVT) Test of expressive vocabulary.

Extended school year (ESY) Special education services beyond the usual school year. This is specified in the Individuals with Disabilities Education Act. Eligibility is determined by a child's IEP.

Free and appropriate public education (FAPE) A right under federal law for children in the United States. All programs and schools that receive federal funding must provide appropriate education to those with disabilities.

Generalization Transferring a skill taught in one place or with one person to other places and people.

Gestalt processing A tendency to process material in its entirety rather than seeing composite parts (often an aspect of learning style in individuals with autism).

Gilliam Autism Rating Scales, 2nd ed. (GARS-2) Diagnostic and assessment instrument for autism.

IDEA *See* Individuals With Disabilities Education Act.

Idiosyncratic language Language use that is unique to the individual, often reflecting his or her own experience;

may be hard to understand for people unfamiliar with the individual; for example, a child with autism might yell "stop that child" when he is upset because the first time he was upset he ran from his mother in a crowded department store and she yelled this phrase at him.

IEP *See* Individualized education plan.

IFSP *See* Individualized family service plan.

Imitation The ability to observe the actions of others and to copy them in one's own actions. Also known as *modeling*.

Inclusion Placing children with disabilities in the same schools and classrooms with children who are developing typically. The environment includes the special supports and services necessary for educational success.

Individualized education plan (IEP) The written plan that specifies the special education and other services (such as occupational or speech therapy) the school has agreed to provide a child with disabilities who is eligible under the Individuals with Disabilities Education Act; for children ages 3 to 21.

Individualized family service plan (IFSP) The written plan that specifies the education and related services to be provided to children eligible for early intervention under the Individuals with Disabilities Education Act and their families; for children birth to age 3.

Individuals with Disabilities Education Act (IDEA) A federal law originally passed in 1975 and subsequently amended that requires states to provide a "free appropriate public education in the least restrictive environment" to children with disabilities. This is the major special education law in the United States.

Infantile autism Same meaning as *autistic disorder* or *childhood autism.*

Intellectual disability Significantly subaverage intellectual and adaptive functioning; also referred to as *mental retardation.*

Intelligence quotient (IQ) A numerical measurement of intellectual capacity that compares a person's chronological age to his or her mental age, as shown on standardized tests.

IQ *See* Intelligence quotient.

Joint attention The activity of engaging with others in watching activities and events and engaging with materials. This typically can be demonstrated readily in normally developing infants; for example, when something interesting or unusual happens, the child will look at it, then turn to the parent to evaluate his or her reaction, then turn back to look.

Kaufmann Assessment Battery for Children, 2nd ed. (KABC-II) A widely used test of intelligence.

Landau-Kleffner syndrome Acquired aphasia with epilepsy.

Least restrictive environment (LRE) The Individuals with Disabilities Education Act requires that children who need special education services must be taught as much as possible alongside children without disabilities.

Leiter International Performance Scale, 3rd ed. (Leiter-3) Nonverbal test of intelligence.

Local education agency (LEA) Agency at the local level that provides educational services.

Mainstreaming *See* Inclusion.

Medical home A primary care practice that provides health care that is comprehensive including preventive, acute, and chronic care; coordinated across primary and specialty care; accessible; continuous from birth through the transition to adulthood; family-centered; compassionate; and culturally sensitive. It should emphasize a partnership with families.

Megadose vitamin therapy Using vitamins in dosages that are at levels higher than the recommended daily allowance.

Mental age Age-equivalent score on a test of intelligence.

Modified Checklist for Autism in Toddlers (M-CHAT) Screening instrument for autism.

Monotonic A style of speech that lacks inflection or prosody; sometimes referred to as *robot-like speech.*

Mullen Scales of Early Learning A developmental test.

Neuropsychological testing Tests of this kind are usually focused on a particular process, such as memory, attention, or particular kinds of problem-solving.

Nonverbal learning disability (NLD) A pattern of strengths and weaknesses that includes better verbal abilities than nonverbal abilities.

Norm-referenced test A test that compares an individual's score against a group of people selected to be representative of the general population. Scores derived from tests of this kind can be presented in various ways, including percentiles, standard scores, and age-equivalent scores.

PDD *See* Pervasive developmental disorder.

Peabody Developmental Motor Scales–2 (PDMS-2) Test of motor skills.

Peabody Picture Vocabulary Test, 4th ed. (PPVT-4) Test of repetitive vocabulary.

Percentile scores Presents a score based on what percentage of scores are lower; for example, an 85th percentile score means the person scored higher than 85% of the people who take the test.

Perseveration Getting stuck on an activity; spending an inappropriate amount of time doing and redoing the same thing.

Personality tests These tests may be paper-and-pencil (self- or parent report) or, in the case of some tests, are individually administered by a psychologist based on a person's responses to stimuli. Tests of personality may include scores related to levels of depression, anxiety, or problem behavior.

Pervasive developmental disorder (PDD) An umbrella category in the DSM-5 for a range of conditions, including autistic disorder, Asperger's disorder, PDD-NOS, Rett's disorder, and childhood disintegrative disorder, and can include symptoms such as difficulties with communication and social skills, unusual interests or habits, and insistence on sameness. The term may be used synonymously with *autism spectrum disorder* in *DSM-5.*

Pica The eating of nonfood substances.

Pivotal response training (PRT) A program developed at University California, Santa Barbara, by Robert and Lynn Koegel that combines aspects of more traditional applied behavioral analysis but in a developmentally informed way that targets issues important for future learning and development. It is evidence-based.

Pragmatics The use of language for social communication.

Preschool Language Scale–4 (PLS-4) Test of language and communication skills.

Projective tests These tests may be paper and pencil (self- or parent report or sometimes individually administered by a psychologist based on a person's responses to stimuli). Projective tests such as the Rorschach inkblot test allow the individual to give a response to a very unstructured stimulus; tests of this kind may be used to look for unusual patterns of thinking or experience.

Prosody The musical aspect of language, often distorted or markedly diminished in individuals with autism. Prosody includes register (loudness), pitch, inflection, and so forth. Lack of prosody may be manifest in monotonic (one-tone) (robot-like) speech.

Public Law 94–142 The Education of All Handicapped Children Act of 1975 that has been revised and is now known as the Individuals with Disabilities Education Act (IDEA).

Reactive attachment disorder A disorder that develops in infants and young children as the result of emotional or physical neglect or abuse; children with the disorder have social skills delays and difficulty bonding with others.

Register The technical term that speech pathologists use to refer to voice volume.

Regression The loss of skill or ability.

Rehabilitation Act of 1973 Prohibits discrimination against anyone on the basis of disability.

Reinforcement Any consequence that increases the likelihood of the future occurrence of a behavior. A consequence is either presented or withheld in an effort to prompt the desired response.

Related services Services that enable a child to benefit from special education. Related services include speech-language, occupational, and physical therapies, as well as transportation.

Repetitive speech Also called *echolalia*. *See also* Perseveration.

Residential services Living arrangements away from home but with supervision.

Resistance to Change A term first used by Leo Kanner in describing the difficulties children with autism had in dealing with any change in the environment.

Respite care Care away from home, often providing relief for the usual caretakers.

Reynell Developmental Language Scales, US ed. Test of language and communication skills.

Rigidity Inflexibility of behavior; needing things to happen a very specific way in order for them to "feel right" to the child.

Screening tests Tests given to groups of children intended to determine which children need further evaluation.

Screening Tool for Autism in Two-Year-Olds (STAT) Screening instrument for autism.

Section 504 Provides accommodations for people with disabilities under the Rehabilitation Act.

Self-help skills Daily living skills needed to live independently.

Self-injury Self-aggression committed by the individual, for example, head banging.

Self-stimulation The act of providing physical, visual, or auditory stimulation for oneself; rocking back and forth and hand flapping are examples.

Sensoro-motor skills Skills in infants and young children involving perception and action; these become the basis of subsequent cognitive and other skills.

Sensory Experiences Questionnaire (SEQ) Test of sensory processing.

Sensory integration The ability to receive input from the senses, to organize it into a meaningful message, and to act on it.

Sensory profile Test of sensory processing.

SLP *See* Speech-language pathologist.

Social communication disorder A new condition included in *DSM-5* for individuals with problems in social interaction and communication but not with repetitive behaviors and restricted interests.

Social Communication Questionnaire (SCQ) Screening instrument for autism.

Social Responsiveness Scale, 2nd ed. (SRS-2) Diagnostic and screening instrument for autism.

Social Security Disability Insurance (SSDI) Money that has been funneled into the Social Security system through payroll deductions on earnings. Workers who are disabled are entitled to these benefits. People who are born with a disability or become disabled before the age of 22 may collect SSDI under a parent's account if the parent is retired, disabled, or deceased.

Social skills Learned abilities such as sharing, turn taking, asserting one's independence, and forming attachments, which allow one to effectively interact with others.

Social Stories A social skills intervention strategy that teaches self-awareness, self-calming, and self-management skills.

Speech-language pathologists (SLPs) A therapist who works to evaluate and improve speech and language skills, as well as to improve oral-motor abilities.

Standard deviation A measurement of the degree to which a given test score differs from the mean (average) score. On many IQ tests, for example, the majority of children score within 15 points above to 15 points below the mean score of 100, so one standard deviation is considered to be 15 points.

Standard score A test score based on the normal distribution curve (the bell curve). In tests scored with standard scores, 100 usually is considered exactly average, with scores from 85 to 115 considered to be in the average range.

Standardized tests Tests that are administered in exactly the same way each time and that are designed so that results can be compared with the performance of other individuals who have taken the test.

Stanford Binet Intelligence Scale, 5th ed. (SB5) Test of intelligence.

Stereotypies Purposeless, repetitive movements or behaviors such as hand flapping.

Substantial gainful activity Used to decide if a person has a disability to determine eligibility for Social Security Disability Income and Supplemental Security Income.

Subthreshold A difference that is so slight that it is not detected by standard tests but may cause some difficulties for the individual.

Supplemental Security Income (SSI)
A program of payments available for eligible people who are disabled, blind, or elderly that is based on financial need, not on past earnings.

Supported employment Employment in a community setting but with support.

TEACCH A statewide eclectic intervention program based in North Carolina but now used widely around the world. It has some unique features and parts of it are evidence-based.

Telescoping effects Problem in recall of temporally remote events in which there is a tendency to recall more recent events as more distant and more distant events as closer in time.

Test of Language Competence (TLC)
Test of language and communication skills.

Test of Visual Motor Integration (VMI) Test of visual-motor skills.

Tics Involuntary, purposeless movements or sounds that occur, for example, in Tourette's syndrome. Tics are usually distressing to a child who has them, in contrast to stereotypic behavior, which children with autism find pleasurable or neutral.

Toddler Infant Motor Evaluation (TIME) Test of motor skills.

Transition The period between the end of one activity and the start of another.

Transition plan Planning for major transitions, most notably between Birth to Three services and school-aged services and again in adolescence.

Validity When used relative to testing, this term typically refers to the notion that the test is indeed measuring what it is supposed to.

Vineland Adaptive Behavior Scales
Test of adaptive skills.

Visual-motor Related to the use of the eyes to process and then motorically respond in tasks, for example, putting a puzzle piece into a puzzle or a key into a keyhole.

Voice synthesizers Technologies that enable a computer to say what someone types.

Wechsler Intelligence Scales Test of intelligence that is widely used; several versions are available and used from preschool to adulthood.

Index

Page references followed by f indicate an illustrated figure; followed by t indicate a table and b indicate a box.